GEOPOLITICS AT THE END OF THE TWENTIETH CENTURY

The Changing World Political Map

Editors

NURIT KLIOT AND DAVID NEWMAN

FRANK CASS
LONDON • PORTLAND, OR

First Published in 2000 in Great Britain by
FRANK CASS PUBLISHERS
Newbury House, 900 Eastern Avenue
London, IG2 7HH

and in the United States of America by
FRANK CASS PUBLISHERS
c/o ISBS, 5824 N.E. Hassalo Street
Portland, Oregon, 97213-3644

Website: www.frankcass.com

British Library Cataloguing in Publication Data:

Geopolitics at the end of the twentieth century : the
changing world political map. – (Cass series in geopolitics
; no. 2)
1. Geopolitics 2. World politics
I. Kliot, Nurit II. Newman, David, 1956 July 4–
320.1'2

ISBN 0 7146 5055 2 (cloth)
ISBN 0 7146 8106 7 (paper)

Library of Congress Cataloging-in-Publication Data:

Geopolitics at the End of the twentieth century : the changing world political map /
editors, Nurit Kliot and David Newman.
    p. cm. – (Cass studies in geopolitics ; no. 2)
Includes bibliographical references and index.
ISBN 0-7146-5055-2 (alk. paper) – ISBN 0-7146-8106-7 (pbk. : alk. paper)
    1. Geopolitics. I. Kliot, Nurit. II. Newman, David, 1956– III. Series.

JC319.G486 2000
327–dc21   00-025891

This group of studies first appeared in a Special Issue on
'Geopolitics at the end of the Twentieth Century: The Changing World Political Map' of
Geopolitics (ISSN 1465-0045) 4/1–2 (Summer–Autumn 1999)
published by Frank Cass.

Printed in Great Britain by Antony Rowe Ltd., Chippenham, Wiltshire

Contents

Introduction:
Globalisation and the Changing World
Political Map

DAVID NEWMAN and NURIT KLIOT

The world political map has undergone many changes during the past decade. In the wake of the collapse of the Soviet Union, many boundaries have been redrawn, or at least re-emerged, while the territorial configuration of states has undergone change. More significantly, the processes affecting territorial sovereignty and statehood in an era of global flows and technological advance, have resulted in new modes of political organisation – locally, regionally and globally. A brief look at a static political map of the world may enable the reader to see the way in which lines have been redrawn, but it hides the more significant and structural changes which have taken place, and which are continuing to take place, in the way that peoples and their governments interact with each other, beyond and between state boundaries.

The collection of essays which follows is based on an international conference, held in Israel in January 1998, examining the changes which have affected the world political map during the past decade. The selected papers are divided into two sections, to be published as two consecutive volumes of the journal, *Geopolitics*, the first dealing with the relationship between geopolitics and globalisation, the second with the changing role of boundaries in the contemporary world political map. The two sections are not unrelated, as the globalisation thesis infers the 'end of the nation state' and a move into a 'borderless, deterritorialised world', in which the territorial configuration of state power is diminished as the trans-boundary processes of globalisation take hold. Many of the papers reflect the geographical focus of most of the writers and, as such, question the extent to which globalisation has indeed brought about an end of the nation state and/or has created a deterritorialised, borderless, world.[1]

Defining Globalisation

Globalisation is conceptualized as a process of linkage and interdependence between territories. A common thread running through most of the views on globalisation is a recognition of the significance of the dramatic reduction in the tyranny of distance, a world in which time-space has shrunk dramatically as a result of technological innovations in transport and communications, especially information technologies. Thus shrinking of the world stems from the increase in range, speed and intensity of social interaction and communication.[2]

Barlow's working definition of globalisation is that it is a process by which places and institutions become integrated into a system that has global dimensions and from a geographical perspective, two fundamental aspects of the process are scale enlargement in the spatial basis of organisations and institutions and increasing levels and intensity of inter-connection across international boundaries.[3] According to Robertson, globalisation is a process which refers both to the compression of the world and the intensification of consciousness of the world as a whole. Globalisation is perceived as an imprecise and developing process, an ideology and programme which challenges the current order.[4]

Globalisation is a hotly contested notion, often reflecting the different disciplinary or cultural perspectives of the proponents of the concept. This is particularly reflected in terms of perspectives on the relationship between the local, the national and the global and the degree to which national states are seen as having been 'hollowed out'.[5] In this respect, the main positions concerning globalisation can be summarised as follows:

1. Globalisation is a process in which capital moves on the globe in search of profit with no constraints on its activities. As a result of this process national states are weakened and deprived of regulatory capacity.

2. While acknowledging the great impact of transnational economies, some authors reject the notion that the globalisation process is accompanied by the hollowing out or weakening process of the national state.[6]

3. Globalisation is a stretching and deepening of social relations and institutions across space and time. Activities and events on the local level are affected by events on the other side of the globe and vice versa.

4. Globalisation processes are explored as a cultural, economic and political process. *Culturally*, it refers to increasing world-wide sharing of symbols and the awareness of a global social entity.[7] To some writers the processes of globalisation are perceived to be a threat to culture in the sense that market opportunity rather than national identity functions as the new reality of international media operations.[8] However, in the debate on global culture, many scholars are abandoning both nostalgic worries about the loss of local culture and the enthusiastic celebration of post-modern tolerance, to focus instead on local interpretation of the

heterogeneous input received through the market.[9] *Politically*, the most important aspects of globalisation is the much contested concept of 'hollowing out' of the nation-state (particularly the European nation-state).[10]

The challenges to the nation-states in the latter part of the twentieth century include: the internationalisation of economic activities and the growth of transnational companies, migration, new technologies, the development of new political movements, demands for regional and local autonomy and religious movements. Following Fukuyama's 1992 essay on the 'End of History' it was claimed that Liberal Democracy now dominates the political culture in most parts of the world. But, according to Johnston[11] even if this claim is accepted, it does not suggest homogeneity in the political practices nor in the economic practices which accompanied Liberal Democracy's rise to hegemony.[12]

Economically, the effects of globalisation are very significant. So fundamental have been the economic changes of space-time compression of measures, such as communication and computer technology, that Luttwak's forecast that geo-economics would displace geopolitics as a global analytical framework whereas geopolitics is state-based.[13] The thrust of geo-economics is towards the elimination of the power of the state.[14] Few critics of the globalisation thesis deny that international companies have increased their share of world trade in recent years or that supranational institutions play an important role in regulating international trade, investment and finance. But Anderson pointed to reality in which societies, cultures and environments exhibit immense variations worldwide, and there are few common global strands. Thus, globalisation needs to be examined in the context of economics, and the study of its various characteristics can be designated geo-economics.[15] In geopolitics the focus is on differences between the locations whereas in geo-economies these differences are suppressed.[16]

Critiques of the globalisation concept, do not accept the notion whereby the nation-state is 'hollowed-out'. Hirst and Thompson insist on the continuing significance of the nation-state.[17] They suggest that globalisation is loaded with political meaning and implies an end-point of systemic interdependence of national economies, genuinely footloose transnational capital, a decline in the power of labor and the transfer of power from national states to supranational bodies. In their criticism of this view they assert that international firms are still largely confined to their home territory in terms of their overall business activity and remain heavily nationally embedded.[18]

The chapters in this volume focus on the dual political and economic dimensions of the globalisation process. Most, but by no means all, of the chapters have been written by geographers and, as such, the spatial and territorial dimension of globalisation occupies a central place in their respective analyses. The first part of the work deals more explicitly with the relationship between globalisation and geopolitical change in the contemporary world, while the second part examines the impact of globalisation on the territorial configuration of states and the changing functional nature of the boundaries within which territories and their respective populations are enclosed.

Political Dimensions of Globalisation

Politically, globalisation refers to the increasing importance of world-wide governance regimes, not exclusively but largely based again on the state system.[19] One of the particularly important aspects of the move 'upwards' of the regulatory powers of national states has been the creation of macro-regions such as NAFTA and the EU as a result of agreements between national states. The penetration of the globalisation process has simultaneously increased both uniformity and diversity. This is despite the superficial current of global homogenisation throughout the world and the apparent development of a uniform global culture, for there is undoubtedly a counter-current of increased religious and/or ethnic identification and confrontation within and across national frontiers often manifested in violent forms.[20] In the closing chapter of this book, Fred Boal argues that, at least in part, ethnic revival in Northern Ireland is a response to globalising forces. Similar arguments could be put forward for other ethnic conflicts around the world. In this respect, it is interesting to note the response of small states which are affected by the economic restructuring that is under way. In his contribution to this volume, Stan Brunn notes that small states will take advantage of this process by 'place promotion' and by seeking an advantage over other large states as well as small states.

On a different spatial dimension, John O'Loughlin shows that concepts and processes of globalisation do not necessarily enter into the sacred halls of American foreign policy. O'Loughlin asserts that US geopolitics of the late 1990s resembles that of the 1920s. He was able to detect seven competing paradigms or geopolitical codes in the current American foreign policy. None of the seven paradigms embodies the global complexity and the new multi-polarity of power and none have broad political support. The doctrine of 'containment', perhaps the true opposite concept of globalisation, isolationist policies and mainly 'regionalist' views, still characterises contemporary American foreign policy.

At the same time, Gearóid Ó Tuathail identifies what he terms as a 'Clinton Doctrine' which responded to the challenges of globalisation, borderless worlds, and the 'Information Age', and which promotes free trade agreements like NAFTA and pursues technological initiatives such as a national information superhighway.

According to Williams,[21] globalisation, together with European integration, changes the context within which civil society is mediated, posing a threat to conventional territorial relationships and simultaneously opening up new forms of inter-regional interaction such as cable television and global multi-service networks. Ethno-linguistic minorities have reacted to these twin impulses by searching for European-wide economies of scale in broadcasting, information networking, education and public administration. They believe that by appealing to the superstructural organizations for legitimacy and equality of group rights they will force the state to recognise their claims for varying degrees of political/social autonomy within clearly identifiable territorial social domains.[22]

Julian Minghi, confirms this assertion in his chapter, which explores the policy of three such linguistic minorities residing in the Alpine margins of Italy. He found that the three regions – Val d'Aosta, South Tyrol, and Friuli – fostered a policy which emphasized the growing role of the European Union in guaranteeing the rights of linguistic minorities within the states of the community. Similarly, Barlow pointed to the importance of the emerging 'national' transborder regions as a middle regional scale in the political organization of space or between the global and local.[23] The main impetus for the formation of transborder regions is economic: by pooling the resource and coordinating development strategies of peripheral parts of two or more states, it is hoped to create an entity that has a higher profile and greater visibility on the supranational economic map.[24] This has recently been explored by Mathew Sparke in his comparative analysis of trans-boundary regions in Western Europe and Cascadia.[25] In addition, sub-state nationalism regions such as Catalonia and Flanders have enjoyed new strength and visibility in the EU, a process which has euphemistically been described by some as constituting a 'fourth world' nationhood.[26] With globalisation reducing the importance of states as economic and spatial units and increasing the importance of supranational economic spaces, it is becoming more plausible for ethnic territories to create a political niche in global system. Thus, few would argue today that the separation of Quebec from Canada is unrealistic on grounds of economic viability assuming that a sovereign Quebec would still be part of an integrated North American economic space.[27]

The processes of globalisation have decreased the capacity of most states to maximise economic regulation functions,[28] but the regulatory power of the state has generally increased in social and political matters, in some cases to the point of over-regulation. In the Asia Pacific region such policies are often intensified by the existence of ethnic diversity where this is associated with ethnic revival, which itself can be seen in part as an intra-state reaction to homogenising globalism.[29]

It has also been argued that globalisation processes have caused instability and insecurity within states. To some extent they have also contributed to the growth in regional organisations for collective security purposes.[30] The emergence of the ASEAN Regional Forum (ARF) in 1994 as a traditional security consultative forum has ensured that new regionalism is no longer solely associated with economic security concerns. Various types of new regionalism are evident in the Asia Pacific regions. These range from region-wide groupings such as the Asia-Pacific Economic Cooperation (APEC) initiative formed in 1989, to sub-regional groups such as ASEAN and a number of interstate growth triangles and development areas located at state peripheries. The gradual deregionalisation of the Asia Pacific Economic Cooperation group which increased its membership around the Pacific Rim is interpreted in this context.[31]

Globalisation – Economic Dimensions

Globalisation has been defined as a process which embodies a certain amount of functional integration among various types of economic activities which are internationally dispersed. Economically, globalisation infers that the world capitalist system has indeed expanded to the global level with no respect for international boundaries and with growing roles of transnational corporations and supernational economic areas.[32] This 'borderless world' argument (to be discussed more fully in the section on boundaries) is accompanied by the 'deterritorialization' thesis, which is discussed in a number of other contributions in this volume.

In his discussion of the deterritorialisation of the financial markets, O'Tuathail presents five new developments since the 1970s. First was the breakdown of the Bretton Woods System of pegged exchanged rates; second was the deregulation of financial markets; third, the introduction of electronic information technology into finance; fourth, the innovation and development of a series of new financial products; and finally, the emergence of a series of new actors in the international financial system. But even the economic implications of globalisation and deterritorialisation is a contested narrative, with the impact of boundaries still playing a role in creating barriers, albeit not with the same intensity as in the past.[33]

The growing significance of processes of globalisation reflects decisions by national states to change the international regulatory framework by participating in institutions such as the IMF, the World Bank and GATT. Despite such growing tendencies, to date there are very few firms and sectors that are organised on a truly global basis.[34] The world trade regime has been constructed through the GATT and its successor World Trade Organisation to promote the particular trading interests of a powerful group of national states dominated particularly by the US and the European Union and multinational companies. Similarly, the IMF effectively erodes the ability of poorer countries to set independent economic policies.[35]

The involvement of such powerful global organisations is seen as increasing inequality within states, resulting in new forms of conflict. In his contribution to this volume, Italian geographer, Fabrizio Eva presents the recent Asian financial crisis as an example for this type of involvement. However, there is evidence to the contrary, as shown by Richard Grant's study of Ghana and Kenya. Grant argues that despite the changing global and national policy domains the state remains a central player; thus the notion of a 'borderless' world appears to be greatly exaggerated.

The proponents of the globalisation thesis do not deal with the many devastating side effects of the process which have become more prevalent throughout the world. In the Asia-Pacific region, the moves towards free-trade are likely to magnify environmental impacts, encourage states to deplete their own resource base and push economies towards narrow export commodities likely to be environmentally damaging. Australia's niche energy-intensive economy ensured non-compliance in global emission's agreements on 'economic' grounds.[36] The current global upsurge in racist politics is in part a reflection of the uncertainty generated by the socio-economic impacts of globalisation.

Boundaries and Territorial Organisation

The second section of the book (volume 4, number 2 of *Geopolitics*) deals with boundaries. The study of boundaries has undergone a significant transition during the past decade.[37] This largely reflects the parallel change in the functions of boundaries themselves as the world political map has experienced changes, not only in terms of the territorial configuration of states and sovereign territories, but also – and perhaps more importantly – in the functional role of boundaries in a globalised world. It does not require one to accept the 'end of nation state' and 'borderless world' thesis, so avidly promoted by economists with their unimpeded flow of capital and global corporatism, and information scientists with a cyberspace that knows no bounds, for one to accept that, to put it simply, international boundaries are not what they once were.[38] Where only ten years ago, boundaries continued to create the barrier functions associated with iron curtains, they have become penetrated during the past decade, thus giving rise to a reassessment of their role in the new world order which has emerged as a result of the collapse of the communist bloc on the one hand, and the advance of global technology on the other.[39]

The paper by Gerard O'Tuathail seeks to problematise the discourses of deterritorialisation within the area of global financial markets. This is an area which is commonly thrown up as an example of an emerging borderless world. Toal argues that rather than dealing with deterritorialisation, we are dealing with a re-arrangement of the identity/border/order complex that 'gives people, territory and politics their meaning in the contemporary world'. Deterritorialisation and reterritorialisation are parts of an ongoing process through which the territorial configurations of world power are constantly changing. Toal concludes by stating that any consideration of the changing world political map must recognise that there are multiple world political maps produced by the territorialities of the inter-state system, alongside dynamic maps of flow produced by new global technologies, and that these must be considered and documented together.

But even in their most conventional sense, international boundaries continue to be demarcated. States continue to contest and redraw the lines separating them from their neighbours. This is mostly reflected in micro-territorial changes along parts of a boundary, rather than in the total redrawing of a boundary altogether. New, sophisticated, techniques of delimitation, coupled with the fact that we live increasingly in a world where the claims of smaller, weaker, States are being posited, has resulted in the reopening of territorial issues which were largely imposed by stronger parties in the past. More sophisticated historical research has enabled past lines of demarcation to be put forward as proof of territorial claims and States are pressing forward with their territorial claims.

Lines are being drawn and redrawn as part of the process of territorial reordering which has taken place in the aftermath of the collapse of the Soviet Union and as other countries seek resolution to ongoing ethno-territorial conflicts. In many cases, the boundaries of new States are no more than the administrative boundaries which separated them during decades of Soviet rule and which, in many cases, reflected the international boundaries in the pre-Soviet era. But the process through which populations have been transferred, often forcefully, has created the sort of ethno-territorial mix within single territories which throws up new political problems.[40]

For as long as they have existed, international boundaries have been linked with territorial conflict.[41] States seek to expand their territorial control and, as such, end up in negotiating, or fighting over, the demarcation of new boundaries. The globalisation era of the 1990's has done nothing to prevent territorial conflicts from taking place. States demand the redemarcation of boundaries to take in ethnic groups of similar national identity, or because of a desire to claim control over scarce and valuable natural resources. Historical injustices in the way that the line was originally drawn are thrown up, while in an era of international human rights and perceived global equality, States often demand a more 'just' allocation of territory than that superimposed upon the landscape by the past colonial rulers. But for most political scientists, boundaries are viewed as constituting a given territorial fact, a static, unchanging feature, rather than one which has its own internal dynamics and which influences, and is influenced by, the patterns of social, economic and political development which take place in the surrounding landscapes – the frontier regions and/or the borderlands.

Gary Goertz and Paul Diehl argue that the fact that most of the world has been divided into States has made boundary disputes much less common than in the past.[42] Nevertheless, they note that the process of territorial expansion is often rooted in the process of national development as States – both old and new – seek to acquire control over additional territory, pushing their boundary outwards to meet demographic, economic or ethnic objectives. In his study of territorial disputes and international conflict, Paul Huth argues that systematic knowledge about the origins, evolution and termination of territorial disputes is limited. His examination of 129 territorial disputes between 1950 and 1990 raises a number of questions concerning the extent to which international boundaries will be disputed between states, and under what conditions such disputes will be settled peacefully through compromise and/or concessions.[43]

In their most concrete dimension, boundaries compartmentalise national territory. These territories contain populations who are expected to retain a loyalty and affiliation to the state within which they reside. National identity is tied up with the territory within which they live and this, despite the fact that most states are multi-national rather than nation-state, and that boundaries are continually changing in such a way as to leave ethnic and national minorities resident of states to which they do not confess a national identity.[44] In this sense, boundaries are very unnatural features in that they do not create the territorial compartments which are compatible with the distribution of the national populations. States attempt to resolve this incompatibility through processes of national and territorial socialisation, applied through such agencies as the media, the formal educational framework, and other means of emphasising the symbolic and mythical elements of the homeland landscape, together with the inviolability of the state boundaries. Anssi Paasi has emphasised the relationship between territory, boundaries and national identity, while focusing strongly on the agents of socialisation which are used by the respective governments to strengthen the feelings of national identity in and around the border zone.[45]

These issues are raised in the chapter by Jason Ackleson, which examines the narratives and representations of territoriality along the US-Mexico borderland. Ackleson explores the relationships between borders, territoriality and collective identity in the borderlands in an increasingly transnational and trans-boundary environment. He argues that in order to thoroughly investigate the notion of 'a border' we need to move away from the familiar and reified understandings of political space and boundaries and adopt an approach which emphasizes a more holistic view of difference and identity. He discusses the notions of integrated borderlands[46] and binational political communities as possible alternatives to communities which are artificially separated by a geographic line, and notes the importance of scale in changing the socio-spatial consciousness of 'borderlanders'.

Ramutsindela's paper on African boundaries also raises important issues of identity. Moving on from the traditional debate concerning the colonial inheritance of Africa's contemporary territorial structure, Ramutsindela asks what should happen to these boundaries in the next stage of decolonisation. He discusses alternative interpretations of African boundaries, ranging from a process of remapping and repartitioning, to one which would retain the present territorial status. A new political map could eliminate threats of ethnic domination by repartitioning space along lines which demonstrate greater ethnic homogeneity This would, in his words, bring about a 'reconfiguration of states, which previously suffered as a result of the forced co-existence of communities'. At the same time, Ramutsindela also notes the argument against changing boundaries because of their 'durability' and their recognition as part of the contemporary international order. In conclusion, Ramutsindela argues that redrawing the map will not necessarily enhance the relationship between territoriality and national identity, and that changes should focus on the functionality of the boundaries, rather than their specific location. Like Ackleson, he argues that the very concept of boundary has to be rethought in changing the character, rather than the physical appearance, of the colonial boundaries.

David Knight's chapter on Quebec builds on his past studies which examine the relationship between geography, nationalism and identity.[47] He discusses the importance of the territory-identity relationship from two contrasting perspectives. The first of these, stressing territory over identity, is the right under international law for an existing state to protect and maintain its existing territory. The second, stressing identity over territory, is the right of a regionally dominant, sub-state people, self defined as a nation, to have self determination and undertake territorial secession, and hence achieve statehood. The issue of boundary definition vis a vis a self defined 'nation', raises the question concerning 'what territory can a seceeding people take with them as they create a new state?'.

There has always remained the chicken and egg question concerning 'what comes first?' – the boundary or the identity? Does the fact that people are spatially compartmentalised within a fixed territory result in the gradual formation of a national identity which is focused on that specific territory, or does the prior formation of cultural and national groups bring about the subsequent demarcation of boundaries around the groups territory – or at least that territory in which they constitute a clear demographic majority? History points to both processes taking place at one and the same time. The so-called 'end of nation state' thesis of the past decade does not stand up well in the light of the return to the nation 'dominant'-state concept which has taken place in the newly independent republics of the former Soviet Union, in the Czech and Slovakian republics, in Yugoslavia, Bosnia, Cyprus, and Israel-Palestine, and the list is endless. The move towards localised autonomy, such as is taking place within Western Europe, points to the importance of what were, until recently, no more than internal administrative boundaries, becoming the new demarcators of ethnic and national territorial identity.

While boundary lines remain largely intact, their functionality has changed dramatically during the past two decades. Where boundaries acted as barriers to all forms of movement in the past, they have become increasingly permeable to movement in the contemporary world. In some spheres of globalisation, such as the dissemination of information through cyberspace and the internet, and the transfer of media images through satellites and cables, boundaries have largely become a relict of the past. Within economics too, the flow of capital in a single global market pays scant attention to the barrier impact of boundaries, while the continued existence of customs and tariffs in some parts of the world is more of an attempt by States to demonstrate their sovereignty than it is a true barrier to economic flows. As people move more freely, they increasingly cross boundaries which were closed to them in the past. The flow of cheap migrant labour from poorer to richer countries, much of it illegal in the sense that the migrants do not possess the official documentation for crossing the boundary and/or remain in their country of work over and beyond the time limits of the initial permits, is indicative of the failure of the boundary to 'keep out' and exclude those groups of people deemed undesirable by the State authorities. The global population has become increasingly mobile, international and trans-boundary travel is no longer limited to the rich elites, while the point of entry into the State has moved away from the boundary at the frontier to the one which exists in the very heart of the state capital, at its air and sea ports.

In other respects, many boundaries remain closed, especially in situations of direct military confrontation between enemy States. Political frontiers, often devoid of civilians and full of military installations are still the order of the day along many boundaries. While ballistic missiles may, in the view of some, have relocated the boundary from the territorial periphery of the State into the heart of the downtown of the capital city, the outer lines of defense remain important for most countries, not least because it continues to demarcate the geographic extent of their territorial sovereignty, and also because even in an era of modern technological war, the threat of an invasion by land troops from across the boundary remains a permanent threat for many countries.

Thus borderlands, rather than borders, have become an important spatial unit of analysis, to the extent that the nature of trans-boundary cooperation and co-existence reflects the extent to which globalisation processes can help dilute inter-ethnic differentiation.[48] Both Minghi's and Boal's chapters focus on different aspects of this process. Minghi's paper on borderland minorities amongst Italy's ethnic communities notes the importance of 'common cause' in consolidating and expanding local political control over the cultural life of each of the minority linguisting groups, while Boal's study of ethnic conflict in Northern Ireland focuses on the 'mutuality solution' as a means of reducing conflict. The location and spatial scale of these two case studies may be very different, as too the intensity of conflict and inter-ethnic differentiation, but they both point to the fact that traditional notions of territorial separation are no longer adequate, in a globalised world, as a means of accomodating difference, otherness and conflict.

Boundaries in a 'Borderless World'

We may live in a world where boundary functions have changed and have become increasingly permeable, but we do not live in a 'borderless' world. One of the fallacies of the globalisation theory is that everything actually becomes global. While globalisation affects people and places throughout the world, it does not affect everyone. Territories, as boundaries, remain spatially differentiated, with some becoming more permeable (such as in Western Europe) while, at one and the same time, others are being constructed as part of a process of conflict resolution and are almost automatically becoming sealed. Where European concepts of fixed boundaries and territory were imposed upon African and Asian societies only fifty years ago, the Western European and North American discourse has now declared the arrival of the 'borderless world', while Africa and Asian countries have only just about moved from their own borderless world to a world full of borders. Thus, while boundaries will continue to be impacted by social and technological change, they will remain differentiated in the extent to which they will be subject to these impacts in different places and at different time periods.

The notion of boundary permeability is associated with transboundary cooperation. In his discussion of African boundaries, Maano Ramutsindela notes that transborder co-operative projects in Southern Africa and elsewhere on the continent (for example transborder peace parks) are viable and pragmatic ways of infusing new meanings into (much disputed) colonial boundaries. This contrasts with the situation described by Jason Ackleson, focusing on the American-Mexico borderland. The present situation in this area reflects the power of globalisation through the formation of NAFTA, transnationalisation of capital and information on the one hand, while preserving the power of exclusionary restrictions on legal and illegal immigration, on the other. Ackleson suggests, however, that in the future a move towards an integrated borderland or a binational political community might be possible. This ties in well with Barlow's[49] discussion of transborder regions as constituting an inevitable outcome of the globalisation process, although some of the inherent difficulties – even in a region of great cultural and socio-economic homogeneity – have been discussed by Sparke in his analysis of the Cascadia region.[50]

The significance of just what boundaries are and what their impact on the political ordering of society is, has also changed. From an almost exclusive focus on the physical nature and demarcation of the territorial lines, the study of boundaries has become multi-dimensional, focusing on the different scales of boundaries, as well as the impact on group and national identities, not all of which are necessarily organised along territorial lines. The nature of boundaries remains strongly linked to the evolution and development of States, but rather than simply looking at the boundary-territory-identity triad in a deterministic fashion, many of the recent studies look at the practices through which these identities and these boundaries are constructed, both by the State (from above) as well as from the populations themselves (from below). All boundaries – be they social or spatial – continue to define the 'us' and the 'them', excluding some and including others. This may not always take place at the territorial level, but territory remains important in the way that many of these lines of exclusion are drawn up in the first place, and the extent to which interaction across these lines of exclusion/inclusion take place.

Concluding Comments

The chapters in these two volumes raise some major questions concerning the validity of the globalisation thesis inasmuch as it relates to geopolitical and territorial issues. The world has not become deterritorialised, although the territorial configurations of state power are changing, as both global and local actors have come into play. The world political map has changed empirically as a result of localised events, such as the break up of the Soviet Union, the coming together of Western Europe, peace processes in Israel-Palestine, Northern Ireland and South Africa, or conflict and warfare in Kosovo, Iraq-Kuwait, and Rwanda. But these changes are no different to the many territorial changes which have continued to take place throughout world history. Where change has taken on a different dimension is the qualitative change, partially impacted by globalisation and technology, in which the traditional components of State power have been challenged, not least the impact and influence of boundaries as constituting the ultimate demarcator of State sovereignty and activity. The geographical and territorial focus of the essays in this volume, while accepting the profound impact of globalisation, demonstrate the constraints which continue to play a role in preserving the territorial focus of power in a changing world political map.

NOTES

1. D. Newman (ed.), *Boundaries, Territory and Postmodernity* (London: Frank Cass 1999).
2. H. van der Wusten, 'Globalisation and geography: editorial', *Geojournal* 45/1–2 (1998) p.1.
3. M. Barlow, 'Globalisation and new regions: government and public administration', *Geojournal* 49/1–2 (1998) p.101.
4. C. Williams, 'Nationalism and Its derivatives in post-1989 Europe', in R. Hudson and A. Williams (eds.), *Divided Europe* (London: Sage 1999) pp.79–106.
5. Hudson and Williams, ibid, Introduction: p.5.
6. R. Boyer and D. Drache (eds.), *States Against Markets: The Limits of Globalisation* (London: Routledge 1996).
7. van der Wusten (note 2), p.1.
8. D. Morley and K. Robins, *Spaces of Identity* (London: Routledge 1995).
9. S. Conti and P. Giaccaria, 'Globalisation: A Geographical Discourse', *Geojournal* 45/1–2 (1998) p.17.
10. K Ohmae, *The Borderless World* (London: Collins 1990); Ohmae, K. *The End of the Nation State* (London: Harper and Collins 1995).
11. R. Johnston (1998), 'The Local Meets the Global in British Geography', *Geojournal* 45/1–2 pp.41–49.
12. Johnston (note 11) p.41.
13. E.N. Luttwak, 'From Geopolitics to Geo-Economics', *National Interest* 20 (1990) pp.17–24.
14. Anderson, E.W., 'The effects of globalisation on geographical perspectives', *Geojournal* 45/1–2 (1998) p.105.
15. Anderson (note 14) p.106.
16. Ibid.
17. P. Hirst and G. Thompson, *Globalisation in Question* (Cambridge: Polity 1996).
18. Hirst and Thompson (note 17) p.98.
19. Van der Wusten (note 2).
20. Williams (note 4) p.102.
21. Ibid, pp.79–106.
22. Ibid, p.102.
23. See Barlow (note 3).
24. Ibid, p.102.

25. M. Sparke, 'From geopolitics to geoeconomics: transnational state effects in the borderland', *Geopolitics* 3/2 (1998) pp.62–98.

26. The notion of 'fourth world' nations in Western Europe is discussed by: B. Nietschmann, 'The "Fourth World": nations versus states', in G.J. Demko and W.B. Woods (eds.), *Reordering the World: Geopolitical Perspectives on the Twenty First Century* (Boulder, CO: Westview Press 1994); R. Griggs and P. Hocknell, 'The geography and geopolitics of Europeans fourth world', *Boundary and Security Bulletin* 3/4 pp.59–67.

27. See Barlow (note 3) p.103.

28. D. Rumley, 'Geography, Interdependence and Security', *Geojournal* 45/1–2 (1998) p.110.

29. Ibid. p.111.

30. Ibid.

31. Ibid.

32. van der Wusten (note 2); P. Taylor, 'Understanding global inequalities', *Geography* 77 (1992) pp.10–21; Barlow (note 3).

33. See: A. Hudson, 'Beyond the borders: globalisation, sovereignty and extra-territoriality', *Geopolitics* 3/1 (1998) p.105; H. Wai-Chung Yeung, 'Capital, state and space: contesting the borderless world', *Transactions of the Institute of British Geographers* 23/3 (1998) pp.291–309.

34. See Hudson and Williams (note 5) p.29.

35. A. Tickell, 'Questions about Globalisation: A Book Review Essay', *Geoforum* 29/1 (1998) pp.1–5.

36. See Rumley (note 29) p.111.

37. The second part of this introductory chapter is based on a recent review looking at the current 'state of art' in boundary studies. See: D. Newman, 'Into the millenium: the study of boundaries in an era of technological and global change', *Boundary and Security Bulletin* 4/4 (2000) pp.63–72, 2000. See also: D. Newman and A. Paasi, 'Fences and neighbours in a postmodern world: boundary narratives in political geography; *Progress in Human Geography* 22/2 (1998) pp.186–207.

38. For various perspectives on the 'borderless world' debate, see: M.J. Shapiro, and H.R. Alker, *Challenging Boundaries: Global Flows, Territorial Identities*, Minneapolis: University of Minneapolis Press, 1996: See also: D. Newman (note 1).

39. D. Newman, 'Boundaries, territory and postmodernity: towards shared or separate spaces?, in M. Pratt and J. Brown (eds.), *Borderlands Under Stress* (London: Kluwer Law International, 2000).

40. V. Kolossov, *Ethno-Territorial Conflicts and Boundaries in the Former Soviet Union.* Boundary and Territory Briefing, No. 2, International Boundaries Research Unit, Durham, England, 1992; T. Forsberg (ed.), *Contested Territory: Border Disputes at the Edge of the Former Soviet Empire* (Cheltenham: Edward Elgar 1995).

41. P. Diehl (ed.), *A Roadmap to War: Territorial Dimensions of International Conflict* (Nashville, TN: Vanderbilt University Press 1999); P. Huth, *Standing Your Ground: Territorial Disputes and International Conflict* (Ann Arbor, MI: University of Michigan Press 1996).

42. G. Goertz and P. Diehl, *Territorial Changes and International Conflict.* (London: Routledge 1992).

43. P. Huth (note 41).

44. T. Wilson and H. Donnan (eds.), *Border Identities: Nation and State at International Frontiers.*(Cambridge: Cambridge University Press 1998).

45. A. Paasi, *Territories, Boundaries and Consciousness: The Changing Geographies of the Finnish-Russian Border* (Chichester: John Wiley 1996).

46. The notion of integrated borderlands is raised by Oscar Martinez, 'The dynamics of border interaction', in C. Schofield (ed.), *World Boundaries Vol I: Global Boundaries* (London: Routledge 1994) pp.1–14.

47. D. Knight, 'Identity and territory: geographic perspectives on nationalism and regionalism', *Annals of the Association of American Geographers* 72 (1982) pp.514–31; D. Knight, 'People together, yet apart: rethinking sovereignty, territory and identity', in G. Demko and W. Wood (eds.), *Reordering the World: Geopolitical Perspectives on the Twenty First*

Century (Boulder CO: Westview Press 1994). See also: D. Hooson (ed.), *Geography and National Identity* (Oxford: Blackwell 1994).

48. Notions of borderlands and trans-boundary interaction are a common theme in recent collections of essays on boundaries. See Martinez (note 47). See also: W.A. Gallusser (ed.), *Political Boundaries and Coexistence* (Berne: Peter Lang 1995); P. Gamster, A. Sweedler, J. Scott and W. Dieter-Eberwein (eds.), *Borders and Border Regions in Europe and North America* (San Diego, CA: San Diego University Press 1997); D. Rumley and J. Minghi (eds.), *The Geography of Border Landscapes* (London: Routledge 1991).

49. M. Barlow (note 3).

50. M. Sparke (note 25).

The Worldviews of Small States:
A Content Analysis of 1995 UN Speeches

STANLEY D. BRUNN

All states have a place on the world political map that is defined by themselves and others. That place becomes significant when there are political and economic changes within states themselves and in the region. Power shifts, new democracies, the ebbs and flows of conflict are examples of the nature of intrastate and interstate dynamics that also lead to defining and redefining a state's place in the world. The past decade provides ample evidence of new states having sought to identify where they fit and belong on regional and world political maps, and also of old states having redefined their roles.[1]

It is not difficult to consider changes in the perceptions and worldviews of major global military, political, and economic players, such as Russia, Germany, China, Japan, or the USA, as these are in key leadership positions in G8 talks, the World Trade Organisation, the European Union, NATO, and the United Nations. They, by their histories of regional and global power and leadership, are among the major players dictating and influencing the world economic and political agendas. Citizens and leaders of other states watch and listen to what these megastate leaders say about themselves, their neighbours, their adversaries, regional hegemons, and pressing global issues. What they express is conveyed to major viewing and listening audiences not only by major transnational media such as CNN and Rupert Murdoch's networks and affiliates, but also by official government pronouncements. Analysts carefully scrutinise the travels of institutional leaders, high-level delegations, and trade and cultural missions: where are they are going and why, not only in the case of friendly states, but also when travelling to sites for conferences and meetings to open dialogue with adversaries or to serve as mediators with disputing parties.

While political and media attention is focused on a few large states, there is another group of states that is far more numerous on the world political map. These are the small states, sometimes also called microstates and mini-states because of their small population or territory, or both. They are important and integral parts of the world map, even though most (and there are exceptions) do not have the economic and political importance of medium-sized and larger states. Small states by their demographies, territory, and economies have concerns and problems not shared by larger states. They may lack a strong agricultural and mineral resource base and access to the world's oceans, and they may be historical or contemporary pawns of larger and more powerful neighbouring states. Size may be a weakness and make them vulnerable to aggressors or a lack of respect and representation in regional and global decision making. Their small size may also mean they are ignored by other states. But regardless of these fundamental features of size, demography, and location, each small state has a worldview of itself and the world. These small states and their worldviews are my focus. I assess these views through a content analysis of the speeches of leaders at the UN's fiftieth anniversary session 22–24 October 1995. At this meeting there were presentations by original and new UN members, large and small states, new and long-standing democracies, and old friends and adversaries, all sitting in the same room.

My purposes are fourfold. First, I review the literature on worldviews and the politics and geopolitics of small states. Second, I examine what these leaders stated in their addresses; I look for key words and common themes. Third, I discern if there were any major issues or problems expressed by those leaders, and whether those problems that were expressed were unique to the state itself or problems expressed at a regional and global scale. I also examine if there were any regional differences. Were those worldviews from European small states any different from those in Africa or the Pacific Basin? The overall objective is to observe whether small states exhibit uniform concerns, or regional or individual concerns, or some combination of all these.

I define small states as those with less than five million people in 1995. There were 78 that met this criterion and made presentations at this UN gathering. Most are in Europe, the Pacific Basin, the Caribbean, and North Africa and Southwest Asia. They range in population from the Holy See (less than 1,000) to Jordan with 4.9 million and in size from 0.44 square kilometres for the Holy See to 1.5 million square kilometres for Mongolia. The 78 states have a combined population of approximately 135 million, which is slightly larger than Pakistan or less than France and Germany together. The combined land area is 8.8 million square kilometres (roughly the size of Brazil or the USA).

Discerning a Worldview

A state's world-views can be measured using a number of variables and indices (Table 1). One measure is how the state depicts itself on regional and world maps. Does it place itself in the centre for maximum eye appeal? What colours does it use to refer to friends and adversaries? How does it demarcate and label conflicting territories, such as Israel/Palestine, Kashmir, and Cyprus? Worldviews are also expressed through diplomatic missions, official visits, and scholarly and citizen exchanges, membership in regional and international organisations, through trade patterns, military alliances, and loans and credits. Speeches represent another opportunity for a state to express its place in a region or the world. Political leaders make statements to their own citizens and to citizens in visiting states and at regional and global conferences. The content of formal addresses will reveal impressions, perceptions, and ideas not only about the leader's own state, but how she or he looks at others. UN voting records may also reveal linkages and associations, for example, among former colonies to a European power or countries with similar religious, linguistic, and cultural heritages. A recent innovation that gives states a new vehicle to display their own history to global audiences is through official World Wide Web homepages. These pages and their hyperlinks often contain symbolic, colourful, graphical, and photographic information about the state for Web users. Text is often at a minimum. The visual contents are designed for tourists, developers, and international investment bankers.

TABLE 1

CRITERIA USED TO MEASURE A STATE'S WORLDVIEWS

Official maps and propaganda cartography
Presentation of history and geography in school texts
Authors of texts
Displays in museums and exhibits
Diplomatic missions: embassies and consulates
Diplomatic exchanges
Official state boosterism: promotion and advertising
Official iconography
Stamps and currency
Official visits
Trade missions and pacts
International trading partners
Membership in alliances: regional and international
Membership in IGOs and NGOs
Content of official WWW homepages

TABLE 2

ELEMENTS THAT HELP TO SHAPE A STATE'S WORLDVIEWS

Historical ties to other states
Experiences in the past, for example, colonialism and occupation
Recent political changes
Images and iconography
Strong personalities
Influences by regional and global superpowers
Internal political changes, for example, civil war and democratisation
Absolute and relative location

Thus the worldview of any state is formed, shaped, and continually being reshaped as a result of a number of processes (Table 2). These changes include historical ties to other units, changes of leadership, independence, and major events such as a conflict or environmental disaster or the passing away of a strong personality. In addition, small states are influenced by the actions of regional powers and superpowers. Relative location also is a key ingredient. Whether the state is central or peripheral to global centres of economic wealth and power is crucial, as is how many states it borders and whether those neighbours are friendly, unfriendly, or neutral. It is important to know whether a small state is landlocked or shelf-locked and how those positions affect its views.

Literature Review

Political and cultural geographers have used a variety of criteria to delimit, measure, and describe the worldviews of countries and regions. In 1904, Mackinder[2] considered Britain's role in a world threatened by continental powers (especially Russia and Germany). His maps became powerful instruments affecting not only Britain's policies, but also other European and North American states. Later, Spykman[3] developed the concept of pan-regions; his maps as well illustrated regional foreign-policy priorities. Security and geopolitics operated hand in hand. Geopolitical and geostrategic views were also integral in the macro-political thinking, power shifts and the results of conflicts and treaties, and how the emerging regional powers were viewed following the Second World War. Cohen's studies[4] looked at global patterns. How individual states saw themselves were the focus of Kristof's[5] study on Russia's homeland, Ginsburg's[6] and Tuan's[7] on China, and Dodds's[8] on the geopolitical imagination in the creation of Argentina.

Worldviews can also be observed through other activities, including diplomatic exchanges and membership in government and non-governmental organisations,[9] the travels of officials,[10] and how political leaders themselves perceive local, regional, and global spaces.[11] UN voting patterns also provide insights into how states look at themselves.[12] The maps a state constructs for school use or official propaganda purposes also convey images about how a state wishes to present itself to its own citizens and to friends and adversaries. Bright colours, eye-catching icons, familiar illustrations, and emotionally laden words when combined with distorted map projections can serve ultra-nationalistic and propaganda purposes.[13] Official maps are symbols of power, and especially if used by the state to advance its own purposes in times of conflict or to generate hostility toward or fear of others.[14] Other state-produced products include textbooks, films produced by national film boards,[15] designs and topics on currency and stamps,[16] flags, anthems, monuments, museum displays, national contests, and recently, the symbolic, graphical and narrative content of official World Wide Web pages.[17] The visits and appearances of dignitaries, and speeches by political leaders, whether as official addresses[18] or words used in debates,[19] also convey their impressions about world events, adversaries, and friendly states.

Small states have been studied by political geographers, political scientists and sociologists, anthropologists, economists, and educators.[20] Most of their works are descriptive, historical, or contemporary case studies of individual states. Few are catholic in perspective, in the sense that they seek to place small-state issues and problems in regional or global contexts. Such states have specific problems because of their small population or territory (or both),[21] their unique cultures and histories,[22] their insular character,[23] and as sites of recent conflict and media images and as landscapes of remembrance.[24] Additional problems occur as they conduct foreign policy,[25] regional political restructuring,[26] security,[27] maintaining defence forces,[28] and public administration.[29] Economic issues on the agenda include not only how they can or might be accommodated in regional trade blocs and globally restructured economies,[30] or issues of sustainability and tourism,[31] but also poor states being adversely affected by international debt considerations[32] and how they see themselves in a larger system.[33] Some states successfully use their size to promote themselves as having a unique role in global affairs, for example, as the headquarters of international agencies or sites for treaties;[34] examples are Sweden,[35] Switzerland,[36] and Finland. Media and telecommunications policies are also of importance to small states.[37] Lastly, there are questions about the future of small states in a larger political arena.[38]

The UN Gathering and Speeches

The fiftieth anniversary session included speeches by 179 heads of state and another 20 intergovernmental and non-governmental organisations, such as the Red Cross and Red Crescent, the South Pacific Forum, the Palestine Liberation Organisation, the Organisation for African Unity, and the European Union. Each speaker was asked to deliver their remarks in 15 minutes, but some took much longer. There were six UN members that did not make presentations: Somalia, Yugoslavia, Eritrea, Ethiopia, North Korea, and São Tomé and Príncipe. The speeches were delivered in 27 different languages; 44 per cent in English, followed by 15 per cent in French, 11 per cent in Spanish, ten per cent in Arabic, and four per cent in Russian. In my analysis, I use English translations.[39]

There was a wide variation in the length of speeches. The longest speeches at the celebration were delivered by Belarus, China, and Croatia, each of 2,500–3,200 words. Of the small states, the shortest was delivered by the United Arab Emirates (448 words) and the longest by Croatia (2,503 words). There were ten speeches of less than 600 words; in addition to the UAE, these were Congo, Armenia. Guinea-Bissau, the Holy See, Laos, Botswana, Panama, St Vincent, and Brunei.

The contents of the 179 presentations can be divided into eight categories. These are: (1) major issues, such as disarmament, women's rights, and expanding the Security Council; (2) immediate problems, such as AIDS, ethnic conflict, or refugees; (3) places, such as Rwanda, Israel/Palestine, and Somalia; (4) regional references, such as the Balkans, Central Asia, or the Pacific Basin; (5) events, including the mentioning of UN conferences, treaties, or the independence of states; (6) a time perspective, usually the coming millennium or next century; (7) symbolic words, such as hope, freedom, and love; and, lastly (8) scale, from the individual state to its region or the entire international community. A given speech would usually include key words and phrases in three or more categories.

The most frequent words included in speeches were 'peace', 'development', 'security', 'conflict', and 'war', all mentioned by two-thirds of all speeches.[40] The next highest frequencies were for 'Security Council', 'human rights', 'future' (including 'millennium' and 'next century'), 'reform', 'poverty', 'co-operation', and 'environment'. It is not surprising that in such a celebratory event there would be words of praise and support for the UN's accomplishments. The words 'small states' appeared in 35 speeches. Most speakers used part of their allotted time to discuss UN history, what it meant to a more peaceful world, and how they envisioned their own place in that world. Words that appeared much less frequently in speeches were 'disarmament', 'Security Council reform', 'terrorism', 'peacekeeping', and 'sustainable development'. Many of these words had regional associations, for example, with 'drugs' and 'terrorism' being more frequently used in speeches by presenters from the North, and 'Security Council reform' (calling for expanding membership) from the South. There were very few references to 'illiteracy', 'famine', or 'well-being'.

Because small states exist in most major world regions, it is to be expected that there would be differences in their worldviews. The list includes those with long democratic traditions, for example, Iceland, Norway, Liechtenstein, and Luxembourg, and others that are emerging democracies, including Kyrgyzstan, Moldova, Palau, and Bosnia. Some have very successful economies, such as the United Arab Emirates, Kuwait, Norway, and Singapore, while others are among the world's poorest, for example, Djibouti, Bhutan and Laos. Some, including Turkmenistan and Namibia, have promising futures because of valuable mineral bases, while others would appear to have less promising outlooks, for instance Nicaragua, Lesotho, and St Vincent. Half of the small states have legacies as former European colonies and many new European and Central Asian states have a Soviet legacy.

Expressions of Worldviews

I examine the small-state speeches with three questions in mind. First, how do these states see themselves in the world? Second, how do they see the world? And, third, how do they envision the United Nations? In regard to the first question, namely, how they see themselves in the world, the addresses varied. Some took the UN anniversary as an opportunity to describe their own identity in the world, an identity that they often traced to historical events. For example, Turkmenistan saw itself as being 'located at a major world crossroads'. Kyrgyzstan described itself as 'an ancient people, but a young nation'; Oman referred to itself as a state that 'has witnessed the most unprecedented level of economic resurgence ever achieved in history'; and Monaco regarded itself as 'a seagoing country that is particularly active, and intends to continue being active in the sphere of protection of seas and oceans, and beyond that, nature in general'. Boosterist statements were not unknown as was a nation commemorating its place in history. Nicaragua was proud that it had 'emerged from the ashes of war'. Macedonia was so proud of 'our constitutional name' that it mentioned the Republic of Macedonia 12 times. Panama's president stated that the country now 'enjoys full democracy, with total freedom and respect for human rights'. Historic and recent events were recorded in other speeches. Armenia reminded the listeners that it 'sent 600,000 to battlefields in the Second World War and nearly half never returned'. Albania declared that it had moved 'from the most isolated and closed country on the planet ... to [being] fully integrated in Europe and the world'. Three states that alluded to recent problems were Samoa, the United Arab Emirates, and The Maldives. Samoa stated, with regard to French nuclear testing in the South Pacific in late 1995, that 'Of the entire United Nations membership, Samoa is located closest to the test site.' The UAE remarked that the 'Iranian occupation of our three islands poses a direct threat.' The Maldives speech was very concerned about the islands' future and expressed a wish to know 'what the UN will do to save the Maldives and other small island nations from being engulfed by the sea', a reference to the negative consequences of global warming. A number of states, large and small, thanked the UN for helping them achieve independence. Bahrain was among these.

How the small states 'see the world' was reflected in statements about the present and future condition of humankind and the planet. Several speakers noted the importance of small states in the world today. Andorra noted that 'small communities can give lessons in peaceful coexistence, cordial understanding, respect and tolerance', this from a country that has had a history of '700 years of peace and tolerance'. Viewing the future with optimism was a common theme in several speeches. Cape Verde expressed the opinion that we are 'at the dawn of a new era'. Bosnia's representative stated that 'We shall win, with God's help.' Gambia's leader commented that he hopes 'that from now on nations will not be guided in their relationships by the law of the jungle or the misguided instinct of might being right'. Other speakers reflected on recent history and wondered what lessons could be learned. Mongolia's leader stated that 'This half century will also be remembered as a time of tremendous waste of human creativity and energy for purposes of destruction,' and St Vincent's that 'the evils of communism ... imposed such monumental waste of our civilization'. A moral tenor was noted in speeches by the Solomon Islands, which contained the phrase 'our problems are ultimately moral and spiritual in nature' and by Ireland, which called for 'a genuine global ethic'. Pacific Island members were among those calling for a world that is better. Vanuatu stated 'Let us build a more pacific world.' New Zealand asked that 'we live in a world without walls' and Uruguay suggested that 'freedom and dreaming are tender plants'. The Holy See speech, delivered by Pope John Paul, noted that the 'future of humanity depends in the final analysis on a willingness to live together'. Not all small states envisioned the world with optimism and without problems. Lesotho noted that the 'economic, social and environmental problems for the majority of humankind still remain bleak'. Djibouti noted the concept of 'nation inflation'.

Most small states saw the United Nations as an organisation that provided them with a forum to express their views. Newly independent states expressed gratitude to the organisation for helping to dismantle colonialism, apartheid, and the lack of freedoms associated with cold-war geopolitics. Croatia referred to the UN as 'a garden of ideas' and St Lucia referred to the organisation as being 'created specifically to help the wretched of the Earth'. Bhutan noted that 'We benefit from the activities of the United Nations ... whose assistance made a real difference in the everyday life of our people.' In a similar fashion, the Barbadian speech stated that the 'United Nations has touched the lives of people in every corner of the world'. The foreign affairs minister of Georgia sums up these last two points: 'If the United Nations did not exist ... [there would be a] need to reinvent it.' Several states referred to the politics of the organisation itself and how it perceives and addresses problems. Ireland referred to the

UN as a 'ritual verbal battle in six languages'. Grenada said it was 'the biggest debating society in the world'. Kuwait, affected by UN intervention during the Gulf War, noted that 'We pray to Allah, the Almighty, to help resolve the human aspirations embodied by the UN.' Slovenia's president noted that members 'must be open to the departure of those who work against the mission of the United Nations'. Samoa noted that 'the power of correction [in the UN] lies not here [in New York], but in the capitals [of its members]'. In spite of all the problems facing the world and the organisation, Antigua's minister of foreign affairs noted that 'history is on the side of the UN'. The president of Palau, one of the UN's newest members, summed up how members see the UN: it is 'at the helm of our planetary spaceship and we are captains, navigators, and crew'.

Regional Variations in Worldviews

Since the worldview of a state is based on how its leaders see themselves, its history, and its place in a region and the world, and because the currents and cross-currents of ideologies and migrations mark the creation of the world political map at any point in time, it is not surprising that small states in many world regions have different perspectives. Inasmuch as the speakers had only a limited amount of time to express what was of utmost concern, the speeches are considered to be useful guides in evaluating what issues mattered to them most. (See Table 3).

Regional variations in speech content existed. These are illustrated in a schematic that 'maps' the content of small-state speeches in 13 major world regions (Figure 1). The key words are categorised into eight major categories: conflict, conflict resolution, human rights, heritage, social and economic issues, self-determination and democracy, environmental issues, and Middle Eastern issues. Speakers from nine regions made comments about conflict; a number included references to Bosnia, ethnic cleansing, terrorism, and civil war. The conflict-resolution category included references to preventive diplomacy, constructive negotiations, peacekeeping, and peace and security; these were themes in speeches from leaders in northern Europe, South America, Southeast Asia, and East Asia. Environmental issues were raised in speeches from northern Europe (sustainable development), South Asia (sea-level rise attributed to global warming), and Pacific Island states (ending nuclear testing by the French in late 1995 and the establishment of nuclear-free zones). The dominant themes in the heritage category were the end of colonialism and apartheid, themes especially important to those leaders in Africa, Central America, and Southeast Asia. The Middle East surfaced as a major theme in speeches by a number of Arab states and also Israel; references were made to the Gulf

TABLE 3

KEY WORDS AND PHRASES USED BY SMALL UN STATES BY MAJOR WORLD REGION

	Europe: Northern	Europe: Southern	Africa: West	Africa: Central	Africa: Southern	South America	Asia: East	Asia: Southeast	Asia: Southwest	Pacific	Caribbean	Central America	Asia: South	Total
End of colonialism	X		X		X			X				X		5
Human rights	X	X	X								X			4
Democratisation	X			X	X									3
Environmental issues	X									X	X	X		4
Drugs and trafficking		X								X	X			3
End of apartheid			X	X	X									3
Self-determination		X					X							2
Terrorism	X	X									X			3
Civil war			X	X										2
Constructive negotiations							X	X						2
Disease			X	X										2
Equality: women							X	X						2
New telecom linkages							X					X		2
Peacekeeping	X					X								2
Political conflicts							X	X						2
Preventive diplomacy	X	X												2
Refugees		X			X									2
Add Japan to the Security Council													X	1
Bosnia and the Balkans		X												1
Economic development						X								1
Elusive Middle East peace									X					1
End of the cold war	X													1
Ethnic cleansing/conflict		X												1
External threats													X	1
Gulf War									X					1
Illiteracy			X											1
International Criminal Court	X													1
Israel's foreign policy									X					1
Nuclear-testing protests										X				1
Nuclear-free zone										X				1
Palestinian rights									X					1
Peace and security						X								1
Poverty and hunger								X						1
Regional conflicts										X				1
Rising sea level													X	1
Unjust economic order						X								1

FIGURE 1
MAJOR ISSUES OF SMALL STATES BY MAJOR WORLD REGION

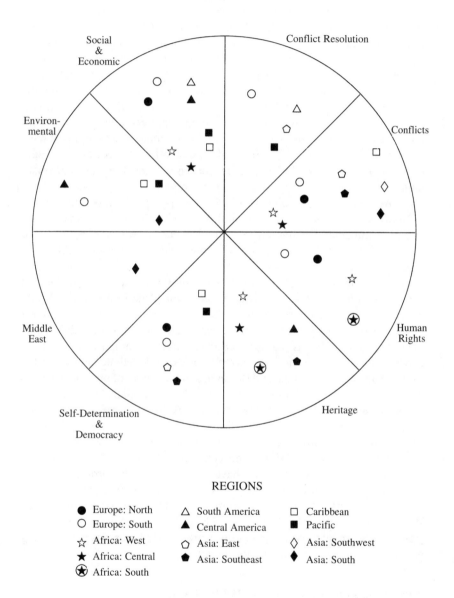

REGIONS

● Europe: North   △ South America   ☐ Caribbean
○ Europe: South   ▲ Central America   ■ Pacific
☆ Africa: West   ⬠ Asia: East   ◇ Asia: Southwest
★ Africa: Central   ⬟ Asia: Southeast   ◆ Asia: South
✪ Africa: South

War, Palestinian rights, and the difficult search for peace. Social and economic issues were incorporated in the speeches by small-state leaders from seven different regions. These issues also illustrated marked regional variations, with drug trafficking and terrorism noted by those in northern Europe, illiteracy in West Africa, poverty and hunger in Southeast Asia, and disease in West and Central Africa. Human rights were a major theme in speeches by leaders from small states in Europe; other issues related to refugees (West and Southern Africa), women (Pacific Islands and the Caribbean), and a World Criminal Court (northern Europe). South America's small states were very concerned about economic development initiatives and also their contributions to international peacekeeping forces.

Which topics speakers ignored is also noteworthy. AIDS was not a topic mentioned in speeches by African leaders, nor were drugs and terrorism mentioned by many from drug-producing regions in Latin America and Asia. Women's rights were not profiled in the speeches by most small states in North Africa, Southwest and Central Asia. While human-rights violations and environmental degradation exist in many states, they were not noted in speeches by many leaders from newly independent countries in Africa or Asia.

The UN presentations by small states illustrated both agreement and variations in how they see themselves and their place in the world. While almost all included references to peace, human rights, democracy, and a Security Council expanded to include Japan and Germany, they differed in identifying the problems that affected them directly. Some stated problems experienced daily by their own citizens, for example, ethnic conflict in the former Yugoslavia, Rwanda, and Burundi, and the fallout of nuclear-weapons testing in the South Pacific. Other speeches, especially from northern European states, dealt with more abstract issues, for example, environmental quality, sustainable development, disarmament, and extensions of human rights to denied groups. Their daily concerns were not civil war or refugees, but stopping the flow of drugs and combating terrorism. The absence of references to certain themes may have been to avoid embarrassment from other states, as might occur if African states had highlighted AIDS or strict Islamic states cited the status of women. In addition, perhaps the lack of stridency in speeches by Israel's neighbours may have been designed to signal a concern by those neighbours to work quietly for efforts guaranteeing greater Palestinian rights and regional harmony.

Small States and Future World Political Maps

Small states have always been integral components of regional and world political maps and they are destined to remain such well into the future. In fact, there will be more of them in the coming decades with renewed calls for self-determination by minority ethnic, religious, and linguistic populations, with new diasporas in transborder and coastal locations, especially in 'gateway' cities and regions, and with regionalist sentiments remaining strong. The appearance of new states and quasi-autonomous states will most likely be in large states where there are old and new population mixes seeking identity and representation and peoples seeking homelands who have been denied such claims. Marginalised populations in peripheral locations, distant from centres of political power, will be among those seeking greater recognition. One might look for fragmented and disenfranchised peoples in Russia, China, Brazil, India, Mexico, the Democratic Republic of Congo, Sudan, and Indonesia to seek autonomy by peaceful and violent means. Also, we might anticipate groups advocating greater representation and autonomy through constitutional means or plebiscites in Australia, Canada, and the USA. Even in states that have long histories as empires, federations or confederations, including France, Italy, Spain, Ukraine, Iran, Nigeria, and Pakistan, new small states might appear.

The functions of new states will be just as varied as they are at present. Political independence, however, does not bring about economic independence. Some poorer states will continue as economic dependencies of traditional powers, that is, there will be a continuation of former colonial status. Others will emerge as transnational havens for favourable banking and investment or for terrorist, insurgent, and rogue activities. New commercial mini-states will surface as centres for global data processing and analysis, publishing, television production, distance learning, money laundering, and gambling (virtual and real), and as conference sites, hosts for regional and global sports events, and for exotic tourism. Some new states may promote themselves as the headquarters of inter-governmental organisations (IGOs) and non-governmental organisations (NGOs) as well as active treaty, mediation and peacekeeping activities. The global economic restructuring that is underway will continue and will result in old and new small states seeking 'place promotion' advantages over large states as well as other small states. In these efforts, the worldviews of new states and how others see them are crucial.

The demographics of future small states will be varied as well. They will exist alongside those in Europe, for example. Some will be small or very small in population or territory, or both; some may even emerge from existing mini-states. Those with larger populations, higher incomes, and favourable geostrategic locations may seek a greater influence in regional and global affairs. With easier transmission of information and rapid communication, many small states will be just as connected to major global markets as are their larger neighbours today.

The political roles and influences of small states will also merit watching. Because of their population 'mixes', cultural and political histories, and economic potential, they are expected to agree on some issues and disagree on others. At times they may side with a larger neighbour, other times with regional interests, and at still other times with other small states regarding global environmental, security, and financial-recovery legislation and on UN restructuring and representation. The analysis above illustrates that the interests of current small states have a strong regional focus. Those near global cores of commerce, wealth, and military power will have different worldviews from those in semi-peripheral and peripheral locations. In this scenario, small SubSaharan African states, which are usually considered 'distant' from global centres of economic and political power, would be expected to emphasise food, population, disease, human survival, and cultural conflict themes. Also, small states in Europe would express interests in human rights, representation, planetary sustainability, regional integration, and environmental quality. Diplomatic networks and roles would be evident in their worldviews. Henrikson[41] posits ten types of small-state diplomacy that will merit watching and analysing; they are: quiet, protest, group, niche, diasporic, multicultural, enterprise, regulatory, summit, and cyber-diplomacy. Rather than one specific mode or model, Henrikson sees the diplomacy of a small state being affected by the actions of neighbours, traditional and emerging political actors within a state, the existing political culture, and advances in telecommunications.

Future Directions

Continued research on small-state worldviews and how larger states perceive small states merits the attention of scholars from different disciplines and traditions. There are five topics that offer promise. The first is to discern whether the small states in a region have worldviews similar to larger states in their region. For example, were the speeches by Ireland, Estonia, Albania, and Luxembourg significantly different from those of Germany, France, Italy, and Britain? The second is to examine the content of UN speeches of new versus old states. Are there any unifying themes among former European colonial states in Africa and Asia that differ from those which have been independent for a much longer period, for example, those in Europe and Central and South America? The third is to determine whether there are any differences in worldviews between states of different sizes. Do those states with a population of less than one million have different worldviews from those that approach five million? One might compare Vanuatu and the Solomon Islands or St Lucia and Dominica with

New Zealand and Singapore or Panama and Uruguay. A fourth topic is whether the small states vote alike in UN General Assembly resolutions or whether they vote in the same way as the larger states in their region. In addition, do small states vote alike on some issues, and if so, what issues? One might examine more closely the Alliance of Small Island States (AOSIS) and the regional associations of small states in the Pacific and Caribbean. The fifth topic is to examine the creation of small-state political culture and discern those critical elements in a small state's past and present that influence how its images and worldviews were shaped and are being shaped, especially with new actors on the global scene and the fuzziness in looking at boundaries, territory, identity, representation, and information and communication technology policy interfaces.[42] In subsequent investigations, I hope to address some of these questions.

ACKNOWLEDGEMENT

I wish to thank Josiah Baker for developing a program to count words in UN speeches.

NOTES

1. A. Holmes, 'Worldviews and theories of international relations', *Journal of International Studies* 24 (1995) pp.148–9.
2. H.J. Mackinder, 'The geographical pivot of history', *Geographical Journal* 23 (1904) pp.421–42.
3. N.J. Spykman, *The Geography of Peace* (New York: Harcourt and Brace 1944).
4. S.B. Cohen, *Geography and Politics in a World Divided* (New York: Oxford University Press 1973); 'A new map of global political equilibrium: A developmental approach', *Political Geography Quarterly* 1 (1982) pp.223–42; 'Global geopolitical changes in the post cold war', *Annals of the Association of American Geographers* 82 (1992) pp.551–80.
5. L. Kristof, 'The state idea, the national idea and the image of the fatherland', *Orbis* 11 (1967) pp.238–55.
6. N. Ginsburg, 'On the Chinese perception of world order', in R.E. Kasperson and J.V. Minghi (eds.), *The Structure of Political Geography* (Chicago: Aldine 1969) pp.330–40.
7. Y-F. Tuan, *Topofilia: A Study of Environmental Perception, Attitudes and Values* (Englewood Cliffs, NJ: Prentice-Hall 1974).
8. K. Dodds, 'Geography and the "envisioning" of Argentina', in K. Dodds and D. Atkinson (eds.), *2000 Geopolitical Traditions* (New York and London: Routledge) pp.150–84.
9. T. Nierop, *Systems and Regions in Global Politics: An Empirical Study of Diplomacy, International Organization, and Trade* (Chichester and New York: John Wiley 1994).
10. J. Hartman and I. Vogeler, 'Where in the world is the Secretary of State?' *Journal of Geography* 92 (1993) pp.2–23.
11. S.D. Brunn, 'The perception of political space', in S.D. Brunn, *Geography and Politics in America* (New York: Harper and Row 1974) pp.27–48.
12. Y. Abate and S.D. Brunn, 'The emergence of African voting blocs and alliances in the United Nations', *The Professional Geographer* 29 (1977) pp.338–46; S.D. Brunn and G.L. Ingalls, 'Identifying voting alliances and blocs in United Nations voting', in N. Kliot and S. Waterman (eds.), *Pluralism and Political Geography: People, Territory, and State* (London and New York: Croom Helm and St. Martin's Press 1983) pp.270–83; S.D. Brunn and G.L. Ingalls, 'Voting patterns in the United Nations General Assembly on uses of the sea', in J. Baylson and N. Ginsburg (eds.), *Ocean Yearbook 7* (Chicago: University of Chicago Press

1988) pp.42–64; R.G. Holcombe and R.S. Sobel, 'The stability of international coalitions in United Nations voting: 1946 to 1973', *Public Choice* 86:1–2 (1996) pp.17–34.

13. L.O. Quam, 'The use of maps in propaganda', *Journal of Geography* 42 (1943) pp.21–32; D.R. Hall, 'A geographical approach to propaganda', in A.D. Burnett and P.J. Taylor (eds.), *Political Studies from Spatial Perspectives: Anglo-American Essays in Political Geography* (Chichester and New York: John Wiley 1991) pp.313–30; J. Pickles, 'Texts, hermeneutics and propaganda maps', in T.J. Barnes and J.S. Duncan (eds.), *Writing Worlds: Discourse, Text, and Metaphor in the Representation of Landscape* (New York: Routledge 1992) pp.192–230; G. Henrik Hebb, 'Persuasive cartography in *Geopolitik* and National Socialism', *Political Geography Quarterly* 8 (1989) pp.290–303.

14. A.K. Henrikson, 'The map as an "idea": The role of cartographic imagery during the Second World War', *The American Cartographer* 2 (1975) pp.19–53; A.K. Henrikson, 'America's changing face in the world: From "periphery" to "centre"', in J. Gottman (ed.), *Centre and Periphery: Spatial Variations in Politics* (Beverly Hills, CA: Sage Publications 1980) pp.79–80; A.K. Henrikson, 'The power and politics of maps', in G.J. Demko and W.B. Wood (eds.), *Reordering the World: Perspectives on the Twenty-First Century* (Boulder: Westview Press 1994) pp.49–70 and (1999, second edition) pp.94–116.

15. K.B. Ryan, 'The "official" image of Australia', in L. Zonn (ed.), *Place Images in the Media: Portrayal, Experience, and Meaning* (Savage, MD: Rowman and Littlefield 1991) pp.135–56.

16. S.D. Brunn, 'Stamps as iconography: Celebrating the independence of new European and Central Asian states', *GeoJournal* (forthcoming).

17. S.D. Brunn and C.D. Cottle, 'Small states and cyberboosterism', *Geographical Review* 87 (1997) pp.240–58.

18. J. O'Loughlin and R. Grant, 'The political geography of presidential speeches, 1946–87', *Annals of the Association of American Geographers* 80 (1990) pp.504–30.

19. C.L. Sutherland and G. Webster, 'The geography of the 1992 U.S. presidential debates', *Geographical Bulletin* 36 (1994) pp.83–93.

20. B. Benedict (ed.), *Problems of Smaller Territories* (London: Athlone Press 1967); C. Clarke and A. Payne (eds.), *Politics, Security and the Development of Small States* (London and Boston: Allen and Unwin 1987).

21. P. Stretter, 'The special problems of small countries', *World Development* 21 (1993) pp.197–202.

22. D. Lowenthal, 'Social features', in Clarke and Payne (note 20) pp.26–49.

23. L. Briguglio and J. Kaminaides, 'Islands and small states. Issues and policies', *World Development* 21 (1992) pp.193–5.

24. K. Dodds, 'Enframing the Falklands: Identity, landscapes and the 1982 South Atlantic war', *Society and Space* 16 (1998) pp.731–56.

25. M.A. East, 'Size and foreign policy behavior: A test of two models', *World Politics* 25 (1973) pp.557–76; R. Vayrynen, 'Small states in different theoretical traditions of international relations research', in Otto Hoell (ed.), *Small States in Europe and Dependence* (Wien: W. Braumuller 1983) pp.83–104; N. Linton, 'A policy perspective', in Clarke and Payne (note 20) pp.214–24; M.F. Elman, 'The foreign policies of small states. Challenging neorealism in its own backyard', *British Journal of Political Science* 25 (1995) pp.171–217; D.J. McGraw, 'New Zealand's foreign policy under National and Labour governments: Variations on the small state theme', *Pacific Affairs* 67 (1994) pp.7–25.

26. K. Mathosa, 'Democracy and conflict in post-apartheid Southern Africa. Dilemmas for social change in small states', *International Affairs* 74 (1998) pp.319–37.

27. R. Espindola, 'Security dilemmas', in Clarke and Payne (note 20) pp.63–79.

28. S.A. Cohen, 'Small states and their armies. Restructuring the militia framework of the Israel Defense Force', *Journal of Strategic Studies* 18 (1995) pp.78–93.

29. C. Farrugia, 'The special working environment of senior administrators in small states', in Clarke and Payne (note 20) pp.221–6.

30. A. Casella, 'Large countries, small countries and the enlargement of trade blocs', *European Economic Review* 42 (1996) pp.389–415; U. Kloti and S. Vondosenrode, 'Adaptation to European integration. Changes in the administration of four small states', *Australian Journal*

of Public Administration 54 (1995) pp.273–81; M. Schiff, *Small Is Beautiful. Preferential Trade Agreements and the Impact of Country Size; Market Share Efficiency and Trade Policy* (Washington, DC: World Bank, International Economics Department, International Trade Division, Policy Research Working Paper 1668, Oct. 1996); H.W. Armstrong and R. Read, 'Trade and growth in small states. The impact of global trade liberalization', *World Economy* 21 (1998) pp.563–85.

31. T. Selwyn, 'Tourism in islands, cities and small states', *Annals of Tourism Research* 21 (1994) pp.850–51; L. Briguglio *et al. Sustainable Tourism in Islands and Small States: Issues and Politics. Vol.1, Images and Policies. Vol.2, Case Studies* (London and New York: Pinter 1996).

32. J. Klaminades and E. Nissan, 'The effects of international debt on the economic development of small countries', *World Development* 21 (1993) pp.227–32.

33. H. Geser, 'Small states in the international system', *Kölner Zeitschrift für Soziologie und Sozialpsychologie* 44 (1992) pp.627–43; J. Overton, 'Small states. big issues. Human geography in the Pacific', *Singapore Journal of Tropical Geography* 14 (1993) pp.265–76; H. Schwartz, 'Small states in big trouble. State reorganization in Australia, Denmark, New Zealand and Sweden in the 1980s', *World Politics* 46 (1994) pp.525–55.

34. S.D. Brunn *et al.*, 'Place, culture, and peace: Treaty cities and national character in contemporary international disputes', *GeoJournal* 39 (1994) pp.331–43.

35. S. Tagil, 'Scale, behavior, and options: The case of Sweden and general considerations for the future', in O. Hoell (note 25) pp.329–41.

36. M. Sieber, 'Switzerland', in O. Hoell (note 25) pp.107–29.

37. A. Grisold, 'Press concentration and media policy in small countries, Austria and Israel', *European Journal of Communication* 11 (1996) pp.485–569; P. Preston, 'Competition in the telecommunications infrastructure. Implications for peripheral regions and small countries in Europe', *Telecommunications Policy* 19 (1995) pp.253–71; P. Preston, 'Network of European Communications Policy and the peripheral regions and small countries', *Telecommunications Policy* 19 (1995) pp.339–44; J.D. Jackson, 'Worldviews on the air. The struggle to create a pluralistic broadcasting system in the Netherlands', *Canadian Public Policy – Analyse de Politique* 24 (1998) pp.129–30.

38. M. Hong, 'Small states in the United Nations', *International Social Science Journal* 47/2 (1995) pp.271–87; J. Niznik, 'The future of small countries. Cooperation is imperative', *Futures* 27 (1995) pp.891–95; Z. Sarder, 'Can small countries survive the future?' *Futures* 27 (1995) pp.883–9; W.J. Davis, 'The Alliance of Small Island States (AOSIS): The international conscience', *Asia-Pacific Magazine* 2 (May 1996) pp.17–22; G.K. Helleiner, 'Why countries worry? Neglected issues in the current analysis of the benefits and costs for small countries of integrating with large ones', *World Economy* 19 (1996) pp.759–73.

39. United Nations. General Assembly. *Fiftieth Session. 35–40th Plenary Meetings. 22–24 October 1995, Official Records.*

40. S.D. Brunn, 'The worldviews of Untied Nations members: Key words in the 50th anniversary speeches', in P. Pagnini and M. Antonsich (eds.), *Europe Between Political Geography and Geopolitics* (Trieste: University of Trieste, forthcoming).

41. A.K. Henrikson, 'Small states in world affairs: The international political position and diplomatic influence of the world's growing number of smaller countries'. Paper presented to a Conference on Small States, St Lucia, Feb. 1999.

42. S.D. Brunn, J.A. Jones, and S.R. O'Lear, 'Geopolitical information and communications in the twenty-first century', in G.J. Demko and W.B. Wood (eds.), *Reordering the World: Geopolitical Perspectives on the 21st Century* (Boulder, CO: Westview Publisher 1999, second edition), pp.292–318; S.D. Brunn, 'A Treaty of Silicon for the Treaty of Westphalia? New territorial dimensions of modern statehood', *Geopolitics* 3/1 (1998) pp.106–31, reprinted in D. Newman (ed.), *Boundaries, Territory, and Postmodernity* (London: Cass 1999) pp.106–31.

Ordering the 'Crush Zone': Geopolitical Games in Post-Cold War Eastern Europe

JOHN O'LOUGHLIN

The mentality of the people in Central and Eastern Europe is characterized by a collective existential fear of a real or imaginary threat of national destruction due to loss of independence, assimilation, deportation or genocide.[1]

Since 1989, one of the main regional foci of post-cold-war geopolitical debates has been eastern Europe.[2] After nearly five decades of ossification induced by the bipolar bloc system that descended on Europe in the late 1940s, the 'crush zone' between the large states of Germany and Russia has once more become a zone of contention. The new geopolitical quarrels within the western strategic community and between pro-NATO and pro-Russian commentators have spurred a renewed interest in the legacy of a debate that reaches back to the end of the last century. At that time, separatist aspirations in the multinational empires of Austro-Hungary and Russia were growing and the great-power rivalry between Germany, the United Kingdom, Russia and the USA was reaching new levels of military spending. Though much has changed in 100 years, especially the replacement of autocracies by democracies and the effacement of imperial borders, three geopolitical issues of late-twentieth-century eastern Europe would look familiar to an informed citizen of the late 1800s: great-power rivalry, military conflicts over the correspondence between national territories and state borders, and the delimitation of the eastern boundary of 'Europe'.

Some of the earliest and most influential geopolitical writings by Sir Halford J. Mackinder, Rudolf Kjellén and Karl Haushofer concerned the newly independent states of eastern Europe that emerged from the battles, truces and forcible settlements of the First World War. While these protagonists offered deeply contrasting policies for their respective countries, they agreed that the region between Berlin and Kiev was a linchpin in the quest for strategic control of Europe and that the Great Powers would continue to vie for dominance in this borderland. The continued strategic importance of eastern Europe was echoed in the opinions of a later generation of geopolitikers, writing in the chaos and aftermath of the Second World War. Then, American strategists such as Nicholas Spykman, Robert Straus-Hupé and George F. Kennan had entered the geopolitical fray and centred their attention on the 'denial principle', that eastern Europe should not fall under the influence of a power that was inimical to American interests. Despite their writings, the Yalta agreement of 1943 sealed the lines of dominance, and eastern Europe was firmly placed in the Soviet zone of influence and geopolitical interest in the region waned as the superpower contest moved to the more unorganised strategic realms of the Third World.[3] In 1989, the geopolitical game in eastern Europe was renewed as a result of the unexpected collapse of the Communist regimes and, subsequently, by the blatant attempts of the new post-Communist regimes to play their national cards for greatest territorial, economic and military advantage. We have thus re-entered an era of geopolitical uncertainty as major domestic and international debates about issues such as North Atlantic Treaty Organisation (NATO) expansion and Russia's relations with her neighbours in the 'Near Abroad' (countries formed from the republics of the former Soviet Union) draw pundits from all perspectives.

In this paper, I will revisit a key concern of the early years of political geography – how to fit a place into a geopolitical order.[4] I will connect the geopolitical visions of external actors, in this case, those of American policymakers and commentators, with the foreign policies of contemporary east-central European states. Earlier geopolitical studies, such as the writings of Mackinder, Bowman, Haushofer and Fairgrieve, always connected the macro-perspective of geopolitics to the micro-scale policies for borders and territories.[5] While not advocating a return to ethnocentric, state-centred geopolitical study, the linkage of geopolitical critique and policy analysis must continue. This paper is a return to classic geopolitical traditions without the national-patriotic baggage that has accompanied earlier, as well as contemporary, works.[6]

The review in this chapter of the contemporary debates in American foreign policy shows that controversies ebb and flow according to the nature and emphasis of the domestic agenda. Other feedback effects emanate from unanticipated developments in strategically important zones and in global economic relations. The short debate from late 1996 to early 1998 in the American political arena about NATO expansion into eastern Europe helps to highlight current political positions and geopolitical perspectives on offer. One of the dramatic features of the NATO debate was the relative lack of attention to historical antecedents and alternative perspectives.[7] Though Russian opposition to NATO expansion as far as the border of the former Soviet Union was generally noted, the great diversity of opinion in that world power was generally simplified or dismissed in a condescending manner. Furthermore, the geographical and historical mosaics of eastern Europe were ignored in the debate and a dichotomy of qualifiers and non-qualifiers for NATO membership summarised whatever attention was paid to the diversity of countries, regions, peoples and politics in the zone between the German and Russian borders.

Geopolitical Controversies in the American World-View

As the western triumphalism of the post-1989 period wanes with growing recognition of intractable territorial disputes that remain unresolved, a decade-long search for a new geopolitical paradigm in the USA has not yet uncovered one capable of 'ordering' a complex world system. This complexity, hidden to US strategists and policymakers blinded by the 'ageographic' lens of the cold-war paradigm, now stands revealed; the US establishment, despite a wish to reorder the post-cold-war world, has not yet uniformly accepted a geopolitical code. The kind of domestic political consensus that emerged in the late 1940s around the 'containment' strategy is not yet evident for any of the proposals for the post-1989 world. Various new paradigms (for example, Huntington's 'civilizational' model)[8] recognise global complexity and a new multipolarity of power, but none has broad political support. US geopolitics of the late 1990s resembles that of the 1920s; indecision and uncertainty in the aftermath of a victory in the First World War resulted in an isolationist withdrawal for two decades. Despite victory in the cold war, the realisation of expectations that have accrued and the limits on foreign-policy activities posed by domestic constraints (not the least of which is the disinterest of most Americans in affairs outside the borders of the USA) have complicated, rather than clarified, the USA's role in the world.

In an attempt to distinguish and highlight current debates, seven 'paradigms' are portrayed in Table 1. In my definition, a geopolitical paradigm is a general world perspective that is moulded by the relative importance and variety of American domestic interests *vis-à-vis* with the state of international relations and the international political economy. Paradigms tend to be associated with specific presidential administrations and become personalised by the global visions that each holder of the presidential office brings to power. 'Mental maps' are strongly influenced by early personal experiences, while others are changed by unexpected global shifts.[9] More than anything else, paradigms offer a fairly abstract blueprint for dealing with international relations and determining the extent and level of US engagement with the world outside its borders.

In contrast to the general perspective, a geopolitical code is defined as 'a set of strategic assumptions that a government makes about other states in making its foreign policy'.[10] While highly ethnocentric and oriented to the perceived needs and interests of the state, geopolitical codes are nevertheless worthy of attention in the interpretation of foreign-policy actions. Codes are the spatial expressions of geopolitical efforts to transform a 'global space into fixed perspectival scenes, and as a two-dimensional register of space [they] would reveal some eternal truths about geography's relationship to politics'.[11] Thus, in order to understand the actions of the USA in post-1989 eastern Europe, we need to examine the place of the region in the competing geopolitical codes of the USA. Each of the respective geopolitical codes that are in vogue, under discussion or have been recently debated in Washington has a clear implication for the nature of the USA's response to changes in eastern Europe consequent on the collapse of Communism in 1989. Though Brown notes how postwar US strategists such as Dean Acheson, Zbigniew Brzezinski, Allen Dulles, Dwight Eisenhower, Alexander Haig, George F. Kennan, Henry Kissinger, Richard Nixon, Paul Nitze and Walter Rostow were influenced by geopolitical theories, a position also held by Sloan, the case for the influence of these theories on US policymaking or plans seems stretched, anecdotal and not yet subject to rigorous analysis.[12] More likely, the general *Weltanschauung* of the times influenced both the geopolitical theorists and the policymakers and generated a geopolitical code that seemed theory based, but was more strongly linked to the operating paradigm in Washington.

The best-known geopolitical code is 'containment' and because its use in Europe and the Middle East in the early days of the cold war is generally viewed as a success of American foreign policy, containment's legacy is powerful and capable of projection to other times and places. Paradigms are not as separate and non-overlapping as a simple list might suggest. Expressions of paradigms often appear in the speeches of policymakers serving in US administrations and are not just issued from the White House. Many foreign-policy speeches mix elements of different paradigms in order to try to bolster public support for a policy, such as a military strike. President Ronald Reagan, for example, combined the 'eagle triumphant', 'world of regions', 'anti-imperialist', and '*noblesse oblige*' paradigms in his televised addresses in the 1980s that argued for support of the Nicaraguan Contras against the Sandinista regime.

Some caveats are in order here. Given the complexity and the shifting lines of geopolitical paradigms, as well as the infrequency of deliberative statements about changing perspectives on world affairs, identification and presentation of contemporary US paradigms must necessarily be imprecise. Overlap between perspectives makes exact identification of all paradigmatic options impossible, but the mix-and-match tendency of speechwriters, often appealing to central tenets of American foreign policy such as the Monroe Doctrine (1823) helps to clarify positions. The seven paradigms listed in Table 1 were isolated after a close reading of official statements in State Department and White House documents, as well as the published writings of administration officials, presidential candidates, leaders in the US Senate and House, and former governmental officials (now foreign-policy pundits) such as Zbigniew Brzezinski, Brent Scowcroft, James Baker and Henry Kissinger. The list of paradigms is deliberately not exhaustive, nor do I claim that it represents a stable array of geopolitical doctrines.

The first paradigm in Table 1, '*noblesse oblige*', takes its title from a report of the Carnegie Endowment National Commission on America and the World. 'Twice before in this century, the United States and our allies triumphed in a global struggle. Twice before we earned the right to be an

TABLE 1

AMERICAN FOREIGN-POLICY PARADIGMS AND GEOPOLITICAL
CODES IN THE LATE 1990s

Paradigm	Geopolitical Code	Policy
1. '*Noblesse oblige*'	Global reach with countries differentiated by need; idealist; for example, JFK's inaugural address	Promote US principles (democracy and the market); US military power and money
2. 'US first'	Identification of 'rogue' states; anti-globalisation; isolationist; for example, Buchananism	Highly differentiated world with big commitments to a few key allies
3. 'Declinist'	Shared effort with allies; careful selection of commitments; US as '*primus inter pares*'; for example, Clinton	Withdraw troops; local allies pay; consult and enlarge the engagement; for example, Bosnia and Kosovo
4. 'Contingency'	USA as global balancing wheel; no geopolitical code; every situation requires an 'ad hoc' response	Respond to crisis after it develops; for example, Somalia or Kosovo
5. 'Eagle triumphant'	Globalist; force without diplomacy; world still dangerous; cold-war-style geopolitics; Pentagon view most important	'Be prepared'; continued high military expenditure
6. 'World of regions'	Identify key regions; regionalist view; focus on places that are important to US welfare; money, allies and troops	Focus on western and central Europe; Middle East; North East Asia
7. 'Anti-imperialism'	Focus on future power emergence; exceptionalism; Russia as a threat; for example, NATO strategists	Continue containment of Russia and China; expand NATO

arbiter of a post-war world. This is our third chance.'[13] The general view of the American 'great and good' (the eastern foreign-policy establishment) is that 'only the United States can do it'; ultimately, only the USA can save the various peoples of the world from disasters of their own making. After a lot of dithering, the *'noblesse oblige'* theme was prominent in President Clinton's 1995 national address at the time of the decision to send troops to Bosnia: 'it's the right thing to do'.[14] A similar perception seemed to have propelled the surprising intervention of the Bush administration in Somalia at Christmas 1992. As trial balloons, some Clinton appointees have suggested that there are some places of the world where the USA should not be taking the interventionist lead (for example, western Europeans should be in the vanguard in Bosnia and Kosovo) and only after the allies have dropped the ball, should the USA step in. Current examples of the idealist paradigm in action are the direct American promotion of peace negotiations in Northern Ireland and Israel/Palestine, and the US lead in the bombing of Yugoslavia to stop Serb attacks on Kosovars.

The supreme example of this kind of 'obligations and burdens' rhetoric and approach to world affairs is President John F. Kennedy's inaugural address in January 1961, when he promised that the USA would 'pay any price, bear any burden' in defence of American values and support of 'freedom'. Earlier, in February 1947, President Truman declared that the USA would help any anti-Communist movements anywhere in the world that requested American help. The approach relies very much on the notion of American exceptionalism and the support for programmes and policies that expand the number of countries that share American principles of free markets, civil liberties and democratic societies. Dick Armey (Republican majority leader) in June 1995 (proposing a much reduced foreign aid bill) said, 'In the history of the world, no nation has ever so much loved freedom that their nation's people have been willing to risk their own peace to secure freedom for other nations…. We are willing to put some part of our treasury behind the dream of freedom and peace for all the world's people.' But rhetoric and reality frequently do not coincide. The debate about foreign aid is a good example. Recent surveys show that American respondents believe that it accounts (on average) for 15 per cent of the federal budget. The actual figure is about one per cent and, interestingly, the average level of support, according to the survey respondents, should be five per cent.[15]

In the USA, the level of interest and concern with foreign questions is now (1999) at an all-time low since the Second World War. Normally, more than ten per cent will cite a foreign-policy issue as a response to the question 'What do you think is the most important problem facing the country today?' The most recent figure is two per cent. On the other hand, 65 per cent of the respondents to a recent Chicago Council on Foreign Relations poll believe that the USA should play 'an active role' in world affairs.[16] Since the 'obligations' can occur in any region of the world, there is no specific geopolitical code associated with this paradigm. Instead, US reach and concern stretches to all corners of the earth, even to previously invisible (in the US public's consciousness) states such as Somalia.

The second paradigm is often now associated with Pat Buchanan, the right-wing Republican presidential candidate noted for his opposition to the North American Free Trade Area and other perceived infringements on US autonomy. We can ascribe this paradigm as 'anti-internationalism' and its catch phrase seems to be 'no aid, no casualties'. With deep and wide support in the Republican party beyond the right wing, this world-view is deeply suspicious of international institutions and especially of the United Nations. While some Americans, especially those in the militias, are rabidly suspicious of non-American agencies such as the UN, this paradigm is not exactly the same as isolationism. As noted by Lawrence Eagleburger, former under-secretary of state, 'Isolationism means a pox on both your houses, don't get involved. I don't think that is what most [Americans] are. They have no real knowledge [of foreign affairs]. They don't care about it. They're focused on domestic problems.'[17] The suspicious basis of this paradigm is well illustrated by the statement by Senator Phil Gramm (Republican, Texas), a former presidential candidate, on foreign aid: 'The US is like a little rich kid in the middle of a slum with a cake, handing out slices yet receiving in return resentment rather than gratitude.' He proposed, instead, that the US should keep the cake, but share the recipe of democracy and market economics.

The liberal Democratic faction is also not immune from similar views. Another former presidential candidate, Reverend Jesse Jackson, has complained of the cost to US taxpayers of the stationing of American troops overseas and how the money could be better used for domestic programmes. One result has been the successful pressure on countries to pay part of the costs of the stationing of US troops in their country. The practical geopolitical output of this approach to foreign affairs is strong loyalty to a few favoured states (Taiwan, Saudi Arabia, Turkey and Israel). Other states either do not register as important places in the US geopolitical orbit or they are rich enough to pay substantially for the stationing of US troops (Japan, South Korea and Germany).

The third paradigm starts from a 'declinist' view that accepts that the USA has slipped from its immediate postwar dominance and now needs the support of allies to promote its global aims. Though the evidence for US decline is mixed and it is clear that the USA stands alone as the military hegemon,[18] there is a widespread perception that the USA can no longer afford all the 'burdens' that President Kennedy was willing to assume in

1961. Consequently, the USA promotes a shared global leadership. As a leading paradigm in Washington DC during the Clinton administration, it holds that the USA is still *'primus inter pares'*. Since global conditions have changed with the growing relative parity of many US allies and the collapse of the Soviet Union, the paradigm holds that other countries of the western camp must share in the global costs of management of the world system in the interests of democracy and free enterprise. The clearest expression of this position was former Secretary of State Warren Christopher's enunciation of four principles. 'First, America must lead. Second, we must seek to maintain productive political and economic relations with the world's most powerful states. Third, we must adapt and build lasting institutions to enhance cooperation. Fourth, we must support democracy and human rights to advance our interests and our ideals.'[19] Like the *'noblesse oblige'* paradigm, the declinist perspective has no specific geopolitical code, though events in countries close to the USA and in Europe attract more attention.

The notion of 'shared leadership' in a kind of regionalised world has been mentioned many times, especially in connection to Bosnia and Kosovo. For more than two years, 1993–95, Clinton administration officials claimed that the Bosnian conflict was intrinsically a 'European question' and the European states should take the lead in resolving the conflict. In the USA, idealists called for more US actions to stop the fighting and for open support for the Bosnian government at a time when the UN and European Union negotiators were trying to ensure a cease-fire. The 'declinist school' has been heavily criticised by the 'American Firsters', who believe that this approach relies too heavily on 'multilateral institutions', especially the UN, of which they are deeply suspicious. However, the overwhelming majority of Americans (74 per cent) believe that 'the US should play a shared leadership role'.[20] The eventual cease-fire in Bosnia in 1995, propelled by US air bombing and later insertion of US-European ground troops, is typical of the approach to crises that will likely emanate from this paradigm, which relies heavily on a shared ideology and closely agreed military operational strategies.

The fourth paradigm does not start from a fixed position, but treats each situation *de novo*. Each situation is viewed as 'contingent' and, therefore, no geopolitical code can be predetermined. Dismissed as 'adhocery' by critics such as former Senator and Republican presidential nominee, Robert Dole, it is partially a result of the current (1999) impasse in Washington DC as Congressional power in foreign affairs continues to grow. Until the First World War, Congress was hardly visible in foreign affairs as such issues were considered essentially to be a presidential prerogative. After blocking US entry to the League of Nations in the early 1920s, Congress began to become more assertive. Despite President Bush's claim of a 'New World Order' at the end of the 1991 Gulf War, the Clinton administration is visibly dismayed by the chaotic nature of the world system in all its varied regional manifestations. The foreign-policy outcome is thus a kind of 'contingency' paradigm rather than an imposition of some sort of global vision on the complex world mosaic. For the first two years of the Clinton administration, the president was focused on domestic affairs and so was the public. The phrase 'It's the economy, stupid' echoed through the 1994 re-election campaign. Lawrence Eagleburger said it best in 1991, after the USA was victorious in the Gulf War: 'it [the USA] finished the war out of breath'. The contingency paradigm can be considered as an extension of the previous declinist view that assumes that local 'policemen' will resolve regional issues, and only after they fail will the USA step in when the conditions and events demand. Somalia, Kosovo and Bosnia are good examples of this progression as these situations were viewed in the USA as humanitarian crises arising as a direct result of UN failures. The USA came riding to the rescue after other options expired, and therefore, no geopolitical code is needed. The actions of the USA in this regard are those of a 'lite power, with a lot of airy rhetoric in its diplomacy and not much kick'.[21]

The fifth paradigm can be termed 'eagle triumphant' and offers a globalist perspective on a 'dangerous world'. It portrays a continued cold-war-style geopolitics accompanied by high military expenditures. It retains a classic 'force without diplomacy' policy, which can be as ineffective as 'diplomacy without force', supposedly the dominant foreign-policy instrument of the early years of the Clinton administration. As a blunt foreign-policy instrument, the globalist view is not now in vogue in Washington and its most visible recent expression was the sounding of the 'triumphalist' notes at the end of the Gulf War (victory parades and so on). The 'Vietnam syndrome' (the public-opinion restraint on US military actions) was supposedly ended at the end of the Gulf War when President George Bush declared: 'We have finally kicked the Vietnam syndrome.' But the Somalia and Kosovo episodes question whether the Vietnam syndrome has indeed been kicked.[22] Use of cruise missiles (as in the August 1998 attacks on Afghanistan and Sudan) and bombers based in safe havens are especially attractive to the proponents of the globalist paradigm as it offers power projection without casualties. The political instability in the former Soviet Union and continuing civil strife in more than 40 locations provides 'evidence' for the dangerous-world perspective. But without a clear and consistent presence of an archenemy, such as the Soviet Union during the five decades of the cold war, this paradigm is hardly credible or sustainable. The geopolitical code associated with the globalist paradigm is global in scope, but differentiated by the relative importance of the allies and foes of the USA. The geographic externalities of foreign-policy actors in these states are explicitly considered and the code does not differ much from that of the Reagan presidency in the 1980s.

A sixth paradigm offers a regionalist alternative to the globalist view and identifies the key regions of Europe, the Middle East and North-East Asia as places most important to the USA. This regionally differentiated world-view harks back to the perspective of George F. Kennan in his 'X' article in 1947.[23] It is especially neglectful of the rest of the Third World and is motivated by the major concerns that were identified in a recent national public-opinion survey. Key threats to the USA were identified as nuclear attack (72 per cent named this item), high immigration (72 per cent) and international terrorism (69 per cent). Asked to identify the places where the USA has a 'vital interest', respondents in 1994 listed Japan (85 per cent), Saudi Arabia (83 per cent), Russia (79 per cent), Mexico (76 per cent), Canada (76 per cent), Great Britain (69 per cent) and China (68 per cent) as the top seven countries, while states such as Egypt (45 per cent), France (39 per cent), Ukraine (35 per cent) and Poland (31 per cent) were well down the list. Four regions matter consistently on these national surveys: North-East Asia (the two Koreas, Japan and China); the Middle East (Saudi Arabia above all other states including Israel); Europe, both central (including Russia) and western; and the Caribbean, including Mexico.[24] The rest of the world has little importance except as 'emerging markets' for US products. Senator R. Dole expressed the linkage between important regional interests and US welfare.[25] For him, the core interests of the USA are 'preventing the domination of Europe by a single power; maintaining a balance of power in East Asia; promoting security and stability in our hemisphere; preserving access to natural resources especially in the energy heartland of the Persian Gulf; strengthening international free trade and expanding US access to global markets; and protecting American interests and properties overseas'. The continued centrality of Europe, including eastern Europe, in this paradigm is a mainstay of a differentiated geopolitical code and recognises both global complexities and the varied relevance of foreign places to the USA.

The final paradigm in Table 1 returns to a world of 'great powers' and treats the USA as the leader of the western bloc coming into conflict with an oppositional Russia and an assertive China. In a sense, it is a return to the bipolar world order of the cold-war years, but the identification of the 'other' is not yet revealed. In any case, it would require ringing the opponent with allies and a containment ring. With the growing uncertainty of the success of the economic and political transitions in Russia and the growing belief that Russia is a 'third world country with nuclear weapons', there is ample opportunity for a return of the 'anti-Sovietism' of the cold-war years. This scenario is even more plausible if the leaders strongly favoured by the USA (the cabal gathered around President Yeltsin) fail to win the continued support of the Russian population and are replaced in an election or a *coup d'état*. This alarmist view of Russia is predicated on the belief that contemporary Russia is the inheritor of the expansionist Russian tradition of hundreds of years. It is especially concerned to push NATO expansion to the borders of Russia, despite the strong opposition of Russians of all political stripes. It anticipates cold-war redux and promotes a geopolitical code based on a bipolar and simple world order. In a return to containment, the USA should fit countries into a geopolitical code that expresses again the half-moon (rimland) of the distribution of American support and attention during the cold war.

The distinctiveness and clarity of these paradigms are rarely evident to the various commentators trying to understand the foreign policy of the USA in the post-cold-war years; they have typically noted the lack of clarity and consistency. Examining the geopolitical codes of Madeline Albright (Clinton's second Secretary of State), Jan Nijman notes that, in comparison to American-born policymakers, those of European origin (Henry Kissinger, Zbigniew Brzezinski and Albright) have a more nuanced, cynical and less idealist perspective.[26] A British journalist, Martin Walker, dismissed the Clinton administration's foreign policy as the 'geopolitics of casual sex', claiming that it involved the 'promiscuous and irresponsible use of US military force without lasting commitment'. Force would only be used in places where quick, casualty-free wins would be certain.[27] Recent cruise-missile attacks on Afghanistan, Iraq and Sudan ('force without diplomacy or casualties') supports Walker's contention.

Major foreign-policy debates have not been prominent in Washington or more broadly in the American body politic since the end of the cold war. Domestic issues have not only dominated political debate, but the sense of peace and security induced by sustained economic growth and a lack of visible threats to Americans at home has not been shaken by terrorist attacks or so-called 'rogue states' such as Iraq, North Korea or Libya. The military budget and overseas troop numbers are down significantly in the past decade (a decrease of about one-third, from an expenditure of $375 billion (1995 dollars) to $260 billion), though that trend will soon reverse.[28] US force levels in East Asia (about 100,000 personnel, mainly in Japan and South Korea) are to be maintained, as are those in Europe (nearly 100,000 plus amphibious forces). The objective, however, remains to be 'capable of prevailing in two nearly simultaneous regional conflicts' in the words of the 1998 US Department of Defense Budget Statement. Concurrent bombing of Yugoslavia and Iraq in spring 1999 is viewed as offering a test of this proposition.

Geopolitical Codes and Eastern Europe

No issue has clarified current geopolitical posturings in the USA like the 1996–98 debate about expansion of NATO into central Europe to admit Poland, the Czech Republic and Hungary and the associated arguments about the USA's role in Europe, especially in the Balkans. Involvement on the European continent as the dominant power in NATO is widely accepted all across the American political spectrum; the debate begins when the specific implications of that involvement come to the forefront of foreign-policy issues. A key element for US policymakers, as for Europeans, is the definition of Europe: which countries meet the criteria for entry into European institutions and which should remain outside Europe, either temporarily or permanently? As noted from the public opinion polls, major European countries are widely accepted as places to which US foreign policy must be directed. The historic association and links between Europe and the USA have been the main axle of US foreign policy, as noted by President Clinton in his major foreign-policy addresses on NATO expansion and on the conflicts in Bosnia and Kosovo. The conundrum of balancing strategic commitment to western Europe while avoiding long-term military involvement in the ethnic wars to the east continues to perplex US strategists. Further expansion of NATO and admission of all qualified states to western institutions remains the cornerstone of US policy. Even Serbia is considered a potential ally. 'Our Alliance remains open to all European democracies, regardless of geography, willing and able to meet the responsibilities of membership, and whose inclusion would enhance overall security and stability in Europe. NATO is an essential pillar of a wider community of shared values and shared responsibility. Working together, Allies and Partners, including Russia and Ukraine, are developing their cooperation and erasing the divisions imposed by the Cold War to help to build a Europe whole and free, where security and prosperity are shared and indivisible.'[29] To examine this conundrum further, the positions of the various players in the NATO-expansion debate will be examined in light of contemporary political and economic changes in the countries of eastern Europe and in light of the historic significance of this region in geopolitical writings and strategic plans.

As domestic events in the USA continue to dominate public attention, eastern Europeans jockey for geopolitical positioning in international fora. The division of Europe into a 'fast-track' incorporation into the western institutions of the European Union and NATO versus 'the others', who are either put into long membership queues (the fate of Turkey for more than a decade) or deemed not to have the free markets and polities necessary for membership of the 'West', can now be anticipated. A recent visit by Leonid

Kuchma, President of Ukraine, to the EU summit in Vienna clarifies the risks, strategies, options and obstacles inherent in the pending classification of countries as eligible and ineligible. Kuchma, like other eastern European leaders, views EU membership as 'an absolute priority for Ukraine' and wants Ukraine to become an associate member of the EU immediately, an option that would reduce tariffs on Ukrainian exports to the EU. For his part, Kuchma tried to portray Ukraine as making steady progress toward a market economy. Significantly, Kuchma opposed a new visa regime on the Polish-Ukrainian border that would treat Ukrainians in the same way as Polish border guards currently treat Russians and Belarussians. Poland, now a NATO member and in the front of the EU queue, has clearly been accepted as 'European' and Kuchma complained that 'the trouble does exist and it troubles us from the point of view of this new splitting of Europe'. Furthermore, Kuchma emphasised Ukraine's non-aligned status with respect to NATO enlargement, but believed that Ukraine must 'move to Euroatlantic structures and the EU as the only alternative to a return to the past'.[30]

Fears and aspirations such as Kuchma's are found from Tallinn to Sofia. To strengthen the case for admission, the depth and length of the European legacy of each country is stressed, most visibly in the new history and geography texts now appearing.[31] In Ukraine, rapprochement with Poland and the other central European states is viewed as an intermediate step toward incorporation into the West and toward separation from Russia. The states that emerged from the former Austro-Hungarian Empire stress their western democratic credentials and fear that the economic problems of the countries to the east might be contagious. As a result, they work to preserve their differences with Ukraine.[32] Overlooked in the triumphalism and joy that accompanied the destruction of the Iron Curtain, the important boundary that separated the Soviet Union from the other eastern European states remains largely intact, with barbed-wire fences and severe restrictions on the movements of goods and people. The post-Soviet governments in Belarus and Ukraine have also maintained tight control of the border crossings to collect tariffs and customs duties and have engaged in intensive struggles with local power elites for control of the lucrative grey trade.[33]

For geopolitical students, of course, this debate about the character and orientation of the eastern European states elicits an overwhelming sense of déjà vu. Eastern Europe is a classic borderland in two senses. At the macro-scale, 'Europe's' limits are generally believed to lie somewhere between the Vistula and the Dnieper, as seen prominently in Huntington's Clash of Civilizations thesis.[34] But at the meso-scale within the region, there are almost innumerable limological uncertainties because of centuries of turmoil, settlement, ethnic cleansing, truce lines, state formation and treaties.[35] Applebaum, in a brilliant travel book, notes that at the peace conferences after the First World War, borders were to be rationally drawn through plebiscites, treaties, and border demarcation. In the end, however, 'borders in the borderlands were drawn by force. During the five-year course of the Russian civil war, no less than eleven armies ... fought for possession of Ukraine.'[36] The linkage between the macro-geopolitics of great powers and the micro-geopolitics of contested territories was clearly made by Karl Haushofer, promoting his notion of 'moveable frontiers'.[37] He perceived borders as temporary battle-lines that moved depending on the relative strengths of the competing neighbouring states. Consequent on the weakening of empires (as happened to Wilhelmine Germany and Tsarist Russia in the First World War), the victors, by creating new states, expected the borderlands to be able to express their own cultures and identities. Decades of war and forced population shifts have now created a 'minority-free' zone of states where minorities constitute less than five per cent of national totals. The zone now covers 15 states (instead of six in 1910), and forms a compact region from The Netherlands to Hungary and from Norway to Slovenia. Conversely, the number of minorities in the European states (Atlantic to Urals) is now 150, 40 per cent higher than it was in 1910, as increasing numbers of states have produced more minorities stranded on the wrong side of the boundaries.[38]

The apposition of land-powers to sea-powers has a century-long legacy in political geography, though Halford Mackinder traced it back to the classical civilisations of the Greeks and the Persians. Like Mackinder, ('who commands Eastern Europe commands the Heartland'),[39] Fairgrieve identified eastern Europe as a buffer zone. The 'buffer zone' principle was developed by Lord Curzon, based on his personal experience in central Asia, and his intent to separate the expanding Russian and British empires of the nineteenth century. Before and after the First World War, eastern Europe was promoted by geopolitikers as a buffer to separate the German and Russian empires. Fairgrieve popularised the term 'crush zone'; this zone of small states in eastern Europe, though separating the two big states, was unstable and precarious due to internal dynamics and external pressures. 'With the organisation of the heartland and the sea-powers, a crush zone of small states has gradually come into existence between them.... With sufficient individuality to withstand absorptions, but unable or unwilling to unite with others to form any larger whole, they remain in the unsatisfactory position of buffer states, precariously independent politically, and more surely dependent economically. This zone of states ... has included Finland, Sweden, Norway, Denmark, ...the Balkan states.... Central Europe, unorganized and broken into small and antagonistic communities, essentially belongs to the crush zone, but organized and powerful is in a very different position.'[40] Turning the idea of the buffer zone on its head, Saul Cohen has recently argued that eastern and central Europe can be an emerging gateway region, a transitional zone that could facilitate contact and interchange between the two realms (Maritime and Continental).[41]

The boundaries of 'Europe' have been gradually moving to the east since 1900. The Russian empire first and the Soviet Union later were unable to make their imperial projects stick in the central European area, and the end result was a proliferation of small states west of Russia. 'The territory of Russia is now smaller than it has been at any time since the late seventeenth century.'[42] Anticipating Huntington's 'clash of civilizations', the Germanophile geopolitiker, Rudolf Kjellén, referred to the divide between Europe and Russia as the 'Great Cultural Divide' and talked about a union of small central European states under German leadership (German-Slavic Union of States) sitting in opposition to the Russian empire.[43] Various geopolitical models for ordering international relations have been proposed since the end of the cold war and assorted geopolitical codes emanate from their spatial expressions. Among the most interesting is the replacement of the bipolar world of the cold war by 'a power-political hierarchy with its centre in Brussels – or alternatively in one of several major West European capitals – with concentric circles extending outwards from the central West European cosmos to the increasingly chaotic regions in the periphery'. This interpretation sees the 'friend-foe' divide along the Iron Curtain of the cold-war years superseded by a 'cosmos-chaos' divide separating the cosmos of the EU or NATO from chaotic eastern Europe and Russia. In relation to the Commonwealth of Independent States (CIS), Russia also appears as a cosmos and Moscow as the centre, with concentric zones of dominance and influence.[44] Unlike the cold-war years, the 'other' is not an implacable foe but a region of 'chaos', more threatening in many respects because the expectation and norms of the great-power geopolitical games do not apply. The geopolitical code of NATO expansion is thus not territorial aggrandisement, as is normally the goal of geopolitical manoeuvrings, but, instead, the promotion of an economic and political agenda to expand the range of the democratic world, centred on Brussels in the case of Europe. Russia, above all, constitutes the chaotic alternative, and if Europe turns its back on the Orthodox/Eurasian/Russian world, we move firmly to a 'cold peace'.[45]

Viewed from the East, the extension of NATO membership and the associated delimitation of the 'West' have had the appearance of a one-sided discussion. Though the USA and the other NATO states issued numerous assurances that enlargement was not directed toward containing Russia, Russian public opinion was not convinced and the suspicions of NATO intentions have reached across the ideological divides. For many westernised Russians, a new division of central and eastern Europe is particularly troublesome. Vladimir Lukin, Chairman of the International Affairs Committee of the Russian Duma, noted that 'the already tense situation is aggravated by the attempts of some presumptuous circles in the Ukrainian political elite to draw a new *de facto* border between the West and the East – somewhere along the Don River as the ancient Greeks did – thus making Ukraine into some kind of "front line of Western civilization"'.[46]

In the wake of the collapse of the Soviet Union, one general perspective and four broad geopolitical tendencies can be identified in Russia. The idea of Russia as a Eurasian country (a world unto itself, neither East nor West) is growing beyond its traditional adherents.[47] The grand debate in Russia about whether Russia is part of the European-western world or the centre of a separate Eurasian sphere has generated four opinion blocks. The 'westerners', such as Vladimir Lukin, want to be part of the Atlantic-European community, though the opponents (nationalists) see westernism as the root of Russia's problems ('neo-democrats' in the language of Brzezinski and Sullivan). The perspectives of the centrists and Communists are less dogmatic, but veer toward the western and the Eurasian ideologies, respectively.[48] A shared belief that NATO enlargement institutionalises a new European wall, bringing it closer to Russia's border, links the otherwise disparate perspectives.[49]

The western debate about NATO enlargement, short and cursory as it was, took little account of divergent Russian opinions or the historical background of east-central Europe. Its proponents stressed the benefits to the alliance and to the three countries (Poland, the Czech Republic and Hungary) selected from the list of applicants and would-be aspirants, while continuing to promise that other countries could join in the future. A crystallisation of geopolitical codes was expected during the NATO enlargement debate, especially in the USA, but the debate seems to have had no lasting impact in an era of 'parachute journalism'. As will be argued in the next section, a strenuous avoidance of geopolitical metaphors that are implicit in many of the paradigms in Table 1 limited the NATO-expansion debate to estimated costs (economic and military), the wish to support new democracies, and a definition of new roles for NATO. In a time of no obvious external threats to American citizens, it is difficult to engage the sustained attention of the public and of the politicians in foreign policy. The NATO-enlargement vote in the US Senate was overwhelmingly positive, but the legacy of the decision will extend significantly, far more than the focus of the debate.

American Geopolitical Codes, the NATO Debate and the Legacy of Geopolitics

As agreed by NATO member states in 1995, prospective members had to meet four criteria for admission, namely (a) demonstrating adherence to democracy, (b) accepting alliance principles, including mutual defence assistance, (c) showing a capability and readiness to contribute to NATO's security functions, and (d) bearing the responsibilities of NATO membership, including any necessary increases in military spending. States were invited to apply for possible membership and 11 countries (Albania, the Czech Republic, Estonia, the Former Yugoslav Republic of Macedonia, Hungary, Latvia, Lithuania, Poland, Romania, Slovakia and Slovenia) entered into dialogue with the NATO partners. Ultimately, three states (Czech Republic, Hungary and Poland) were accepted for membership beginning in March 1999.

In a report to the US Congress in February 1997 on the 'rationale, benefits, costs and implications' of the enlargement of NATO, the Bureau of European and Canadian Affairs of the State Department made the case for NATO expansion into east-central Europe. Among the myriad of benefits of expansion were listed 'the broader goal of a peaceful, undivided and democratic Europe'. Other benefits to the West that were specifically identified were 'democratic reforms', a 'stronger defence capability', 'improved burden-sharing', a 'better environment for trade, investment and economic growth', and 'improved relations among the region's states'. Of the total costs of expansion, European allies would be expected to pay $18–23 billion over ten years, while the USA would be expected to pick up about $9–12 billion in additional costs. The report to Congress stressed the minimal costs to the American taxpayer of NATO expansion and it also downplayed any extra financial burdens that might be placed on the applicant countries. The report briefly noted the opposition of the Russian government and people, but stressed that the expansion was not directed against any one country and was designed to assure the stability and democracy of east-central Europe. 'Thus far, Moscow has pursued a two-tracked policy. On the one hand, the Russian government and political elite continue to voice opposition to enlargement. On the other hand, President Yeltsin, Foreign Minister Primakov and other senior Russian officials are now engaging in an intensive dialogue with the US, other key allies and NATO about the enlargement process and prospects for developing the NATO-Russia relationship.'[50] The report further asserted that Russian public opinion was relatively indifferent to the issue of NATO expansion.

Fundamentally, the pro-enlargement argument was based on the 'New Strategic Concept' for NATO developed in 1991, which 'moved beyond the

Cold War NATO stress on positioned forward defense to place a new emphasis on the development of multinational force projection, supported from extended lines of communication and relying on deployable and flexible logistics support capabilities for crisis management operations. Since then, NATO has taken steps to put these ideas into practice. It has led to the military mission in former Yugoslavia.'[51] Only a half-page in the report was devoted to the wider geopolitical implications of the expansion under the heading 'Putting geopolitical costs in perspective'. In this section, the main emphasis was on the message that failure to expand would deliver to the NATO applicants, including the assertion that such an action 'would falsely revalidate the old and now-arbitrary divisions of the Cold War at a time when Western policy is committed to overcome them. The resulting sense of isolation and vulnerability would be destabilizing to the region.'[52]

Numerous critics in the West of NATO enlargement generally have also avoided a geopolitical argument, emphasising instead economic, cultural, military and strategic costs. Amongst the anti-enlargement arguments were (a) the increased nuclear danger because of the failure of the Russian Duma to ratify the START II treaty, (b) the increased military costs of forces' integration with the new members (Czech Republic, Hungary and Poland) and with the USA, (c) confusion in the NATO mission as it switches from a North Atlantic to a North American and western and central European alliance, (d) the alienation of populations in countries not offered membership (Bulgaria, Rumania and the Baltic states), (e) the strengthening of the anti-West factions in Russia, and (f) the further alienation of Russia as future NATO expansion is planned in parts of the former Soviet Union.[53]

The geopolitical argument, that NATO enlargement risks the delimitation of a new dividing line in Europe, was made most forcibly by George F. Kennan. On one side of a new geopolitical divide would be the 19 members of NATO and on the other side, Russia, Ukraine and Belarus. With plans for future incorporation of the Baltic states, this division could become even more controversial because of the presence of ethnic Russians in these states and the growing sense of encirclement that would undoubtedly grow across the Russian political spectrum, with a subsequent growing appeal of the anti-West blocs. Kennan called NATO expansion the 'most fatal error of American policy in the entire post-cold-war era'.[54] As Nijman argues persuasively, the current US administration, under the leadership of Secretary of State Madeline Albright (a native of the Czech Republic), has deliberately avoided a geopolitical quarrel and moved the debate instead to geography, suggesting that the new members are part of a democratic, capitalist, historical Europe.[55] What was most noticeable was the *ahistorical* nature of the NATO discussion in the USA. By contrast, a pro-expansion argument resting on traditional geopolitical arguments by the central European émigrés, Zbigniew Brzezinski and Henry Kissinger, stood out dramatically.[56]

As was shown earlier in this paper, the 'crush zone' of east-central Europe figured prominently in the geopolitical codes of the Great Powers from the late-nineteenth century to 1945. After a half-century of relative obscurity due to the clear domination of the Soviet Union in the region, the geopolitical strategists once again have the chance to consider 'Mitteleuropa' in all its regional dimensions. While Russian strategists and political leaders clearly want to keep central Europe as a neutral or transition zone, the West in the guise of NATO wants to incorporate the region firmly into the European world. Rather than accepting or even debating the proposition that the area between the Oder and the Dnieper has always been a 'shatterbelt' or 'crush zone', western leaders, such as Madeline Albright, claim that NATO expansion into this region returns it to Europe, in effect releasing the 'occident kidnappé', in Milan Kundera's phrase.[57] The near total avoidance of geopolitical language and concepts is both clever and short-sighted; historical geopolitical memories in the region could eventually undermine the strategic decision to expand NATO or at least, the challenges sown by the geopolitical fragments that continue to resonate in the region could tie NATO down in more Kosovo-like conflicts.

Conclusions

Gertjan Dijkink defines a geopolitical vision as 'any idea concerning the relation between one's own and other places, involving feelings of (in)security or (dis)advantage (and/or) invoking ideas about a collective mission or foreign policy strategy'.[58] Both Dijkink and David Campbell argue that there is a pervasive connection in US foreign policy between the fear of disunity at home and the fear of unrest abroad in countries and regions in which the USA has a strategic interest.[59] The end of the cold war has clouded the clarity of a divide between self and other. Conservative American commentators decry the resulting 'hollow hegemony' as the USA has 'lost faith in its own ideals'.[60] To the average American, the world appears more confusing, chaotic and unruly than ever before and no amount of US foreign aid or military assistance appears to be able to bring it to order.

For scholars writing in the critical geopolitical tradition, the foreign policy of the USA provided an easy foil in the years of the cold war. In the post-cold-war dilemmas posed by the bloody events in Bosnia, Chechnya and other nationalist battlegrounds, the USA has been caught between intervention, now promoted by humanitarians to prevent more 'holocausts', and isolationism, supported by most of the public who are fearful of another

Vietnam-style 'quagmire'.[61] The lack of consensus is clearly reflected in the menu of geopolitical codes that are currently on offer (Table 1). As a consequence of the uncertain global role for the USA, critical geopolitical works have become less 'critical' and more speculative. As the foreign-policy ground keeps shifting and geopolitical debate is assiduously avoided, critics of US foreign policy find themselves with little recourse except either to bemoan the lack of attention to foreign events on the part of a great power or to try to comprehend an erratic policy.

Classic geopolitical concepts, such as the 'crush zone' or 'shatterbelt', do not change meaning or location, except over the long haul. The absence of geopolitical memory, now endemic in the US foreign-policy establishment, requires that political geographers explain the importance of geopolitical precedents and regional legacies. No place has a more troubled and prominent history of local and international conflict than eastern Europe, and the attempt to patch over the legacy of these wars through the extension of NATO to the Polish eastern border does not resolve the issue of where Europe ends. As the Ukrainian political establishment clamours that their country is (historically) an integral part of Europe and plans to extend NATO to the Baltic states in the future augur a shift of the 'European' border to the east, a new geopolitical divide seems destined to appear on either the western or eastern border of Ukraine. The future geography of 'Europe' thus remains undecided and there appears little chance that it will ever include 'unruly' Russia. At this historical juncture, the Clinton administration has tried to avoid taking a stand while sweeping away out of sight the geopolitical debris of past wars and the geopolitical uncertainties of contemporary foreign relations.

NOTES

1. A. Miller, 'Europe's East or East of Europe' (*Vostok Evropa ili na vostok iz Evropa*), *Pro et Contra* 3/2 (1998) p.5 (in Russian).
2. In this paper, I will refer to the region between the Oder and the Dnieper by various names. Though the term 'eastern Europe' is most widely used in English to describe the area, other terms that are commonly used include 'east-central Europe', '*Mitteleuropa*' and 'central Europe'. By most accounts, the region includes the former Communist countries of Poland, the Czech Republic, Slovakia, Hungary, Bulgaria, Moldova, Ukraine, Belarus, Romania and the three Baltic states (Latvia, Estonia and Lithuania). Though physically part of the Oder-Dnieper world, the Russian enclave of Kaliningrad is typically not included in the region and neither are the Balkan states of the former Yugoslavia and Albania.
3. The geopolitical manoeuvrings of the USA and the Soviet Union in the Third World during the second cold war, 1979–85, are described in J. O'Loughlin, 'World-power competition and local conflicts in the Third World', in R.J. Johnston and P.J. Taylor (eds.), *A World in Crisis* (Oxford: Basil Blackwell 1986) pp.289–332.
4. The concept of 'geopolitical order' is elaborated in P.J. Taylor, 'Geopolitical world orders', in P.J. Taylor (ed.), *The Political Geography of the Twentieth Century* (London: Belhaven Press 1993) pp.33–61.

5. Among these studies are H.J. Mackinder, *Democratic Ideals and Reality: A Study in the Politics of Reconstruction* (London: Constable 1919); K. Haushofer, *Grenzen in ihrer geographischen und politischen Bedeutung* (Berlin: Karl Vowinckel Verlag 1927); I. Bowman, *The New World. Yonkers on the Hudson* (New York: World Book Company 1921); and J. Fairgrieve, *Geography and World Power* (London: University of London Press 1915).

6. For examples of state-centred geopolitical analyses, the reader can look at any issue of *Strategic Review, Journal of Strategic Studies* or any of the main foreign-affairs journals, such as *Foreign Affairs, Foreign Policy, Orbis, World Policy Journal, Washington Quarterly* or *International Organization*.

7. George F. Kennan was a notable exception to this statement. In his opposition to NATO expansion, Kennan emphasised the continuities of Russian fears of encirclement, a fear that he had first highlighted in his famous 'X' article, 'The sources of Soviet conduct', *Foreign Affairs* 25 (1947) pp.566–82.

8. For his thesis about the 'clash of civilizations', see S.P. Huntington, *The Clash of Civilizations and the Remaking of World Order* (New York: Simon & Schuster 1996).

9. For studies of the 'mental maps' of US leaders, see A. Henrikson, 'The geographical mental maps of US foreign policy makers', *International Political Science Review* 1 (1980) pp.495–530; and J. O'Loughlin and R.J. Grant, 'The political geography of presidential speeches, 1946–87', *Annals, Association of American Geographers* 80 (1990) pp.504–30.

10. This definition is from P.J. Taylor, *Political Geography: World-System, Nation-State and Locality*, third edn. (London: Longman) p.91. Taylor elaborates that a geopolitical code 'will have to incorporate a definition of a state's interests, an identification of external threats to those interests, a planned response to such threats and a justification of that response' (p.64). This concept is similar to that of 'image plans' as described by Henrikson and the term 'geopolitical code' was first used in J.L. Gaddis, *Strategies of Containment* (New York: Oxford University Press 1982).

11. The quote is from T. Luke and G. Ó Tuathail, 'Global flowmations, local fundamentalisms, and fast geopolitics: "America" in an accelerating world order', in A. Herod, G. Ó Tuathail and S. Roberts (eds.), *An Unruly World?: Globalization, Governance and Geography* (London: Routledge) pp.72–94.

12. S. Brown, 'Inherited geopolitics and emergent global realities', in E.K. Hamilton (ed.), *America's Global Interests* (New York: W.W. Norton 1989) pp.166–77; and G.R. Sloan, *Geopolitics in United States Strategic Policy, 1890–1987* (Brighton: Wheatsheaf Books 1988).

13. The quote is the opening lines of a report by the Carnegie Endowment for International Peace, National Commission on America and the New World, *Changing Our Ways: America and the New World* (Washington DC 1992).

14. For details on the dilemma facing the Clinton administration in Bosnia, caught between a 'quagmire' and a 'holocaust', see G. Ó Tuathail, *Critical Geopolitics: The Politics of Writing Global Space* (Minneapolis, MN: University of Minnesota Press 1996).

15. The figures are reported in S. Kull, 'What the public knows, what Washington doesn't', *Foreign Policy* 101 (winter 1995–96) p.109.

16. The figures are reported in J.D. Rosner, 'The know-nothings know something', *Foreign Policy* 101 (winter 1995–96) p.124.

17. The Eagleburger quote is found in R.S. Greenberger, 'Dateline Capitol Hill: the new majority's foreign policy', *Foreign Policy* 101 (winter 1995–96) p.162.

18. J. O'Loughlin, 'Fact or fiction?: The evidence for the relative decline of the US, 1966–1991', in C. Williams (ed.), *The Geography of the New World Order* (London: Belhaven Press and New York: John Wiley 1993) pp.148–80.

19. W. Christopher, 'America's leadership, America's opportunity', *Foreign Policy* 98 (spring 1995) p.8.

20. This according to the Chicago Council of Foreign Relations poll cited in Kull (note 15). In a similar poll by the *Wall Street Journal* and reported in the same article, 72 per cent said that the USA should let other countries and the United Nations take the lead in solving international crises and conflicts.

21. B. Buzan and G. Segal, 'The rise of lite powers: A strategy for the postmodern state', *World Policy Journal* (autumn 1996) pp.1–10.
22. Maybe it has been replaced by a 'Somalia syndrome' as a result of the death of 18 US troops in a shoot-out in Mogadishu in 1993. After this fire-fight, US troops were pulled out immediately, though the fact that US troops killed 3,000–5,000 Somalis in that conflict seemed lost on the public with its fetish on US casualties. As noted by Buzan and Segal (note 21) p.3, 'the weakening of shared identity means that individuals are not as prepared as in the past to die for their country, although they may be perfectly willing to risk their lives in dangerous sports or by excesses of consumption'. In recent military actions, 'America's impressive demonstration of high-tech military power was offset by its equally impressive desire to avoid both casualties and entanglement' (Buzan and Segal, note 21, p.8).
23. Kennan (note 7).
24. Chicago Council on Foreign Relations surveys 1990 and 1994, as reported in Kull (note 15).
25. R. Dole presents his list in 'Shaping America's global future', *Foreign Policy* 98 (spring 1995) p.35.
26. J. Nijman 'In search of Madeline Albright's geopolitical vision', *Geojournal* 44 (1999 forthcoming).
27. Cited in Ó Tuathail (note 14) p.206. In a similar vein, Ó Tuathail reports the jokes of a late-night television comedian: 'we do deserts; we don't do jungles. Or mountains.'
28. Stockholm International Peace Research Institute (SIPRI), 'Military expenditure database', *SIPRI Yearbook* (Stockholm: SIPRI 1998) Ch.6. There is a substantial increase proposed for the Pentagon budget in fiscal year 2000.
29. The Washington Declaration, signed and issued by the heads of state and government participating in the meeting of the North Atlantic Council, Washington DC, 23 and 24 April 1999.
30. The quotes from Leonid Kuchma are reported in N. Hodge, 'Kuchma curries European favor, aid', *Kiyiv Post* (20 Oct. 1998) p.1.
31. V. Kolossov and J. O'Loughlin, 'New borders for new world orders: Territorialities at the *fin-de-siècle*', *Geojournal* 43 (1999) pp.259–73. For a recent example of this kind of geographical placement, see O. Subtelny, *Ukraine: A History* (Toronto: University of Toronto Press 1993). This book firmly places Ukraine in Europe and Russia in the East. For an example of the new geographical texts, see O. Shablij, *Social-Economic Geography of Ukraine* (*Sotsialno-ekonomicheskaya geografiya ukrain'i*) (L'viv: Svit 1995) (in Russian).
32. A. Moshes, 'Ukraine's geopolitical quest: Central and eastern Europe in Ukraine's foreign policy' (*Geopoliticheskie iskaniya Kieva: Tsentral'naya I vostochnaya Evropa v politike Ukrain'i*), *Pro et Contra* 3/2 (spring 1998) pp.95–110 (in Russian).
33. T. Warner, 'The second Iron Curtain', *Kiyiv Post* (23 Oct. 1998) p.5.
34. Huntington (note 8).
35. For a very useful treatment and an analogy, see M. Foucher (ed.), *Fragments d'Europe: Atlas de l'Europe médiane et orientale* (Paris: Fayard 1993).
36. A. Applebaum, *Between East and West: Across the Borderlands of Europe* (New York: Pantheon Books 1994) p.xii.
37. Haushofer (note 5).
38. V. Kolossov and A. Treivish, 'The political geography of European minorities', *Political Geography* 17 (1998) pp.523–4.
39. The full text of the famous Mackinder aphorism is 'Who Rules East Europe Commands the Heartland; Who Rules the Heartland Commands the World Island; Who Rules the World Island Commands the World'. It was first published in *Democratic Ideals and Reality* (1919).
40. J. Fairgrieve, *Geography and World Power*, eighth edn. (London: University of London Press 1941) pp.329–31.
41. S.B. Cohen, 'Global geopolitical change in the post-cold-war era', *Annals, Association of American Geographers* 81, pp.551–80.
42. G. Parker, *Geopolitics: Past, Present and Future* (London: Pinter Publishers 1998) p.92.
43. R. Kjellén, *Der Staat als Lebeurform* (Leipzig: S. Hirzel, 1917).
44. O. Tunander, 'Post-cold war Europe: Synthesis of a bi-polar friend-foe structure and a hierarchic cosmos-chaos structure?' in O. Tunander, P. Baev and V.I. Einagel (eds.),

Geopolitics in Post-Wall Europe: Security, Territory and Identity (Thousand Oaks, CA: Sage Publications 1997) p.18.

45. Tunander (note 44) p.37. Regarding the concentric circles around Brussels, see also O. Waever, 'Imperial metaphors: Emerging European analogies to pre-nation-state imperial systems', in Tunander, Baev and Einagel (note 44) p.67.

46. V. Lukin, 'Our security predicament', *Foreign Policy* 88 (autumn 1992) p.63.

47. See the articles in Z. Brzezinski and P. Sullivan (eds.), *Russia and the Commonwealth of Independent States: Documents, Data and Analysis* (Armonk, NY: M.E. Sharpe 1997), especially Brzezinksi on the Eurasian tradition in Russia in 'Introduction: Last gasp or renewal?' pp.3–9. Alexander Solzhenitsyn is a prominent spokesperson for the Eurasianist perspective.

48. I.B. Neumann, 'The geopolitics of delineating "Russia" and "Europe": The creation of the "other" in European and Russian traditions', in Tunander, Baev and Einagel (note 44) pp.148–50. Brzezinski and Sullivan use the terms 'neo-democrats', 'national-patriotic', 'pragmatists' and 'left extremists' to designate the same four geopolitical ideologies.

49. Neumann (note 48) p.171. Y. Borko, 'Possible scenarios for geopolitical shifts in Russian-European relations', in Tunander, Baev and Einagel (note 44) p.206 reports that public opinion in Russia is highly variable and is a contrasting mosaic. Most Russians are suspicious of plans for NATO expansion, but 33 per cent were favourable to the EU, while 19 per cent were neutral and only seven per cent had a negative attitude, according to *Central and Eastern Eurobarometer* 6 (1996).

50. Bureau of European and Canadian Affairs, US Department of State, *Report to the Congress on the Enlargement of the North Atlantic Treaty Organization: Rationale, Benefits, Costs and Implications* (24 Feb. 1997) p.19. The State Department also distributed a glossy 24-page brochure entitled *The Enlargement of NATO: Why Adding Poland, Hungary and the Czech Republic to NATO Strengthens American National Security* (Washington DC: Feb. 1998). The brochure prominently featured the most widely known quote by Secretary of State Albright: 'A larger NATO will make us safer by expanding the area in Europe where wars simply do not happen.' (7 Oct. 1997.)

51. Bureau of European and Canadian Affairs (note 50) p.10. These new NATO aims were formally certified at the fiftieth anniversary meeting of the organisation in Washington DC, April 1999.

52. Bureau of European and Canadian Affairs (note 50) p.9.

53. For criticisms of the NATO enlargement, see A. Perlmutter and T.G. Carpenter, 'NATO's expensive trip east', *Foreign Affairs* 77/1 (1998) pp.2–6; M Brown, 'The flawed logic of NATO expansion', *Survival* 37, pp.34–52; and P. Kennedy and M. Gorbachev, 'The false pretence of NATO expansion', *New Perspectives Quarterly* 14/3 (1997) pp.62–4.

54. G.F. Kennan, 'A fatal error', *New York Times* (5 Feb. 1997) p.13.

55. J. Nijman (note 26).

56. See Z. Brzezinski, 'A geostrategy for Eurasia', *Foreign Affairs* 76/5, pp.50–71 and Z. Brzezinski, *The Grand Chessboard: American Primacy and the Geostrategic Imperatives* (New York: Basic Books), while an early statement on NATO enlargement was provided by H. Kissinger, 'Expand NATO now', *Washington Post* (19 Dec. 1994) p.27.

57. M. Kundera, 'Un occident kidnappé ou la tragédie de l'Europe centrale', *Le Débat* 27/11, pp.2–24.

58. G. Dijkink, *National Identity and Geopolitical Visions: Maps of Pride and Pain* (London: Routledge 1997) p.11.

59. Dijkink (note 58) pp.49–57 and D. Campbell, *Writing Security: United States Foreign Policy and the Politics of Identity* (Manchester: Manchester University Press). For a specific example of NATO actions in Bosnia, see D. Campbell, 'Apartheid cartography: The political anthropology and spatial effects of international diplomacy in Bosnia', *Political Geography* 18 (1999) pp.395–435.

60. F. Zakaria, 'Our hollow hegemony: Why foreign policy cannot be left to the market', *New York Times* (1 Nov. 1998) pp.44–5, 47, 74, 80.

61. G. Ó Tuathail (note 14) Ch.6.

Economic Globalisation: Politics and Trade Policy in Ghana and Kenya

RICHARD GRANT

Political geographers[1] have applied geopolitical analyses to understand the contemporary world order. In particular, their most important contributions to understanding geopolitical change are in their theories about the spatial effects of the rapid changes unfolding in the world economic and political system. Political geographers have disputed the idea of a 'borderless world' purported by some international business and international relations scholars.[2] Instead, they have re-centred the new world order debate by emphasising fragmentation over homogeneity through the varying territorial dimensions of global geopolitics and the real variations in political phenomena at all scales.

More recent approaches to geopolitics emphasise the growing significance of economic factors in defining patterns of world order. Some now consider geo-economics (the struggle for national economic or industrial supremacy) as a replacement for traditional geopolitics.[3] Power in the geo-economic world is measured in terms of global market share rather than military capabilities or acquired territorial space. Political geographers have even gone beyond separating political and economic realms, and researchers from the emerging school of critical geopolitics have linked the globalisation of political spaces to the economic world of connections and flows.[4] In particular, they note that both territorial states and non-state actors now operate in a world in which state boundaries have become permeable to decisions and flows emanating from networks of power not captured by singularly territorial representations of space. This has led to a shrinking of the world and a tighter enmeshment of states and societies in global networks and systems of interaction. The spatial consequences are evident in the more complex and messy appearance of political and economic life, where the foreign and the domestic are no longer neatly separated as distinct analytical categories.

Political geographers[5] also emphasise that hegemony is no longer based on any single nation-state, but is being replaced by a new ideology of the market (and of market access) which is being embedded in, and reproduced by, a powerful constituency of liberal states and international institutions. This ideology of 'transnational liberalism' is introduced by structural adjustment policies (SAPs), especially via trade-liberalisation policies. The pre-eminence of trade liberalisation is revealed by statistics showing that more than 60 per cent of structural adjustment loans have gone for trade-related reforms in Africa.[6] Trade liberalisation includes the removal of tariff restrictions, the rationalisation of tariff structures, and the establishment of export-promotion measures, such as the removal of export taxes and the creation of export-processing zones. Trade liberalisation results in reconfigurations of state-local relations and new political geographies. As the national economy is 'depoliticised' new opportunities are available for political groups to capture economic rewards.

A number of observations need to be made about the study of globalisation from a geopolitical perspective. First, political geographers have concentrated mostly on the macro-scale and on the broader theoretical issues of global change, rather than on the measurement and mechanisms of global engagement. Political geographers' treatment of globalisation has lacked precision; globalisation has thus been studied as a total entity. Apart from the examination of the globalisation of financial flows, studies of other economic dimensions of globalisation (that is, trade) are rare. Second, political geographers have not adequately distinguished the different realms of globalisation (economic, political, and cultural). There are obviously relationships between the different areas of globalisation, but understanding all aspects of globalisation and linking this knowledge to geopolitics is simply too large a task for any one study. Third, the nexus of global-local bridging of the economic and political realms that has been theorised by political geographers has rarely been examined in detailed case studies. Our knowledge base about globalisation is especially thin regarding regions such as Africa, where case studies have been particularly rare.

To further our understanding of globalisation, this article focuses on economic globalisation (only one dimension of the process of globalisation) in Ghana and Kenya. Economic globalisation is defined as the mechanisms by which the national economy is linked to global economic activities. It has triggered worldwide processes of systematic convergence and competition in economic relations as well as in the behaviour of governments, which pursue similar policies to enhance national competitiveness. Ghana and Kenya make a useful comparison because of their similar post-independence development strategies, high levels of ethnic diversity, and shifts toward trade liberalisation since the 1980s (for example, Kenya commenced trade liberalisation in 1980 and Ghana initiated SAPs in 1983). Their performances on trade liberalisation have received markedly different reviews from the World Bank and other international organisations. For instance, Ghana has been labelled 'the star pupil of adjustment'[7] and merited President Clinton's first stop on his five-state African tour in 1998. By contrast, Kenya is known for 'its patchy and intermittent commitment' to reform[8] as well as its flagrant abuses of human rights.

To understand the specifics of economic globalisation, I first examine the domestic national political process in which trade-liberalisation policies are introduced. The national trade environment is mediated by domestic institutional politics and turf battles over the timing and the content of trade reforms. Institutional theorists have deduced the main political and societal conditions necessary for the successful implementation of trade reforms.[9] I summarise their research findings in the next section to guide the study of the implementation of liberalisation policies. I follow this theoretical section with detailed case studies of Ghanaian and Kenyan experiences to uncover the factors that result in the differentiation of economic globalisation.

Second, I discuss the international environment which also shapes Ghanaian and Kenyan integration into the global economy along two routes. One is the national business climate by way of the international business community's perceptions of the reform process in both countries. International business has spearheaded the globalisation of commerce, and their assessments of the reform process represent an important link between the domestic politics of trade reform and the level and type of global engagement. I assemble data from a variety of organisations on the effects of reforms on transparency and levels of corruption. Corruption is viewed as a national factor that can slow or reverse international economic integration. In later sections, I discuss international perceptions of the business climate in both countries and then detail an index of those perceptions (at the time of reform, 1987–90, and in the current period, 1994–97).

The second route is to measure empirically the nature and extent of contemporary economic globalisation in both countries. Researchers, surprisingly, have not developed an index of economic globalisation that can measure the intensification of state-global relations. Globalisation theorists hypothesise increases in foreign business activity in the form of direct investment, multinational corporations, stock investors, tourist flows, and the intensification of trade ties (both globally as well as intraregionally).[10] I construct an index based on the compilation of these indicators. In the concluding section, I offer a number of observations about the differentiation of globalisation.

Global Differentiation: An Institutional Framework and a Political Geographic Framework

The introduction of trade liberalisation overturned the crony state capitalism[11] and the extensive government intervention that had characterised African national economies following independence. This brought to an end the various state-led development efforts that had been represented as inefficient, market distorting and 'anti-trade' oriented.[12] The signing of SAP agreements with international financial institutions (IFIs) committed African governments to market reforms that in theory promised more global economic engagement.

The trend toward liberalisation across the developing world since the 1980s affords political geographers two important research opportunities: first, to examine the complex connectivity between the two limiting geographic-scale possibilities (the state and the global); and, second, to examine geographic differentiation under economic globalisation. An institutional framework is appropriate for studying the interactions between the global economy and national politics and for assessing the activities and choices of state officials situated between these domains.[13] Institutionalists have pointed to factors that are sources of both continuity and change in trade policymaking arenas and that shape unique political geographies of power. Drawing on evidence from 13 developing countries' experiences, Williamson and Haggard highlight institutional conditions that have shaped the degree of trade liberalisation and the framework for global integration. Common prerequisites for the successful introduction of trade liberalisation have included:

- Authoritarianism (authoritarian governments found it easier to introduce trade reform, but typically once trade reforms were well underway more democracy was introduced)

- A honeymoon period (economic reformers enjoyed greater freedom of political manoeuvre immediately after they took office, when difficult decisions could be blamed on the legacy of the outgoing government)

- A solid political base of support (implementing reforms required a solid foundation of governmental support, whether societal or legislative, or both)

- A fragmented and demoralised opposition (this ensured that no group could challenge the unpopular reforms)

- A visionary leader (leaders with a sense of history were individuals prepared to take a long-term view of what was at stake, regardless of the short-term political risks)

- A coherent economic team (sustained reforms required the economic team to include individuals with conflicting views on economic policy so that the president could benefit from competing views)

- 'Technopole' leadership (this involved the president relying on the advice of experts, most typically from trade and finance ministries), and

- 'Voodoo' politics (the economic team often operated behind the scenes to convince groups that reform was in their interest).[14]

Institutional research has documented strong anti-liberalisation currents in society, emanating from urban dwellers, especially informal workers, and civilian and military employees who before trade reform benefited disproportionately from subsidised food and consumer goods, access to political leaders and civil service employment, and who realised rents through their involvement in trade.[15] Some opposition parties have also joined the anti-liberalisation camp in an attempt to position themselves for elections by championing resistance to unpopular austerity measures.[16] With the deepening of trade liberalisation over time, opponents have begun to coalesce with more anti-globalisation groups within societies (the latter typically oppose liberalisation based on cultural as well as economic reasoning).[17] Anti-globalisation groups are difficult to identify: they are fragmented and their level of discontent varies markedly. However, they remain susceptible to being ignited to attack the visible expressions of globalisation. For instance, anti-globalisation groups are noted for some ferocious assaults on cultural symbols of globalisation, such as Coca Cola, McDonald's and Planet Hollywood, and on political symbols, such as US embassies in Africa.

There is a large theoretical literature on economic globalisation that explains the processes that primarily determine the nexus of state-global economic development.[18] A combination of mechanisms (flows of trade, foreign direct investment, finance and people, and liberalisation policies) is typically employed to explain how states become more closely tied to the global economy. Investigation of the nature and the extent of economic globalisation presents us with a reverse challenge to that of the institutionalists: to ground economic globalisation theories in geographic case studies of real-world policy environments. Many political geographers' theoretical notions concerning the territorial mediation of economic globalisation require examination. For example, we need to move beyond theoretical abstractions of an ideal pattern of economic globalisation (a fully globalised economy) or random flows and networks toward explanations of the current state of affairs of global differentiation. While institutionalists have highlighted institutional factors that account for the different territorial impacts of economic globalisation, their list of variables is by no means exhaustive. Political geographers have noted that economic governance and the politics of trade and ethnicity are equally important determinants of global engagement.[19] According to Dunning and Hamdani, policymakers' abilities in the economic policy arena are a critical determinant in accounting for states' marginalisation or integration into the global economy.[20]

The Trade-Liberalisation Experience in Ghana

Ghana acceded to the General Agreement on Tariffs and Trade (GATT) in 1957, but did not adhere to GATT principles prior to adjustment. Before SAPs the economy was regulated by a highly protectionist, inward-looking trade regime. For instance, a 40 per cent tariff was levied on imports, non-tariff barriers such as licensing were widely used,[21] and the state controlled 130 parastatals.[22] Trade regulation varied from total control over imports to a more open export system where exporters were permitted to retain part of their foreign-currency earnings to pay for imports essential to their production without the requirement of a licence. In practice, exporters abused the licensing arrangement by purchasing foreign consumer goods for highly profitable domestic resale.[23]

The government's protectionist trade policy was strongly undermined by the economic downturn of the 1980s, beginning with the collapse of prices for Ghana's leading export (cocoa) in the early 1980s. Ghana had been highly dependent upon foreign exchange generated from commodity exports; it was indispensable to the entire economy because most sectors depended on importing inputs. A series of additional disastrous events (including drought, fires, murders of judges, and the expulsion of one million Ghanaian workers from Nigeria) all conspired to bring about economic collapse. The economy was in such a ruinous condition that by early 1983 'even senior civil servants found it difficult to obtain food'.[24]

The government announced SAPs in April 1983 and immediately devalued the cedi and made, or remade, trade a state monopoly. According to Minister for Finance Kwesi Botchwey, 'This should put an end to the corruption of officials in charge of import licensing, while ensuring that the benefit of all commissions and discounts offered to foreign manufactures would accrue to the government rather than individual importers.'[25] In early 1984, the government announced a ban on all imports not covered by government licences. To combat black-market traders, the government required importers to be licensed or to pay all import duties plus a ten per cent penalty. The import-licensing system remained in place until January 1989, when illegal trade abated in cocoa (but not in other areas, such as diamonds).[26] Regaining state control of trade enabled the Ghanaian government to collect 45.3 per cent of its tax revenues from trade taxes in 1985–90.[27] The new revenues were used by the government to solidify support among groups that that did not endorse President Jerry Rawlings' coming to power. These funds were used to mitigate partially the social hardships of adjustment (growing urban unemployment and so on) as well as to build roads and bring electricity to rural areas. From the beginning of SAPs Rawlings understood the economic and political logic even if he did not comprehend the far-reaching implications that they would have on Ghana. There is considerable evidence that Rawlings received strong backing from indigenous businesses in a position to benefit from liberalised trade.[28]

The economic recovery programme entailed a restructuring of trade institutions.[29] In 1981, when Rawlings came to power and the parliament was dissolved, most laws governing trade were made obsolete. At the commencement of SAPs, an Economic Management Team (EMT) was installed, comprising of the ministers of finance and economic planning, trade and tourism, industry, science and technology, and agriculture, as well as the chief statistician and the head of the research section of the Bank of Ghana, to coordinate and guide trade liberalisation.[30] Outside the EMT no permanent advisory trade body existed, and the government, with strong IFI backing, remained hegemonic in its pursuit of trade liberalisation. For instance, it overlooked a proposal from national economists to establish a Council of Economic Advisors to facilitate their involvement. Moreover, the EMT was sidelined over time and trade policy was implemented by decree following secret agreements among the IIEs, the ministry for finance and the president. Leadership of the reform programme was handed to technocratic finance ministers (initially, Kwesi Botchwey and subsequently Richard Kwame Peprah). Nevertheless, despite the high profile accorded to the finance minister, the president still held onto the final say in all trade-policy decisions. However, since the tilt toward democracy (following the 1996 election), it has become expedient to consolidate a more solid base of support within the cabinet for trade liberalisation. The reappointment of Peprah in 1997 for a second term as finance minister was largely based on his ability to maintain cabinet support for liberalisation.

In efforts to reverse the urban-rural terms of trade, control smuggling (estimated to be about 15 per cent of cocoa production),[31] and boost export earnings, the price paid to cocoa producers was progressively raised from cedis 12,000 per ton in 1982 to cedis 224,000 in 1991, and to cedis 1.8 million in 1997.[32] The Ghana Cocoa Board was restructured, and 40 per cent of its employees were trimmed to increase efficiency, cut costs, and control political rents. The latter entailed removing 25,000 'ghost workers' from the payroll, and approximately 100,400 workers from various sectors have been retrenched since 1985.[33] The government also sought to rehabilitate gold and timber exports, and attempted to diversify exports through incentives to promote non-traditional exports (for example, pineapple juice, cut flowers, vegetables, spices, and so on). This rehabilitation of trade was accompanied by bureaucratic reform, whereby export procedures were made less cumbersome and export licences were phased out by 1990 (except for minerals). By the early 1990s, the number of steps required for exporting had been reduced from 32 to eight.[34]

Over time Rawlings' political bases of support (outside his home region of Volta) has changed from an initial urban, labour, radical and populist base toward diffuse and precarious support from some rural groups that benefited from trade reform. The government sought to consolidate rural support by regularly praising farmers for their contribution to reform, but the dispersal of small farmers over wide areas prevented mass mobilisation and their organisation into a powerful national political group.[35] One particular government initiative to build rural support for trade liberalisation was the establishment of export-promotion villages (EPVs) for non-traditional exports (especially handicrafts and vegetable production). The EPV scheme entailed community-based discussions on the formation of export-based companies with a guarantee of financial, data, and administrative support from the government. This high-profile political involvement has yielded mixed results. There has been a nationwide interest in non-traditional exports, but severe financial constraints arising from the government not honouring its commitments curtailed the programme: to date, only five EPVs have been established.[36] Despite governmental rhetoric to promote export diversification, non-traditional exports account for only a small share of exports (less than seven per cent in 1997). Another government attempt to build rural support involved political decentralisation and the introduction of District Assembly elections. This effort increased support for the ruling party, the People's National Democratic Council (PNDC), in many rural areas and most importantly encouraged political leaders seeking office to co-opt the trade-liberalisation discourse.

The Ashanti region, however, stands out as a failure in regional politics: the PNDC has failed to establish support in the area, despite the large cocoa producers there benefiting greatly from trade reforms. The largest opposition party, the New Patriotic Party (NPP), continues to have a strong hold on the region. The high proportion of top-ranking government officials originating from the Akan, Ewe, and Northern regions has added to resentment of the government.[37]

In addition, urban and public-sector workers, national unions such as the Trade Union Congress (TUC), the lower ranks of the army, and the universities have protested strongly against trade reforms. According to TUC estimates, in 1991 manufacturing employment was half that of 1983.[38] To temper urban opposition, censorship of the press was introduced, requiring all newspapers to be licensed after March 1989. The official justification was that it was necessary to save newsprint, a scarce commodity, and that many papers had 'become pornographic'.[39] In 1992, censorship of the media was relaxed somewhat and opposition newspapers regularly criticised 'unbridled trade liberalisation'.[40] The government's response has been to continue in its efforts to build more urban support. The negative, heavy-handed approach used to deal with public protests was replaced with a blend of firmness and conciliation in the 1990s. The government also became opportunistic of political situations. For example, it took advantage of a million-dollar timber-smuggling scandal involving Lebanese and Indian expatriates by rallying opposition to these two unpopular, but successful, economic groups well known to have associations with corrupt trade officials.[41] Further efforts to identify with the austerity of the urban poor included the government's introduction of a super sales tax of 50–500 per cent in February 1990 to curb luxury imports, such as mineral water, fruit, champagne, and automobiles.

The anti-trade-reform sentiment reached a peak in May 1995, when the government attempted to introduce a value added tax (VAT) of 17.5 per cent to raise more revenue. During anti-VAT rioting in Accra, five people were killed. Urban opposition to the tax united labour unions, small businesses, university employees and students, and even government supporters. The protesters' criticisms also spilled over to include the government's record on SAPS, and paradoxically there were calls for more globalisation. As one opponent noted, 'it is not that we have been left behind by globalisation, it is more that we haven't started yet'.[42] It seems that, in the public's view, foreign direct investment and trade liberalisation are separate matters, and few draw the connections between the policy environment that facilitates globalisation and the end result (a fully globalised economy). Worst of all, this dispute highlighted divisions within the government itself over the phasing and timing of reform. Subsequently, the finance minister and the minister for trade and industry were used as scapegoats and resigned. Such high-level resignations suggest that the economic policymaking staff is always insulated from politics, especially when the government faces widespread social upheavals. The extent of the VAT opposition has slowed down its reintroduction. Currently, the government is engaging in a public-relations campaign to educate Ghanaians on VAT fundamentals, and a 12.5 per cent rate is being steadily implemented.

In general, trade liberalisation has opened the economy, even if political obstacles (for example, corruption and regional and urban opposition) remain. By 1991 the average tariff rate was ten per cent, down from a 30 per cent rate prior to SAPs (Table 1), and tariffs have been lifted for agriculture.[43] Non-tariff barriers have been eliminated, except in agricultural and mineral commodities. Furthermore, government monopolies are now limited to the importation of petroleum and wheat, cocoa exports, shipping, and telecommunications (except mobile phones).[44]

To a large extent the government's trade policy is a 'top-down' approach to development. Exports are promoted without giving farmers and other social groups an institutional voice in policymaking. The whole trade-policy

TABLE 1

AVERAGE IMPORT TARIFFS RATES IN GHANA (percentages)

Product category	1980–83	1987–90	1994–97
Raw materials	25	10	10
Capital goods	30	15	10
Consumer goods	30	20	20
Luxury goods	30	25	25

Sources: GATT, *Trade Policy Review. Ghana* (Geneva: GATT 1992); Government of Ghana, *Customs and Excise*, Tariff Interpretation Order No. 1 (Accra: Ministry for Finance 1998).

planning process is closely monitored and censored by official appointees, who unconditionally endorse trade-liberalisation policies enacted by the central government. The Ghana case study confirms the vast majority of Williamson and Haggard's institutional assumptions about trade reform.[45] The main exception is the prerequisite of solid bases of support. Despite its impressive implementation record, the government has sustained only a moderate support basis for trade liberalisation. The social costs of liberalisation have been immense. Even the World Bank now acknowledges that the social costs in most countries (increasing poverty, higher costs of living, and greater social and spatial polarisation) have outweighed the few economic benefits to states.[46] In addition, there always remains the possibility that liberalisation could be easily derailed. Matters beyond the government's liberalisation policies could conspire to swell opposition to the government's policies, for example, the current electricity shortages due to climatic factors (lower water levels in Lake Volta) as well as rapid urbanisation (the estimated growth of Accra's population from 1.5 million in 1970 to 3.5 million in 1998).

The Trade-Liberalisation Experience in Kenya

Kenya became a member of GATT in 1964 and adhered to many free-trade principles until the early 1970s. Average tariff rates reached their lowest levels to date in 1974 at 22 per cent. The 1973 oil shock was the first in a series of severe balance of payments crises that forced the government to shift toward protectionism.[47] The end of the 1977–78 coffee price boom intensified Kenya's financial crisis. High world prices for coffee had encouraged the government to borrow and spend at levels that required coffee prices to remain high. The 1980s brought about a decline in commodity prices, and coffee prices plummeted. Faced with a fiscal crisis the government decided to raise more taxes by entertaining protectionism and increased the average tariff rate to 30 per cent48 (Table 2). Moreover, use of protectionism became more irregular over time: tariff rates became highly discretionary and varied widely by commodity (for example, tobacco at 138 per cent, garments at 100 per cent and books at zero per cent). Levels of protection became more a function of politics (that is, the ability of economic interest groups to persuade the government to designate a sector as 'strategic') than of economics. Government involvement in trade also extended to exports, and a licensing arrangement was introduced for agricultural exports. An export tax was initiated for unprocessed products in an effort to increase processing content and improve the balance of payments.[49]

TABLE 2

AVERAGE IMPORT TARIFFS RATES IN KENYA (percentages)

Product category	1980–83	1987–90	1994–97
Raw materials	40.0	37.3	30.0
Capital goods	40.0	30.2	20.0
Consumer goods	n/a	51.2	40.0
Luxury goods	n/a	53.6	50.0
Average tariff	30.0	38.5	34.0

Sources: GATT, Trade Policy Review. Ghana (Geneva: GATT 1992); Dun and Bradstreet, Exports Encyclopedia (New York: Dun and Bradstreet International 1998).

Prior to SAPs the government linked trade and manufacturing policies with import-substitution policies. Importers had to obtain a 'no-objection certificate' from local manufacturers before importing any product made domestically. High duties were levied on processed imports that competed with domestic manufacturers and consumer goods, whereas tariffs on raw materials, intermediate products, and capital goods were lower. Moreover, import-substitution policies were framed in the context of ethnic discrimination. For instance, the government attempted to 'Africanise' industry by removing citizens of Indian descent from the manufacturing sector in an effort to ensure black Kenyan control.[50] A combination of racially biased industrial policies, rent-seeking behaviours, and importers violating their trade privileges charted a course along which illegal practices in trade flourished.[51]

By contrast, agriculture was driven more by comparative advantage than by government intervention.[52] Kenya's pricing policy for principal exports (coffee and tea) differed from Ghana's in that the government did not set producer prices. Instead, it adopted a policy of 'throughput' whereby the world market price was approximated after percentages were deducted for government handling, transportation, processing, and parastatal operating costs. This pricing policy introduced farmers (in tea, coffee, cotton, pyrethrum, and maize) to far more market discipline than was the case in the manufacturing sector.[53] Regional differences in quality were also reflected in payments to growers, as each factory calculated its own producer prices. This translated into higher incomes in regions with better soils, which favoured the Kikuyu group, the largest ethnic group in Kenya. Farmers' interests were, furthermore, co-opted by the political elite by a democratic process that ran contrary to governmental authoritarianism. For instance, elections provided conduits connecting the state to farmers and institutionalised rural interests.[54] Even small farmers had some policy influence via their participation in rural community organisations and commodity-based organisations, such as the Kenya Coffee Growers Association.[55]

The Kenyan government first attempted structural adjustment in 1980 when it shifted from import-substitution to export-oriented trade.[56] To promote manufacturing exports, a compensation scheme was instituted whereby manufacturing exporters could claim a refund of 20 per cent of duty paid on components. In addition, a guarantee scheme provided insurance against the risk of non-payment. As early as January 1981, however, the government reversed its trade-liberalisation policy: all textile imports were banned, and all imports henceforth required a licence. The government's commitment to trade liberalisation fizzled out by 1982. Compliance had been limited to a small cadre of top civil servants, and enforcement proved too difficult as local governments were both unwilling and unable to implement reform.[57]

During Kenya's two trade-liberalisation experiments (1980–82 and 1987–97), economic policymaking was characterised by a struggle between the reforming arm of government (the minister of finance, economic planning and development commerce, and the Central Bank) and anti-reform ministries. Anti-trade-liberalisation ministers railed against cheaper imports, accusing the government of 'promoting employment in Taiwan at the expense of the Kenyan worker'.[58] Intragovernmental rivalries over trade policy meant that cabinet reshuffles became expedient (eight from 1986 to 1998) to keep ministers in check. Himbara described a breakdown among the ministries to collect taxes and a lack of coordination in implementing reforms and intense intracabinet rivalry.[59] Repeated backtracking on trade liberalisation meant that no individual minister was accorded insulation from anti-liberalisation groups or could even be assured of the president's support. For instance, George Satori, a former minister for finance, is currently implicated in a fraud scandal that involves the government paying $100 million in gold and diamond export subsidies to the Goldenberg International Company. The president has done all in his power to distance himself from this corruption case and the policies pursued by his ministers while in office.

Moreover, the cabinet itself has rarely acted as a coherent economic team, and 'voodoo' politics has characterised internal cabinet struggles. For example, the president took some important policymaking decisions without consulting the finance and trade ministries, such as favouring and promoting wheat growing in Kalenjin, the president's home province, at the expense of the Kikuyu region, comparatively advantaged in agriculture.[60] Cabinet ministerial rivalry has intensified since the 1996 elections as cabinet members now publicly position themselves for the next presidential election (the current president, Daniel Arap Moi, is legally prohibited from seeking another term). Fracas rather than dialogue has now become common in economic policymaking. For instance, in April 1998, Simeon Nyachae, the minister of finance, along with six other cabinet members attended an IFI-sponsored summit without consulting the president, who, outraged, called a special parliamentary session to admonish the wayward cabinet members, but was unable to secure large parliamentary support.[61]

During the second experiment with trade liberalisation (1987–97), Moi's strategy was to shatter potential opponents' power bases through the sponsorship of rival competitive groups and regional areas. Disruptions to businesses became commonplace. For instance, Unga, the main milling company, was forced to stop production periodically for several weeks because its owners refused to cede a share of control to the government.[62] Parastatal appointments were used to promote high-ranking officials from within Moi's constituencies, and civil service retrenchment was employed to remove opposition supporters, many of them Kikuyu.[63] In particular, the Kikuyu group was targeted for the harshest government treatment in an effort to curtail their economic participation. For example, the government reorganised the Kenya Tea Development Authority and various coffee co-operatives, which translated into higher prices and higher quotas for smallholder farmers in the Rift Valley and Western Provinces at the expense of the Kikuyu in the Central Province.[64] The government single-mindedly introduced these policies even though they resulted in declining tea exports and eroded Kenya's international market share for its principal exports. Furthermore, state budgets became political instruments, with the largest allocations earmarked for special projects in Moi's areas of support.[65] The government's interference in the economy even extended to the president brazenly promoting the economy of his hometown (Eldoret), which has since become a manufacturing centre that rivals Nairobi in terms of African-owned firms. Moi, in 1995, went so far as to propose an international airport for Eldoret to rival Nairobi, a proposal vetoed by the IFIs, but acted upon by the government.[66] Kikuyu power in government was also eliminated: after 1989 no Kikuyu was granted a cabinet position. The state's strategy, whenever possible, was not to draw an explicit connection between the

Kikuyu and its opposition. Accordingly, the government blamed all anti-government protests on the 'Mwakenya', a shadowy organisation supported by intellectuals, socialists, and some Kikuyu, but not known to have a clear geographical or ethnic base. The government's heavy-handed interference eventually remade the economy, and global economic factors were of lesser importance in shaping national economic development. The Moi regime marks the first time in Kenya's history that the presidency, and hence the state sector, is ethnically separate from a traditionally dominant group in the urban and large-holder export sectors.

Opposition to state policies has escalated ethnic tension and engendered an 'ethnic terror'. It is estimated that 1,060 Kikuyu have been killed and another 250,000 driven out of the Rift Valley or pressured to sell their land to Kalenjin at low prices.[67] Other ethnic groups have also been alienated from politics and the economy. For example, the government's policy of redistributing trade rewards excludes Luo participation.[68] Opposition to governmental trade policies, however, is not wholly ethnic in character; it also includes lawyers, other professionals, and church leaders, who are increasingly concerned about the lack of democracy in every sphere of economic and political life. Furthermore, the deterioration of agricultural producer prices by 26 per cent since 1981 has eroded some farmer support, even from those who benefit from the ethnic character of government targeting.[69] Large-scale demonstrations of public disaffection with government policies have occurred across the country, especially among the Kikuyu people. Wrong sums up the current Kenyan economy as being caught in 'a destructive downward spiral' brought about 'by government sleaze and economic irrationality'.[70]

One of the unintended consequences of state trade policies has been to encourage Kenyan Indian and Kikuyu involvement in other non-government-controlled sectors, such as horticulture. This area differs from most Kenyan trade in that it is dominated by private enterprises.[71] Horticultural exports have become the most dynamic export sector and since 1992 have been consistently among the top three exports (along with tea and coffee) as well as a major employer (two million workers were employed in this sector in 1998).[72] Horticulture exporters' success is largely in spite of the state sector, rather than because of it, and it illustrates how comparative advantage can be arbitrarily created and more contingent on structural changes in domestic politics than the global economy.

The fiscal problems for the state have been intensified by the government's authoritarianism in the economy, which has resulted in the state capturing fewer rewards from trade. For instance, in 1990, trade taxes amounted to 16.8 per cent of total taxes collected, compared to 38.1 per cent in Ghana.[73] Also, IFIs decided in August 1997 to cut off structural adjustment assistance, which was subsequently followed by the systematic withholding of all bilateral aid. It is now estimated that the fiscal crisis is so extreme that 95 per cent of government expenditure is spent on wages and debt repayments, leaving only five per cent for national economic development.[74] Because of Kenya's deplorable record in maintaining political and economic freedom, political conditionality is increasingly attached to loans; it has become an African test case for the linking of economic and political freedoms. Conditions are expected to worsen in Kenya before improving, and most analysts do not expect IFIs to have returned there before 2000.

Kenya has backtracked several times on trade liberalisation and has terminated liberalisation on two occasions: the first time, the state ended its experiment; the second time, the international community halted its support.[75] In terms of numerical indicators, it has abruptly raised and then gradually liberalised tariffs. The government's approach to the economy is based more on a struggle of power, succession, and personality than on long-term policy goals. In Kenya, the whole process of implementation has been subverted by the need to meet immediate political demands. Its liberalisation derailments make it distinctive from Ghana and the other adjusting countries that have been studied by Williamson and Haggard.[76] In many ways, the prominence of domestic political struggles and ethnicity in Kenya over national economic development and global engagement has contributed to irrationality in the economic sphere. The whole deliberation of trade policy is limited to the president and a few close associates, and there is no room for trade and other governmental institutions to influence policy.

International Business Perceptions of the Reform Climates in Ghana and Kenya

The advancement of economic globalisation has heightened the international business community's attention toward regularly making global comparisons and assessments of the business climates in developing countries. These assessments are based on individuals' experiences, and they provide an important check on the effects of trade liberalisation on facilitating international business, especially in the areas of corruption and transparency. Because the international business community participates in day-to-day transactions with developing countries, its experiences are as important as those of IFIs. For instance, international businesses' designation of a country as 'an emerging market' can facilitate trade, investment, and stock market investments. Alternatively, international businesses' labelling of a business climate as restrictive (for example, Nigeria) can encourage global disengagement.

However, there is no agreed-upon measure for comparing and assessing the business climate across the globe. As mentioned earlier, political scientists and economists have recently addressed the issues of corruption and economic globalisation.[77] Several organisations now provide independent assessments of economic freedom based on aggregations of the perceptions of a variety of groups (such as journalists, consultants, executives in middle management, and policy analysts). Following in the tradition of Elliott,[78] an index of economic corruption (Table 3) is compiled from summaries of the individual country reports for Ghana and Kenya from such organisations as Business International, Political Risk Services, the Institute for Management, and the Heritage Foundation. Each rating is based on aggregating various responses to survey questions about the business climate. These surveys solicited opinions about the degree to which improper practices (such as illegal payments) are necessary to facilitate business transactions. The *World Competitiveness Report*, in particular, has received a lot of media publicity in recent years with its annual country rankings based on indicators for economic competitiveness. While these surveys are not scientifically sampled and may be more complete for some countries than for others, they provide an important global assessment of the reform process. The summary index is divided into three periods: (1) 1980–83, representing the state of affairs at the commencement of trade liberalisation; (2) 1987–90, illustrating the period after a decade and a half of trade liberalisation; and (3) 1994–97, the most recent period.

There was a high level of consistency across the ratings of the business climate in Ghana and Kenya over time (Table 3). At the introduction of trade liberalisation, both countries scored on the high end in terms of corruption and bribery in the economic arena. A trend toward transparency in the Ghanaian business environment occurred over time. However, surprisingly, since the transition from military to democratic rule in December 1996 the ratings for Ghana have not improved. There is contradictory evidence on recent achievements in Ghana. On the one hand, Ghana's successful record in implementing trade liberalisation has resulted in a lot of positive international publicity. For instance, President Clinton praised Ghana in March 1998 for its economic and political achievements and noted that 'Ghana again lights the way for Africa' in that 'business is growing and trade and investment are rising'.[79] On the other hand, however, domestic issues temper Ghana's positive image abroad. For one, the 1998 energy crisis (projected to last a number of years) is damaging.[80] In addition, the US government's decision to close temporarily its embassy in Accra (although this is unrelated to any change in the Ghanaian political environment) exposes the vulnerability of doing business abroad. Most

TABLE 3

INDEX OF ECONOMIC CORRUPTION OR TRANSPARENCY

Source	Survey	Subject Asked	Ratings Ghana	Kenya
Reform Period (1980–83)				
Business International	Assessment by staff (journalists)	Degree to which business transactions involve questionable payments	high	moderate /high
Political Risk Services	Assessment by staff (consultants)	Likeliness to demand special and illegal payments throughout government levels	high	high
Reform Period (1987–90)				
Business International	Assessment by staff (journalists)	Degree to which business transactions involve questionable payments	moderate /high	high
Political Risk Services	Assessment by staff (consultants)	Likeliness to demand special and illegal payments throughout government levels	moderate /high	
World Competitiveness Report, Institute for Management, Lausanne	Executives in top and middle management	Improper practices such as bribing or corruption in the public sphere	n/a	high
Reform Period (1994–97)				
Political Risk Services	Assessment by staff (consultants)	Likeliness to demand special and illegal payments throughout government levels	moderate /high	moderate /high
World Competitiveness Report, Institute for Management, Lausanne	Executives in top and middle management	Improper practices such as bribing or corruption in the public sphere	moderate /high	high
Heritage Foundation	Staff	Restrictions on freedom to participate in the economy	partly free	mostly not free

Sources: Business International, *Handbook for International Corporations* (New York: Business International 1983); Freedom House, *The Index of Economic Freedom* (Washington DC: Heritage Foundation 1996); Heritage Foundation, *1997 Index of Economic Freedom* (Washington DC: Heritage Foundation and Dow Jones 1998); HYPERLINK http://www.gwdg.de/~uwvw/icr.htm; Political Risk Services, *Political Risk Annual* (Syracuse, NY: Political Risk Services 1980–98).

importantly, there has been a widespread domestic belief that corruption is on the increase and lawlessness more prevalent. A recent opinion poll in the *Daily Graphic* confirms this trend: 57 per cent of respondents believed that corruption was the biggest problem in Ghana.[81] Even President Rawlings was forced to address the issue of corruption in his first speech of the year to parliament in January 1998, during which he announced his 'zero tolerance policy'. Over the next few months hundreds of individuals were arrested on criminal charges, including one high-ranking police official.[82] Increasing urbanism and a squeeze on the rewards that can be made from legitimate employment are said to be forcing individuals into illegal activities such as diamond smuggling, drug trafficking, prostitution, and so on. Furthermore, the government's threat to retrench the civil service more in 1998 has continued the practice of bribing or 'dashing' as individuals use any means at their disposal to capture what they can from the state.

In Kenya, the climate for conducting business has deteriorated over time, and the country was scored at the high end of economic corruption in the most recent period. The *World Competitiveness Report* rated Kenya as the third most corrupt country in the world for business in 1996. Similarly, the Heritage Foundation's 1997 freedom survey noted that 'human rights violations and harassment of political opponents have increased and the government has not shown a willingness to eliminate the system of business patronage which the ruling party depends on for survival'.[83] The level of corruption and the extent of human-rights violations have been so widespread in Kenya that in August 1997 the international community withdrew all funding from the country. Amnesty International has accused the government of 'divide and rule tactics', 'spiralling violence and intensifying ethnic hatred'.[84] On 3 April 1998, the US State Department issued a business and travel advisory announcement for Kenya, warning its citizens about 'instability, street crime, banditry, unreliable mail and improper protection against credit card and check theft'.[85] The 7 August 1998 terrorist attack on the US embassy in Nairobi (killing 258 people) also injured Kenya's international image as a safe place to conduct business. The Kenyan government has responded to these claims by announcing the establishment of a corruption commission mandated to clean up the business environment[86] and by advocating a get-tough policy on crime. However, it remains to be seen whether these efforts will accomplish anything or simply become additional persecution vehicles at the president's disposal.

Economic Globalisation?

After a decade or more of implementing trade-liberalisation policies some African policy elites are converts to free-market principles. The liberalisation intellectual current drew inspiration (rightfully or not) from the upward economic mobility (up to recently) of the so-called newly industrialising countries (NICs), particularly those in East Asia, such as South Korea and Malaysia. Officials in both Ghana and Kenya have made future projections about the globalisation of their economies. According to President Moi, 'Kenya is now ready for the next stage of global economic transformation along the path taken by South Korea, Taiwan...'.[87] The director of the Private Enterprise Foundation claimed, 'Ghana's Tema and Takoradi ports can become the gateway ports for all of Africa's global business.'[88] Similarly, the African media embraced globalisation. For instance, *West Africa* referred to Africa as 'the last emerging global market'.[89]

The conversion of trade-liberalisation policies and speculation about the globalisation of economies into global engagement is, however, significantly more complex, especially considering the global financial turmoil that began in 1997. Few researchers have gone beyond the abstract notion of globalisation to assess the reality of global engagement. Because there is no agreed-upon criteria for assessing the extent of economic globalisation, as a preliminary step toward its measurement, I constructed an index for Ghana and Kenya over time (Table 4), which is based on the various criteria highlighted by globalisation theorists.[90]

The indicators' trends are quite revealing. The number of affiliates of the world's largest 450 multinational corporations (MNCs) have declined in both countries since the introduction of trade liberalisation (dropping from seven to four in Ghana and dramatically from 25 to seven in Kenya). It should be acknowledged, however, that this trend has been offset by a growth in foreign presence in these economies (for example, joint ventures, foreign-controlled smaller companies, and foreign equity shares).[91] The trend for the largest MNCs suggests that liberalisation policies alone are not sufficient to attract their involvement. Instead, larger MNCs appear to follow the crowd more in locating abroad, and locations such as Ireland, China and eastern Europe are favoured over Africa. The average number of trading partners also registered a decline over the reform period, suggesting that international trade linkages are dependent on more than the degree of marketisation and much more likely to be determined by the types of commodities produced as well as the level of technology incorporated into the goods. Both Ghana's and Kenya's trade predominately flows on a North-South axis, which is reminiscent of the early days of post-colonialism. Both countries still conduct most of their trade with traditional partners, despite the globalisation current. Their attempts to foster non-traditional exports and to develop new products for new markets fail to register as a success at this level of aggregation. This suggests that both

TABLE 4

INDEX OF ECONOMIC GLOBALISATION

Reformer	Indicator	Pre-reform	1987–90	1994–97
Ghana	Number of MNCs	7	6	4
	Business travellers (1,000s)	na	46	103
	Foreign investments ($)	10	10	239
	Number of trading partners	55	53	49
	Trade outside Africa (per cent)	84	88	80
	Stock-market listings	na	11	21
	Tourist receipts ($)	na	55	233
Kenya	Number of MNCs	25	24	7
	Business travellers (1,000s)	na	66	96
	Foreign investments ($)	26	43	7
	Number of trading partners	73	57	51
	Trade outside Africa (per cent)	88	90	83
	Stock-market listings	20	56	58(20)
	Tourist receipts ($)	na	56	58(20)

Notes: The number of MNC affiliates refers only to affiliates of the largest 450 MNCs in the North and underestimates the total number of MNCs operating in both countries.

The Ghana stock exchange opened in 1990 and companies were listed provisionally until 1991. On the Nairobi stock exchange 58 companies are listed in the most recent period but only 20 companies are offered for foreign investors.

The number of business travellers in the third period relate to the year 1995.

Sources: D. Stafford and R. Purkis, *Directory of Multinationals* (New York: Stockton Press 1989); Macmillan, *Macmillan Directory of Multinationals* (New York: Macmillan 1998); Dun and Bradstreet, *Exports Encyclopedia* (New York: Dun and Bradstreet International 1998); UNCTAD, *World Investments Reports* (New York: United Nations 1993–98); for Ghana stock exchange (1996): http://ourworld.compuserv.com/homepages/khaganu/stockex.htm; for Nairobi stock exchange (1997): http://mbendi.co.zulexke.htm; *IFC, Emerging Stock Market Factbook* (Washington, DC: IFC 1996); World Tourism Organization (1998): http://www.world-tourism.org/; IMF, *Direction of Trade Statistics* (Washington, DC: IMF 1982-98).

government and IFI expectations about the benefits of economic globalisation are not realised for Ghana's and Kenya's international trade. We can conclude that the structure and composition of international trade are much more difficult to alter than national policy.

A major difference between the countries is that Ghana has been much more successful than Kenya in attracting foreign direct investment. Foreign investment has risen dramatically from $10 million before SAPs to $239 million in the most recent period. In 1997, Ghana became the sixth most important foreign direct investment destination in the developing world. A similar positive trend is registered in the growth in the number of companies listed on the national stock market. The Ghanaian stock exchange opened for business in 1990 and listed 21 companies in the most recent period. By 1996, Ghana had the sixty-first largest stock market in the world in terms of the number of shares traded, and its market capitalisation was valued as $1,873 million.[92] Kenya's financial environment has exhibited contrary trends. Foreign investment has almost dried up in Kenya (averaging $7 million for the 1995–97 period). The Nairobi stock market, despite being one of Africa's oldest and largest (in terms of the number of countries listed) stock markets, has declined in relative importance. Presently, only 28 of the 58 companies listed are available to foreign investors, and its market capitalisation has stagnated to a level just below the new Ghanaian market ($1,846 million in 1996).[93]

Positive reviews of Ghanaian trade liberalisation and of its economy in general attract more business travellers, the number of which has more than doubled since the early 1990s. In the last year, Ghana received more than 103,000 business travellers, thus surpassing the number in Kenya for the first time. The area where Ghana is still far behind Kenya is in international tourism, even though Ghanaian tourist receipts have more than quadrupled since the second period of reform. Kenyan tourist receipts, although stagnating in recent years, are still highly significant. At $456 million for the most recent period, this high value helps negate some of the declines registered for many of the economic globalisation indicators. However, it is anticipated that Kenya's negative international image will eventually undermine its tourist business.

Conclusions

The Ghanaian and Kenyan case studies illustrate very different state experiences with economic globalisation, trade liberalisation, and domestic trade politics. The case studies call into question a 'mono-economic' understanding of developing economies and globalisation. In both cases, the state was instrumental (albeit in very different ways) in mediating pressures 'from above' and 'from below'. State interactions occur in an environment where the ground is shifting underneath established arrangements and where territoriality is being partially 'unbundled' by diminished sovereignty through the implementation of SAPs. Despite the changing global and national policy domains, the state remains a central player; thus, the notion of a 'borderless' world appears to be greatly exaggerated.

Economic globalisation is geographically differentiated and does not impact countries in the same way. It is not essentially global, but rather highly particularistic. The processes of economic globalisation are selective and uneven, and the emerging political realities are a mixture of old and new or are hybrid forms with varying degrees of territorial integrity. The state has reverted to regionalism in a pre-modern form in Kenya, which even challenges the territorial integrity of the post-independent state. In Ghana, the state has embraced globalisation and there remains the possibility of entering a post-modern form with multiple levels of authority and engagement for economic activities. Rather than seeing that state in the singular in an era of globalisation, we need to appreciate that states (in the plural) have assumed and will continue to assume a variety of forms as they adapt to the changing historical and geographical circumstances of globalisation.

How states mediate globalisation is a function of different trade-policy, institutional, and ethnic variables. The histories of trade reform in Ghana and Kenya call for the addition of ethnic and regional variables to the institutional trade framework. Both case studies illustrate that ethnic politics (government versus Ashanti and government versus Kikuyu) provided an important backdrop for governmental policies. However, ethnicity and regional interests are far from a 'mono-political' explanation. For instance, the Ghanaian government sought to include the Ashanti and rural farmers early in SAPs, whereas the Kenyan government excluded the Kikuyu at any cost. These case-study findings indicate that the constraints imposed by ethnicity are elastic and difficult to predict; the relationship between government stimuli and internal responses often worked in entirely unexpected ways. For instance, in Kenya, this translated into Kikuyu dominance in horticultural exports.

The promises of economic globalisation are not fulfilled in either state. Ghana and Kenya remain on the margins. Neither the policies of economic liberalisation and the tilt toward political liberalisation in Ghana nor the authoritarian statist alternative followed by Kenya are capable of delivering levels of economic growth or development that are remotely comparable to what has been achieved in globalised economies such as the USA. Moreover, the permeability of state borders by economic globalisation also works in the reverse way. For instance, economic globalisation opens up the state to wide swings in the behaviour of global speculators, and fragile states and the poor are susceptible to being swept away during economic crises in the rush to rebalance portfolios (for example, Thailand and South Korea in 1997–98). The contagion of the 1998 global financial crises resulted in the Accra stock market losing 19 per cent of its value and the Nairobi market losing 15 per cent.[94] In many ways, it was fortuitous that the Ghanaian and Kenyan economies were not more globalised as they would have experienced more capital flight along the lines of the South Asian NICs (for example, the Bangkok and the Seoul stock markets lost more than 55 per cent of their values).[95] Statist barriers such as non-convertible currencies and exchange controls provided some insulation.

The lesson that we can learn from the introduction of SAPs in Ghana and Kenya is that development cannot be externally imposed, but it may be learned. Learning is not merely applying formulas and reducing barriers; it is also about institution building, which is a longer term undertaking. Institution building depends on the ability to respect and delegate authority, on the capacity to conceptualise and implement a distinction between the 'public' interests of a trade institution and the 'private' interests of the individuals within it, and on conceptions of obligation and accountability, which are ultimately moral and societal in nature. Learning is above all about using local knowledge to shape the type of policies pursued by the global community. The current global climate affords African states an important opportunity to put forward their own proposals for economic development and for IFIs to incorporate the specificities of individual country's experiences into their macro-economic policies.

NOTES

1. J. Agnew, *Geopolitics. Re-Visioning World Politics* (New York: Routledge 1998); J. Agnew and S. Corbridge, *Mastering Space. Hegemony, Territory and International Political Economy* (New York: Routledge 1995); A. Herod, G. Ó Tuathail and S. Roberts (eds.), *An Unruly World? Globalization, Governance, and Geography* (New York: Routledge 1998).
2. K. Ohmae, *The Borderless World. Power and Strategy in the Interlinked Economy* (London: Fontana 1993); R. O'Brien, *Global Financial Integration: The End of Geography* (New York: Council on Foreign Relations Press 1992).
3. E. Luttwak, 'From geo-politics to geo-economics', *The National Interest* 20 (1990) p.17.
4. Herod, Ó Tuathail and Roberts (note 1).
5. Agnew and Corbridge (note 1) p.196.
6. C. Fitzpatrick and J. Weiss, 'Trade policy reforms and performance in Africa in the 1980s', *Journal of Modern African Studies* 33 (1995) p.286.
7. C. Leechor, 'Ghana: Frontrunner in adjustment', in I. Husain and R. Faruqee (eds.), *Adjustment in Africa. Lessons from Country Studies* (Washington DC: World Bank 1994) p.153.
8. G. Swamy, 'Kenya: Patchy, intermittent commitment', in I. Husain and R. Faruqee (eds.), *Adjustment in Africa. Lessons from Country Case Studies* (Washington DC: World Bank 1994) p.193.
9. J. Williamson, *The Political Economy of Policy Reform* (Washington DC: Institute for International Economics 1994).
10. P. Hirst and G. Thompson, *Globalization in Question* (Cambridge: Blackwell 1996); D. Harvey, 'Globalization in question', *Rethinking Marxism* 8 (1995) pp.1–17; E. Cater, 'Consuming spaces: Global tourism', in J. Allen and C. Hammett (eds.), *A Shrinking World? Global Unevenness and Inequality* (New York: Oxford University Press 1995) pp.183–232; G. Burtless, R. Lawrence, R. Litan and R. Shapiro, *Globaphobia: Confronting Fears about Open Trade* (Washington DC: Brookings 1998).
11. This refers to the post-independence practice whereby governments permitted corruption in the economy to reward supporters. For the most part, governments concentrated on the political as opposed to the economic dimensions of power.
12. J. Sender and J. Smith, *The Development of Capitalism in Africa* (London: Methuen 1986).
13. Williamson (note 9); S. Haggard and S. Webb, 'What do we know about the political economy of policy reform?' *World Bank Research Observer* 8 (1992) pp.143–68.
14. J. Williamson and S. Haggard, 'The political conditions for economic reform', in J.

Williamson (ed.), *The Political Economy of Policy Reform* (Washington DC: Institute for International Economics 1994) p.563.

15. H. Bienen, 'The politics of trade liberalization in Africa', *Economic Development and Cultural Change* 38 (1990) pp.713–32; J. Herbst, *The Politics of Reform in Ghana, 1982–1991* (Berkeley, CA: University of California Press 1993).

16. R.H. Bates and P. Collier, 'The politics and economics of policy reform in Zambia', in R.H. Bates and A.O. Krueger (eds.), *Political and Economic Interactions in Economic Policy Reform* (Oxford: Blackwell 1993) pp.387–443.

17. D. Rodrik, *Has Globalization Gone Too Far?* (Washington DC: Institute for International Economics 1997).

18. Hirst and Thompson (note 10); Harvey (note 10); J.H. Dunning and K.A. Hamdani, *The New Globalism and Developing Countries* (New York: United Nations University Press 1997); Rodrik (note 17); M. Waters, *Globalization* (New York: Routledge 1995).

19. Herod, Ó Tuathail and Roberts (note 1).

20. Dunning and Hamdani (note 18).

21. World Bank, *Adjustment in Africa. Reforms, Results, and the Road Ahead* (New York: Oxford University Press 1993).

22. J.R. Nellis, 'Public enterprises in sub-Saharan Africa', in B. Grosh and R.S. Mukandal (eds.), *Public Enterprises in Sub-Saharan Africa* (Boulder: Lynn Rienner 1994) pp.3–24.

23. Economist Intelligence Unit, *Ghana, Country Profile* (London: EIU 1983) p.19.

24. J.C. Leith and M. Lofchie, 'The political economy of structural adjustment in Ghana', in R.H. Bates and A. Krueger (eds.), *Political and Economic Interactions in Economic Policy Reform* (Cambridge: Blackwell 1993) p.234.

25. Economist Intelligence Unit (note 23) p.9.

26. K. Anyemedu, *The Effects of Trade Liberalization on Industry and Labour in Ghana* (Accra: Friedrich Ebert Stiftung 1995).

27. F. Foroutan, *Trade Reform in Ten Sub-Saharan Countries. Achievements and Failures*, World Bank Policy Research Working Paper 1222 (Washington DC: World Bank 1993).

28. G. Mohan, 'Adjustment and decentralization in Ghana: A case of diminished sovereignty', *Political Geography* 15 (1996) p.91.

29. Foroutan (note 27).

30. GATT, *Trade Policy Review. Ghana* (Geneva: GATT 1992).

31. P. Nugent, 'Educating Rawlings: The evolution of government strategy toward smuggling', in D. Rothchild (ed.), *Ghana. The Political Economy of Economic Recovery* (Boulder: Lynn Rienner 1991) p.72.

32. J. Kraus, 'The political economy of stabilization and structural adjustment in Ghana', in D. Rothchild (ed.), *Ghana. The Political Economy of Economic Recovery* (Boulder: Lynn Rienner 1991) p.123; 'Cocoa to regain dominance in the export sector', *Daily Graphic* (8 Aug. 1998) p.3.

33. M. Barratt-Brown and P. Tiffen, *Short Changed: Africa in World Trade* (London: Pluto 1992) p.47; P.B. Arthilsbah, *Trade Unions and Economic Structural Change in Ghana. The Ghanaian Experience* (Accra: Ghana Trades Union Congress 1994).

34. Anyemedu (note 26) p.20.

35. 'Reform supports workers', *Daily Graphic* (2 Jan. 1990) p.3; Herbst (note 15).

36. Ministry for Trade and Industry, *Export Promotion Villages* (Accra: Government of Ghana 1998).

37. In the 1996 presidential election, Rawlings won a majority of votes in all regions except the Ashanti region, where rival presidential candidate John Kufour won 65.8 per cent of the votes. T. Callaghy, 'Political passions and economic interests: Economic reform and political structure in Africa', in T. Callaghy and J. Ravenhill (eds.), *Hemmed In: Responses to Africa's Economic Decline* (New York: Columbia University Press 1993) pp.463–519.

38. Anyemedu (note 26) p.29.

39. Economist Intelligence Unit, *Ghana, Country Profile* (London: EIU 1989) p.4.

40. 'ICU: Review trade liberalization', *Public Agenda* (1 July 1996) p.12.

41. Economist Intelligence Unit, *Ghana, Country Profile* (London: EIU 1991) p.11.

42. 'Ghana's foreign investment climate', *Daily Graphic* (15 May 1997).

43. Government of Ghana, *Customs and Excise*. Tariff Interpretation Order No.1 (Accra: Ministry for Finance 1998).
44. World Bank (note 21) pp.236–7.
45. Williamson and Haggard (note 14).
46. K. Kapoor, *Africa's Experience with Structural Adjustment*. World Bank Discussion Paper No.288 (Washington DC: World Bank 1995).
47. Swamy (note 8).
48. World Bank (note 21).
49. GATT, *Trade Policy Review. Kenya* (Geneva: GATT 1994) pp.2, 23.
50. D. Himbara, 'The failed Africanization of commerce and industry in Kenya', *World Development* 22 (1994) pp.469–82.
51. C. Leys, *The Rise and Fall of Development Theory* (Bloomington: Indiana University Press 1996).
52. M. Lofchie, 'Trading places: Economic policy in Kenya and Tanzania', in T. Callaghy and J. Ravenhill (eds.), *Hemmed In: Responses to Africa's Economic Decline* (New York: Columbia University Press 1993) pp.398–462.
53. B. Grosh, *Public Enterprises in Kenya. What Works, What Doesn't, and Why* (Boulder: Lynn Rienner 1991) pp.206–9.
54. J. Herbst, 'The politics of sustained agricultural reform in Africa', in T. Callaghy and J. Ravenhill (eds.), *Hemmed In: Responses to Africa's Economic Decline* (New York: Columbia University Press 1993) pp.332–56.
55. J. Barkan and F. Holmquist, 'Peasant-state relations and the social bases of self-help in Kenya', *World Politics* 41 (1989) pp.359–80; N. Ng'ethe and K. Oders, 'Farmers' organizations in Kenya. State agents or civil institutions', *African Rural and Urban Studies* 1 (1994) pp.31–55.
56. Government of Kenya, *Sessional Paper No.4* (Nairobi: Government of Kenya 1980).
57. Swamy (note 8).
58. Economist Intelligence Unit, *Kenya, Country Profile* (London: EIU 1998) p.12.
59. D. Himbara, 'Domestic capitalists and the state in Kenya', in B. Berman and C. Leys (eds.), *African Capitalists in African Development* (Boulder: Lynn Rienner 1994) p.73.
60. F. Holmquist, F. Weaver and M. Ford, 'The structural development of Kenya's political economy', *African Studies Review* 37 (1994) pp.69–105.
61. Economist Intelligence Unit (note 58) p.14.
62. Leys (note 51) p.160.
63. Economist Intelligence Unit, *Kenya, Country Profile* (London: EIU 1985) p.4.
64. J. Widner, 'Two leadership styles and patterns of political liberalization', *African Studies Review* 37 (1992) p.163.
65. Holmquist, Weaver and Ford (note 60).
66. The first scheduled flights took off from Eldoret international airport in summer 1998.
67. Economist Intelligence Unit (note 58) p.12.
68. Lofchie (note 52).
69. World Bank (note 21) p.244.
70. M. Wrong, 'Kenya's economy, hit by sleaze, debt and El Nino, is caught in a destructive spiral', *Financial Times* (22 April 1998) p.4.
71. Himbara (note 59).
72. S. Jaffee and P. Gordon, *Exporting High-Value Food Commodities. Success Stories from Developing Countries*. World Bank Discussion Paper 19 (Washington DC: World Bank 1993); Economist Intelligence Unit (note 58) p.29.
73. Foroutan (note 27) p.49.
74. Wrong (note 70) p.5.
75. World Bank (note 21) p.231.
76. Williamson and Haggard (note 14).
77. K.A. Elliott, *Corruption and the Global Economy* (Washington DC: Institute for International Economics 1997).
78. Elliott (note 77).
79. See http://www.usia.gov/regional/at/prestrip/w98023a.htm.

80. 'How Volta dims Ghana's lights', *The Sun* (Baltimore, MD: 11 June 1998) p.2.
81. 'Survey of public opinion', *Daily Graphic* (1 June 1997).
82. Economist Intelligence Unit, *Ghana, Country Profile* (London: EIU 1998) pp.12, 23.
83. Heritage Foundation, *1997 Index of Economic Freedom* (Washington DC: Heritage Foundation and Dow Jones 1998) p.56.
84. See http://www.amnesty.org/ailib/aipub/1998/AFR/132019981.htm.
85. See http://www.travel.state.gov/Kenya.htm/.
86. Economist Intelligence Unit (note 58) p.23.
87. Economist Intelligence Unit, *Kenya, Country Profile* (London: EIU 1995) p.10.
88. Interview with Kwesi Abalesi (Accra: 16 July 1996).
89. I. Gambari, 'Africa in the new world order', *West Africa* 80 (1997) p.12.
90. Hirst and Thompson (note 10); Harvey (note 10); Cater (note 10); Burtless, Lawrence, Litan and Shapiro (note 10).
91. Ghana Investment Promotion Centre, *Statistics on Registered Projects* (Accra: GIPC 1998).
92. International Finance Corporation (IFC), *Emerging Stock Market Factbook* (Washington DC: IFC 1997).
93. Ibid.
94. See http://www.africaonline.com.gh/ and http://www.africaonline.com.ke/.
95. J. Sachs, 'Making it work. Global capitalism', *The Economist* (12 Sept. 1998) p.24.

Geopolitical Change and the Asia-Pacific: The Future of New Regionalism

DENNIS RUMLEY

The main purpose of this paper is to outline a preliminary framework for the analysis of the nature of geopolitical change in relation to interactions among globalisation, the state and regionalism for the Asia-Pacific region. Overall, it is clear that the combination of globalisation with the 'collapse' of bipolarity has ensured that regionalism and regionalisation will become increasingly important in world politics.[1] There is a need for post-realist spatial structures and policies to cope with all of these outcomes, and regionalism can potentially play an important 'intermediary' role in which the re-establishment of security and stability can be facilitated. The emergence of 'new regionalism' in the Asia-Pacific is potentially well suited to these requirements, although its structure and function are highly contested.

The post-cold-war period has seen a continuation of the relative shift of global economic power to the Asia-Pacific region (the recent currency 'crisis' notwithstanding) and it is estimated that by 2020 four of the world's five largest economies will be located in the region.[2] At present, however, the cold war has yet to end in that region; indeed, it has even been suggested that the Asia-Pacific has yet to achieve post-postwar status (Figure 1).[3] Most writers believe that the end of the cold war has significantly reduced the level of global threat, and yet questions of security and instability are paradoxically central during the present period. It is argued here that one of the main reasons for this is that the processes of globalisation are among the principal causes of uncertainty, insecurity and instability within states. In particular, the rise of global financial markets has increasingly constrained economic and political sovereignty.[4]

The present discussion is in three parts. The first part is a brief overview of geopolitical change which emphasises the centrality of security and analyses the implications of globalisation for the role of the state. Second, the functions of regionalism are outlined before undertaking a comparative evaluation of 'old' and 'new' regionalism and a description of some of the current patterns of new regionalism. Third, some contested 'orders' for the Asia-Pacific region are critically reviewed and the discussion concludes with an appraisal of the future prospects for new regionalism.

FIGURE 1

THE ASIA-PACIFIC REGION

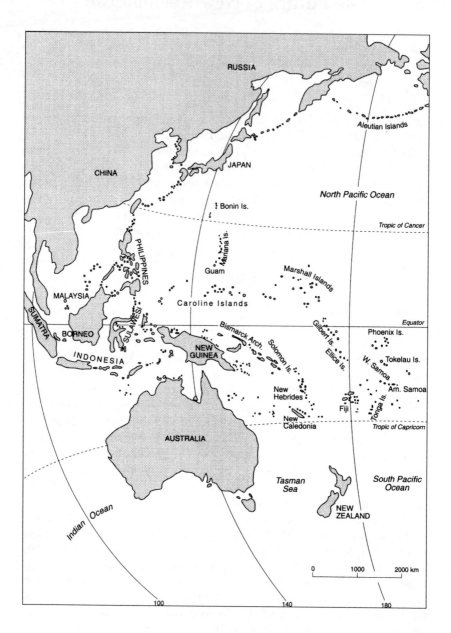

Globalisation, the State and Security

It appears that globalisation is a contested process. It has been defined as being more complex than 'internationalisation' in the sense that it embodies a certain amount of functional integration among various types of economic activities which are internationally dispersed.[5] Furthermore, the process of globalisation, involving deepening forms of economic interdependence, is not a recent phenomenon, but rather has been in progress for centuries.[6] To some writers, the process of globalisation is perceived to be a threat to culture in the sense that market opportunity rather than national identity functions as the 'new reality' of international media operations.[7] In short, globalisation impacts upon a wide range of aspects of security and state regulation functions (Table 1). It is therefore preferable to think of globalisation as comprising a set of processes rather than as an overarching, unidimensional concept.[8]

The Centrality of Security

It is no coincidence that the Brundtland Report was published in the final stages of the cold-war period.[9] The global implications of the interdependence of society, economy, politics and environment were explicitly enunciated for the first time and the centrality of a multidimensional post-realist concept of security was affirmed. Thus, for example, ecologically sustainable development was seen to be necessary in order to maintain *environmental security*. Second, economic participation needed to be maximised to guarantee *economic security*. Economic inequalities would likely lead to social insecurity. Third, representation and participation ought to be maximised in order to ensure *political security*. Clearly, while environmental movements can have an impact on political security, government policies can influence the extent of environmental security. In sum, the degree of stability and security, and thus peace and conflict among and within states, are determined by this set of interrelationships.[10] The search for real security can no longer be found at the scale of the family, neighbourhood or the state. The best guarantee of *regional* security in the Asia-Pacific, for example, is via regional co-operation.[11]

Globalisation and State Regulation Functions

Globalisation and the nature of global geopolitical change have ensured that the power of the state in the Asia-Pacific region and elsewhere has been limited in at least four principal ways: the growth in weapons and communications technology impacts upon the state's traditional security function; the resurgence of cultural identity and ethnicity influences the state's representation and participation functions; the globalisation of the economy affects the state's capacity to undertake economic regulation; and environmental degradation necessarily involves states in environmental security issues beyond their international boundaries.

Above all, the process of globalisation has decreased the capacity of most states to maximise economic regulation functions. It has been suggested, for example, that the transition from a primarily nation-based to a primarily global form of economic regulation has resulted in a 'new colonialism' in which nation-states face a distinctive brand of colonisation by capital. State economic functions are therefore reduced to administering the coloniser's needs by organising resources for the benefit of global banks and corporations.[12] In brief, nation-states have lost their role as meaningful units of participation in the global economy.[13]

Nonetheless, while the regulatory power of the state continues to exist to varying degrees in economic matters, it has generally increased in social and political matters, in some cases to the point of over-regulation.[14] Increases in both domestic economic deregulation and socio-political regulation are direct consequences of the globalisation process (Figure 2). This is especially relevant in post-colonial societies, where state institutions are generally not as strong and where the nation-building process is an explicit component of government policy. In the Asia-Pacific region, such policies are often intensified by the existence of ethnic diversity where this is associated with 'ethnic revival', which itself can be seen in part as a reaction to homogenising globalism. In such cases, where the legitimacy of the state is challenged or where instability is perceived or contrived by ruling elites, or both, then the outcome can often be the application of a set of control policies[15] or the maintenance of the political *status quo* among weak states.[16]

Globalisation, the State and Economic Deregulation

As has been pointed out, nation-states have lost their capacity to control exchange rates and protect their own currencies. Indeed, the foreign exchange market has itself become one of the largest investment instruments.[17] It has been argued that the recent currency crisis in the Asia-Pacific region was caused by 'western financial speculators', although a combination of large increases in foreign debt, inadequate regulatory controls, some loss of competitiveness and 'crony capitalism' must have been contributory factors. For some regional states, the necessary 'structural reforms' may well be associated with a decrease in authoritarianism and an increase in democracy, such as may be happening presently in Indonesia (Figure 2).

FIGURE 2

SOME GLOBALISATION-REGIONALISM-STATE INTERACTIONS

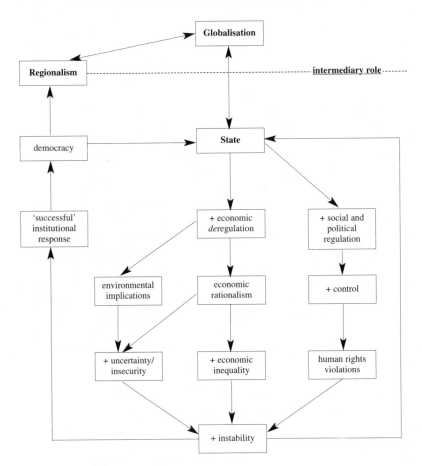

Given the limits placed by globalisation on the performance of economic regulation policies, the state is more likely to be concerned with the implementation of various aspects of deregulation policies. Increases in economic deregulation can have at least two broad sets of implications and outcomes: environmental and economic rationalism. From an environmental viewpoint, economic deregulation ensures that, for the most part, states 'compete away' their environmental heritage. This is especially the case for many industrialising states possessing significant overseas debts. In the Asia-Pacific region, moves toward freer trade are likely to magnify environmental impacts, encourage states to deplete their own resource base and push economies toward narrow export commodities likely to be environmentally damaging.[18] Thus, any state which has a particular resource (especially energy) niche in the global economy is also likely to be caught in an 'environmental trap'. For example, at the December 1997 Kyoto Climate Change Conference, the Australian government 'successfully' argued that emissions targets should not be universally applied because of what it saw as a global 'environmental catch-22', that is, Australia's niche energy-intensive economy (a product of the global economy) ensured non-compliance in global emissions agreements on 'economic' grounds. When Australia was 'allowed' an eight per cent increase on 1990 greenhouse-gas emission levels to 2012, conservative politicians, coal corporations and sections of the media described this outcome as a 'diplomatic victory' and a 'win for Australian jobs'.

Economic rationalist policies, on the other hand, can be generally recognised by their adherence to deregulation on the one hand and privatisation on the other.[19] They are closely linked to the rise of managerialism, whose principal aim is that of reshaping government organisations into control agencies. This is achieved in part by the strict application of 'managerialist logic' – 'if it moves privatise it; if it doesn't restructure it'. The growth and application of such 'logic' has facilitated increasing social, economic and spatial inequality and has resulted in social instability.[20] It has therefore been suggested that there is a need to create institutions which go beyond the market and the state and which enhance the power and dignity of working people.[21]

Globalisation, the State and Socio-Political Regulation

While globalisation is responsible for economic deregulation and the resultant outcomes of economic rationalism, there has been an associated intensification of socio-political regulation in most Asia-Pacific states during the post-cold-war period. Economic threats to state legitimacy are inversely related to increased social and political regulation expressed as control. Invariably, this leads to an increase in human rights violations, especially among minority and other groups, such as women, children and the aged (Figure 2). Indeed, minority group 'control' is a commonplace in many parts of the world. The current global upsurge in 'racist politics' is in part a reflection of the uncertainty generated by the socio-economic impacts of globalisation.

There are at least two important geopolitical outcomes of these processes. First, as we have seen in the post-cold-war period, most major conflicts now tend to occur within, rather than between, states. Second, questions related to the future internal structure of states, security broadly defined, possible state expansionism, and the problems of the political viability of some post-colonial states are collectively likely to accelerate the trend toward greater regional co-operation.

The Role of Regionalism

Regionalism has been narrowly defined as 'a form of intergovernmental political collaboration whose principal objective is to foster economic co-operation among participating states'.[22] Clearly, regionalism is much broader in scope and potentially embodies a range of other functions (Table 1). It is an especially appropriate mechanism for international co-operation at a spatial scale between unsatisfactory national approaches and unworkable universal schemes.[23] In this sense, regionalism can be seen as having an intermediary role between a narrowly defined nationalism and an overly broad globalism.[24] Two of the options offered by globalisation include either a rejection of nationalism or a rejection of global competition. On the one hand, the global market might be embraced; on the other hand, the nation-state might be defended.

However, there is a danger of representing regionalism as being antithetical to globalisation (Table 1). Rather than being antithetical, globalisation and regionalism are in fact complementary processes which can occur simultaneously and interact. Increasing globalisation and deregulation associated with a decline in national economic control induces a 'compensatory' regional process.[25]

TABLE 1

ANTITHETICAL REPRESENTATION OF GLOBALISATION AND REGIONALISM

Globalisation	Regionalism
Top down	Bottom up
Rigid	Flexible
Authoritarian	Voluntaristic
Control	Consociation
Homogenisation	Diversity
Alienation	Community
Insecurity	Confidence building
Competitive	Humane

The Functions of Regionalism

Regionalism can be attractive to states and groups of states for a wide range of reasons. It can be perceived as one means of consolidating state power, for addressing the structural problems of the state and for solving regional problems.[26] It can thus be aimed at creating regional benefits and at increasing the power or autonomy of the region as a whole with respect to other 'non-regional' states and organisations.[27] Apart from a perceived enhancement of security in the broadest sense, states can be inclined toward regionalism since they see it as one potential means of controlling the behaviour of other 'local' states.[28]

Regionalism can also function to improve human values. For example, it has been suggested that, in the post-cold-war environment, regionalism can play a significant role in the achievement of peace, social justice, human rights and democracy in at least four main ways.[29] First, regionalism can operate to contain negative aspects of globalism, such as insensitivity to human suffering, insufficient attention to ecological sustainability and the tendency toward polarisation and marginalisation. Second, regionalism can serve to mitigate 'pathological anarchism', such as acute political disorder engendered by genocide and large-scale famine. Third, regionalism can promote 'positive globalism' by avoiding excessive centralism and by taking account of social and spatial diversity. Lastly, 'positive regionalism' can be used to incorporate human values while resisting any renewal of western hegemony.

However, it is arguable whether a post-cold-war 'order' based around regionalism will necessarily produce greater stability. Certainly, the combination of a relative loss in state economic power, the end of the bipolar structure and a relative decline in US power has helped to facilitate the development of regionalism. Furthermore, regional co-operative initiatives inevitably increase the cost of regional conflict.[30]

On the other hand, it has been suggested that the emergent triadic world economic system is inherently unstable compared with the cold-war bipolar structure.[31] Nonetheless, a *multi*-region world which contained stronger regions would probably possess greater stability-inducing elements.[32]

Old and New Regionalism

In the Asia-Pacific region, the emergence of 'new regionalism' in the 1970s has been contrasted with the 'old regionalism' typical of western Europe[33] in that it tends to be global in scale, more outward looking in orientation, is concerned with interregional linkages and possesses a broad and flexible interaction pattern (Table 2). The very flexibility of new regionalism enables the state to enhance its regional economic regulation function and its socio-political legitimacy. In essence, it represents a shift away from a Eurocentric 'order'. Furthermore, from an economic viewpoint, new regionalism is market driven rather than politically driven and incorporates states at different stages of economic development.[34] Old regionalism has been described as 'hard' and concerned with exclusive institution building, while new regionalism is 'soft', informal and based on inclusive networks.[35]

TABLE 2

OLD AND NEW REGIONALISM

	Old	New
Emergence	1950s/1960s	1970s/1980s
Regional application	Mainly western Europe	Worldwide
Orientation	Inward turning ('closed' regionalism)	Outward looking ('open' regionalism)
Connectivity/control	Interregional autonomy	Linkages
Structure	Regional organisations	Broad and flexible interactions
Other salient features	Politically driven among economics with similar levels of development	Market driven among economies at different stages of development
	'Hard'/institutional	'Soft'/informal
	Exclusive institution building	Inclusive networks
	Confronting an adversary	Confronting uncertainty
	Form a military alliance	Promote confidence building among like-minded states
		Incorporate sources of uncertainty
Examples	EC, NATO	APEC, ARF

Sources: Elek and Soesastro, 1994; Katzenstein and Shiraishi, 1997; Palmer, 1991.

The emergence of the ASEAN Regional Forum (ARF) in 1994 as a traditional security consultative forum has ensured that new regionalism is no longer solely associated with economic security concerns. From a politico-security perspective, while old regionalism was closely related to the realist assumptions of the cold-war era, in the post-cold-war environment, the 'adversary' in the Asia-Pacific of new regionalism is uncertainty. Thus, sources of uncertainty (for example, non-Communist and Communist) are incorporated into the new regionalism in order to maximise confidence building. As has been pointed out, the 'geopolitical fault lines' in the Asia-Pacific region are in the process of being stabilised, in contrast to the European situation in which contrasts between the continent and its neighbourhood are being accentuated.[36]

Current Patterns of New Regionalism

Regional groupings within the Asia-Pacific region have generally been promoted on the basis of a number of perceived economic benefits to member states. In particular, they have been preferred as a result of a range of economic security concerns. It has been hoped that regionalism will produce high growth rates for individual nation-states. Furthermore, it has been felt that greater internal interaction will decrease the prospect of conflict between states.

Various types of new regionalism are evident in the Asia-Pacific region. These range from region-wide groupings, such as the Asia-Pacific Economic Cooperation (APEC) initiative formed in 1989, to subregional groups, such as ASEAN and a number of interstate 'growth triangles' and development areas located at state peripheries. The most recent of the latter, the Australia-Indonesia Development Area (AIDA) created in April 1997, was the first subregional agreement developed by Indonesia outside of ASEAN.[37]

The emergence of regional forums such as APEC clearly gives some support to the view that the Asia-Pacific possesses a range of common economic and other interests. The extent to which such forums will continue to develop will inevitably depend on the degree of internal commitment by member states to a collective regional consciousness and collective regional goals. Malaysia's reluctance to attend some of the APEC Summit meetings and Japan's concern over the protection of its food market could be interpreted as negative signs in this regard.

Nonetheless, the degree of intraregional trade within APEC has grown at a faster pace than within the EU during the post-cold-war period (Table 3). In 1980, for example, intraregional trade in both regions was virtually the same in percentage terms. There was a considerable increase in intraregional trade even before the creation of APEC, however. During the same time period (1980–85), the relative importance of EU intraregional trade marginally declined. Following APEC's creation in 1989, the percentage of intraregional trade has grown slowly from 68.3 per cent in 1990 to 70.7 per cent in 1993 and to 73.3 per cent in 1994. However, from 1990 to 1993 the total volume of intra-APEC trade grew by 32 per cent compared with a fall of 15 per cent for intra-EU trade during the same period. The Japanese Economic and Trade Organisation (JETRO) attributes this relatively high growth in total intra-APEC trade to dynamic economic growth in East Asia. In addition, to some extent it also reflects the deepening of mutual dependence among member states.

The issue of APEC member states has not been without controversy since its inception. From an original conception as a West Pacific grouping

TABLE 3

INTRAREGIONAL TRADE: APEC AND EU

		1980	1985	1990	1993
US$m	**APEC**	344,345	492,357	897,859	1,187,325
	Per cent of total	56.0	67.7	68.3	70.7
US$m	**EU**	385,170	353,169	828,184	704,095
	Per cent of total	55.7	54.4	60.6	55.4

Source: Japanese Economic and Trade Organisation (JETRO)

which would likely have excluded North America, by 1994, APEC had become a select Pacific-rim grouping of 18 states. However, at the most recent APEC Leaders' Meeting in Vancouver in November 1997, rather than adding India to its membership as was earlier expected, Peru, Russia and Vietnam were admitted. Vietnam is explicable because of its ASEAN membership and Peru 'fits' the Pacific-rim concept. However, the admission of Russia can be interpreted as a 'consolation prize' for US opposition to its entry into NATO. It seems that APEC has now become too much influenced by global politics over Asia-Pacific questions, since it is unlikely that Russian membership will restrict discussion only to its Far East region. This decision, which appears to eventuate from pressure from China, Japan and South Korea with US support, has been severely criticised by many Australian journalists.[38]

Toward a New Geopolitical Order in the Asia-Pacific

The notion of 'order' has been commonly used in geopolitical discourse, although it is clearly a contested concept.[39] On the one hand, it implies either the imposition of some outside set of controls or some innately given scientific structure to which states inevitably comply. On the other hand, the phrase implies the opposite of chaos and uncertainty and thus embodies a normative condition to which politicians and diplomats readily subscribe in the face of a congenital incapacity to deal effectively with any alternative. Order intuitively appeals in the face of uncertainty. During the cold-war period, the term also had hegemonic overtones since the global 'order' was to be imposed through western dominance. With the end of the cold war, the 'new world order' became a contested concept among, for example, traditionalists (maintain cold-war structures and attempt trilateral accommodation with Japan and Europe), revisionists (maintain a pentapolar world), idealists (maintain an era of everlasting peace) and post-revisionists (maintain collaboration in international police work with former enemies).[40]

Contested 'Orders' in the Asia-Pacific

There is a great deal of conjecture over the future of the Asia-Pacific region and it is neither immediately apparent what kind of regional order is emerging nor whether there is regional agreement among alternative orders.[41] Some writers have discounted the relevance of the 'end of history' thesis for the region.[42] The 'clash of civilisations' hypothesis, on the other hand, would envisage an Asia-Pacific conflict between the 'western' group (Australasia) and 'the rest', that is, the Islamic (Indonesia and Pakistan), Sinic, Hindu, Buddhist and Japanese 'civilisations'.[43] From what has already been argued, the ongoing process of new regionalism in the Asia-Pacific has been designed to enhance regional security and minimise possible intraregional conflicts. Indeed, for the region as a whole, any potentially destabilising forces, such as territorial disputes, religious fundamentalism and nationalism, are presently outweighed by stabilising factors.[44]

Having said this, the Asia-Pacific could be destabilised by a process of first-order power competition, especially among China, Japan and the USA. The combination of China's large size, its 'market Leninism' and its development imperative is likely to ensure a constructive regional role for the foreseeable future. Japan's role in creating regional economic interdependence and regional co-operation is without parallel. It is the regional role of the USA which has been a debating point in the post-cold-war period. On the one hand, most Asia-Pacific leaders want the USA to remain as a 'strategic balancer' in the region.[45] On the other hand, there are some who prefer a post-cold-war 'voice of Asia' model in which Japan can begin to disengage from the West, in which no US military presence is needed in Asia, and in which regional security is guaranteed by regional co-operation.[46] For its part, the USA appears to wish to prevent the emergence of any alternative regional power while maintaining access to the huge regional market through the application of its Asia-Pacific 'new regional order'.[47]

The Future of New Regionalism in the Asia-Pacific

Given the above, it comes as no surprise that there are 'competing logics' for the future of new regionalism in the Asia-Pacific.[48] Asia-Pacific regionalism is therefore 'contested'[49] and this is based both on structure and on policy. In terms of regional structure, there are essentially four broad options.[50] The first is an 'inclusive' and expanded APEC, and the Vancouver Summit has ensured a forum for four of five global poles, created a medium-to-long-term danger of alienating the other West Pacific states (partly through perceived big-power domination), and has effectively excluded India through its ten-year membership moratorium. Furthermore, the Vancouver outcome is suggestive of a new global bipolar order which foreshadows 'the other' as being the European Union (EU).

However, the current size (21 states) and structure of APEC has both weakened its 'regionality' and its capacity to act quickly and effectively. Furthermore, given APEC's 'opposition' to the EU, beginning with the 1994 Bogor Declaration, it is likely that its first-order powers will increase the pressure for 'closure' and for greater trade liberalisation and, as a result, create some difficult internal tensions. Greater APEC 'institutionalisation' is likely to meet stiff opposition, particularly from many of the Asian members. As a result, as one commentator has forecast, APEC may well have a 'short half-life'.[51]

A second broad regional alternative is a return to an early concept of APEC as a West Pacific grouping including Oceania. In part, the relevance of this option will depend on the emergent nature and function of the North American Free Trade Area (NAFTA), Japan-USA economic relations and the attitudes toward APEC goals of political elites in developing states in the region. In addition, APEC is seen by some as a vehicle for assuring the economic interests of non-Asian states using Australia as a surrogate for promoting and maintaining United States entry into the West Pacific.

A third 'exclusive' alternative is an 'Asian' Pacific grouping which excludes Oceania. The principal driving force of this option has been Malaysian Prime Minister Mahatir, first via his 1990 East Asian Economic Grouping (EAEG) and then his East Asian Economic Caucus (EAEC). The inaugural Asia-Europe Meeting (Asem) in Bangkok in March 1996 is also a manifestation of the felt need to exclude western (Oceania and North America) influence from an Asian grouping based on Asian values. The ten Asian states at the Asem meeting were the same as the proposed membership of EAEC. By rejecting western hegemony, such a grouping at the same time drives a wedge through the Pacific Ocean.

Given insufficient agreement either on the future of APEC, on a West Pacific or on an Asian grouping, the future regional structure of the Asia-Pacific might well assume the form of a loose association of emergent groupings (for example, ANZ plus ASEAN plus Northeast Asia plus SAARC plus NAFTA), that is, a looser two-tier and even more open APEC with less stringent Action Plans.

Conclusion

It has been argued that the processes of globalisation have caused instability and insecurity within states. For many industrialising states in the Asia-Pacific region, it has been suggested that the solution to the financial crisis is to 'de-globalise'. This would involve a much greater reliance on the domestic market, a greater dependence on domestic capital resources as well as closer co-operation with neighbouring economies.[52]

It has also been suggested that regionalism can play an intermediary role, although its likely structure and function is highly contested in the Asia-Pacific. Certainly, future research needs to investigate more fully the question of how regional and global tendencies will likely coexist.[53]

From a western perspective, one of the Asia-Pacific's key areas of 'weakness' is in the area of political development.[54] Few states in the region respect most human rights.[55] A consideration of such 'local' characteristics is also necessary in any full analysis of future state and regional stability.

Above all, the regional and global role of Japan will necessarily be instrumental in the future development of new regionalism in the Asia-Pacific.[56] In the final analysis, however, the success of this will probably depend on how all major non-European powers use regional and other international groupings and organisations to build a multipolar system of relations.[57]

NOTES

1. P.J. Katzenstein and T. Shiraishi (eds.), *Network Power: Japan and Asia* (Ithaca: Cornell University Press 1997) p.41.
2. E.K.Y. Chen, 'Dynamic Asian economies: Retrospect and prospect', in Chan Heng Chee (ed.), *The New Asia-Pacific Order* (Singapore: Institute of Southeast Asian Studies 1997) p.21.
3. D. Rumley, T. Chiba, A. Takagi and Y. Fukushima (eds.), *Global Geopolitical Change and the Asia-Pacific: A Regional Perspective* (London: Avebury 1996) p.329.
4. W. Hutton, *The State We're In* (London: Vintage 1996) p.312.
5. P. Dicken, *Global Shift: The Internationalization of Economic Activity* (London: Chapman 1992) p.1.
6. R. Hayter, *The Dynamics of Industrial Location* (Chichester: Wiley 1997) p.1.
7. D. Morley and K. Robins, *Spaces of Identity* (London: Routledge 1995).
8. J. Camilleri, 'Making sense of globalization', in J. Wiseman (ed.), *Alternatives to Globalization: An Asia-Pacific Perspective* (Fitzroy: Community Aid Abroad 1997) p.6.
9. G.H. Brundtland, *Our Common Future* (Oxford: OUP, Australian edn., 1990).
10. D. Rumley, 'Geography, interdependence and security', *Geojournal* 45/1–2 (1998) pp.109–14.
11. M. Mahatir and Ishihara Shintaro, *The Voice of Asia* (Tokyo: Kodansha 1995) p.121.
12. P. McMichael, 'The new colonialism: Global regulation and the restructuring of the inter-state system', in D.A. Smith and J. Böröcz (eds.), *A New World Order? Global Transformation in the Late Twentieth Century* (Westport: Praeger 1995) pp.37–55.
13. K. Ohmae, *The End of the Nation-State* (London: Harper Collins 1995) p.11.
14. E. Kofman and G. Youngs (eds.), *Globalization: Theory and Practice* (London: Pinter 1996).
15. D. Rumley and O. Yiftachel, 'The political geography of the control of minorities', *Tijdschrift voor Economische en Sociale Geografie* 84/1 (1993) pp.51–64.
16. M. Alagappa, 'Systemic change, security and governance in the Asia-Pacific', in Chan Heng Chee (ed.), *The New Asia-Pacific Order* (Singapore: Institute of Southeast Asian Studies 1997) p.41.
17. Ohmae (note 13).
18. C.L. Harper, *Environment and Society: Human Perspectives on Environmental Issues* (New Jersey: Prentice-Hall 1996) pp.375–6.

19. S. Rees and G. Rodley (eds.), *The Human Costs of Managerialism* (Leichhardt: Pluto Press 1995).
20. Hutton (note 4) p.194.
21. J. Buchanan, 'Managing labour in the 1990s', in S. Rees and G. Rodley (eds.), *The Human Costs of Managerialism* (Leichhardt: Pluto Press 1995) p.65.
22. J. Ravenhill, 'Competing logics of regionalism in the Asia-Pacific', *Journal of European Integration* 28/2–3 (1995) pp.179–99.
23. Katzenstein and Shiraishi (note 1) p.3.
24. N.D. Palmer, *The New Regionalism in Asia and the Pacific* (Lexington: Heath 1991) p.175.
25. Katzenstein and Shiraishi (note 1) pp.343–4.
26. P. Taylor, *International Organization in the Modern World: The Regional and the Global Process* (London: Pinter 1993) pp.28–9.
27. W.A. Axline (ed.), *The Political Economy of Regional Cooperation* (London: Pinter 1994) p.192.
28. Ravenhill (note 22) p.192.
29. R. Falk, 'Regionalism and world order after the cold war', *Australian Journal of International Affairs* 49/1 (1995) pp.1–15.
30. S. Harris, 'U.S.-Japan relations in the new Asia-Pacific order', in Chan Heng Chee (ed.), *The New Asia-Pacific Order* (Singapore: Institute of Southeast Asian Studies 1997) p.175.
31. I. Wallerstein, 'The global possibilities, 1990–2025', in T.K. Hopkins, I. Wallerstein, *et al.*, *The Age of Transition: Trajectory of the World-System, 1945–2025* (Leichhardt: Pluto Books 1996) p.230.
32. Taylor (note 26) p.13.
33. Palmer (note 24).
34. A. Elek and H. Soesastro, 'Framework for future multilateral and regional cooperation', in East Asia Analytical Unit, *Expanding Horizons: Australia and Indonesia into the 21st Century* (Canberra: DFAT 1994) pp.263–81.
35. Katzenstein and Shiraishi (note 1).
36. Katzenstein and Shiraishi (note 1) p.27.
37. R. Crappsley, 'Postmodernism and trans-boundary security issues', Honours Dissertation (University of Western Australia: Department of Geography).
38. G. Sheridan, 'Moscow entry a membership bridge too far', *The Australian* 27 (Nov. 1997) p.8.
39. Harris (note 30).
40. Rumley *et al.* (note 3) p.5.
41. Harris (note 30).
42. Ohmae (note 13).
43. S.P. Huntington, *The Clash of Civilizations and the Remaking of World Order* (New York: Simon and Schuster 1996).
44. Alagappa (note 16) p.63.
45. Harris (note 30) p.174.
46. Mahatir and Ishihara (note 11).
47. R. De Castro, 'U.S. grand strategy in post-cold war Asia-Pacific', *Contemporary Southeast Asia* 16/3 (1994) pp.342–53.
48. Ravenhill (note 22).
49. Katzenstein and Shiraishi (note 1) pp.9–10.
50. D. Rumley, *The Geopolitics of Australia's Regional Relations* (Dordrecht: Kluwer Academic 1999).
51. M.S. Dobbs-Higginson, *Asia-Pacific: A View on its role in the New World Order* (Hong Kong: Longman 1993) p.389.
52. W. Bello, 'The answer: de-globalize', *Far Eastern Economic Review* 1652/17 (1999) p.61.
53. A. Gamble and A. Payne (eds.), *Regionalism and World Order* (Basingtoke: Macmillan 1996) p.16.
54. Alagappa (note 16) p.50.
55. C. Humana, *World Human Rights Guide* (Oxford: OUP, third edn., 1992).
56. G. Hook, 'Japan and the construction of Asia-Pacific', in A. Gamble and A. Payne (eds.), *Regionalism and World Order* (Basingstoke: Macmillan 1996) pp.169–206.
57. F. Ching, 'New world order emerging', *Far Eastern Economic Review* 160/498 (1997) p.40.

Global Stability Through Inequality Versus Peace Processes Through Equality

FABRIZIO EVA

The World Order is Still Working

In the early 1990s, the end of the bipolar world and the apparent absence of major ideological conflicts encouraged the idea that it would be possible to establish a new world order that could guarantee peace and international security. The end of geopolitical control by the two opposing blocs enabled military operations against Iraq in 1991 by a huge alliance of states, as well as the 'humanitarian' intervention in Somalia in 1992, both of which took place under the UN banner. The active role of these operations seemed to pave the way to setting up a world government responsible for the problems of peace, security, democracy, and the safeguarding of human rights.

The historic agreement between Rabin and Arafat created hope for an international climate conducive to accords rather than conflicts. After some initial disorientation caused by the disappearance of the 'enemy', NATO, rather than dissolving (like the Warsaw Pact), appeared as a support to active peace policies, in particular on behalf of the UN. Its initial use as a military threat (such as the bombing of Serbian targets in Bosnia), and then as an instrument of territorial control in Bosnia following the Dayton Agreements, were elements that seemed to point to a new world order.

The critics, doubters, and opponents of this idea have cited numerous local and internal conflicts to underline its weaknesses and the unfeasibility of developing a true order. In reality, however, current world dynamics display several precise empirical indicators that show that there has been a world order for some time and that it is working.

The role of the UN remains uncertain. But with the disappearance of the USSR, a transitional phase began in which it appeared that the UN might assume a clearer and better defined role, since within the UN there have been 'legal and political developments that point towards the possibility of a new organising principle for international relations'.[1] It is not possible to speak of a new order, however, since existing international relations are founded on geopolitical premises that have been in place for some time (such as the Westphalia System) and which have not altered dramatically.[2] International relations are likewise based on the tacit acceptance of a 'fiction' that pushes into the background the irreconcilable disparities between declarations of the principle of 'equality' and the functional reality of the hierarchy of states.[3] The main element of the existing world order, which is also an accepted 'ideological' concept, is inequality of power (and therefore of action and rights) between states. On the basis of the geopolitical indicators provided daily (crisis areas, conflicts, tensions, international agreements, respect or otherwise of the rules, embargoes, the statements of leading politicians, military actions, and so on), it is possible to formulate a framework of the world hierarchy of states as follows. (See Figure 1).

FIGURE 1

HIERARCHY OF POWER AND IMPORTANCE IN THE WORLD ORDER

Superpower and supranational world organizations

USA
UN
IMF - WB
UN Security Council
GB FR   RUSSIA   CHINA
G5 Level   GERMANY   JAPAN
G7 Level   Canada   Italy
Level A   supranational organizations
NATO
EU
INDIA
(special "isolated" position)
OCDE
APEC (Australia)
Level B   supranational organizations
NAFTA   ARAB LEAGUE   ASEAN
(Mexico)   (Islamic Conference Org.)
(Egypt)

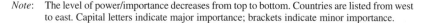

Regionally significant countries

Brazil   Indonesia

Areas/countries of "first step" importance

LATIN AMERICA   BLACK AFRICA   Malaysia
Nigeria   Thailand
South Africa

Note: The level of power/importance decreases from top to bottom. Countries are listed from west to east. Capital letters indicate major importance; brackets indicate minor importance.

Despite the fact that, in general, the main feature of this power structure and hierarchy is stability, the structure shown above is subject to change, depending on real geopolitical dynamics.[4] However, the fundamental structure has not changed. Indeed, the USA, the G7 (G8 with Russia), and NATO have seen their roles strengthened. In contrast, the role of the UN as an international mediator has deteriorated greatly, as has the value of its stamp of approval for military operations.

The acceptance of the world hierarchy of states ('the due recognition of the need of this hierarchy in any system of security')[5] leads to a general expectation that it is the action of the most powerful states that will guarantee (or achieve) so-called 'peace in security'. The effects of this modern-day 'cosmopolitical model of Holy Alliance'[6] are mainly seen in instruments of territorial containment of conflicts, and the maintenance of internal stability within political structures, irrespective of their nature. 'It has been demonstrated that the superpowers tend much more towards stability than continual expansion of their power.'[7] Indeed, 'the superpowers and the international organisations dependent on them silently exercise, in the name of the world order, a policy of – for want of a better term – "non-proliferation of states"',[8] 'but the ultimate authority of the United States is expressed openly'.[9] Moreover, the situation in Kosovo in mid-1999 (with the province occupied by NATO, but still formally under the sovereignty of the defeated Yugoslavia) testifies to the conceptual resistance to changes to the world political map and the desire to maintain the existing states.

Through stability and territorial control even the USA-USSR confrontation guaranteed widespread peace, which preserved inequalities of power within the two alliances. This irresolvable conflict between the blocs centred on the freedom of movement of capital (and goods) and the right to private property. Where there were local situations of contested or unstable territories (Korea, Vietnam, the Congo, Afghanistan, and so on), there were limited armed conflicts.

Today, with the demise of the bipolar world, the potential for the movement of capital and the spread of consumer goods, the capitalist production system and private property has grown considerably. Under these new conditions, the potential for the penetration, diffusion, and influence of the mass media and of the phenomenon of tourism has also increased. This has not, however, modified the hierarchical structure of world power since 'many of these exchanges [culture and communication] are the result of the exportation of a particular culture'[10] (that of the modern West) and do nothing to halt the perpetuation of 'an unequal framework for cultural exchange'.[11] Western countries occupy the majority of the dominant positions within the world order.

Despite the existence of several local conflicts, which sometimes occupy a greater space on the television news, not one of them is currently a 'global' danger from the standpoint of traditional geopolitics, one must conclude that today the world is substantially at peace and is secure. Most present conflicts are within states (that is, they are territorially contained) and pose no threat to international stability. Potential conflicts (between China and Taiwan, North Korea and South Korea, Greece and Turkey, and so on) have a good chance of being offset and negotiated in some international setting. This is partly due to the direct action of the more powerful states, especially the USA. Conflicts in Africa seem to have a relative global significance for the international community; in fact it does not appear very much involved.

By way of admonishing the opponents of the current world order, the defeat of Iraq was a crystal-clear example of inequality in military power. The bombing of Serbia in 1999 marked the official baptism, since World War II, of a geostrategy involving preventive military intervention without UN authorisation by a military organisation that declares itself to be defensive and aimed at influencing the internal affairs of a sovereign state. If, on the one hand, there has been a symbolic re-evaluation of the universal condemnation of genocide and crimes against civilians, on the other, the bases have been established (or at least a 'legal' precedent has been set) for reinforcing a world order based on inequality. After all, 'the flip side of hierarchy is inequality'.[11]

However, factors exist that threaten this stability, and since they extend beyond state borders, they also threaten world order. Such factors stem from cultural and economic causes and basically consist of: (1) religious fundamentalism and ethnic-national revindication, the two often being combined, (2) migratory pressure, and (3) imbalances and crises within the international financial system. All these factors are difficult to contain within territories. Therefore, if they threaten the stability of states, they can also threaten the stability of a world order founded essentially on these states.

Factor (1) is difficult to control since, besides involving the cultural dimension of human beings, it exists with no regard for the ideological premise of inequalities between states. Indeed, belief in the pre-eminence of a collective identity (religious and ethnic, for example) is often directed against the most powerful nations (most often the USA), who are seen as enemies dedicated to cultural colonisation. The pragmatic objective of the world order is to keep these cultural, religious, and ethno-national phenomena contained within areas or states. When these factors cross borders it is often in the form of terrorism; the fight against so-called international terrorism is based on the expectation (on the part of the leaders of the world order) that individual states will support the common struggle and those that do not (or who are thought not to) will become the subject of ostracism, embargoes, diplomatic isolation, and so on. This was the case with Libya and Iran.

Factor (2) is combated both by exerting pressure on the countries of origin of the migrants and by strengthening the borders of destination countries. Such actions are, however, inadequate, since migration stems from a systemic condition of economic inequality between 'the nationalities favoured by the West and the expectations of endless masses of people belonging to regional or sub-continental areas that are undeveloped and have high populations'.[13]

Factor (3) is offset through the combined action of international bodies, the International Monetary Fund (IMF), the World Bank (WB), the World Trade Organisation (WTO) and pressure exerted by the USA[14] and the G7 countries. This is supplemented by the complementary action of the governments and private banks of the rich countries that draw the greatest advantages from the dynamics of international finance and, therefore, may suffer more from the instability. An example is the Asian financial crisis of 1997–99.

During the cold war, factors (1) and (2) were rigidly controlled by the two blocs, while self-exclusion of the socialists from the market to some degree limited the negative effects of international financial imbalances. Today, the spatial dimension of these factors is more planetary than global. By 'planetary' I mean that while these factors are at work simultaneously in many parts of the planet, they do not behave according to a univocal or global mechanism. Although caused by substantially homogenous factors, local dynamics are influenced by numerous elements. I am also using the term 'planetary', here, in a 'horizontal' sense (that is, contemporaneous), rather than the word 'global', to which a 'vertical' meaning is often attached (that is, an interconnection between the 'high' of the centres of power and economics and the 'low' of other places on earth). Without denying the hierarchical nature of the globalisation process, this is not a world order, and the view of an almost preordained all-encompassing action aimed at producing a 'single thought' is less than entirely convincing.[15]

In the recent past, the USA and USSR were symbolic combatants representing two alliances. Since their conflict was ideological, the inequality factor was hidden. The limited possibility for action by states in either bloc seemed to stem from tactics rather than hierarchical structure. The existence of a common threat meant that individual states limited their criticism of the *status quo*, while those that did take a stand were accused of betrayal or plotting with the enemy. Because of this ideological-cultural constriction, which persisted for many years, we are unable, even today, to free ourselves of the mind-set of that time when assessing geopolitical dynamics.

The ideological premises of the alliance left in the wake of the bipolar world remain parliamentary democracy (in the sense of the power of the majority) and the market (that is, freedom of movement for capital and unlimited private property). The most widely accepted political (and geopolitical) views of the mass media and those responsible for international relations support the idea that the strengthening of the UN and other international bodies (even if structured according to the traditional inequality approach) can lead to peace in security and a more effective response to the problems that beset the international community. The values of democracy and the market represent the 'egalitarian' principles that justify, and even make 'correct',[16] the existence of a hierarchical structure. The handling of the recent Kosovo crisis is a clear example of the application of this approach.

We are already living in what is, at root, a situation of peace and security, where the dangers and negative effects that can occur are 'acceptable' in that they are inversely proportional to the power of states – that is, the number of states, the sole representatives of individual rights,[17] affected by geopolitical crises is small and does not include those occupying the upper echelons of the world order. The play-off between costs and benefits is therefore attractive. There is an obvious parallel here with the ideology of natural inequality between human beings that can be compensated for by the equal theoretical and democratic possibility for all humans to improve their lot – a possibility that could only exist in a free market economy.

At the international level there is concern for human rights, poverty, the welfare of children, women's issues, famine, disease, the environment, the oceans, the Antarctic, and so on, and major conferences are held to discuss these issues. The decisions made on these questions must, however, be compatible with the world order. This is partly because international measures and initiatives can almost exclusively be promoted and supported by the main players of the world order. For the supporters of the 'democratic' world order, there are no other solutions that are more efficient or 'fair' – conflict only arises out of conservative opposition to modernisation and globalisation.

Inequality as a Constant Source of Conflict

Viewed from a different perspective, inequality can be seen as a constant source of conflict and, within the 'cosmopolitical model of Holy Alliance', a means of territorial control that necessarily involves flowing with events and dynamics without being able to promote real peace processes. Any intervention of force may stabilise a situation for a time, but only at a high cost, even if such intervention may be beneficial for certain important industries; the rush to win contracts for the reconstruction of Kosovo is a case in point. Where outcomes have been positive, the main agent of peace appears to have been time rather than the initial action of force. Certainly, actions of force may create situations conducive to peace, but the costs (particularly the human cost) are generally very high.

The holy alliance of the most powerful states has a vision of peace as being all-encompassing for the system and with priorities that are strictly dependent on their political and economic interests. It does not have sufficient tools or the capacity pragmatically to resolve the causes of conflict over time. It is believed that addressing problems in terms of state, population, and different interests will resolve the contradictory nature and uncontrollable diversity of the psychology and identities of human beings in a *rational* and *modern* way. The results are several unequal socio-political structures, but diversity does not automatically and necessarily mean inequality.

The inequality factor is a source of conflict in any territory and in any culture. It exists, or coexists, in three main areas.

1. *Inequalities of power*. This factor is obvious in authoritarian regimes and where identifiable ethnic groups control the state (such as the Serbians in Yugoslavia, the Protestants in Ulster, and the Tutsis in Rwanda). It is also present, however, in parliamentary democracies, since it stems from numerical relationships that, through elections, identify a majority – that is, the general will of the people that determines how territory and society are administered. The mechanism through which this majority is determined inevitably leads to a merging of the 'general will' with the socio-political moderate centre, which may swing from right to left, but can never bring about significant changes in the short term. Under these conditions, the control of power (exercised by the representatives of the majority) is also determined by other factors of inequality, such as available finances, social class, the role or function of politicians (image) and control of the media, all of which can exert influence on voters' choices.

2. *Inequalities in economic conditions*. At the world level, such inequalities differ from country to country and from population to population.[18] Within individual nations, wealth-production mechanisms (which are global in the case of the capitalist model) are based on the slogan 'opportunity for all'. But the slogan cannot be true for all. The idea of 'competition producing wealth' is founded on numeric relationships of a clearly and freely acknowledged pyramidal nature (one earns success) and the promise of unlimited private property, the latter being an extremely powerful hierarchical driving force. The psychology of capitalism explains its conceptual acceptance, even where it offers no real advantage for the individual at a lower socio-economic level, in that it offers the hope of improvements that often do not occur (or that do occur, but over a long, uncertain time-span) and are subject to numerous imbalances.

The prospect of greater wealth and a better future is the same hope that inspires millions of people to risk their lives to reach the country of their dreams or, more simply, a country where there are more options.

Inequalities of wealth are what drive the mechanism,[19] and no other solutions for containing the uneven distribution of wealth would appear to be more effective. Human beings are always on the move,[20] but there is a difference in terms of society and potential conflict between mass migration and the movement of small groups diluted over time. A comparison of world social stratification and freedom of movement demonstrates the inequalities in opportunities and the resulting potential grounds for conflict (Figure 2).

FIGURE 2

WORLD SOCIAL STRATIFICATION AND FREEDOM OF MOVEMENT

World social stratification
(socio-economic opportunities decrease)

Freedom of movement
(socio-economic opportunities decrease)

owners of capital — capital

consumers — goods

workers — workers

dropouts — dropouts

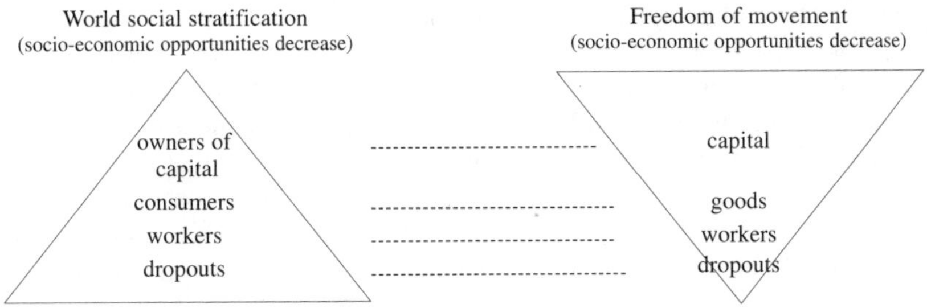

The involvement of the IMF during the Asian financial crisis exemplified both the inequality of power (the IMF's internal decision-making mechanisms operate on the basis of quotas, which sees the countries of the western world again holding the upper hand) and the 'power' inherent in inequalities in the availability and control of capital (to obtain immediate financing, South Korea had to make speedy modifications to its economy, which it had refused to do for years, while Indonesian President Suharto gave up his position during his seventh term because of his economic shortcomings).

Apocalyptic commentators (such as 'fundamentalist' ecological organisations, for example) see the world's recurring financial crises, the crossing of the threshold of environmental sustainability in the name of growth, and population explosions as signs of a looming global collapse that will place the survival of the human race in jeopardy. Less extreme observers[21] cautiously predict a global demographic transition that will last around a century, which, in combination with economic dynamics and environmental degradation, will potentially produce a 'grave crisis', using this term to indicate a dramatic situation that will not be controllable using current methods of international geopolitical and geo-economic management.

3. *Inequalities in the recognition of rights.* The symbolic and universal

term 'human rights' should override numeric relationships of majority and minority on the basis of the universality of the individual and the citizen. Human rights should exist beyond culture and social structure. The reality is, however, that in differing degrees the recognition and exercise of rights throughout the world is largely dependent on the existence of economic and power inequalities. The result of this situation is relativity in the rights of the individual and a hierarchisation of the enjoyment of freedom.

Inequalities in the recognition of rights are accepted out of habit, ignorance, and where symbolic elements (nation, religion, tradition, ethnicity, ideology, and language) 'justify' or camouflage them. In a situation of psychological or concrete crisis or uncertainty, or both, the consciousness of inequalities between individuals and groups leads to a desperate search for new presumed or imagined equalities, these often being drawn from a mythical past. Equality is therefore sought within a group of equals (equal in language, religion, ethnicity (real or imagined), and so on) and not on the basis of universal rights. This is the reason that geopolitical situations that have been stable for some time may fall into conflict and why others become stable when there is an acceptance of a new equilibrium in the symbolic elements that justify inequality (often found in a common enemy).

The cessation of conflict normally comes about when one side wins (such as the Croatian offensive in Bosnia), when a kind of blackmail is exerted by one or more external forces (NATO bombings, for example), or because of the depletion or fatigue of the adversaries (all these factors were present in Bosnia, for example). Such factors most often result in temporary solutions doomed to again deteriorate into conflict with the passing of time, the arrival of new players, or the emergence of new conditions.

The collective identity of a group of human beings is a factor that camouflages inequality. The strength of group identity lies in its 'capacity to conceal its origins in human beings so that it appears to be a naturally occurring fact. In the case of territoriality and the universalising of the principles that accompany this identity, its effects are to be feared. Concepts of group identity aim to give territory the unequivocal role as a natural attribute of the claimed identity. The belief that derives from this is clear and increasingly widespread: an identity must correspond to a territory.'[22]

Within one's individual space (one's own room, with one's family) negotiation is either unnecessary or minimal: the sense of homogeneity that stems from blood relationships or choice (marriage) satisfies the need for security. In the community space, however, there is need for negotiation with others regarding behaviour, attitudes, ideas, and the space itself. The more homogenous the cultural composition of a society, the more the need for negotiation (and the quality of that negotiation) is reduced. In such situations, the community is understandable to all its members and is perceived as being protective. Anything that frees us human beings from fear is regarded as desirable, and it is therefore understandable how the satisfaction stemming from this psychological condition has consequences at the level of ideological justifications.[23] The presence of different ethnic groups and different potential symbols of identity (religion, dialect, or traditional customs) can become a psychological escape route by which a claim is made to a territory in which to 'confine' one's own group in the name of freedom and equality of customs rather than rights.

This condition of inequality for groups that justifies inequalities in power, social conditions, and rights must be opposed since it generates conflict and prevarication. The conceptual weapon for doing this is claiming the right to diversity, but not at the expense of others, and individually and not collectively.

If one thinks of society as a space for citizens[24] that is founded upon the rights of humans as such and not as members of a homogenous group identity, then the role of common laws (which need to be recommendatory rather than coercive) and their application throughout the territory may become a powder keg as far as existing social structures are concerned. In particular, in the presence of declared principles of egalitarianism and universality, which treat the individual as an individual and not as a member of a group, the application of egalitarian laws within the space immediately reveals injustices, that is, inequalities in rights, powers, and conditions. References to inequality highlights 'the two-pronged approach that seems to characterize the new international law: the rights of populations and the rights if humans'.[25] We are currently witnessing a transitional phase that not only involves groups, but also certain aspects of the make-up of human society that have become established over an extended period – and time itself is a factor that deserves particular attention.

The technological revolution we are currently seeing in the communications sector is founded on greatly speeded up processes. This speed is leading to a new conception of space (both real and virtual) as well as cultural disaggregation, which in turn leads to crises of identity. Some of the traditional cultural justifications for inequality are now losing their persuasiveness, while others are unable to find a new equilibrium. This situation is provoking conflict and tension.

A principal element of cultural diversity is differences in the concept of time, in particular as it concerns change (which remains inevitable).[26] This is the position taken by the keenest observers from traditional cultures, who, despite often wanting a further opening up of their own culture, are aware of the explosive differences that exist between their cultures and culture of the West, which is so technological and so 'fast'. Such individuals emphasise the importance of the time factor[27] in pursuing new social balances without triggering conflict. This, however, runs counter to the speed factor so highly prized by the supporters of globalisation.

Equality as an Interpretative Key

Peace processes can lead to a final and lasting equilibrium if they take equality (that is, respect for the individual) as their guiding principle and objective. While such a statement emphasises individual rights over the rights of the 'people', it is necessary not to place the individual and the group in opposition. This can be done.

The concept of equality has been very much a part of European and western thought for a very long time, although it has figured more in declarations of principles than in practice. One may even interpret a large part of European history as a continual struggle between the theoretical assertion of the principle of equality and resistance to it, as represented in the concept of territory and by human behaviour. The Greek *polis*, Christianity (early and monastic), Brother Dolcino and the mendicant orders, the Waldensians, the Levellers and the Diggers, the French Revolution (particularly Babeuf, but also the destabilising effect of the Code Napoléon on Europe's *ancien régime*), and socialism (in its anarchic and Marxist forms) are just a few examples that show the long history and importance of the principle of equality.

When this principle is taken as the guiding light for peace processes, nothing new is achieved since the principle derives from European thought, which is the basis of the current world order. As in the past, the principle cannot do otherwise than provoke strong resistance. This does not mean, however, that it is not valid or that there is no chance for it to prevail.

To promote peace processes, peaceful principles must be proposed to achieve peaceful lands. The objective is to change initial conditions. It is therefore important to consider the time factor, since positive geopolitical factors need considerable time. The re-establishment of an equilibrium must occur over a long period for it to be stable. Peace processes therefore require both time (it is useful, for example, to indicate the duration of a process and set the times for negotiation and assessment) and rebalancing (that is, those actions that reduce the inequalities behind the conflict).

The passing of time, however, can also consolidate conflicts and make it more difficult to exit from them. It can also consolidate inequalities in the sense that it makes the ways and conditions that have been brought about by the conflict stable and 'normal', particularly for young people or new arrivals. A long series of conflicts has taken place within relatively stabilised situations (Israel-Palestine, Northern Ireland, Lebanon, and Cyprus, to mention just a few of the better known and local examples) for which reason the original conditions have radically changed. Stabilisation through time is an important factor and should not be overlooked in formulating peace processes. The viewpoint of inequality or the historical approach in determining good and bad do not generally take the time factor into account. They produce solutions that have their roots in the past (that is, making the situation return to the way it was) or do not eliminate the original cause (in many cases, some inequality).

The principle of equality cannot rely on the actions of a handful of parties, who are often forced to repeat actions to constrain conflicts that constantly resurface. Again, the former Yugoslavia is emblematic. It is necessary to create or to stimulate the development of elements that will bring about change, and this becomes possible the more numerous and diverse the players involved are. Those involved must be made to feel responsible and a part of the process.

According to the model proposed by Jean Gottmann of the dialectic between iconography and the movement factor (or circulation), time has the function of stabilising (iconography) the effects of a process, while the relationship between the players and between them and the aims of the process provide the push toward movement, the fuel of dynamics (the movement factor).

Effective peace processes can remain stable and be successful if they are based on respect for human beings as individuals and their individual freedom as holders of the rights of citizens. This means guaranteeing within a particular space the right to chose one's own diversity and to which group one wishes to belong, the option of change, the negotiation of rules, and the negotiation of space (the mobility of borders).

Another essential building block is the limitation of inequalities (economic and of power, that is, the rejection of privilege and exclusion). This is something more than a generic 'majority will' democracy offers. If we take equality as our starting point, we are forced to view things through different eyes and to propose new strategies.

Equality of Power

Equality of power means accepting, as regards the nation-state in particular, a limit to sovereignty and the progressive setting up of decision-making forums at various levels (not only supranational) through mechanisms that allow for changes in the dimensions of the bodies involved and the characteristics of agreements.[28] On this basis, one could envisage certain modifications to the United Nations: first and foremost, to make it a forum with genuine equality, without privileges such as the right of veto and permanent membership of the Security Council. This would be a UN with a flexible structure based in various regions with bodies set up to deal with particular issues and problems. This overhauled UN would look for solutions that viewed the planet as a whole. The General Assembly could be paralleled by at least one other assembly whose members would not be chosen on the basis of state (human groups, movements, and non-governmental organisations (NGOs)) so as to achieve a constant dialectic factor.[29] This would be a more influential UN, since it would be seen to be impartial. It would not use coercive tactics, but would rely more on the pressure of members and leading by example.[30] Such a UN would respect the cultural identities of individual groups, who would, however, not only have to accept formally confrontation and debate with other cultures, but also guarantee citizens the right to individual choice.

The current view of the state as the sole guarantor of the (formal) equality of citizens and the balancing out of the different needs of various sectors of society must give way to the centrality and sovereignty of the individual. In turn, the individual's support legitimises and gives sovereignty to other bodies of every type and size (from municipalities to regional assemblies).

Economic Equality

Social and economic equality is a fundamental yardstick for measuring formal democracy. Respect for the rights of the individual has as its logical consequence the limitation of private property, which must nevertheless be protected as a guarantee of the survival of the individual, but limited as a means for accumulating wealth. This can come about through the social use of territory – that is, limiting the ownership of land and the use (and ownership) of certain commodities that can be seen to belong to the common wealth (air, water, vegetation, animals, and so on).

The aim of economics is (or should be) to improve the quality of life, which may come about through free production and trade, and the channelling of 'collective' money into socially useful purposes. Respect for the rights of the individual makes it impossible to accept production's current hierarchical structure. This structure must be reorganised on a co-operative basis without divisions between employer and employee.[31] Obviously, such a proposal flies in the face of the entire make-up of the current economic-financial system, in which it is believed that a higher quality of life is the automatic outcome of the globalisation of consumption and the mobility of capital. The as-yet unsuccessful attempt by the OECD countries (the most developed) to codify a global financial system (the Multilateral Agreement on Investment) that is restrictive as far as states are concerned, but liberal as regards those who control capital and international production, clearly points to which are the dominant 'unequal' interests.[32] It is clear that these interests are, and always will be, a source of conflict.

Equality of Rights

Enforcing limits on discrimination means opposing the absolutism of cultural homogeneity by encouraging contact between groups and the sharing and exchange of experiences. It means the increasing rejection of the traditional value of group membership through birth (ethnicity), family (religion, socio-economic group), or society (language). Such limits are not intended to remove (abolish by law) individual space, but to guarantee all persons a margin of individual protection and security that is not to the detriment of others. Although this is a fundamental condition, it is not sufficient in itself to create a society that is dynamic and founded on equality. Indeed, the conservative approach regards individual security as a defence of the principle of private property (unlimited, however) and of the precedence of the individual over the state (which must, however, be sufficiently strong to protect this private property and guarantee that it is unlimited).

The ideal point of reference here is the principle of *egaliberté* (equality and freedom combined),[33] in the sense of the actual condition of psychological security discernible throughout a territory that stems from the knowledge that it is possible to act positively, that is, that sense of individual freedom that, since it is guaranteed to all on the basis that they are equal, leads individuals to accept the limits or guarantees of protection or negotiate these with others. If *egaliberté* is taken as the conceptual point of reference, the problem of who is to act as the guarantor of this principle is no longer relevant: municipality, province, region, state, and other groupings represent degrees in scale, but not substance – each acts as guarantor. This presupposes the creation of organs for mediation and negotiation freed from the reasoning typical of states. Although there have been international debates and interesting proposals made, the obstacles to be overcome are formidable.

Along with a few other nations, the USA and China voted against the treaty containing the statute for the International Criminal Court (Rome, July 1998), which in turn did not receive media support for other humanitarian operations, such as Kosovo. In 1986, the USA, which denounced Milosevic to the International Criminal Tribunal for the Former Yugoslavia in The Hague, withdrew its support for the International Court of Justice in The Hague after its ruling concerning the use of mines in Sandinista-controlled ports in Nicaragua. An international legal order can only be conceived on a planetary basis, with one rule applying to all. President Clinton, however, states that he supports 'such a court in principle, but wants more protection for US armed forces overseas'.[34] There are, nevertheless, signs of progress in the constitution of a 'global civil society', although some commentators are perhaps overoptimistic.[35]

Schemes for a Comparison

To allow a comparison of real situations, I outline and compare two schemes below for analysing peace processes based on the principles of equality and inequality as discussed above. The differences between the two schemes are immediately clear: processes originating from 'above' and initiated by a handful of recognised and authoritative players correspond to the inequality scheme; processes that involve numerous players are flexible, involve self-empowerment originating from 'below', and correspond to the equality scheme.

From the point of view of political representatives, official mediators, and the organisations and states involved, the process underlying the equality principle is fraught with dangers, since it affects various taboo areas, including borders, power hierarchies, and the self-management of territory. The question of whether the principle of equality presupposes peaceful processes, or if it can involve the use of arms or armed groups, or both, merits in-depth discussion. Nevertheless, in general, it is possible to say that the use of arms may also occur in a process originating from below. Processes originating from above always involve an armed deterrent and, generally, one or more of the armed groups is a state or equivalent body. The use of arms also changes according to the reference principle.

The recent crisis in Kosovo is a real example to which the scheme can be applied. The events as they unfolded would appear to have had much in common with the case history of the inequality scheme, particularly if we look at the so-called Rambouillet peace plan, which involved: a few authoritative mediators (with the USA occupying a special position); representatives for the most part being chosen by the mediators; scant consideration of the historical and cultural characteristics of either side; any consideration of rights being almost restricted to collective rights; the 'stability' of the recognised political leader (Milosevic); and involved existing states remaining untouchable (according to stability and territorial containment principles). Given these premises, the objective of a peaceful division of territory between the two groups was difficult, and was made all the more problematic by the fact that interest in the events on the part of the so-called international community (that is, the leaders of the world order) was only aroused after many years of apathy concerning the Kosovars' peaceful internal resistance.

Approaching these events from the perspective of equality may have produced some useful outcomes. In the first place, among the greatest obstacles to peace was the attitude of the Serbs to Kosovo – that is, the ethno-national consciousness according to which Kosovo is the cradle of the Serb nation. One does not fight with arms or decrees for a nation that only exists in a people's collective consciousness; it is necessary to manufacture another image with the appropriate tools (television in particular). It is insufficient to indicate the terms of the process and speak generically of self-determination; it is much more important to establish that the process can be altered and indicate how this can be done. Permanent forums for negotiation must exist both within and without the contested territory. More players must be involved, including a greater presence by local representatives (Kosovars and Serbs). In negotiation, separate tables and representatives that refuse to meet other delegations should not be allowed. Financial aid should be directed to encourage the self-administration of mixed local groups through structures for the use of all (schools, hospitals, social centres, and so on) with priority given to individual aid (or for families) for personal needs (housing, business, and so on).

The main aim of negotiation is not 'symbolism' (independence, identity, history, borders, sovereignty, and so on), but the guaranteeing of individual rights and freedom within a territory and within daily life. If necessary, small separate spaces should be established to avoid conflicts in the larger shared spaces. Encouraging bilingualism (in hospitals, for example) and having set areas for the use of minority languages (schools, for example) encourages wider acceptance of a different official language when it occurs in other contexts (courts, for example). These are the kinds of practical problems that would have needed attention.

Efficient mediation does not only come from above. It could also come from locally present external observers or mediators (one, for example, in each Kosovo village with mobile telephones or other means for rapid communication) who could contribute to resolving daily conflicts. These observers would prevent paramilitary groups and nationalist guerrilla groups going unpunished. Such observers would have to be very conscious of the fact that they were not 'whites' in the land of the savages, and, in the case of danger, it would have to be possible to remove them quickly from the situation. It would be necessary to provide the greatest protection possible for these people, but their role would still be a risky one. Their main role would be to be present, so they need not be soldiers, but their predicament would be more dangerous than that of soldiers.

Lastly, it is worth mentioning a comment by the great cellist Rostropovitch, who, as regards a solution for preventing the events in Kosovo, proposed guaranteeing both the Serbs and Kosovars $3 billion (less than the total cost of the bombings and reconstruction) for building cities, schools, houses, nursery schools, and hospitals.[36] To discuss how this could be done, a huge table would be set up on the border between Serbia and Kosovo with plenty (but not too much) vodka (or slivovic) on hand. This is decidedly a proposal from below and with greater structure perhaps it would have worked.

Schemes for Assessing Peace Processes Based on the Principles of Equality and Inequality

It is essential to consider the time factor when dealing with the issue of equality, that is:

- The duration of the process, and the timeframes and methods for assessing and adjusting agreements, and

- Understanding the historical-cultural characteristics of the human groups involved in the process.

TABLE 1

SCHEMES FOR ASSESSING PEACE PROCESSES BASED ON THE PRINCIPLES OF EQUALITY AND INEQUALITY

EQUALITY	INEQUALITY
Power	*Power*
The players in the process are:	The players in the process are:
• numerous, internal and external	• few, internal and external
• at different levels	• formal institutions or important figures
There are permanent forums for negotiation.	• negotiation takes place at high levels in the hierarchy only
Economics	*Economics*
• efforts are made to compensate for imbalances	• differences remain as they are either ignored or no action is taken
• financing is directed	• those who possess more retain greater scope for action
• individuals (and groups) can organize themselves	
Rights	*Rights*
• numerous players are involved	• some players are devoid of rights
• attempts are made to accommodate different views through continual negotiation to achieve ongoing solutions to conflicts	• only a few cultural values are recognized (ethnicity, religion, language etc.)
• recognition of individuals rights to choice (as wide as possible)	• collective rights are recognized to homogenous groups
• sovereignty and borders can be modified through negotiation	• privileges are retained
• spaces are shared	• the forums for action of the process are set
	• spaces are separate

Conclusions: Geography for Peace or Global Security?

Good geographical analysis should be particularly sensitive to space and time.[37]

Geography is nothing more than history within space, just as history is geography within time.[38]

In the past, geographers were called in as consultants for the negotiation of agreements, the drawing of borders, and to suggest 'geopolitical' (in the old, 'Kjellenian' sense of the word) strategies. Now that geography is less cartographic and military, and more open (including to compromise), the number of geographers directly involved in geopolitical dynamics or who are called upon by the media to discuss current issues has fallen dramatically. Perhaps this is because it is difficult to confine current events to borders that were the result of peace or armistice treaties.

So, is geography no longer capable of interpreting events? Hardly. Geography is probably even too good at doing this and has more critical ability today than ever before. But criticism stemming from geography is not what those who hold the reigns of power within the world order are looking for; it is better to 'use' the experts in International Relations, who accept more easily the world order hierachy.

Geography will maintain its capacity for comparison and analysis provided it continues to occupy a relevant place in the discussion, which it can do by rethinking its conceptual points of reference. In this regard, Johnston, Taylor, and Watts identify six remappings as 'fundamental for a basic understanding of the current trajectory of our world',[39] proposing them as points of reference for accurate geographical analysis:

(1) The reconfiguration of capitalism
(2) The promotion of markets as resource allocators in an increasingly deregulated world
(3) The challenge to state sovereignty
(4) The construction of new civil society
(5) The environment question transcending (state) borders, and
(6) The actual debate on modernity (in relation to so-called post-modernism).

Similar to geopolitical dynamics, geographical analysis, particularly if it is critical in nature, has interpretative keys. The equality and inequality schemes are also effective within these remappings, in particular as regards points (1) to (5). Each of these five points can be interpreted from the perspective of equality or inequality, which begs the question of the relationship between politicians and geographers and the neutrality of science (in its broader sense). The lively debate surrounding critical and post-modern geography[40] has also demonstrated how 'political' point (6) can be.

In the conclusion of *Geographies of Global Change*,[41] Johnston, Taylor, and Watts say that 'all of these remappings imply profound social change', but this social change can only be achieved through political action.

Geography is an investigative tool that identifies and analyses dynamics, and compares differences (and inequalities). It can even attempt to anticipate effects and make predictions. Whether we like it or not, by doing this it is performing what is essentially a political function.

Geographers can play an important role in defining and analysing peace processes. In doing this, the dividing line between the geopolitician and the politician proper becomes blurred or is continually crossed in either direction. Reclus and Kropotkin were well aware of this, declaring themselves to be both geographers and politicians, specifically in reference to equality.

Inequalities within a territory are always abundantly clear (even solely from the perspective of the layout of a town) and for any peace process to have a chance of success, it cannot avoid aiming to change both social and environmental conditions. This is a political action that cannot do without the input of geography as one of the most effective tools for environmental analysis available. Herein lies the insoluble link between the two.

As academics we can explore the possibility and validity of several interpretative keys (indeed, we must do it), but we cannot escape the political character of our analyses. The choice between the approaches of equality and inequality lies with each individual geographer, but the effect on their work, and of their work, is inevitable and has various repercussions on the dissemination and acceptance of the main ideas expressed. The choice lies in deciding if one wants geography to exist in history or to observe history.

NOTES

1. D. Held, *Democrazia e ordine globale* (Trieste: Asterios 1999) p.103.
2. Ibid., p.103.
3. F. Eva, 'International boundaries, geopolitics and the (post)modern territorial discourse: The functional fiction', *Geopolitics* 3/1 (summer 1998, special issue).
4. For example, the positions of NATO and the EU as presented in Jan. 1998 at the third Israeli Seminar in Political Geography, were changed during the Kosovo crisis (with a 'higher' position for NATO), while the role of APEC, ASEAN, Indonesia, Malaysia and Thailand now seems quite different following the Asian economic crisis of 1997–99.
5. I. Clark, *The Hierarchy of States: Reform and Resistance in the International Order* (Cambridge: Cambridge University Press 1989) p.166.
6. D. Zolo, *Cosmopolis. La prospettiva del governo mondiale* (Milan: Feltrinelli 1995). English version (Cambridge: Polity Press).
7. Ibid., p.129.
8. Ibid., p.179.
9. D. Binder and B. Crossette, *As Ethnic Wars Multiply, United States Strives for a Policy.* Quoted in Zolo (note 5) p.179.
10. D. Held (note 1) p.131.
11. Ibid., p.131.
12. Ibid., p.86.
13. D. Zolo (note 5) p.164.

14. '[Although] always with the transparency of formal agreements, which constitute the perfect application of the hegemony and consensus model that has been the pivot on which the United States has turned since the end of the cold war.' M. Platero, *Il Sole 24 Ore*, 14 Jan. 1998.
15. I. Ramonet, *Il Pensiero Unico e i nuovi padroni del mondo* (Rome: ASEC 1996).
16. M. Walzer, *Just and Unjust Wars* (New York: Basic Books 1992).
17. Ibid.
18. The wealth of the three richest people in the world (Bill Gates, the Sultan of Brunei, and the Walton family) is greater than the total GDPs of the 43 poorest countries. UN report quoted in the *International Herald Tribune*, 14 July 1999.
19. J.T. Fawcett, 'Networks, linkages, and migration systems', *International Migration Review* XXIII, 3 (1989) pp.671–80.
20. M. Livi Bacci, *Storia minima della popolazione del mondo* (Turin: Loescher 1989); F. Eva, '*Geografia delle migrazioni*', in E. Damiano (ed.), *Homo Migrans* (Milan: Franco Angeli 1998).
21. Umberto Melotti and Nanni Salio, Conference *Nord/Sud, migrazioni e capitalismo* (North/South, migration and capitalism). Milan, 17 Jan. 1998.
22. B. Badie, *La fine dei territori* (Trieste: Asterios 1996). Originally published as *La fin des territoires. Essai sur le désordre international et sur l'utilité sociale du respect* (Paris: Fayard 1995).
23. 'The Christian equality, unless the rigidly, hierarchical structure of the life on earth.' H. Arendt, *Tra passato e futuro* (Florence: Vallecchi 1970).
24. R.A. Falk, *Positive Prescriptions for the Near Future*, Paper No.20 (Princeton: Center for International Studies 1991).
25. G. Harrison, '*Antropologia culturale dei processi migratori e dei diritti umani*', in E. Damiano (ed.), *Homo Migrans* (Milan: Franco Angeli 1998) p.180.
26. 'The one unchanging fact of our world – that is forever changing.' Johnston, Taylor, and Watts (eds.), *Geographies of Global Change* (Oxford: Blackwell 1995) p.381.
27. See, for example, the comments of author Moussa Konaté and director Adama Drabo made in reference to changes in customs in African societies during a special broadcast on France2 recorded in Mali in the presence of the president of the republic, 11 Jan. 1998.
28. E. Malatesta, '*Ancora di repubblica e rivoluzione*', *Pensiero e Volontă*, No.12 (15 June 1924), as well as many of the propositions of David Held (D. Held (note 1) p.279) in his model of cosmopolitical democracy.
29. D. Archibugi, R.A. Falk, D. Held, and M. Kaldor, *Cosmopolis? Possibile una democrazia sovranazionale?* (Rome: Manifestolibri 1993).
30. E. Malatesta, *Pagine di lotta quotidiana* (Carrara: Movimento Anarchico Italiano 1975).
31. P.J. Proudhon, *Qu'est-ce que la propriété? Ou recherches sur le principe du droit et du gouvernement* [1840]. Italian translation, *Cos'è la proprietă?* (Bari: Laterza 1967).
32. L.M. Wallach, 'Le nouveau manifeste du capitalisme mondial', *Le Monde Diplomatique* (Feb. 1998).
33. E. Balibar, *Le frontiere della democrazia* (Rome: Manifestolibri 1993); F. Buonarroti, *Cospirazione per l'uguaglianza, detta di Babeuf* (Turin: Einaudi 1971).
34. *International Herald Tribune*, 13 July 1999, p.8.
35. Falk (note 23).
36. Interview with Riccardo Chiaberge, *Corriere della Sera*, 16 June 1999.
37. Johnston, Taylor, and Watts (note 25) p.7.
38. E. Reclus, *L'Homme et la Terre* (Paris: Librairie Universelle 1905–08).
39. Johnston, Taylor, and Watts (note 25), p.383.
40. Inaugural International Conference in Critical Geography, Vancouver, 10–14 August 1997. International Conference 'The City and Post-modern Geographical Praxis', Venice, 10–11 June 1999.
41. Johnston, Taylor, and Watts (note 25) p.383.

Reclaiming Geopolitics: Geographers Strike Back

VIRGINIE MAMADOUH

J. Agnew, *Geopolitics: Re-visioning World Politics*. London: Routledge, 1998.

J. Agnew and S. Corbridge, *Mastering Space: Hegemony, Territory and International Political Economy*. London: Routledge, 1995.

G.J. Demko and W.B. Wood (eds.), *Reordering the World: Geopolitical Perspectives on the 21st Century*. Boulder: Westview, 1994, 1999.

G. Dijkink, *National Identity and Geopolitical Visions: Maps of Pride and Pain*. London: Routledge, 1996.

K. Dodds, *Geopolitics in a Changing World*. Harlow: Prentice Hall, Pearson Education, 2000.

M. Heffernan, *The Meaning of Europe, Geography and Geopolitics*. London: Arnold, 1998.

Y. Lacoste (ed.), *Dictionnaire de géopolitique*. Paris: Flammarion, 1993, 1998.

J. O'Loughlin (ed.), *Dictionary of Geopolitics*. Westport: Greenwood, 1994.

D. Newman (ed.), *Boundaries, Territory and Postmodernity*, London, Frank Cass, 1999.

G. Ó Tuathail, *Critical Geopolitics: The Politics of Writing Global Space*. London: Routledge, 1996.

G. Ó Tuathail and S. Dalby (eds.), *Rethinking Geopolitics*. London: Routledge, 1998.

G. Ó Tuathail, S. Dalby and P. Routledge (eds.), *The Geopolitics Reader*. London: Routledge, 1998.

A. Paasi, *Territories, Boundaries, and Consciousness; The Changing Geographies of the Finnish-Russian Border*. Chichester: Wiley, 1996.

G. Parker, *Geopolitics: Past, Present and Future*. London: Pinter, 1998.

'Geopolitics' is a fashionable term, much used at the end of the twentieth century, as is shown by the titles of many publications and by the name of this very journal. Things were much different three or four decades ago, when it was hardly pronounced by geographers. It then stood for a dark episode in the history of their discipline, namely, the relationship between the German school of *Geopolitik* and the Nazi regime during the 1930s and the Second World War, as well as for similar bonds between students of geopolitics and totalitarian regimes in other countries (Italy, Japan, Argentina, and so on). The most influential of these German geographers, Karl Haushofer, was inspired by a Swedish political scientist, Kjellén (who had coined the neologism 'geopolitics' in 1899) and the Anglo-American school of geostrategy led by the British geographer Sir Halford J. Mackinder. Mackinder's ambition was to enlist 'geography as an aid to statecraft and strategy'.[1]

As a result of the disastrous consequences of the enlistment of the work of German geopoliticians by Nazi ideologists, geographers turned their back on power politics for several decades. But the beginning of the 1980s witnessed a major revival of political geography (including the establishment of a journal, *Political Geography Quarterly*) and the rehabilitation of geopolitics. As John O'Loughlin and Henning Heske so accurately put it, it was 'time to reclaim the geopolitical theme from its hijackers in the strategic community' (1991: 37). It was time to strike back and reinsert geopolitics into the research agenda of (political) geographers.

In the past two decades, geographers have effectively reclaimed geopolitics: they have repossessed its terminology and, most importantly, they have taken up again the eminently important issue of power relations and space. This review article is meant to provide an overview of geographers' efforts during the past decade. It focuses especially on books by geographers and special issues of geographical journals. A short presentation of the old geopolitics will be given before reviewing these new developments. Some three ways of reclaiming geopolitics are distinguished: one in which geography is an aid to political action (to paraphrase Mackinder) and two academic stances in which geography is pulled back into academia. These two partly overlapping perspectives consist of the conventional and primarily positivist approach of neutral scholarship, 'new geopolitics', and a critical approach to geopolitics, which has established itself in the past decade under the tag 'critical geopolitics'. They will be discussed in chronological order of appearance, but the review may seem somewhat unbalanced because the latter approach has been extremely productive over the past two years.

The Past of Geopolitics

Friedrich Ratzel is generally presented as the founder of political geography on account of his book *Politische Geographie* (1897), but it is a Swedish political scientist who coined the neologism 'geopolitics' in 1899. Like

Ratzel (and many of their contemporaries), Rudolf Kjellén had an organic theory of the state. He introduced five neologisms to conceptualise the core features of the state. *Geopolitik* was a term used to describe the location, the form, and the surface and physical characteristics of the territory of the state, and also the study of these features. The term 'geopolitics' was borrowed by German geographers, who established their journal, *Zeitschrift für Geopolitik*, in 1924. Classical geopolitics was closely associated with geostrategy, a discipline that originated in the work of the British geographer Sir Halford Mackinder and the American admiral Alfred T. Mahan. It emerges as a school of thought in a period of global closure: the expanding European states had conquered most of the world and were left to compete with each other. Geopolitical thinking was instrumental to state policies, conceptualising the influence of geographic factors in the power relations between states. In addition, classical geopolitics was deterministic: geography was expected to determine politics.

As mentioned above, the enlistment of geopolitics by the Nazi regime led to its rejection altogether, not so much in the strategic community, but certainly among geographers. The traditional approach to geopolitics and geostrategy still exists, albeit in a less deterministic flavour, in military and, more specifically, naval academies, as well as in circles of foreign-policy advisers (for recent examples, see Brzezinski 1997).

Political Activism: *Géopolitiques*

In past decades, geographers have reclaimed geopolitics, but they did it differently. In France, the revival of geopolitics is rooted in the solidarity of some French geographers with anti-colonial and anti-imperialist struggles in the Third World. Yves Lacoste has been the major motor of an approach to geopolitics that reclaims it for political action. These geographers also reclaim the heritage of a brilliant nineteenth-century geographer, Elisée Reclus, who has been neglected in academic circles because of his anarchist ideas.

This alternative and subversive approach to geopolitics has matured over 20 years in the Journal *Hérodote*, which was founded in 1976. The approach focuses on the conflictual character of geopolitical representations and claims. These geographers often use the plural while the conventional writing of *géopolitique* in French is singular. Territorial conflict, rather than the state or the state system, is the unit of analysis. Besides, geopolitics is not the prerogative of the state, therefore, these geographers also deal with internal geopolitics (what others may call electoral geography and administrative geography). The continuous and sustained effort to develop this approach to geopolitics can be traced in *Hérodote*, with its four thematic issues a year. Among the topics discussed in recent issues are nations (Spain in No.91), regions (the Mediterranean in No.90 and southern Europe-North Africa in No.94), coastlines (No.93), and public health (No.92).

Lacoste has been influential among French and also Italian geographers. An Italian adaptation of *Hérodote* was produced between 1978 and 1984 (first as *Hérodote-Italia*, then as *Erodoto*). In the 1990s, two more journals, sharing the same name and dealing with geopolitics, were established: the Italian and the French *LiMes*. A selection of *Hérodote* articles was introduced to the English-speaking community as early as 1987 (Girot and Kofman 1987). Moreover, geopolitics have become a particularly popular topic in France, even if many geographers interested in geopolitics and world politics do not join these ranks, for example, most of the contributors to the forthcoming special issue of *Geopolitics*, whose guest editor is Jacques Lévy (see also Claval 1994).

Monographs inspired by this approach to geopolitics include the work of Michel Korinman (1990; 1991) on German geopolitics, Michel Foucher (1991; 1993; 1996) on borders, and more recently the work of Barbara Loyer (1997) on Basque nationalism. Yves Lacoste has also edited numerous reference works, to begin with a *Dictionnaire de géopolitique* (Lacoste 1993, 1998). It is voluminous book of about 1,700 pages. The entries are extremely diverse in content and size. They consist of geographical objects (all the states in the world, territorial subdivisions, cities, mountains and rivers which are or have been at stake in geopolitical conflicts), as well as geopolitical actors (associations and organisations, political movements, and religions), geopolitical vocabulary ('state', 'border', and so on), and terms pertinent to the geopolitical approach promoted by Lacoste. There are numerous maps to summarise the key features of concrete geopolitical conflicts.

The book does not discuss the evolution of geopolitics as a discipline or the many possible approaches of geopolitics. But, it contains an extensive introduction in which Lacoste presents his specific approach. The dictionary is also a valuable tool as an introduction to existing geopolitical conflicts, and as such it can be used to make sense of events reported by the mass media by framing them in a historical and geographical context. The same kind of information is provided in another *Dictionnaire de géopolitique*, the one published in 1998 by two specialists of international relations, Chauprade and Thual (1998).

An updated edition of the Lacoste dictionary was released in 1995, as well as a CD-ROM version. In addition, a more limited edition, consisting only of the articles dealing with states, was produced under the title *Dictionnaire de géopolitique des états* (the last update of which is Lacoste 1998a). For November 1999, a *Dictionnaire des idées et notions de géopolitique* has been announced. It is as yet unclear to me if the volume will also consist of an updated selection of articles from the original dictionary or if it is a new text elaborating on Lacoste's recent essay regarding the nation (Lacoste 1998b).

Neutral Scholarship: New Geopolitics

The attitude of Anglo-Saxon political geographers has been very different. They were eager to reclaim geopolitics from the state and the military, but did so by pulling it back into academia. Political geography regained some popularity at the end of the 1970s and the beginning of the 1980s, a fact that was institutionalised in the creation of a new journal, *Political Geography Quarterly*, in 1982. Geopolitics was only one of the many themes on the new research agenda; it was conceived as a political geography of international relations. The term 'geopolitics' itself is either avoided or used carefully to distinguish between the practical or applied geopolitics of the politicians and diplomats (a practical body of knowledge instrumental to the conduct of foreign affairs) and formal geopolitics as an academic body of knowledge. They also distinguish between old geopolitics (serving the foreign policy of a particular state) and new geopolitics as a geographical perspective on the relations between states.

These political geographers have effectuated their claims on geopolitics in several volumes dealing with the political geography of international relations (such as Pepper and Jenkins 1985; Kliot and Waterman 1991; O'Loughlin and Van der Wusten 1993; Taylor 1993; and Williams 1993). Many articles have been published in *Political Geography Quarterly* and its successor, *Political Geography*, including two special issues (Vol.6, issue 2 in 1986, and Vol.8, issue 4 in 1989) and an ongoing series of articles presenting national traditions of geopolitics (for example, Fukushima 1997). By the mid-1980s, two major books were available. In the first, Patrick O'Sullivan (1986) presented a model approach to the study of spatial relations between states (see also his more recent account of geopolitical force fields, O'Sullivan 1995). The second was an account of the evolution of western geopolitical thought by Geoffrey Parker (1985).

In 1994, the *Dictionary of Geopolitics* was edited by John O'Loughlin, one of the two editors of *Political Geography* (and before it *Political Geography Quarterly*). This dictionary is a valuable reference book, despite some structural deficiencies. The introduction is too succinct to give us a sound account of the evolution of the field; the selection of entries often seems fortuitous; and there is not a single map to illustrate the concepts discussed. On the other hand, the content of the 200 plus articles is very informative, and a comprehensive bibliography of almost 600 titles is provided. It is, of course, partly outdated by the recent upsurge of geopolitical publications, but this dictionary remains a valuable reference volume for those interested in the history of geopolitics as a discipline because it offers an account of core concepts and key authors, and of important schools and journals.

Reordering the World, a volume edited by George Demko and William Wood in 1994 and revised in 1999, is closer to American foreign-policy practice than could be expected of neutral geopolitics, as the second editor is affiliated to the Office of the Geographer of the US State Department. Nevertheless, most contributors work in an academic tradition. The book is divided into three parts: the first deals with recurring themes in political geography in the past century; the second with the linkage between societies and their environments; and the third with new arenas of geopolitical research. Part one includes an introduction to the political geography of international relations (Demko and Wood 1994b), to new geopolitics (Cohen 1994), the power of maps (Hendrikson 1994), territory, identity and sovereignty (Knight 1994), international boundaries (Thomas 1994), and electoral geography (Morrill 1994). Part two addresses natural resources (Cutter 1994), global environmental hazards (Kasperson 1994), global ecopolitics (Mofson 1994), and demographic issues such as international migration (Demko 1994; Wood 1994). Part three deals with international law (Murphy 1994), fourth-world theory and the resistance to state building (Nietschmann 1994), the United Nations and non-governmental organisations (NGOs) (Drake 1994), political economy (Agnew 1994; Corbridge 1994), and information and communication (Brunn and Jones 1994). These contributions are interesting introductions to a broad range of geopolinomical[2] issues at the end of the twentieth century, but they largely stand on their own; therefore, the volume as a whole does not provide the sense of order promised by the title. In the 1999 edition, four contributions have disappeared (Kasperson, Nietschmann, Drake, and Corbridge), revised versions have sometimes been given a new title (Wood and Demko 1999b; Wood 1999a; Brunn, Jones and O'Lear 1999), and three new contributions have been included. The first deals with time and scale (Flint 1999), the second with data and tools for sustainable development (Wood 1999b), and the third with non-governmental organisations (Price 1999).

In 1998, the British political geographer Geoffrey Parker published his textbook on geopolitics under the title *Geopolitics: Past, Present and Future*. It traces the history of geopolitics from its origins to its rediscovery by geographers from the 1970s onward. The book is conventional in scope and treatment. The book consists of ten chapters and an epilogue. In the introduction, Parker assesses the origins and uses of the terms 'political geography' and 'geopolitics'. Whether the latter is conceived as a sister discipline or a subdiscipline of the former, it is defined as the spatial study of international relations. The first three chapters deal with geopolitical traditions: the origins of geopolitics (Kjellén and Ratzel), *Geopolitik* (the interbellum, the war, and German geography), and *géopolitique* (the French school of political geography and the reinvention of geopolitics in the 1970s). The following chapters deal with the world political map. Chapter five investigates the spatial typology of the state by reviewing different paths of state formation, assessing the predominant form of geopolitical organisation at different times (opposing nations and empires), and contrasting large and small states, Alexandrine and Platonic states following Jean Gottman, and extensive and intensive states following Yves-Marie Goblet (see his older work on the dominance of states over others, Parker 1988). Chapter six presents the different scales of geopolitical analysis (micro, meso, and macro). Parker then distinguishes three different ways to interpret the world as a whole from a geopolitical perspective. He distinguishes the bipolar world (chapter seven), the pluralist or multipolar world (chapter eight), and the unitary view (centre-periphery, in chapter nine). In chapter ten, Parker deals with geopolitics as process, contrasting two types: the Normative Geopolitical Process that results in the domination of one (Alexandrine or extensive) state over others and the Alternative Geopolitical Process in which smaller states aim at maintaining their independence and order in the international scene through association. The book is illustrated with many maps and includes a consequential glossary (about 70 terms). The entries consist mainly of the key notions of different geopolitical theories, including French, German, and Italian terms. Last but not least, in his epilogue about the future of geopolitics, Parker also mentions the contribution of critical geopolitics. He sees the major task of geopolitics as being the reconfiguration of the significance of territory in the age of globalisation.

Critical Scholarship: Critical Geopolitics

Critical geopolitics has been established as a post-structuralist approach to geopolitical discourses. The term seems to originate from the Ph.D. thesis completed by Gearóid Ó Tuathail (also known as Gerald Toal) in 1989 under the supervision of John Agnew at Syracuse University[3] (see also Ó Tuathail and Agnew 1992; and Ó Tuathail 1992). Another early publication deconstructing geopolitical discourses is Simon Dalby's account of the second cold war (1990), and one should also mention Peter Taylor's account of the geopolitical transition in British foreign policy toward cold war (1990). During the past decade, critical geopolitics has established its own research agenda, focusing on the deconstruction of present and past geopolitical discourses and the exploration of spatial concepts. Another characteristic of critical geopolitics is its interest in popular geopolitics (as expressed in the mass media and popular culture) on top of practical and formal geopolitics. Lastly, it includes a wide range of topics under the umbrella of geopolitics, being receptive to cultural geography, cultural studies, and feminist theory. Although critical geopolitics is politically engaged, it is more involved in the business of 'speaking truth to the face of power', as Michel Foucault phrases it,[4] than in practical and applied geopolitics as advocated by Lacoste.

Apart from various articles, critical geopolitics has established itself through two important special issues, both edited by Gearóid Ó Tuathail and Simon Dalby. The first was published in 1994 in *Environment and Planning D: Society and Space*. Entitled *Critical Geopolitics, Unfolding Spaces for Thought in Geography and Global Politics* (Ó Tuathail and Dalby 1994), it consisted of seven articles (Dodds and Sidaway 1994; Ó Tuathail 1994a; Weber 1994; Routledge 1994; Charlesworth 1994; Dalby 1994; and Luke 1994). The second was published two years later in *Political Geography*, demonstrating the width of the range of topics addressed (Dalby and Ó Tuathail 1996). It consisted of eight articles (Clarke, Doel and McDonough 1996; Luke 1996; Routledge 1996; Crampton and Ó Tuathail 1996; Sharp 1996; Dodds 1996; Dalby 1996a; and Sparke 1996) and a discussion about writing critical geopolitics (Herbert 1996; Ó Tuathail 1996b and 1996c; and Dalby 1996b). Both journals have published numerous articles in this tradition (for recent examples, see Häkli 1998a or Slater 1997) as has *Transactions*, in particular, a discussion between Slater (1993; 1994) and Ó Tuathail (1994b).

In that same year, Gearóid Ó Tuathail published his *Critical Geopolitics* (1996a) subtitled *The Politics of Writing Global Space*. The book consists of seven essays investigating the geopolitical imagination. The first two deal with geopolitics and critical geopolitics; the next two with British imperial geopolitics (Mackinder!) and American views on German geopolitics during the Second World War. In chapter five, Ó Tuathail discusses critical approaches to 'geopolitics' by reviewing the work of Karl Wittfogel, Isaiah Bowman, Yves Lacoste, Richard Ashley, and Simon Dalby. The last two chapters investigate the American geopolitical imagination of the 1990s; the first deals with 'Bosnia, 1991–1994' and the second presents visions of the global space at the end of the twentieth century, discussing more specifically Luttwak and Huntington.

Two books by John Agnew should be mentioned: *Geopolitics: Re-visioning World Politics* and an earlier volume, *Mastering Space*, written in collaboration with Stuart Corbridge in 1995. The later book was broader in scope, discussing international political economy and the hegemony of the USA. The first part of *Mastering Space* deals with geopolitics, assessing the existence of three geopolitical orders and their corresponding geopolitical discourses. Civilisational geopolitics fits the British geopolitical order of the Concert of Europe (1915–75); naturalised geopolitics fits the geopolitical order of inter-imperial rivalry (1875–1945); whereas ideological geopolitics fits the cold-war geopolitical order (1945–90). The closing chapter deals with the 'territorial trap', an expression coined by Agnew to reveal the specific character of the modern state and our tendency to be blind to other spatial forms. The second part of the book examines the present American hegemony and its perceived decline. In his newest book, Agnew (1998) specifically addresses geopolitics and, more precisely, what he calls the modern geopolitical imagination. In his first chapter, he discusses the visualising of global space (a necessary condition for speaking of world politics). The second chapter is devoted to a second element of the geopolitical imagination, namely, turning time into space. Chapter three, entitled 'A world of territorial states', deals with the territorial trap. The following chapter investigates the social origins of great powers and the pursuit of primacy. The three ages of geopolitics are discussed in chapter five. The text is clearly conceived as an introduction to geopolitics, as is also shown by a list of recommended reading materials at the end of each chapter and a concise glossary of 19 terms.

The Geopolitics Reader (Ó Tuathail, Dalby and Routledge 1998) is an anthology of exemplary pieces of geopolitical discourse introduced by three major contributors to the establishment of critical geopolitics: Gearóid Ó Tuathail, Simon Dalby, and Paul Routledge. The 39 excerpts from academic articles, speeches, and books are divided into five sections, each introduced by a review essay providing information about the selection of the texts, the background of the authors, and supplying references for further reading. Gearóid Ó Tuathail wrote the general introduction, a plea to think critically about geopolitics and to scrutinise the production of geographical knowledge. The first three sections (introduced by Ó Tuathail) correspond to what many expect to be the subject of geopolitics. They deal with different periods and different geopolitical discourses: imperial geopolitics, which focuses on the rivalry between the United Kingdom and Germany; cold-war geopolitics centred around the rivalry between the USA and the Soviet Union; and new world order geopolitics revolving around the remaining superpower. The last two sections illustrate the broader scope that critical geopolitics wants to address. The first (introduced by Dalby) deals with environmental geopolitics, that is, visions about global environment change; the second (introduced by Routledge) with resistance to geopolitics, regarding which he distinguishes colonial anti-geopolitics opposing imperial geopolitics, cold-war anti-geopolitics and new world order anti-geopolitics. Simon Dalby wrote the general conclusion, reassessing that critical geopolitics is about questioning what is taken for granted in geopolitical discourses. As with any reader, *The Geopolitics Reader* can be criticised for the inclusion of certain excerpts and the neglect of others, and for the consistency of the collection. Still, the volume offers a fascinating anthology of geopolitical discourses, introducing authors as different as it is possible to be (Samuel Huntington and Edward Said, Adolf Hitler and Martin Luther King, and Robert D. Kaplan and the Chiapas rebel Marcos).

Gearóid Ó Tuathail and Simon Dalby are also the editors of the voluminous collection of essays entitled *Rethinking Geopolitics*. Their introduction assesses the importance of developing a critical geopolitics (Ó Tuathail and Dalby 1998b). They sum up the differences between this approach and a more conventional approach in five points. It is a much broader cultural phenomenon than that which practitioners of statecraft have in mind. It is about the construction of the boundary between the inside and the outside (rather than the outside of the state only). It refers to a plurality of representational practices (they distinguish a practical geopolitics of diplomats and politicians, a formal geopolitics of the strategic community, and a popular geopolitics). It seeks to disturb objectivism by underlining that geopolitics is situated knowledge and it cannot be politically neutral.[5] Lastly, it seeks to theorise the development and use of geopolitics.

The volume consists of 14 contributions. Gearóid Ó Tuathail (1998) discusses the possible existence of a post-modern geopolitics in a review of Agnew's typology of modern geopolitical imaginations (see above) and Luke's work on globalisation. Marcus Doel and David Clarke (1998) address the direct, but rarely acknowledged, link between the concept of *Lebensraum* coined by the founding father of political geography, Friedrich Ratzel, and enlisted by the Nazis, and the genocidal practices of the Nazis (*Entfernung*). Anders Stephanson (1998) explores the origin of the term 'cold war'. His essay is organised into 14 notes, sketching a history of the conceptual pairing of war and peace, including not only presidents of the two superpowers, Clausewitz and other expected classics, but also Augustine, Don Juan, and James Bond. Carlo Bonura (1998) revisits Almond and Verba's classic *The Civic Culture* (1963) and Inglehart's *Culture Shift* (1990), revealing how their comparative approaches to national political cultures take national entities for granted and, consequently, participate in the construction of national subjectivities so necessary for geopolitical discourse and conflict. Kim Rygiel (1998) discusses the attempt of the Turkish state to accommodate ethnic and religious diversity in its construction of a unitary 'modern' state; she addresses especially the regulation of Kurdish identity and the regulation of gender. Jouni Häkli (1998b) offers an account of the shaping of the Finnish provinces, exploring the encounters between governmental 'geographs' and popular 'geographs'. The administrative reform effectuated in 1992 followed no less than 34 state initiatives and eight reform proposals drafted by state committees. Häkli emphasises the strength of popular resistance to the provincial concept provided by governmental discourses of objectification and universalisation.

Popular geopolitics is the topic addressed by Joanne Sharp (1998) in her exploration of post-cold-war American movies and by Klaus Dodds (1998) in his analysis of cartoons by Steve Bell about the events in Bosnia in the early 1990s, more specifically about international (non-)intervention. Matthew Sparke studies the Oklahoma bombing. The bomb blast that killed 168 persons in downtown Oklahoma City in April 1995 was first attributed to Islamic terrorists. Instead, it was the work of an American veteran of the Gulf War and a 'militia man next door'. Sparke (1998) underlines the connection between the geopolitics of the Gulf War and that of McVeigh's representation of the federal government. James Sidaway (1998) describes the emergence of the 'Persian Gulf' as a region of 'strategic anxiety'. Once crucial for the British imperial script, the Middle East was not a primary focus of concern during the cold war, until the oil crisis. The formula 'arc of crisis' was coined in 1979 by Brzezinksi, the national security advisor of President Carter, and from then on the region was represented as strategically vital, which then makes the Gulf War more 'natural'.

The last four papers are concerned explicitly with 'informationalisation'. Paul Routledge (1998) presents the case of the Zapatista insurgency in Chiapas and its informational war against the Mexican state and the North American Free Trade Agreement (NAFTA). James Der Derian (1998) examines virtual realities, addressing the similarities between warfare scenarios (such as training exercises) and popular culture (such as videogames). Timothy Luke (1998) discusses the implications of the growth of electronic communications and cyberspace. Contrasting real life and virtual life, atom-state and bit-state, his infography investigates the revolutionary potential of the digital revolution, nonetheless acknowledging the limited portion of humanity that has access to digital highways. Lastly, Simon Dalby (1998) investigates the geopolitics of the global, that is, those discourses about global security that frame environmental degradation as a global threat. He stresses the importance of identities in the production of geopolitical representations of the poor (the Third World) as a threat to the affluent (the North), closing the book with what he calls the POGO syndrome, that is, the persistence of 'Political Organizations to Generate Others'. *Rethinking Geopolitics* may not be easy reading for those unfamiliar with critical theory, but they should persevere, because it offers a challenging and fascinating collection of critical geopolitical studies.

The most recent contribution to critical geopolitics is a textbook by Klaus Dodds entitled *Geopolitics in a Changing World* (Dodds 2000). It is a short and concise text of about 180 pages, with numerous illustrations and maps. Dodds emphasises the contested nature of geopolitics. He conceives the lively academic developments in political geography as a process of negotiating geopolitics, and he explicitly pleads for a broad definition and a critical approach. Dodds does not present a history of geopolitics as a (sub)discipline, but an introduction to critical geopolitics. The book consists of seven thematic chapters addressing contemporary geopolitics, globalisation, North-South relations, popular geopolitics, nuclear proliferation, environmental issues, and human rights.

Opening with a discussion of key visions of world politics after the end of the cold war (Fukuyma versus Huntington), Dodds then sums up the key features of today's global system: global information and financial networks, the 'sovereign' state, regionalism, and the role of the media in wars and humanitarian emergencies. His second chapter deals with theoretical approaches in the field of international relations and political geography, opposing critical geopolitics to realism and liberalism. Realism matches the Westphalian model (world politics as a system of sovereign states), idealism the United Nations model, and critical geopolitics the globalisation of world politics. The chapter closes with a summary of arguments for and against the globalisation thesis. 'Global Apartheid' is the title of the third chapter, which deepens the analysis of North-South relations. The fourth chapter is much different in kind. It deals with a less conventional topic: popular geopolitics. Dodds exposes geopolitical visions in popular culture, such as in film, television, magazines, and music, but he only mentions the Internet to assess its potential, as if the area still needs to be examined by critical geopolitics.[6] The following three chapters deal with the globalisation of danger through nuclear proliferation, environmental issues, and humanitarianism respectively. In his conclusion, Dodds emphasises the increasing inequality in world politics caused by the globalisation process, which amplifies original differences in capacities between the different peoples, states, or regions of the world. The book also contains a geopolitical quiz, a glossary, and references for further reading. All things considered, this textbook is a challenging and highly recommendable introduction to critical geopolitics.

Also worth mentioning are two other books, somewhat older and somewhat different in kind; one was published by a Dutch geographer, the other by a Finnish one. Gertjan Dijkink explores the relation between national identity and geopolitical visions (Dijkink 1996). The book presents nine concise, but fascinating, portraits of the geopolitical visions of several states in the light of their geography and history. The selected cases cover all continents but Africa, and consist of Germany, Great Britain, the USA (at two different periods), Argentina, Australia, Russia, Serbia, Iraq, and India. In the second of these books, Anssi Paasi elaborates on the relations between geopolitics, nationalism, and the institutionalisation of territories in his detailed study of the Finnish-Russian border (Paasi 1996). The book includes a theoretical discussion of the formation of regions, the role of boundaries, and geography and nationalism. Furthermore, it consists of a multiscale analysis of the institutionalisation of the Finnish territory, dealing with geopolitics and nationalism before and since independence and with the local experience of the Finnish-Russian boundary in the locality of Värtsilä.

More recently, the British historical geographer Michael Heffernan published *The Meaning of Europe: Geography and Geopolitics* (1998). Heffernan analyses visions of Europe, the actors that voice them, and the context in which they operate. The book is organised chronologically. The first chapter is devoted to the territorialisation of power in secular Europe from the Renaissance to the late-nineteenth century. It presents the main stages of the evolution of the modern political map of Europe, both nationally (the formation of specific states) and internationally (the Treaty of Westphalia in 1648, the Napoleonic Wars, and the Treaty of Vienna in 1815). The second chapter deals with *fin de siècle* geopolitics, a period that witnessed the culmination of European hegemony and the horrors of industrial warfare. Chapter three covers the interbellum and Second World War, while chapter four deals with cold-war geopolitics, the division of Europe into East and West, European integration, the 1989 revolutions, and the umpteenth redrawing of the political map of Europe. A short concluding chapter explores the prospects of the idea of Europe for the twenty-first century. With a substantial bibliography and more than 60 maps, the book is an outstanding introduction to the evolution of Europe's political geography.

Lastly, we should turn to journals. The French and Italian journals *Hérodote* and *LiMes* have already been mentioned, as has *Political Geography*. The repossession of geopolitics by geographers is illustrated by the change of name of a young journal into *Geopolitics* (it was established in 1995 as *Geopolitics and International Boundaries*). Its new editorial staff consists of political geographers, the two editors David Newman and John Agnew, and two associate editors, Gearóid Ó Tuathail and Mark Bassin. This journal, like *Political Geography*, presents contributions from the two academic approaches to geopolitics distinguished above.

The first issue edited by David Newman (Vol.3, issue 1) has also been published as a book, entitled *Boundaries, Territory and Postmodernity* (Newman 1999). The editor introduces the collection of nine papers with an assessment of the comeback of geopolitics. He defines geopolitics as a multidisciplinary approach focusing on the changing role of the state and the dynamic nature of the relationships between states. He then presents five key themes of the contemporary research agenda: globalisation and the changing function of state sovereignty; the deterritorialisation of the state and its consequences for boundaries; the study of geopolitical texts, maps, narratives, and traditions; the geopolitical imagination (that is, the conception of the relative location of a state in the global system); and, lastly, 'reterritorialisation' in the light of the importance of ethnic identities and the strength of territorial ideologies (Newman, 1999b). The first paper, by Mathias Albert (1999), examines post-modernist analyses in the field of international relations (the discipline), especially regarding the study of borders and boundaries. Then come three papers dealing with the impact of globalisation on state organisation. Fabrizio Eva (1999) discusses the fiction of the 'anarchy' of the Westphalian state system and the informal system of world government already in place. Gearóid Ó Tuathail (1999) opposes the Westphalian and post-Westphalian classifications of the world political map in the light of their notion of risk. During the cold war, risks and threats were primarily territorial ones, while present discourses underline global dangers. Simon Dalby (1999) discusses the position of the underdeveloped world in the global system. Instead of globalisation, he speaks of global apartheid in order to expose the uncomfortable condition of poor countries. The analogy points at the apartheid system in South Africa, where homelands were seen as both a source of labour for the white regime and perceived by it as a major threat to the system.

    The next three papers deal more specifically with the changing role of boundaries and issues of territorial compartmentalisation. Alan Hudson (1999) examines institutional mechanisms for the management of border disputes and extraterritorial jurisdictional claims (when regulatory authorities seek to extend their authority beyond their own borders). Stanley Brunn (1999) explores the impact of new information and communication technologies on the internal policies and the external relations of the state. Increased flows of transborder information make nodes more important than territory. To replace the Treaty of Westphalia, we may need a Treaty of Silicon. Anssi Paasi (1999) discusses the role of boundaries by contrasting deterritorialisation (prompted by processes of globalisation) and reterritorialisation (through nationalist and ethno-regionalist mobilisations). To replace the modernist conception of boundaries as fixed lines, he conceptualises them as social processes. They are used as instruments of social distinction. For his empirical illustration, he examines the changing meanings of the Finnish-Russian border (see above). The last two papers present case studies of the process of reterritorialisation. Vladimir Kolossov and John O'Loughlin (1999) discuss pseudo-states as a challenge to the stability of the state system. The breakdown of the Soviet Union has led to the creation of many of these pseudo-states. The two authors present a comparison of the conflicts in four of them (Transniestra, Abkhazia, Chechnya, and Nagorno-Karabahk) and a case study of the Transdniester Moldovan Republic. Lastly, Mira Sucharov (1999) examines the decision by Israel and the PLO to enter into negotiations related to the 1993 Oslo accords. His findings reveal the importance of ideational and discursive factors in the pursuit of the resolution of territorial conflict, especially the degree of exclusionary discourse used to consolidate political community.

Obviously, this journal is likely to become an important forum for those interested in geopolitics, geographers or otherwise (see the present issue or the forthcoming issue on French geopolitical approaches mentioned above), but general geographical journals have also been paying attention to the topic. A recent special issue of *GeoJournal* (Vol.46, No.4) was devoted to it. The introduction by the special issue's editor, Herman Van der Wusten (1998), presents the six contributions and sums up a few important problems that are not tackled in the collection but need our attention, such as the change in the nature of the state system, the bias of geopolitical analysis toward the analysis of certain states and certain regions (leaving other states under-researched), and the increasing competition between states over the use of the seas and airspace. It is followed by a comprehensive review of geopolitical publications in the 1990s by Virginie Mamadouh, who distinguishes four approaches (neo-classical geopolitics, subversive geopolitics, non-geopolitics, and critical geopolitics), but emphasises the shift from geostrategical toward geo-economical stakes common to all four approaches (Mamadouh 1998a; 1998b). Hermann Kreutzmann (1998) analyses the evolution of Huntington's analysis from modernisation theory in the 1960s to the *Clash of Civilizations* in the 1990s. Jan Nijman (1998) discusses the foreign-policy views of Madeleine Albright, the current US Secretary of State, and especially her policy regarding the enlargement of NATO. She differs from both her typically American predecessors (such as George Schultz, James A. Baker III, and Warren Christopher), who had no prior interests in international relations and were not particularly concerned with European issues, and most influential European-born practitioners involved in US foreign policy, namely, Henry Kissinger and Zbigniew Brzezinski. Albright (born in Prague in 1937) combines a European awareness of geopolitics with an American idealism. While she is very sensitive to the problematic of central and eastern European countries, she ostensibly denies the influence of geography and history upon their near future. Jacques Lévy (1998) addresses the current changes in France's geopolitics regarding its international relations (especially French policy in Africa) and the changing discourses of scholars and experts. Klaus Kost (1998) discusses anti-Semitism in German geography in the period 1900–45, exposing the prevalent anti-Semitism of geographical publications and underlining the continuity with the later school of *Geopolitik*. The contribution by Gertjan Dijkink (1998) sketches a cross-national research agenda for the study of the relationship between the geopolitical codes of those practising statecraft and popular representations.

Conclusion

This review article only reveals part of the huge body of literature produced by geographers in the field of geopolitics, not to mention the related work of scholars from neighbouring disciplines, especially international relations (for a more comprehensive review, see Mamadouh 1998a). It has been limited to the main books, key journals, and special issues. It should be enough to convince the reader that geographers have successfully reclaimed geopolitics, and that a huge research agenda has been outlined for geographers in general and for this young and renamed journal in particular.

More of this literature has been published, and there is more to come. Kathleen Braden and Fred Shelly, two American geographers, have prepared a textbook entitled *Engaging Geopolitics* and intended to provide an 'introduction to the influence of geography, demography and economics on politics and international relations'. Moreover, a volume edited by Klaus Dodds and David Atkinson is coming out soon, and will cover a century of geopolitical traditions. It includes studies of national traditions (Japan, Spain, and Italy), but also religious traditions (for example, Jesuits and Hindus) and recent renegotiations of geopolitics (*Hérodote* in France, changing discourses in Israel, popular representations, and ecological discourses). Also forthcoming is a special issue of *Geopolitics* devoted to French geopolitics with contributions by Lévy, Raffestin, Retaillé, Dollfus, Badie, Smouts, Laïdi, Lacoste, Foucher, Prevalikis, and Debie. Last but certainly not least, books by Davis Slater, Timothy Luke, and Gearóid Ó Tuathail have also been announced.

NOTES

1. Quoted in J.R. Short (1993: 18). See also W.H. Parker (1982).
2. 'Geopolinomics' is a neologism underscoring the addition of economics to geopolitics (Demko and Wood 1994b: 10–11, 13; Corbridge 1994: 297–8).
3. See Ó Tuathail (1996a: 56 and 270, note 10).
4. Quoted in Dodds (2000: 158).
5. There is no view from nowhere, as Agnew puts it (1998: 125).

6. However, there are already fascinating accounts of the digital world, such as the contributions to *Rethinking Geopolitics* (Ó Tuathail and Dalby 1998a) (see above).

REFERENCES

Agnew, J. 1994. Global hegemony versus national economy: the United States in the new world order. In *Reordering the World: Geopolitical Perspectives on the 21st Century*, eds. Demko, G.J. and Wood, W.B., 1994a, pp.269–79. Boulder, Westview.

—— 1998. *Geopolitics: Re-visioning World Politics*. London, Routledge.

Agnew, J. and Corbridge, S., 1995. *Mastering Space: Hegemony, Territory and International Political Economy*. London, Routledge.

Albert, M. 1999. On boundaries, territory and postmodernity: An international relations perspective. In *Boundaries, Territory and Postmodernity*, ed. Newman, D., 1999a. London, Frank Cass.

Almond. G. and Verba, S. 1963. *The Civic Culture: Political Attitudes and Democracy in Five Nations*. Princeton, NJ, Princeton University Press.

Bonura, C.J. Jr. 1998. The occulted geopolitics of nation and culture: Situating political culture within the construction of geopolitical ontologies. In *Rethinking Geopolitics*, eds. Ó Tuathail, G. and Dalby, S., 1998a, pp.86–105. London, Routledge.

Brunn, S.D. 1999. A Treaty of Silicon for the Treaty of Westphalia? New territorial dimensions of modern statehood. In *Boundaries, Territory and Postmodernity*, ed. Newman, D., 1999a. London, Frank Cass.

Brunn, S.D. and Jones, J.A. 1994. Geopolitical information and communications in shrinking and expanding worlds: 1900–2100. In *Reordering the World: Geopolitical Perspectives on the 21st Century*, eds. Demko, G.J. and Wood, W.B., 1994a, pp.301–22. Boulder, Westview.

Brunn, S.D., Jones J.A. and O'Lear, S. 1999. Geopolitical information and communications in the twenty-first century. In *Reordering the World: Geopolitical Perspectives on the 21st Century*, eds. Demko, G.J. and Wood, W.B., 1999. Boulder, Westview.

Brzezinski, Z. 1997. *The Grand Chessboard, American Primacy and its Geostrategic Imperatives*. New York, Basic Books.

Charlesworth, A. 1994. Contested places of memory: The case of Auschwitz. *Environment and Planning D: Society and Space*, 12:5, pp.579–94.

Chauprade, A. and Thual, F. 1998. *Dictionnaire de géopolitiques: états, concepts, auteurs*. Paris, Ellipses.

Clarke, D.B., Doel, M.A. and McDonough, F. 1996. Holocaust topologies: Singularity, politics, space. *Political Geography*, 15:6/7, pp.457–89.

Claval, P. 1994. *Géopolitique et géostratégie. La pensée politique, l'espace et le territoire au XXe siècle*. Paris, Nathan.

Cohen, S.B. 1994. Geopolitics in the new world era: A new perspective on an old discipline. In *Reordering the World: Geopolitical Perspectives on the 21st Century*, eds. Demko, G.J. and Wood, W.B., 1994a, pp.15–48. Boulder, Westview.

Corbridge, C. 1994. Maximizing entropy? New geopolitical orders and the internationalization of business. In *Reordering the World: Geopolitical Perspectives on the 21st Century*, eds. Demko, G.J. and Wood, W.B., 1994a, pp.281–300. Boulder, Westview.

Crampton, A. and Ó Tuathail, G. 1996. Intellectuals, institutions and ideology: the case of Robert Strausz-Hupé and 'American geopolitics'. *Political Geography*, 15:6/7, pp.533–55.

Cutter, S.L. 1994. Exploiting, conserving, and preserving natural resources. In *Reordering the World: Geopolitical Perspectives on the 21st Century*, eds. Demko, G.J. and Wood, W.B., 1994a, pp.123–40. Boulder, Westview.

Dalby, S. 1990. *Creating the Second Cold War, the Discourses of Politics*. London, Pinter.

—— 1991. Critical geopolitics: Discourse, difference and dissent. *Environment and Planning D: Society and Space*, 9, pp.261–83.

—— 1994. Gender and critical geopolitics: Reading security discourse in the new world disorder. *Environment and Planning D: Society and Space*, 12:5, pp.595–612.

—— 1996a. Reading Rio, writing the world: The *New York Times* and the 'Earth Summit'. *Political Geography*, 15:6/7, pp.593–613.

1996b. Writing critical geopolitics: Campbell, Ó Tuathail, Reynolds and dissident skepticism. *Political Geography*, 15:6/7, pp.655–60.

1998. Geopolitics and global security: Culture, identity, and the 'POGO syndrome'. In *Rethinking Geopolitics*, eds. Ó Tuathail, G. and Dalby, S., 1998a, pp.295–313. London, Routledge.

Dalby, S. 1999. Globalization or global apartheid? Boundaries and knowledge in postmodern times. In *Boundaries, Territory and Postmodernity*, ed. Newman, D. 1999a. London, Frank Cass.

Dalby, S. and Ó Tuathail, G. 1996. Editorial introduction: The critical geopolitics constellation: Problematizing fusions of geographical knowledge and power. *Political Geography*, 15:6/7, pp.451–6.

Demko, G.J. 1994. Population, politics, and geography: A global perspective. In *Reordering the World: Geopolitical Perspectives on the 21st Century*, eds. Demko, G.J. and Wood, W.B., 1994a, pp.179–90. Boulder, Westview.

Demko, G.J. and Wood, W.B. (eds.) 1994a. *Reordering the World: Geopolitical Perspectives on the 21st Century*. Boulder, Westview.

1994b. Introduction: International relations through the prism of geography. In *Reordering the World: Geopolitical Perspectives on the 21st Century*, eds. Demko, G.J. and Wood, W.B., 1994a, pp.3–13. Boulder, Westview.

1999. *Reordering the World: Geopolitical Perspectives of the 21st Century*. Boulder, Westview.

Der Derian, J. 1998. 'All but war is simulation'. In *Rethinking Geopolitics*, eds. Ó Tuathail, G. and Dalby, S., 1998a, pp.261–73. London, Routledge.

Dijkink, G. 1996. *National Identity and Geopolitical Visions: Maps of Pride and Pain*. London, Routledge.

1998. Geopolitical codes and popular representations. *GeoJournal*, 46:4, pp.397–403.

Dodds, K. 1996. The 1982 Falklands War and a critical geopolitical eye: Steve Bell and the If... cartoons. *Political Geography*, 15:6/7, pp.571–92.

1998. Enframing Bosnia: The geopolitical iconography of Steve Bell. In *Rethinking Geopolitics*, eds. Ó Tuathail, G. and Dalby, S., 1998a, pp.170–97. London, Routledge.

2000. *Geopolitics in a Changing World*. Harlow, Prentice Hall, Pearson Education.

Dodds, K. and Sidaway, J.D. 1994. Locating critical geopolitics. *Environment and Planning D: Society and Space*, 12:5, pp.525–46.

Doel, M.A. and Clarke, D.B. 1998. Figuring the Holocaust: Singularity and the purification of space. In *Rethinking Geopolitics*, eds. Ó Tuathail, G. and Dalby, S., 1998a, pp.29–61. London, Routledge.

Drake, C. 1994. The United Nations and NGOs future roles. In *Reordering the World: Geopolitical Perspectives on the 21st Century*, eds. Demko, G.J. and Wood, W.B., 1994a, pp.243–67. Boulder, Westview.

Eva, F. 1999. International boundaries, geopolitics and the postmodern territorial discourse: The functional fiction. In *Boundaries, Territory and Postmodernity*, ed. Newman, D., 1999a. London, Frank Cass.

Flint, C. 1999. Changing times, changing scales: World politics and political geography since 1890. In *Reordering the World: Geopolitical Perspectives on the 21st Century*, eds. Demko, G.J. and Wood, W.B., 1999. Boulder, Westview.

Foucher, M. 1991. *Fronts et frontières: un tour du monde géopolitique, Nouvelle édition entièrement refondue*, (first edition 1988). Paris, Fayard.

(ed.) 1993. *Fragments d'Europe: Atlas de l'Europe médiane et orientale*. Paris, Fayard.

(ed.) 1996. *Les défis de sécurité en Europe médiane*. Paris, La Découverte.

Fukushima, Y. 1997. Japanese geopolitics and its background: What is the real legacy of the past? *Political Geography*, 16:5, pp.407–21.

Geopolitics and International Boundaries (1995–), since 1999: *Geopolitics*.

Girot, P. and Kofman, E. (eds.) 1987. *International Geopolitical Analysis: A Selection from Hérodote*. London, Croom Helm.

Häkli, J. 1998a. Discourse in the production of political space: Decolonizing the symbolism of provinces in Finland. *Political Geography*, 17:3, pp.331–63.

1998b. Manufacturing provinces: Theorizing the encounters between governmental and popular 'geographs' in Finland. In *Rethinking Geopolitics*, eds. Ó Tuathail, G. and Dalby, S., 1998a, pp.131–51. London, Routledge.

Hefferman, M. 1998. *The Meaning of Europe, Geography and Geopolitics*. London, Arnold.

Hendrikson, A.K. 1994. The power and politics of maps. In *Reordering the World: Geopolitical Perspectives on the 21st Century*, eds. Demko, G.J. and Wood, W.B., 1994a, pp.49–70. Boulder, Westview.

Herbert, S. 1996. The geopolitics of the police: Foucault, disciplinary power and the tactics of the Los Angeles Department. *Political Geography*, 15:1, pp.47–57.

Hérodote: Stratégies-géographies-idéologies (1976–), since 1982: *Hérodote: revue de géographie et de géopolitique*.

Hudson, A. 1999. Beyond the borders: globalisation, sovereignty and extra-territoriality. In *Boundaries, Territory and Postmodernity*, ed. Newman, D., 1999a. London: Frank Cass.

Inglehart, Ronald. 1990. *Culture shift in advanced industrial society*. Princeton, NJ: Princeton University Press.

Kasperson, R.E. 1994. Global environmental hazards: Political issues in societal responses. In *Reordering the World: Geopolitical Perspectives on the 21st Century*, eds. Demko, G.J. and Wood, W.B., 1994a, pp.141–66. Boulder, Westview.

Kliot, N. and Waterman, S. (eds.) 1991. *The Political Geography of Conflict and Peace*. London, Belhaven.

Knight, D.B. 1994. People together, yet apart: Rethinking territory, sovereignty, and identities. In *Reordering the World: Geopolitical Perspectives on the 21st Century*, eds. Demko, G.J. and Wood, W.B., 1994a, pp.71–86. Boulder, Westview.

Kolossov, V. and O'Loughlin, J. 1999. Pseudo-states as harbingers of a new geopolitics: The example of the Trans-Dniester republic (TMR). In *Boundaries, Territory and Postmodernity*, ed. Newman, D. 1999a. London, Frank Cass.

Korinman, M. 1990. *Quand l'Allemange pensait le monde; Grandeur et décadence d'une géopolitique*. Paris, Fayard.

1991. *Continents perdus: les précurseurs de la géopolitique Allemande*. Paris, Economica.

Kost, K. 1998. Anti-Semitism in German geography 1900–1945. *GeoJournal*, 46:4, pp.389–95.

Kreutzmann, H. 1998. From modernization theory towards the 'clash of civilizations': Directions and paradigm shifts in Samuel Huntington's analysis and prognosis of global development. *GeoJournal*, 46:4, pp.359–69.

Lacoste, Y. (ed.) 1993, 1998. *Dictionnaire de géopolitique*. Paris, Flammarion.

(ed.) 1998a. *Dictionnaire de géopolitique des états*. Paris, Flammarion.

1998b. *Vive la Nation! Destin d'une idée géopolitique*. Paris, Fayard.

Lévy, J. 1998. A twilight zone: Identity crisis in French geopolitics. *GeoJournal*, 46:4, pp.383–88.

LiMes: rivista italiana di geopolitica (1993–)

LiMes: revue française de géopolitique (1996–)

Loyer, B. 1997. *Géopolitique du Pays Basque, nations et nationalismes en Espagne*. Paris, L'Harmattan.

Luke, T.W. 1994. Placing power/sitting space: The politics of global and local in the New World Order. *Environment and Planning D: Society and Space*, 12:5, pp.613–28.

Luke, T.W. 1996. Governmentality and contragovernmentality: Rethinking sovereignty and territoriality after the Cold War, *Political Geography*, 15:6/7, pp.491–507.

Luke, T.W. 1998. Running flat out on the road ahead: Nationality, sovereignty, and territoriality in the world of the information superhighway. In *Rethinking Geopolitics*, eds. Ó Tuathail, G. and Dalby, S., 1998a, pp.274–94. London, Routledge.

Mamadouh, V. 1998a. Geopolitics in the nineties: One flag, many meanings. *GeoJournal*, 46:4, pp.341–57.

1998b. Reference books on geopolitics: A lexicon, a reader and three dictionaries. *GeoJournal*, 46:4, pp.405–9.

Mofson, P. 1994. Global ecopolitics. In *Reordering the World: Geopolitical Perspectives on the 21st Century*, eds. Demko, G.J. and Wood, W.B., 1994a, pp.167–77. Boulder, Westview.

Morrill, R. 1994. Electoral geography and gerrymandering: Space and politics. In *Reordering the World: Geopolitical Perspectives on the 21st Century*, eds. Demko, G.J. and Wood, W.B., 1994a, pp.101–19. Boulder, Westview.

Murphy, A.B. 1994. International law and the sovereign state system: Challenges to the *status quo*. In *Reordering the World: Geopolitical Perspectives on the 21st Century*, eds. Demko, G.J. and Wood, W.B., 1994a, pp.209–24. Boulder, Westview.

Newman, D. (ed.) 1999a. *Boundaries Territory and Postmodernity*. Cass Series in Geopolitics, No.1. Frank Cass, London.

1999b. Geopolitics renaissant: Territory, sovereignty, and the world political map. In *Boundaries, Territory and Postmodernity*, ed. Newman, D., 1999a. London, Frank Cass.

Nietschmann, B. 1994. The fourth world: Nations versus states. In *Reordering the World: Geopolitical Perspectives on the 21st Century*, eds. Demko, G.J. and Wood, W.B., 1994a, pp.225–42. Boulder, Westview.

Nijman, J. 1998. Madeleine Albright and the geopolitics of Europe. *GeoJournal*, 46:4, pp.371–82.

O'Loughlin, J. and Heske, H. 1991. From '*Geopolitik*' to '*géopolitique*': Converting a discipline for war to a discipline for peace. In *The Political Geography of Conflict and Peace*, eds. Kliot, N. and Waterman, S., pp.37–59. London, Belhaven.

O'Loughlin, J. and Van der Wusten, H. (eds.) 1993. *The New Political Geography of Eastern Europe*. London, Belhaven.

O'Sullivan, P. 1986. *Geopolitics*. New York, St Martin's Press.

1995. Geopolitical force fields. *Geographical Analysis*, 27:2, pp.176–81.

Ó Tuathail, G. 1992. 'Pearl Harbour without bombs': A critical geopolitics of the US-Japan FSX debate. *Environment and Planning A*, 24, pp.975–94.

1994a. (Dis)placing geopolitics: Writing on the maps of global politics. *Environment and Planning D: Society and Space*, 12:5, pp.525–46.

1994b. Critical geopolitics and development theory: Intensifying the dialogue. *Transactions of the Institute of British Geographers*, 19, pp.228–33.

1996a. *Critical Geopolitics: The Politics of Writing Global Space*. London, Routledge.

1996b. Review essay: Dissident IR and the identity politics narrative: A sympathetically skeptical perspective. *Political Geography*, 15:6/7, pp.647–53.

1996c. The patterned mess of history and the writing of critical geopolitics: A reply to Dalby. *Political Geography*, 15:6/7, pp.661–5.

1998. Postmodern geopolitics? The modern geopolitical imagination and beyond. In *Rethinking Geopolitics*, eds. Ó Tuathail, G. and Dalby, S., 1998a, pp.16–38. London, Routledge.

1999. De-territorialised threats and global dangers: Geopolitics and risk society. In *Boundaries, Territory and Postmodernity*, ed. Newman, D., 1999a. London, Frank Cass.

Ó Tuathail, G. and Agnew, J. 1992. Geopolitics and discourse; Practical geopolitical reasoning in American foreign policy. *Political Geography*, 11:2, pp.190–204.

Ó Tuathail, G. and Dalby, S. 1994. Critical geopolitics: Unfolding spaces for thought in geography and global politics. *Environment and Planning D: Society and Space*, 12:5, pp.513–4.

(eds.) 1998a. *Rethinking Geopolitics*. London, Routledge.

1998b. Introduction: Rethinking geopolitics: Towards a critical geopolitics. In *Rethinking Geopolitics*, eds. Ó Tuathail, G. and Dalby, S., 1998a, pp.1–15. London, Routledge.

Ó Tuathail, G., Dalby, S. and Routledge, P. (eds.) 1998. *The Geopolitics Reader*. London, Routledge.

Paasi, A. 1996. *Territories, Boundaries, and Consciousness; The Changing Geographies of the Finnish-Russian Border*. Chichester, Wiley.

1999. Boundaries as social processes: Territoriality in the world of flows. In *Boundaries, Territory and Postmodernity*, ed. Newman, D., 1999a. London, Frank Cass.

Parker, G. 1985. *Western Geopolitical Thought in the Twentieth Century*. London, Croom Helm.

1988. *The Geopolitics of Domination*. London, Routledge.

1998. *Geopolitics: Past, Present and Future*. London, Pinter.

Parker, W.H. 1982. *Mackinder, Geography as an Aid to Statecraft*. Oxford, Clarendon Press.

Pepper, D. and Jenkins, A. (eds.) 1985. *The Geography of Peace and War*. Oxford, Basil Blackwell.

Political Geography Quarterly (1982–), since 1992: *Political Geography*.

Price, M.D. 1999. Nongovernmental organizations on the geopolitical front line. In *Reordering the World: Geopolitical Perspectives on the 21st Century*, eds. Demko, G.J. and Wood, W.B., 1999. Boulder, Westview.

Routledge, P. 1994. Backstreets, barricades, and blackouts: Urban terrains of resistance in Nepal. *Environment and Planning D: Society and Space*, 12:5, pp.559–79.

1996. Critical geopolitics and terrains of resistance. *Political Geography*, 15:6/7, pp.509–31.

1998. Going globile: Spatiality, embodiment, and media-tion in the Zapatista insurgency. In *Rethinking Geopolitics*, eds. Ó Tuathail, G. and Dalby, S., 1998a, pp.240–60. London, Routledge.

Rygiel, K. 1998. Stabilizing borders: The geopolitics of national identity construction in Turkey. In *Rethinking Geopolitics*, eds. Ó Tuathail, G. and Dalby, S., 1998a, pp.106–30. London, Routledge.

Sharp, J.P. 1996. Hegemony, popular culture and geopolitics: The *Reader's Digest* and the construction of danger. *Political Geography*, 15:6/7, pp.557–70.

1998. Reel geographies of the new world order: Patriotism, masculinity, and geopolitics in post-cold war American movies. In *Rethinking Geopolitics*, eds. Ó Tuathail, G. and Dalby, S., 1998a, pp.152–69. London, Routledge.

Short, J.R. 1993. *An Introduction to Political Geography*, second edition. London, Routledge.

Sidaway, J.D. 1994. Geopolitics, geography and 'terrorism' in the Middle East. *Environment and Planning D: Society and Space*, 12:3, pp.357–72.

1998. What is in a gulf? From the 'arc of crisis' to the Gulf War. In *Rethinking Geopolitics*, eds. Ó Tuathail, G. and Dalby, S., 1998a, pp.224–39. London, Routledge.

Slater, D. 1993. The geopolitical imagination and the enframing of development theory. *Transactions of the Institute of British Geographers*, 18, pp.419–37.

1994. Reimagining the geopolitics of development: Continuing the dialogue. *Transactions of the Institute of British Geographers*, 19, pp.233–9.

1997. Geopolitical imaginations across the North-South divide: Issues of different development and power. *Political Geography*, 16:8, pp.631–53.

Sparke, M. 1996. Negotiating national action: Free trade, constitutional debate and the gendered geopolitics of Canada. *Political Geography*, 15:6/7, pp.615–39.

1998. Outsides inside patriotism: The Oklahoma bombing and the displacement of heartland geopolitics. In *Rethinking Geopolitics*, eds. Ó Tuathail, G. and Dalby, S., 1998a, pp.198–223. London, Routledge.

Stephanson, A. 1998. Fourteen notes on the very concept of the cold war. In *Rethinking Geopolitics*, eds. Ó Tuathail, G. and Dalby, S., 1998a, pp.62–85. London, Routledge.

Sucharov, M. 1999. Regional identity and the sovereignty principle: Explaining Israeli-Palestinian peacemaking. In *Boundaries, Territory and Postmodernity*, ed. Newman, D., 1999a. London, Frank Cass.

Taylor, P.J. 1990. *Britain and the Cold War, 1945 as Geopolitical Transition*. London, Pinter.

(ed.) 1993. *Political Geography of the Twentieth Century: A Global Analysis*. London: Belhaven Press.

Thomas, B.L. 1994. International boundaries: Lines in the sand (and the sea). In *Reordering the World: Geopolitical Perspectives on the 21st Century*, eds. Demko, G.J. and Wood, W.B., 1994a, pp.87–99. Boulder, Westview.

Van der Wusten, H. 1998. Geopolitics: Its different faces, its renewed popularity. *GeoJournal*, 46:4, pp.338–40.

Weber, C. 1994. Shoring up a sea of signs: How the Caribbean Basin Initiative framed the US invasion of Grenada. *Environment and Planning D: Society and Space*, 12:5, pp.547–8.

Williams, C.H. (ed.) 1993. *The Political Geography of the New World Order*. London, Belhaven.

Wood, W.B. 1994, Crossing the line: Geopolitics of international migration. In *Reordering the World: Geopolitical Perspectives on the 21st Century*, eds. Demko, G.J. and Wood, W.B., 1994a, pp.191–205. Boulder, Westview.

1999a. International migration: One step forward, two steps back. In *Reordering the World: Geopolitical Perspectives on the 21st Century*, eds. Demko, G.J. and Wood, W.B., 1999. Boulder, Westview.

1999b. Geo-analysis for the next century: New data and tools for sustainable development. In *Reordering the World: Geopolitical Perspectives on the 21st Century*, eds. Demko, G.J. and Wood, W.B., 1999. Boulder, Westview.

Wood, W.B. and Demko, G.J. (eds.) 1999. Introduction: Political geography for the next millennium. In *Reordering the World. Geopolitical Perspectives on the 21st Century*, eds. Demko, G.J. and Wood, W.B., 1999. Boulder, Westview.

Borderless Worlds?
Problematising Discourses of
Deterritorialisation

GEARÓID Ó TUATHAIL (GERARD TOAL)

We live, we are constantly told, in an era of revolutionary changes. In contrast to the revolutions of earlier times, our contemporary revolutionary movements are technological and informational, economic and geographic. They promise utopian futures and limitless freedoms, though the utopian future they envisage is a technologically enveloping design for digital living, and the limitless freedom they project is the freedom of unleashed markets and a borderless world of friction-free capitalism.[1] Instead of liberation by social and nationalist movements, it is socio-machinic networks, collectives of corporations and computers, that will overthrow the oppressive ancient regime of the state and deliver us from taxes and territory. Instead of soil, we will have software. Instead of territorial being stuck in place, we will have telemetrical becoming on the world wide web. Our capitalist technoculture already proclaims this promise of transcendence: 'Where do you want to go today?' (Microsoft); 'Solutions for a small planet' (IBM); 'Is this a great time or what?' (MCI-World Com).

Deterritorialisation, the French critic Paul Virilio declared some time ago, is the question for the end of this century.[2] The term is one amongst many others – globalisation, glocalisation, postcolonial, postnational, transnational, third space, cyberspace – that have been coined to try to describe the rearranging and restructuring of spatial relations as a consequence of the technological, material and geopolitical transformations of the late twentieth century.[3] Deterritorialisation is the name given to the problematic of territory losing its significance and power in everyday life. Territory, the concept suggests, is no longer the stable and unquestioned actuality it once was. Rather than it being an assumed given, its position and status are now in question.

Historically delimited in the process of state formation and nation building, the concept of territory is contextually dependent upon the development of state bureaucratic powers (agencies empowered with instruments of visualisation and survey), military institutions and technology capabilities (especially the logistical systems enabling spatial occupation and movement), identity regimes and socialisation structures (like schools, churches and civil society networks), and telecommunication systems (like national literacy and media institutions).[4] Rather than territory we should really speak of culturally contextual and technopolitically contingent territorialities or regimes of territoriality. Territory, therefore, should never be conceptualised in isolation for it is part of a complex of state power, geography and identity. Put somewhat differently, territory is a regime of practices triangulated between institutionalisations of power, materialisations of place and idealisations of 'the people'.

To speak of deterritorialisation in contemporary discourse is to speak of a generalised dismantling of the complex of geography, power and identity that supposedly defined and delimited everyday life in the developed world for most of the twentieth century. It is to speak of a new condition of speed and informationalisation, of the transgression of inherited borders, the transcendence of assumed divides, and the advent of a more 'global' world. Though regimes of territoriality are constantly in flux and under negotiation, discourses of deterritorialisation tend to ascribe a unique transcendency to the contemporary condition, defining it as a moment of overwhelming newness.[5] Such functionally anti-historical notions of deterritorialisation find a variety of different expressions in political, economic and techno-cultural knowledge.

Politically the idea of deterritorialisation is a central notion in the Clinton administration's consciousness of change. President Clinton's first inaugural address declared that '[c]ommunications and commerce are global; investment is mobile; technology is almost magical; and ambition for a better life is now universal…There is no longer division between what is foreign and what is domestic – the world economy, the world environment, the world AIDS crisis, the world arms race – they affect us all'.[6] In office, Clinton's administration moved to define a so-called 'Clinton Doctrine' that responded to the challenges of globalisation, borderless worlds and 'the Information Age' (a concept that was central to the administration's rhetoric and self-image) by promoting free trade agreements like the NAFTA, pursing technological initiatives like a national information superhighway, and pushing the enlargement of the world community of so-called 'market democracies'.[7]

Economically, deterritorialisation is held to be a consequence of an unstoppable globalisation of previously discrete national markets and economies. The Clinton administration's former Labour Secretary Robert Reich proclaimed the coming irrelevancy of corporate nationality as previously national champions restructure themselves into global webs of production, sub-contracting, strategic alliances and sales. '"American" corporations and "American" industries', he declared, 'are ceasing to exist in any form that can meaningfully be distinguished from the rest of the global economy. Nor, for that matter, is the American economy as a whole retaining a distinct identity…'.[8] Reich's work is a strategic response to such deterritorialisation, a 'work of nations' agenda emphasising educational training, infrastructural investments, and skills development for state administrators to promote and cultivate upon their territorial patch of the global economy.

Kenichi Ohmae's work suggests organisational strategies for transnational business managers to take advantage of what he sees as the coming borderless world and the death of the nation-state.[9] In Ohmae's idealised world 'multinational companies are truly the servants of demanding consumers around the world'.[10] 'Old-fashioned bureaucrats', however, keep trying to hinder the natural development of a borderless world. 'They create barriers and artificial controls over what should be the free flow of goods and money.'[11] Inflating observations of the Japanese marketing strategy of global localisation, the borderless organisational possibilities of global telecommunications, the emergence of a transnational 'foreign exchange' market, and the increasing importance of foreign direct investment as an economic development strategy for states, Ohmae envisions a world where national interest has lost much of its meaning and where the 'national soil' refers not to identity but to the supportive environment needed by companies trying to grow their businesses.[12] He celebrates this emergent condition of statelessness and nationlessness, declaring in conclusion that he would happily begin paying a third of his taxes to an international fund dedicated to solving the world's problems, a third to his local community and the last third to his country which, he adds, 'each year does less and less for me in terms of security or well-being and instead subsidises special interests.'[13]

This striking disillusionment with the state and disenchantment with national territory and soil is evident also in the digital culture that has grown up around the spread of informational technologies in the advanced industrial world.[14] Lurking within this culture is a strong desire to delink from territory, detach oneself from soil, and leave the physical world of territory, trouble and taxes behind.[15] Information, as the digerati are wont to declare, just wants to be free.[16] In their hubristic 'Magna Carta for the Knowledge Age' sponsored by Newt Gingrich's Progress and Freedom Foundation, the neoliberal digerati Esther Dyson, George Gilder, Jay Keyworth and Alvin Toffler proclaim that the 'central event of the twentieth century is the overthrow of matter.'[17] The longstanding power of territorial matter is being undermined by emergent telemetrical power. Existing notions of politics, territoriality and communal identity are under challenge and will eventually be replaced by a new informational civilisation. 'The meaning of freedom, structures of self-government, definition of property, nature of competition, conditions for cooperation, sense of community and nature of progress will each be redefined for the Knowledge Age – just as they were redefined for a new age of industry some 250 years ago.'[18] Yet the transcendent truths of 'the American idea' remain relevant. In keeping with the Progress and Freedom Foundation's mission to create 'a positive vision of the future founded in the historic principles of the American idea',[19] the 'Magna Carta' conceptualises cyberspace within the terms of classic American exceptionalist myths of the frontier and exploration. Cyberspace is a land of knowledge with a 'bioelectronic frontier' demanding discovery and colonisation. Exploring this frontier is 'civilisation's truest, highest calling'.[20] Although declared to be universal and borderless, cyberspace is nevertheless represented as quintessentially American.

Like Ohmae, the digerati see state bureaucracies, old-fashioned border builders, as a threat to progress on the bioelectronic frontier. Governments in the cybernetic knowledge age need to get out of the way of the pioneers of the information age. Their industrial policy should focus on 'removing the barriers to competition and massively de-regulating the fast-growing tele-communications and computing industries'.[21] Freed from the constraints of the old spatial order, cyberspace promises to open up closed markets and liberate repressed peoples, to unify an increasingly free and diverse world. In another irony lost on the neoliberal digerati, the future of human freedom supposedly lies in cyberspace, that most machinic and surveillant of domains.[22]

These different examples of discourses of deterritorialisation are, of course, sweepingly superficial representations of the complexity of boundaries, territory and the world map at the century's end. Seriously flawed though they are as conceptualisations of the contemporary world, the confident hyperbole of these discourses nevertheless has considerable ideological power and rhetorical force. This paper seeks to problematise such discourses of deterritorialisation in a general way by examining one of the more precise articulations of the phenomenon of deterritorialisation, the so-called 'end of geography' in the domain of financial markets. On the face of it, the case of global financial integration would seem to be a particularly strong instance of deterritorialisation. Rather than understanding the issue, however, as a mere confirmation of an unproblematised deterritorialisation, this paper makes three arguments about deterritorialisation discourses generally, using the case of global finance. The first argument is that discourses of deterritorialisation are ideological discourses that do not describe actuality but seek to discursively constitute and represent certain complex tendencies as both inevitable and positive developments in contemporary capitalist society. Discourses of deterritorialisation, in other words, are part of the self-interpretation of contemporary informationalised capitalism. They combine elements from many longstanding Western discourses (con)fused in a contradictory and unstable unity. For example, digital culture discourses combine a strong humanistic inheritance emphasising human freedom, liberation and fulfilment; a capitalist discourse concerning the virtues of open and transparent markets; and a discourse of technophilia which celebrates technological systems as wondrous entities that enhance human capacities and capabilities.

The second argument is that what we are dealing with is not deterritorialisation alone but a rearrangement of the identity/border/order complex that gives people, territory, and politics their meaning in the contemporary world. Deterritorialisation is not qualitatively and overwhelmingly new. Further, there is no pure transcendence of the existing complex of nationality, territoriality and statism but a rearranging of their practical functioning and meaning in a globalising and informationalising capitalist condition. The human practices organising borders, states and territories are co-evolving with socio-technical networks and informationalised capitalist relations of production and consumption. It is not simply that there is no de-territorialisation without re-territorialisation, but that both are parts of ongoing generalised processes of territorialisation.

The third argument is that the consequence of de- and re-territorialisation at the century's end is the creation of a world political map that is paradoxically more integrated and connected yet also more divided and dislocated as a result of the uneven development of the trends and tendencies associated with informationalisation and globalisation. While transformations in markets and telecommunications are creating a global village, this village is characterised by a functional global apartheid that separates and segregates certain affluent and wired neighbourhoods from other deprived and disconnected zones and neighbourhoods.[23] The development of borderless worlds does not contradict but actually hastens the simultaneous development of ever more bordered worlds characterised by stark inequalities and digital divides. The concept and practice deconstruct themselves.

Finally, the paper concludes by going beyond these arguments to question how political geographers can and should approach the technological systems that underpin many claims of deterritorialisation.

The End of Geography? Deterritorialisation and Financial Markets

One of the traditional markers of state sovereignty and territorial power is the ability of a government to print its own money and control its own financial destiny. While this power was not realised by many states, financial markets were nevertheless considered to be predominantly and undeniably territorial until the last few decades. Since the early 1970s a number of developments and tendencies have thrown the state territorial character of financial markets into question. The first of these developments was the breakdown of the Bretton Woods system of pegged exchange rates in 1971 and 1973. This ushered in a new era of floating exchange rates and stimulated the development of an extensive foreign exchange sector dedicated to managing, monitoring and profiting from the daily fluctuations of national currencies. Transnational corporations were forced to develop their own foreign exchange departments. Financial services companies became increasingly important to the conduct of international business and trade. In many instances transnationals began to borrow money outside their home country to fund their overseas projects. American transnationals in Europe, in particular, started to engage in this practice. The largest and most significant foreign exchange market that developed in the early 1970s was the so-called 'eurocurrency market', a market of and for state currencies beyond the territory of the state. The original eurocurrency market was a eurodollar deposit account made up of Chinese and Soviet government dollar deposits looking for a safe haven from hostile US government regulations. Subsequently, the market developed into a series of deposit, credit, bond and foreign exchange markets, all with the common characteristic of being beyond the national regulatory restrictions governing the currencies they were handling. The Bank of England allowed British banks to take deposits and make loans in dollars in 1958. The London subsidiaries of American banks were also allowed to do this. The eurodollar market began to grow in the 1960s as a consequence of the movement of dollars abroad by US banks to avoid restrictive financial regulations (such as the Interest Equalisation Tax and Regulation Q) and to finance the expansion of American transnationals in Europe. These markets grew tremendously after the oil price rise of 1973 and the influx of petrodollars from OPEC members looking for high rates of return, something the euromarkets could offer because they were not subject to the same reserve requirements and interest-rate restrictions as national markets and financial institutions. By the end of the 1980s the size of the eurodollar market was estimated at $2.8 trillion.[24]

A second important development was the deregulation of financial markets in the late 1970s and 1980s as a consequence of the political triumph of neoliberal ideologies in Great Britain under the rule of Margaret Thatcher and in the United States under Ronald Reagan. The abolition of many rules restricting access to certain financial centres and regulations governing national financial markets helped create a more open, international and nominally more transparent financial system in the 1980s. The best example of this tendency was the 'Big Bang' deregulating business practices in the City of London in 1986, though other reforms, such as rules governing the Tokyo Stock Exchange, were also significant.

A third development was the introduction of electronic information technology into finance and the consequent development of a whole series of new capabilities. On-line transaction processing, electronic wire transfers, automatic transaction machines and electronic data interchange radically altered the space-time relationships governing the financial sector, integrating regional financial markets, encouraging global 24 hour trading horizons, and enabling faster transactional and response times. As Martin notes, 'Market participants no longer have to be in the same centre, the same country or even the same continent for trading to take place: in terms of contact between financial firms and institutions, new information technologies allow propinquity without proximity.'[25]

A fourth development was the innovation and development of a series of new financial products as a consequence of conditions created by the synergy of deregulation and technological change. It was now possible for groups of banks from different countries to come together to syndicate loans to institutions, corporations and countries. Financial markets became increasingly securitised as a global equity and bond markets developed in the 1980s. Most famously, a plethora of derivative markets were created which built upon the structure of currency, equities, bonds and debt markets. Disintermediation also became possible as corporations cut banks out of the lending and borrowing process.[26]

A final development was the emergence of a series of new actors in the international financial system. With financial deregulation, financial services companies became vital players in the world economy. Institutional investors also began to play a key role in shaping the geography of money. Pension and insurance funds carried enormous financial weight in the marketplace. In the 1980s mutual fund managers became key players in conditioning flows of investment capital across the globe. Particularly significant for central banks was the emergence of a transnational elite of speculators and hedge fund managers searching for opportunity in the gap between the economic performances of national economies and the political commitments of governments.

Clearly, all of the developments were radically restructuring the scalar relations, power relationships and time-space logics conditioning the geography and territoriality of finance in the late twentieth century. Some commentators, however, went further and proclaimed the 'end of geography'. O'Brien defined this as 'a state of economic development where geographical location no longer matters in finance, or matters much less than hitherto'.[27] The deterritorialisation of finance for O'Brien is a multidimensional process. The last few decades were characterised by the erosion of national financial sovereignty. 'Financial market regulators no longer hold full sway over their regulatory territory; that is, rules no longer apply solely to specific geographical frameworks, such as the nation-state or other typical regulatory jurisdictional territories.' Information technology and worldwide electronic networks now made it possible for financial firms to decentralise their operations and not be as locationally dependent as they once were. Stock markets are also deterritorialising with some markets generating virtual trading floors in cyberspace and not even requiring actual physical trading floors. 'Stock markets are now increasingly based on computer and telephone networks, not on trading floors. Indeed, markets almost have no fixed abode.'[28] Finally, the emergence of the array of new financial products and choices is interpreted as part of the denationalisation of financial services and the advent of a new era of 'global choice' for consumers.

O'Brien's argument about global financial integration marking the 'end of geography' is, however, both overstated and poorly conceptualised. Despite making grand claims about the end of geography, he concedes that differences between markets and products are not about to disappear and that geography will remain an important reference point in the international financial system. His argument, rather, is that we are *naturally moving towards* the end of geography. The end of geography is represented as an inevitably tendency and process driven by information technology and regulatory change. He comes close to technological determinism when declaring that '[t]o a great extent the end-of-geography story is a technology story, the story of the computerisation of finance.'[29] But deregulation is also crucial to his claims for it provides greater ease of access and transparency in pricing and information. 'Transparency encourages the end of geography by revealing the cost of regulatory barriers – both discriminatory ones, imposed by national and other laws, and non-discriminatory ones, imposed by customs, cultures and market practices.'[30] The end-of-geography thesis, thus, is implicitly a thesis about markets and how global financial markets are manifestly destined to approximate the 'perfect market' – a market characterised by full transparency, no friction of integration and perfect information – conjured up by contemporary finance theorists.[31]

The argument that global financial integration leads to the end-of-geography is a conceptualisation flawed in three distinct ways. First, despite the erosion of national economic sovereignty, states are still central to the operation and functioning of the world financial system. While many smaller states are at the mercy of world financial markets, the co-ordinated actions of the G7 states still set the rules for the world financial system.[32] End-of-geography discourse which represents deregulation and technological change as both natural and inevitable processes is often a stalking horse for normative discourse on why geography *qua* state power *should* end. O'Brien's argument comes close to this. 'Money', according to O'Brien, 'being fungible, will continue to try to avoid, and will largely succeed in escaping, the confines of the existing geography'.[33] According to this reasoning, the efforts of national states to restrict the free movement of money are ultimately doomed to fail. Free markets are held to be more efficient and rational than regulated ones. Regulations only create distortions in the marketplace and inhibit the natural development of perfect markets. Deregulation is the most rational and sensible policy option, for global financial integration is an ineluctable process.[34]

In this instance deterritorialisation discourse is a part of neoliberal ideology. It strives to denaturalise and limit the power of states while naturalising and bolstering the virtues of markets. The contemporary world financial system, however, is not the product of natural forces and tendencies but of a new working relationship between states and markets promoted, in part, by the states themselves. The hegemony of neoliberal ideology in the 1980s in the United States and Great Britain helped make the integration of financial markets seen in that decade possible. Martin notes that a new 'bankers' bargain' between the state and finance capital replaced the former 'social bargain' between the state, labour and national capital resulting in the state ceding considerable power to financial markets organised at a supra-state level. This move, which expressed itself in the state's inclination towards financial interests and its deregulation of financial institutions, tilted power towards financial markets and reduced the bargaining power of the state. As Martin notes, '[i]t is a bargain that has encouraged more risky activity, raised the likelihood of panics and bankruptcies, and rendered government ever more captive to the sentiments of the market. The loss of national autonomy to global finance is thus not some benign outcome or necessity of world market forces, but has a political origin.'[35] End-of-geography discourse tends to naturalise the deterritorialisation of financial markets and obscure the complicity of certain political forces within states with this tendency.

Second, end-of-geography discourse fails to demonstrate how deterritorialisation is in actuality also a reterritorialisation. Geography is not so much disappearing as being restructured, rearranged and rewired. Global financial integration has, in fact, produced a new geopolitical complex of territory, technology, states and markets on a global scale. At the pinnacle of this complex are a series of integrated global financial centres. As Sassen, Thrift and others have noted, the development of a globally integrated financial system has not rendered place less significant but more significant.[36] Even O'Brien concedes that face to face contact is extremely important at the upper levels of the global financial system. Thrift argues that international financial centres have become centres of social interaction on an expanded scale. Rather than these centres dissolving into an electronic space of flows, the volume and speed of such flows 'may make it even more imperative to construct places that act as centres of comprehension'.[37] In pointing out how global financial markets are not perfect markets Clark and O'Connor underscore how national regulations make a difference in conditioning markets. 'There is, in effect, a robust territoriality to the global financial industry.'[38]

Third, the end-of-geography discourse fails to acknowledge and engage the construction of new geographies of financial exclusion across the planet. The de-territorialisation of national financial spaces and the creation of an integrated global financial space has changed the rules of world economic affairs for both developed and developing economies. In order to attract capital and foreign direct investment to spur economic development, states have to present themselves before a geo-financial panopticon of market makers and market analysts.[39] They have to adopt neoliberal creeds in their economic management philosophy, undertake certain structural reforms deregulating 'national monopolies' and privatising state assets, and be prepared to be evaluated on a daily basis by the 'electronic jury' of interlinked international markets.[40] States that do not play by these rules are effectively excluded from global investment capital. While the changes of the last decade have enabled certain developing states who have followed neoliberal nostrums to obtain considerable investment capital, this has come at a cost. Global financial capital tends to be impatient capital and exceedingly volatile. In times of crisis, capital will take flight to 'safer' and more 'predictable' markets, devastating national economies and development strategies in the process. The economic and social dislocations caused by this process are considerable, destroying economic resources and investments built up over years in a few days or less. As a consequence of the 'emerging market contagion' of 1997–98, income inequalities between the developing and developed world have widened considerably.

Policies of discrimination and 'red-lining' credit exclusion also operate at more local level, creating multiple classes of 'financial citizenship' in many states.[41] 'Happy' neoliberal discourse on the convenience of 'electronic trading' and 'internet banking' elide the world where certain groups cannot even obtain access to ordinary credit facilities and regular banking services.

Borderless Worlds for Whom?

The superficialities of deterritorialisation discourse in financial markets have their equivalents in digital culture. For example, MIT media technologist Nicholas Negroponte describes the revolution unleashed by computers as a world transforming qualitative transition from a world of 'atoms' (large, heavy, inert mass) to a world of 'bits' (microscopic, light digital code).[42] The atomic mass of territory is eclipsed by the light flexibility of telemetricality. In the warp drive of an informationalisation powered by Moore's law (the doubling of computer capacity every eighteen months), the world economy will become a 'seamless digital workplace'.[43] 'A self-employed software designer in Peoria will be competing with his or her counterpart in Pohang. A digital typographer in Madrid will do the same as one in Madras.' 'Bits', Negroponte assures us, 'will be borderless, stored and manipulated with absolutely no respect to geopolitical boundaries'.[44]

Discourses touting the inevitable borderlessness of a coming informationalised world tend to be discourses peddling neoliberal visions of what informationalisation should create, namely a 'friction-free market'. Such discourses also tend to hyperbolise the 'borderlessness' and 'global' character of the information age, presenting images of its penetration into the smallest Italian villages or the remotest monasteries as signs of a 'globality' that is ultimately parochial to 'virtual capitalism' and its 'virtual class'.[45] Finally, these discourses dismiss the tremendous informational inequalities across the world and within states, a world where most people do not even have access to a POTS (plain old telephone service).[46]

'Borderless world' discourses need to be problematised by old political economy questions: Who benefits? What class promotes the discourse of 'borderless worlds'? For whom is the world borderless? Martin and Schumann provide the context for some answers in their description of a 80:20 world where one fifth of the world's population will be sufficient to keep the world economy running while four-fifths will be excluded from its high-speed lanes of power and privilege.[47] The top 20 per cent are the 'wired technological classes' connected across the planet to each other and disconnected from the rest living in the same territorial state as themselves. The majority will remain trapped in the 'space of places' pacified by entertainment industries or uneasily contained by prisons and the police. Robert Reich provides a similar vision of a one-fifth/four-fifths society where the successful one-fifth ('symbolic analysts') are 'secessionists' living in similar gated communities across the globe and resolutely seeking to avoid territorial taxes in order to pay for Reich's 'work of nations' agenda.[48] Luke pushes this further, provocatively suggesting that for the top fifth 'nodality' is displacing 'nationality' as identity, community, sovereignty and territory are re-configured by the vast informational networks of cyberspace.[49] In the coded environment of network places, connectivity spaces, and digital domains, these national citizens are reinventing themselves as freelance 'netisens', hyper-individualised 'digital beings' net-working on the world wide web.[50] The 'borderless world' is their self-interpretation, the utopian community imagined for them by informational capitalism. Yet this cyber-community of fantasy and play is also a harsh performative workplace where work for even the most privileged and rewarded requires routine 'overwork'.[51]

Such visions of the geo-economics and geopolitics of an emergent cyberspatialised world dominated by transnational informational capitalism or what Eisenstein terms the 'cyber-media complex of transnational capital'[52] are themselves simplified and overstated, complicitious in some cases with the technologically deterministic hyperbole of that which they seek to criticise. Nevertheless, such visions do underscore the fact that contemporary transnational informational capitalism is deepening inequalities across the globe and rearranging, not abolishing, borders, boundaries and territories. For all peoples across the world processes such as class, gender, race, educational opportunity, wealth, citizenship and political power are perpetually producing borders. 'Borderless world' discourses are the fantasies of the few that can dream of becoming digital in a world where just being is a persistent struggle for so many.

Theorising the Techno-Political

For political geographers interested in conceptualising the changing world political map, discourses of deterritorialisation are significant as signs and symptoms of geopolitical change. They are the language of the latest round in the ongoing re-configuring of boundaries and territoriality in the modern world system. As such, they need to be treated as important ethnographic clues to the discursive formations characterising the contemporary geopolitical condition and world order. They provide insight into the consciousness of certain elites – economic, technological, cultural and political – and the fantasies that live large in their geoeconomic and geopolitical imaginations. They are, in addition, ideological expressions of material interests linked to the changing structure of what is now a deeply informationalised capitalism. Such discourses need to be contextualised within the histories, geographies and political economies of struggles over boundary processes and regimes of territoriality. Their rhetoric of 'newness' and metaphors of 'waves', 'impacts', and 'revolutionary change' needs to problematised for its overstating of and implicit normalisation of technologically deterministic visions of change. Specific spatial tropes within these discourses like 'borderless worlds', 'the death of distance' and the 'end of geography' need to be deconstructed to reveal their situated seeing of geography and the blindness to other geographies that make this situated seeing possible, a task geographers have begun to do.[53]

Discourses of deterritorialisation are also a window into an under-studied problematic in contemporary political geography, namely the long relationship between technological systems and the world political map. Driving most contemporary claims of deterritorialisation is a 'skein of networks' (Latour) comprising complex technical systems from micro-radio communications and satellite transmission systems to transcontinental optical cable lines.[54] These in turn enable everything from ebusiness on the Internet to 24 hour television broadcasting and deep space navigation. These telecommunications networks, as Hillis notes, have a long history and are much more than 'tools' or 'conduits' for the transmission of information.[55] Rather, they are socio-technical networks that envisage, enframe and in-site 'worlds'. In Latour's terms, they are 'actor-networks' that combine humans and machines in co-evolving arrangements of mutual constitution and dependence.[56] Actor-networks have important techno-political geographies that are often invisible or neglected. Political geographers have been slow to theorise the implications of such deeply geopolitical actor-networks as radar, trans-continental bombers, inter-continental ballistic missiles and space travel programmes in the past. Today's spy satellite systems and global television networks, overwhelmingly owned and dominated by a few Western states and transnational corporations, have also not received the attention they deserve. Neither has the Internet which, while a supposed 'global network' is dominated by US-centric traffic and dependent upon thirteen root-name servers, only three of which are located outside the United States.[57] Such invisible actor-network geopolitics has multiple visible geopolitical implications and consequences, such as the ability to monitor foreign policy crises in near real time and the capacity to co-ordinate rapid military responses across many different locations.

Any consideration of 'the changing world political map' on the eve of the twenty first century must recognise that there are multiple world political maps, state-centric maps produced by the territorialities created by the inter-state system but also dynamic maps of flow produced by the telemetricality created by informational capitalist corporations and well funded state institutions. New types of atlases are required to visualise these techno-political geographies of the info-sphere and a critical geopolitics of cyberspace is needed to deconstruct the latest manifestations of techno-political discourse. Characterised not by a transcendence of territoriality but by centralised routing stations, interconnected nodes, dense concentrations of flows, and sharp digital divides, this geopolitics of cyberspace is layered upon, wired across and embedded within existing territorial relations of power. Documenting the multidimensional spatiality and complex regime of boundaries and territorialities produced by an informational capitalist world economy, a networked transnational civil society, and informationally rich and digitally disadvantaged states is one of the great challenges facing political geography in the twenty-first century.

NOTES

1. L. Bryan and D. Farell, *Market Unbound: Unleashing Global Capitalism* (New York: Wiley 1996); E. Dyson, *Release 2.0: A Design for Living in the Digital Age* (New York: Broadway 1997); B. Gates, *The Road Ahead*, revised edition (New York: Penguin 1996); T.W. Luke, 'Running flat out on the road ahead; Nationality, sovereignty and territoriality in the world of the informational superhighway', in *Rethinking Geopolitics*, G. Ó Tuathail and S. Dalby (eds.) (London: Routledge 1998) pp.274–94; A. Toffler, and H. Toffler, *Creating A New Civilisation: The Politics of the Third Wave* (Atlanta: Turner Publishing 1994).
2. P. Virilio and S. Lotringer, *Pure War* (New York: Semiotext(e) 1983).
3. M. Crang, P. Crang and J. May (eds.), *Virtual Geographies* (London: Routledge 1999).
4. A. Giddens, *The Nation-State and Violence* (Berkeley: University of California Press 1987); A. Paasi, *Territories, Boundaries and Consciousness* (New York: Wiley 1996).
5. G. Ó Tuathail, 'Political geography III: Dealing with deterritorialisation', *Progress in Human Geography* 22 (1998).
6. W. Clinton, Inaugural address, 1993. Available from http://www.whitehouse.gov
7. M. Walker, *Clinton: The President They Deserve* (London: Vintage 1997).
8. R. Reich, *The Work of Nations: Preparing Ourselves for Twenty First Century Capitalism* (New York: Knopf 1991) p.77.
9. K. Ohmae, *The End of the Nation State* (New York: Free Press 1995) and *The Borderless World* (New York: Harper Business 1990).
10. *Borderless World* p.x.
11. Ibid. p xii.
12. Ibid. pp.204–8.
13. Ibid. p.215.
14. A. Kroker and M. Kroker (eds.), *Digital Delirium* (New York: St. Martin's Press 1997).
15. J.D. Davidson and W. Rees-Mogg *The Sovereign Individual* (New York: Simon and Schuster 1997); K. Robins, *Into the Image* (London: Routledge 1996).
16. K. Auletta, *The Highwaymen: Warriors on the Information Superhighway* (New York: Random House 1997); J. Brockman, *Digerati: Encounters with the Cyber Elite* (New York: Hardwired 1996).
17. E. Dyson, G. Gilder, J. Keyworth and A. Toffler, 'A Magna Carta for the Knowledge Age', *New Perspectives Quarterly* 11/4 (1994) pp.26–37.
18. Ibid. p.27.
19. Ibid. p.26.
20. Ibid. p.28.
21. Ibid. p.33.
22. J. Brook and J. Boal (eds.), *Resisting the Virtual Life* (San Francisco: City Lights 1995).
23. J. Brecher and T. Costello, *Global Village or Global Pillage?* (Boston: South End Press 1994); S. Dalby, 'Globalisation or global apartheid? Boundaries and knowledge in postmodern times', *Geopolitics* forthcoming; R. Falk, *On Humane Governance* (University Park, PA: Pennsylvania University Press 1995).
24. R. Martin, 'Stateless monies, global financial integration and national economic autonomy: the end of geography?' in S. Corbridge, R. Martin and N. Thrift (eds.), *Money, Power and Space* (Oxford: Blackwell 1994) p.258.
25. Ibid. p.262.
26. A. Leyshon, 'Dissolving difference? Money, disembedding and the creation of 'global financial space', in P.W. Daniels and W.F. Lever (eds.), *The Global Economy in Transition* (Harlow: Longman 1996) pp.62–80.

27. R. O'Brien, *Global Financial Integration: The End of Geography* (New York: Council on Foreign Relations 1992) p.1.
28. Ibid. p.1.
29. Ibid. p.8.
30. Ibid. p.19.
31. G. Clark and K. O'Connor, 'The informational content of financial products and the spatial structure of the global finance industry', in K. Cox (ed.), *Spaces of Globalisation* (New York: Guilford 1997) pp.89–114.
32. P. Hirst and G. Thompson, *Globalisation in Question* (Cambridge: Polity 1996).
33. O'Brien, *Global Financial Integration*, p.2.
34. Martin (see note 24) pp.270–71.
35. Ibid. p.271.
36. S. Sassen, *Global Cities* (Princeton NJ, Princeton University Press 1991); N. Thrift, 'On the social and cultural determinants of international financial centres: the case of the city of London', in S. Corbridge, R. Martin and N. Thrift (eds.), *Money, Power and Space* (Oxford: Blackwell 1994) pp.327–55.
37. Thrift (note 36) p.337.
38. G. Clark and K. O'Connor (note 31) p.90.
39. G. Ó Tuathail, 'Emerging markets and other simulations: Mexico, Chiapas and the geofinancial panopticon', *Ecumene* 4 (1997) pp.300–17.
40. S. Gill, 'The global panopticon? The neoliberal state, economic life, and democratic surveillance', *Alternatives* 20 (1995) pp.1–49; and A. Herod, G. Ó Tuathail and S. Roberts (eds.), *An Unruly World? Globalisation, Governance and Geography* (London: Routledge 1998).
41. A. Leyshon and N. Thrift, *Money/Space: Geographies of Monetary Transformation* (London: Routledge 1997) pp.225–59.
42. N. Negroponte, *Being Digital* (New York: Knopf 1995).
43. D. Tapscott, *The Digitial Economy: Promise and Peril in the Age of Networked Intelligence* (New York: McGraw Hill 1996).
44. Negroponte (see note 42) p.228.
45. A. Kroker and M. Weinstein, *Data Trash: The Theory of the Virtual Class* (New York: St. Martin's Press 1994).
46. H. Schiller, *Information Inequality* (New York: Routledge 1996); W. Wresch, *Disconnected: Haves and Have-Nots in the Information Age* (New Brunswick: Rutgers University Press 1996).
47. H. Martin and H. Schumann, *The Global Trap* (London: Zed 1997).
48. Reich (see note 8).
49. T.W. Luke, 'From Nationality to Nodality: How the Politics of Being Digital transforms Globalisation'. Paper presented at the APSA meeting, 3–6 Sept. 1998.
50. M. Castells, *The Rise of the Network Society* (Oxford: Blackwell 1996).
51. W. Greider, *One World, Ready or Not: The Manic Logic of Global Capitalism* (New York: Simon and Schuster 1997); J. Schor, *The Overworked American* (New York: Basic Books 1992).
52. Zillah Eisenstein, *Global Obscenities: Patriarchy, Capitalism and the Lure of Cyberfantasy* (New York: New York University Press 1998).
53. Stephen Graham, 'The end of geography or the explosion of place? Conceptualising space, place and information technology', *Progress in Human Geography* 22/2 (1998) pp.165–85; David Newman and Anssi Passi, 'Fences and neighbors in the postmodern world: boundary narratives in political geography', *Progress in Human Geography* 22/2 (1998) pp.186–207; Anssi Paasi, 'Boundaries as social processes: Territoriality in the world of flows', *Geopolitics* 3/1 (1998) pp.69–88; David Newman, 'Geopolitics Renaissant: Territory, Sovereignty and the World Political Map', *Geopolitics*, 3/1 (Summer 1998); H.W. Yeung, 'Capital, state and space: contesting the borderless world', *Transactions, Institute of British Geographers* NS 23 (1998) pp.291–309.
54. Bruno Latour, *We Have Never Been Modern* (Cambridge, MA: Harvard University Press 1993).

55. Ken Hillis, 'On the margins: the invisibility of communications in geography', *Progress in Human Geography* 22/4 (1998) pp.543–66.
56. Latour (see note 54). See also Mike Crang, Phil Crang and Jon May (eds.), *Virtual Geographies* (London: Routledge 1999).
57. V. Shannon, 'What's lurking behind those slow downloads', *International Herald Tribune*, 27 May, p.6. This report is based on the study *TeleGeography 1999* by the Washington-based research firm TeleGeography Inc.

Discourses of Identity and Territoriality on the US-Mexico Border

JASON M. ACKLESON

That fence over there – the Americans make a big deal of it
Charles Boyer, *Hold Back the Dawn* (1941)

Introduction

At the stroke of midnight on 19 September 1993, the 'Thin Green Line' swept along the banks of the Rio Grande river. Four hundred and fifty US Border Patrol Agents moved within line of sight of one another along twenty miles of the US-Mexico boundary that thinly divides El Paso, USA and Juarez, Mexico. Using night scope goggles and electronic sensors, and employing a cadre of agents who maintained a watchful gaze across the river, 'Operation Blockade' began as a vigil to seal the international boundary from unofficial incursions into the United States, chiefly undertaken by undocumented Mexican citizens seeking work.

The Operation (later renamed 'Operation Hold the Line') – and its supporting narratives – have become exemplary of the new territorial discourse of the boundary, changing policy on the ground and playing a major role in how people understand and reconstruct the border. It came at a time of both increased dynamism and tension; the booming *maquiladora* (twin assembly plant) industry and free trade under the North American Free Trade Agreement (NAFTA) have injected a surge of transnational economic opportunity and development into the border matrix while increased exclusionary restrictions on legal and illegal immigration temper the mix. These economic and political developments take place against a long historical backdrop of extensive cultural and social interaction across the state frontier. In fact, in many ways border cities on both sides of the boundary can be considered single communities that enjoy a variety of economic, social, and cultural ties that span the line and constitute a unique 'zone' or 'borderland' extending hundreds of miles into each state (Figure 1).

The situation in the US-Mexico borderlands at the opening of the twenty-first century is representative of the kinds of challenges – especially those posed by the transnationalisation of capital, production, and information – facing nation-states and border regions globally. To fully

FIGURE 1

US–MEXICO BORDERLANDS

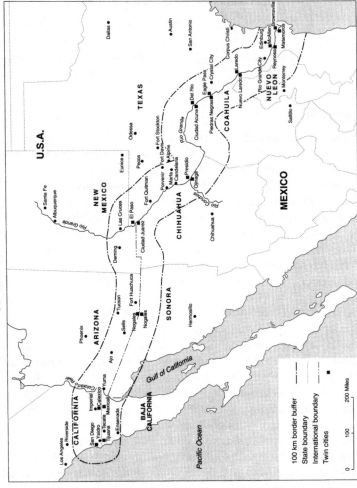

Source: Digital Chart of the World, La Paz; William Longewiesche, *Cutting for Sign* (New York: Vintage, 1993).

understand these issues, however, a multifaceted and transdisciplinary approach is necessary to explore what exactly the US-Mexico border *is* beyond simply a 2,000 mile political frontier that separates an information age superpower and a rapidly developing state. That kind of analysis involves looking at what kind of *socio-politically constructed* borders of identity – economic, ethical, and psychological – operate in both spatial and non-spatial contexts; this is particularly important as the developments of globalisation and nationalism affect the lives of the over 22 million citizens who live in border communities. From that, some theoretical and policy implications of these changes for the post-Cold War era might be drawn.

More specifically, this comment asks several research questions: (1) How have the narratives and representations of territoriality and identity in the US-Mexico borderlands changed under new American policies of 'border control'? (2) How do these new patterns of inclusion and exclusion implicate modern forms of territoriality and identity and the concomitant discursive and conceptual structures which support them? (3) What are the relationships between borders, territoriality, and collective identity in the borderlands in an increasingly transnational and 'turbulent' moment of late modernity?

These questions are explored through both a critical theoretical analysis and an empirical case study on 'Operation Hold the Line', illustrative of the current situation in the borderlands. The paper that argues the policy is an attempt to react against shifts and mixing in identity and culture in the borderlands as economic and socio-cultural transnationalism fosters deterritorialisation and challenges existing nation-state structures. Thus, new normative patterns of exclusion and identity *are* being fostered on the border, discouraging the development of an 'integrated' borderland or binational community.

More importantly, however, the launch of the Operation recast the discursive social and historical *construction* of the US-Mexico borderlands and changed what Paasi calls 'socio-spatial' consciousness whereby individuals and communities are socialised as members of a territorially bound community.[1] This struggle over the redefinition of space is directly related to a new understanding of social consciousness that creates a clearer notion of identity by illuminating the 'us' and the 'Other' division. That dichotomy is both symbolised and reinforced by the existence of the territorial boundary as well as the Border Patrol's tighter policy along it. In this case, collective identity is being partly reshaped through the vehicle of nationalism and supportive discursive strategies.

Any theoretical moves in International Relations (IR) and geopolitics, then, towards deterritorialisation must account for the freeing of space for capital and communication, but not – at this stage – identity and people. In other words, different kinds of 'bounded communities' and patterns of inclusion and exclusion are emerging, especially in the peripheries. The discourse of US-Mexico border – and in particular that surrounding this case study – affords an important laboratory to examine the mounting challenges these developments are posing to many nation-states in the post-Cold War era and offers us an opportunity to reflect on the theoretical tools we use to examine borders.

The paper proceeds by first examining the conceptual literature on borders and border theory to outline the problematic of analysis. Borders are a rich, yet relatively undertheorised phenomenon; most traditional examinations of borders in political geography and IR either have focused exclusively on international political boundaries or have not yet hybridised emerging critical thinking about other, no less important kinds of 'borders' that demarcate difference, identity and change in an increasingly heterogeneous world. The 'turbulent'[2] world scene, borders and 'boundedness' in a moment of late modernity are then explored by looking at both challenges to traditional territorial understandings of world politics. The next section reads the US-Mexico borderlands as an emerging, dynamic, and unique zone of intense economic and social interaction presenting numerous questions of policy and theory. Here transnational forces for free trade and socio-cultural interaction clash with new restrictions on the movement of labour.

This analysis is followed by a theoretical review of the relationship between borders and identity – focusing particularly on collective national identity – and the critical implications of a questioning of bounded space. The anchoring case study of 'Operation Hold the Line' and its impact on trends in the borderlands for identity and community follows, employing a hermeneutic approach to understand border residents' and policymakers' views on the exclusion and inclusion of undocumented workers on the border as illustrated by discourse, particularly the rhetoric, symbols, and metaphors employed in the debate over 'Operation Hold the Line'. This examination is supported by an interpretive methodology that situates identity in terms of spatial demarcations, borders and narratives, asking how several participants in the public discourse make sense of reality and construct meaning through the use of language, metaphors and images of the border. The impact of nationalism on border policy and the identity of border residents is included as a factor that shapes the reconstruction of consciousness, boundaries, and space.

Borders

The construction of reality, quite simply, depends on borders. Meaning, content, form, and discourse in the physical, social, and political worlds require distinct delimitations, differentiations, differences – all of which are formulated by, through, over and under different kinds of borders and boundings. But traditional examinations of borders have tended only to take on narrow applications of this fecund concept. Political analysis of the nature and dynamics of borders and borderlands, for example, has traditionally occurred either in a spatially oriented, 'classic', conflict-based, territorial manner or through a 'modern' approach which focuses on the socio-cultural ordering of late modernity which, as Connolly suggests, 'is a systematic time without a corresponding political space'.[3]

Geography, in particular, has until recently proceeded along classic lines, forming a boundary tradition, as pointed out by Newman and Paasi in an excellent review of the literature, that has a 'long, descriptive, and relatively nontheoretical history'.[4] These studies typically concentrate on discerning boundaries, legal issues and disputes and have focused on generally accepted concepts of the state and international boundaries.

Contemporary trends in global politics, however, certainly recommend analysis of borders along a more multidimensional, 'modern' line; the heightened political influence of non-state actors and multinationals, the resurgence of new patterns of ethnicity and identity, the further internationalisation of national economies, and the widening gap between the world's rich and poor are but a few examples of this pattern.[5] Standard understandings (typically influenced by epistemic realism) through 'bordered' theoretical and empirical representations of sovereignty and territoriality are, happily, beginning to evolve towards more nuanced notions of transnationalisation, globalisation and territoriality and their accompanying implications for identity. One notable recent effort by Herb and Kaplan, in fact, examines the complicated link between identities of nation, territory, and space – and the power relations which constitute them.[6]

Territorial space manifested as a form of modernity – essentially the Westphalian, sovereign state system – is particularly relevant to an understanding of this modern border discourse.[7] As Taylor submits 'territoriality is directly linked to sovereignty to mold politics into a fundamentally state-centric social process...the modern world is premised upon territoriality'.[8] Indeed, the modern Westphalian state has successfully enveloped social relations and shaped them through its territoriality – creating a wider system disjointed and mutually exclusive in nature. Control and distinction of a state's boundaries is a hallmark of sovereignty traditionally understood; this is, as Giddens formulated it, political domination over a spatial extension, and this can also be viewed in non-spatial terms.[9] Contact with the Other, for example, can also raise the intensity of territorial awareness.[10]

As the processes of transnationalism, globalisation, the impact of non-state actors, and other factors promote deterritorialisation (in Ruggie's terminology 'unbundled territoriality') and challenge the traditional statist discourse of modernity, some go so far as to suggest 'today's borders have become rubbery'.[11] But to effectively evaluate empirical developments, to begin to understand how the lines of the post-Cold War world are being drawn, we need to investigate thoroughly the notion of a 'border' and return to the richness of the original concept. We need to take a step away from easy, familiar, and reified understandings of political space and boundaries and instead explore a more holistic view of difference and identity.

Borders can be a possible vehicle of analysis here – they are all around us, an essential part of every system or object, a ubiquitous 'metapattern'[12] found throughout the social world which constructs reality while structuring and defining what is in and out, who 'we' are and who 'they' are.[13] 'Define' in fact, derives from the Latin word for 'boundary', *finis*. Indeed, our entire social order is predicated on the flexible or rigid theoretical and practical ways in which we separate or 'border' things – our family from strangers, moral from immoral, Americans from Mexicans.[14]

Accordingly, from cell walls to social stratification, borders and borderlands – particularly those that are socially created – are intriguing transdisciplinary phenomena increasingly attracting artists, writers, and scholars from several disciplines, including cultural studies, literary theory, anthropology, gender studies, Chicano studies, IR, and geography (particularly critical geopolitical analysis).[15] This swelling of interest is largely due to the fact that borders may be 'simultaneously historical, natural, cultural, political, economic, or symbolic phenomena'.[16] They present themselves as interfaces and points of transitions between ideas, concepts and movements and thus make themselves viable 'sites' for various lines of inquiry. Moreover, they open themselves to change – as socially constructed enterprises, they are always in the process of *becoming* – thus creating the possibility for critical transformation.[17]

This new kind of 'border analysis', beyond 'classic' and 'modern' approaches (while isolated still to select and often marginalised spheres of social theory), has, 'as much as any other manifestation in the early 1990s', however 'marked a new stage in the debates over postmodernism, cultural studies, and postcolonialism'.[18] Of particular interest are the 'borderlands' of not only international boundaries, but also other identities, spaces, and orders with unique ethnic, social, and cultural dimensions. While Kaplan argues borderland identities, in particular, are complicated zones of state, cultural, and national identities – more 'cracks' of seemingly stable identities (regional, ethnic, and otherwise) emerge here first.[19] The borderlands are, as Gloria Anzaldúa writes, 'a vague and undetermined place created by the emotional reside of an unnatural boundary'.[20] The discourses of these personal and political zones will increasingly be relevant on global basis given the force of transnational change and emerging identity patterns of heterogeneity and diversity.[21]

With this kind of a larger understanding of borders and borderlands, we can see the state not as the sole 'power container' of economic, cultural and social forces but as a 'leaking container', which trickles at its borders and view it as only one historically unique category.[22] More importantly, we can begin to denaturalise the state and its boundaries and the concepts that support them.[23] Heterogenous and fluid borderlands in reality pose significant questions about the relationship between borders, territory and identity; the non-spatial – conceptual, normative, or analytic – borders here are of particular interest since they underpin our understandings of reality and help produce discourse. Sovereignty and nationalism, for instance, are the socially constructed mechanisms of imposing political difference and distinction. These 'boundary maintaining structures' are the kind of non-spatial borders designed to keep a system differentiated from the environment and have intriguing dynamics.[24] Contemporary nationalist movements and exclusionary or 'hardening' initiatives like the case study, 'Operation Hold the Line', are good examples of this on the US-Mexico border but, to be better understood, must be read under this new approach.

Reading the US-Mexico Borderlands

The US-Mexico borderlands constitute one of the most economically, socially, and politically important boundary zones in the world. Considered as a region, it is the 'fourth member of NAFTA' with a population of over 22 million and a gross product of $300 billion a year.[25] An astounding 450 million crossings occur over the border each year.[26] The growing number of Latinos on the border has fostered extensive social and cultural linkages and interdependency.[27] The situation of the borderlands presages changes in the US as a whole: the Latino population in the United States is now at 11 per cent and is the fastest growing ethnic group, set to become the nation's largest ethnic minority.[28] These trends, combined with rapidly growing, ethnically diverse border populations and their transnational ties, point to an increasingly salient political force along a boundary Asiwaju calls 'the most spectacular land border between the First and the Third World'.[29]

Interdependence and interaction are a way of life in the borderlands; borderlanders (in both the US-Mexico case and in general) are generally unique individuals who are often shaped by a transnational processes and an environment that is distant from the 'centres'.[30] Around the world, those living on borderlines are impacted by conflict and accommodation, separateness and transnational interaction – a kind of 'borderlands milieu'.[31] The 'international' environment of borders gives borderlanders numerous opportunities for symbiotic interaction, trade, tourism, migration, information, and generally exchange. US residents and recent immigrants, for example, often travel and communicate on a daily basis with Mexican nationals. The twin-city phenomenon too is particularly illustrative; Ciudad Juarez, Mexico and El Paso, USA share an economic relationship to a degree that peso devaluations in Juarez destabilise and depress downtown El Paso, forcing numerous shops to close just as over 10,000 El Pasoeans head to work everyday in the *maquiladoras* in Juarez.[32] Cultural exchanges are frequent; border literature and art is vibrant and expanding, and binational schools are being developed in some areas.

The US-Mexico border fits a model of 'interdependent' borderlands since a relatively stable international relations and economic climate exist between the two nations.[33] The border differs from many other boundary situations, however, because of the remarkable economic asymmetry apparent along the border; the zone is indeed where the developing world meets the developed. Production capital in the industrialised nation often utilises raw materials and inexpensive labour on the other side, as is the pattern along the US-Mexico border with the *maquila* industry and agricultural labour. Because interaction and interdependence will likely only increase as Mexico develops economically, though, more opportunities for 'transculturation' will become available.[34]

Where do these patterns fit in the midst of wider global developments? The region is marked historically by shifts in the strength of the boundary, but as Kearney suggests, not in its sovereignty.[35] The border has experienced varying degrees of centralised control, ranging from benign neglect to allow *de facto* migration and, as we will see, more recently, heightened militarisation as a response to domestic economic and political difficulties. Consequently, the US-Mexico border pattern coincides with some of the worldwide trends in sovereignty: the political border is strengthened, but increasingly the non-spatial forces of interdependence and globalisation are gaining momentum but apply in uneven ways.[36] One of the most important manifestations of this trend is transnationalism, defined by Kearney as a 'blurring' or 'reordering...of the binary cultural, social and epistemological distinctions' of the modern state system.[37] Interdependent borderlands like the US-Mexico border are marked by this kind of reconstruction. They suggest what Peter Marden points to in his sense that 'a new geography may be emerging: one that is about the reconstitution of identity and place...it may in fact be a geography where our prior texts concerning spatial association in social, cultural and political life have to be rewritten'.[38]

Borders and Identity: A Theoretical Angle

The link between borders and identity is an increasingly theorised dynamic.[39] This section explores two theoretical aspects related to this nexus: critical theory and collective identity formation. Critical theory is a non-realist, post-positivist, way to examine some of the central concerns of the post-Cold War era – such as collective identity, nationalism, and boundaries – since these forces are kinds of 'boundings' that politically and ethically include and exclude.[40] While a full discussion is beyond the scope of this argument, aspects of critical theory can be applied to border analysis, especially as it can 'stress[es] how human beings learn to include some within, and exclude others from, their bounded communities' within a larger emancipatory matrix which seeks greater freedom in socio-political relations.[41]

By 'questioning all social and political boundaries' and 'distinctions between insiders and outsiders', critical theory can be extremely helpful for studies of collective identity formation because it explores how the national or ethnic bonds between citizen and community are formed, deepened, widened, or narrowed.[42] Especially relevant to studies of borders is critical theory's ability to question 'perspectives which naturalize what is essentially social and historical', to unpack constructions.[43] Political boundaries are an important case in point; borders and issues of collective identity (such as nationalism) directly interface how members of bounded communities understand their separateness. Borders drive right to the heart of the bonds between citizen and state, creating distinction against the Other, establishing the limits of state sovereignty which encapsulate citizens' legal rights by demarcating territory, and encouraging the 'national' idea within them.

Changing Bounded Communities

This dynamic, however, is increasingly complex and subtle given contemporary global political movements which are marked by a seeming paradox noted in the globalisation literature: the global order appears to tend both at once towards integration and fragmentation.[44] Increased change, fluidity, and an upsurge in nationalism, ethnic and intrastate conflict are all driven by new patterns of identity formation which were partly kept in check during the Cold War. Concurrently, however, the traditional condition of boundary maintenance is problematic as communities are linked and widened in this pluralist, post-Cold War 'milieu' – a time of globalisation, interdependence, and transnationalism. Bauman suggests an emerging reality: 'in today's world the great modern project of achieving a unified, managed and controlled space is facing its most critical challenge'.[45]

Even while Europe, for example, removes internal borders in favour of inclusionary unification and perhaps an embryonic supranational identity, nationalist and alternative identities surge. Similarly, as North America unifies economically under NAFTA, goods and capital are flowing across the US-Mexico border at unparalleled rates while walls are erected along the border and US Border Patrol agents seal the boundary in 'Operation Hold the Line', a policy of exclusion – not of capital, but of people.

The forces of collective identity and nationalism – seen through the lens of critical theory – can help manage the paradox of integration, fragmentation and boundedness characteristic of some emerging patterns of globalisation.[46] Various kinds of boundaries and bounded communities are emerging in the post-Cold War milieu; in the face of globalisation, the borders – and discourses – of bounded communities appear to be changing in two ways. First, they may be softened through an inclusionary policy of individuals and cultural influences while nationalistic and ethnic demands may reassert themselves but in a more fragmented, regional or quasi-supranational nature (such as in the European Union). Second, spatial borders may be hardened in an exclusionary fashion, not to exclude capital but individuals, particularly in cases where elites manipulate them in an instrumentalist fashion to promote or demote ethnic or national identity.

Both of these responses are advanced as the state's 'leaks' that spring at its borders and are allowed to drip unless governments attempt to 'plug' them. The case study of state inclusion and exclusion in the US-Mexico border region supports this argument as recent policy indicates economic interdependence but a resistance to social integration which manifests itself through nationalistic boundary maintenance by elites. This kind of boundary maintenance coheres with some post-structural readings of borders as foci of power relationships that define space.[47]

Collective Identity and Nationalism – A Brief Theoretical Perspective

Before turning to an examination of how borders and bounded communities are related to collective identity and nationalism in the post-Cold War era, we need to set up a few theoretical markers for this discussion of a prominent territorial discourse: nationalism. The nation-state constitutes an important kind of modern 'bounded community' with socially constructed and reproduced borders forming the bounds.[48] Through the framework of critical theory, we can see how nationalism conditions the borders of bounded states which in turn inform the inclusionary and exclusionary control of who and what cross in and out. Identity, in many ways, determines these impulses which set the solidity of state borders.

Nationalism, in this study, is understood as a modern, socially constructed phenomenon with a role for elites and susceptible to change.

Scholars who support this instrumentalist perspective include Hobsbawm and Brass.[49] As Motyl suggests, while different theorists provide different answers on how the nation is formed, most 'premise their arguments on the centrality of elites'.[50] Hobsbawm, for instance, argues the nation is an modern, 'invented' tradition devised by political elites to legitimise their power – collective identity, then, is an artificial and epiphenomenal phenomenon that can be manipulated.[51]

For these thinkers, the study of elite competition and manipulation is the key to an understanding of nationalism. Moreover, the modernist perspective is compelling because it can explain the growing fluidity of identities drawn out and overlapped in part by the breakdown of multinational states as well as rapid technological, social and economic transformations.[52] As it is put aptly by Anthony Smith, ethnic and national units afford convenient 'sites' for generating mass support in the universal struggle of elites...ethnic symbols and boundaries are able to evoke greater commitment...under a single banner'.[53] This view, Smith asserts, holds ethnicity as fundamentally instrumental, lending support to the argument here identities are socially constructed and able to be altered and manipulated as the political community widens or narrows.

Borders and Collective Identity: Theoretical Overviews

Borders are critical to the study of nationalism, but are often overlooked. Conversi, in fact, maintains that 'nationalism is a struggle over the definition of spatial boundaries' which has a 'crucial border-generating function'.[54] Similarly, Paasi contends that 'the existence, limitations, and symbols of boundaries between states...express the sovereignty of states'.[55] Ultimately, boundaries are needed to provide distinction between groups and symbolise important aspects of national identity. Lanternari places the debate back in the realm of critical theory: 'groups tend to define themselves, not by reference to their own characteristics, but by *exclusion*, that is by comparison to 'strangers' (emphasis added).[56] Nationalism and collective identity formation thus become a process of 'bordering', excluding and differentiating against the Other. Such boundaries, Wolin asserts, 'are a metaphor of containment' that proclaim identity and difference.[57]

The prominent Norwegian anthropologist Fredrik Barth reinforces this argument through an early discussion of the symbolism of borders, border guards, and border mechanisms which create separation and differentiation and thus formulate social attitudes.[58] Boundaries, then, both attribute and cause the 'principles of separation' the national community is concerned with – they differentiate the Other and thus define the self. 'The ethnic boundary', Barth reminds us, 'defines the group, not the cultural stuff that it encloses'.[59]

Similarly, John Anderson's symbolic analysis follows Barth's model, 'emphasiz[ing] [the] various "border guards", symbols that make the barriers between 'us' and 'them' (the strangers and outsiders) visible'.[60] These kinds of distinction are precisely the kind of analysis critical theory seeks because they allow us to begin to question about how we understand 'separateness'. Through what Conversi calls 'transactionalism', that is the exchanges and relationships between human groups, 'separateness' of identity and nationality are constructed.[61] The contesting forces over and under boundaries ultimately create this difference.[62]

Case Study: The US-Mexico Borderlands and 'Operation Hold the Line'

The most recent trend in the history of the US-Mexico border is the 'hardening' of the international boundary. The new policy was introduced in the wake of NAFTA which liberalised trade between the US and Mexico but amid increased unemployment and social and environmental distress on the border. The policy is an example of 'boundary maintenance' designed to influence discourse and reinforce national sentiment through a security problematic and construction of the Other. The 'militarisation' or hardening of the border complete with physical fortifications, armed military forces, and high tech surveillance equipment, taken in conjunction with Border Patrol policies of exclusion such as 'Operation Hold the Line' are – this paper argues – elite attempts to manipulate nationalism and create distinction against the backdrop of a border wide open under NAFTA to capital and trade.[63]

Militarisation and Operation Hold the Line attempt to 'seal' the border, signalling a major change in the territorial discourse of the boundary. The initiatives are seen, in the eyes of their planner, Border Patrol Sector Chief (and now US Congressman) Sylvestre Reyes, as 'an overwhelming success of historical proportions' and are being emulated elsewhere.[64] The policy reversed a tacit understanding that allowed many undocumented workers access to El Paso, particularly to work in the informal sector of the economy (such as domestic work) for wages that far exceeded those in Mexico. The blockade also effectively cut off the informal crossings of many residents of Juarez who could not afford official papers to work or visit friends and families in El Paso.

The following section is illustrative of both border residents and policymakers' understandings of their identity, their communities, and Operation Hold the Line.[65] The study of the narratives which support boundaries, identity, and border policy is a relatively undeveloped enterprise and has yet, generally, to utilise new perspectives on discourse analysis and critical theory.[66] The approach here, however, is highly qualitative and interpretive, designed to uncover the respondent's experiences, attitudes, beliefs and thoughts – and the accompanying policy discourse. This is a hermeneutic turn which 'seeks to discover ... meaning ... by examining how the individual consciousness [of the subject] reflects and refracts the spirit of the age.'[67] It largely follows Paasi's study of the social and historical construction of boundaries and socio-spatial consciousness; his methodology understands that 'the representation of state boundaries [are] laden with strong visible/non-visible, local/non-local, ideological, and metaphorical dimensions.'[68] The subjects of study here, then, are the constructed texts, symbols, and rhetoric – elements of a discourse seen as 'the representation and constitution of the real' – which support and depict social forces and actions: nationalism, identity, and ultimately the distinctions between 'us' and 'them'.[69] The metaphors, rhetoric and symbols involved are major factors in the social delimitating of space and the articulation of political-religious narratives of identity and nationalism, as well as being constitutive of the 'discourse strategies' designed to support them.[70]

Reading the Discourse of the Borderlands: Selected Themes

Americans and the Other

The Other is an important theme in critical social science accounts, prevalent since the 1970s. The premise behind the construction of the Other, Paasi contends, is 'an external entity against which 'we' and 'our' identity is mobilized'.[71] The dichotomy suggested here flows from an understanding of symbolic, social, and psychological 'borders' alluded to earlier in this comment. Nationalisms and other conceptions of collective identity spring from these boundaries which are developed partly in relation to difference.[72]

The US-Mexico international boundary is of course the ultimate symbolisation of the us–Other schema because it structures both social and territorial space. But that symbolic representation was only extended and reinforced with Operation Hold the Line:

> The Operation is to reinforce American versus Mexican. That's the worse thing about it. It flows out of this historical condition.[73]

The respondent, an immigrants' rights advocate and outspoken opponent of the initiative, starkly identifies how she feels about being cast in strokes of nationalism along the border, but the Border Patrol disagrees, emphasising the 'disorder' caused by undocumented workers entering the borderlands:

> There is very serious havoc that can be reeked by unchecked illegal immigration.[74]

This comment, by the Border Patrol spokesman, reflects the agency's new policy of tighter border control and serves to reinforce spatial consciousness in response to the 'havoc' of a more interactive, 'disordered', and fluid situation brought on by the increased interdependence and trans-nationalisation that tends to characterise the border region.

Several of the respondents also addressed the national question as they discussed the broadly positive reaction to Hold the Line in the Mexican-American community. Their comments are insights into concepts of identity, the Other, and citizenship:

> There is this misperception that non-Mexicans have that the Mexican population is very homogeneous population that breeds this inbred loyalty and nothing could be further from the truth. [Reyes] wedged down that wedge because of the rhetoric he surrounded the operation with and with the context he really exploited the image. There's a definite case of 'us' versus 'them'.[75]

The interviewee here, a local journalist and opponent of the policy, nods to Reyes' role in forcing 'a wedge' into the community – a clear symbol of what she feels he and the operation did to change both sides of the border – specifically reconstructing the Other. This also served to help strengthen the bond between citizen and state for many Americans, especially new citizens.

Part of the construction of national identities involves the collective representation of identity by 'depersonalising' membership through a stereotype of collective features.[76] The use of stereotypes is also a basis for deligitimation and moral exclusion.[77] This borderlander, also publically opposed to the policy, addresses this representation as well as her feelings about the painting of the 'illegal alien' as the Other:

> The enemy is the undocumented worker who is here taking jobs...in the public eye, the enemy is the brown Mexican. Why are people so frightened of this poor Mexican? Why is there this stereotype, this misperception that they are all on welfare? It's just not true. So you have all these indisputable facts and yet the bias remains.[78]

This language of the 'brown Mexican' is in line with Barth's understanding of ethnic boundaries and their role in constructing identity. As we will see in the next section, this use of stereotypes as foils for identity is prevalent in the discourse strategy surrounding the initiative.

Reyes as a Political Elite and the Forging of National Sentiment

Border Patrol Chief Reyes was a focal point for several of the respondents. He is seen by some respondents as an elite who capitalised on the latent Other sentiment in the community and then led, constructed and galvanised a discourse of national sentiment and identity, in part for personal political gain. Reyes was indeed successful in attracting increased attention and funding for border control operations; Congress approved massive funding for thousands more agents and enhanced Border Patrol operations. The head of the Immigration and Naturalization Service Commission called the operation 'an extraordinarily successful innovation'.[79] The local *El Paso Times* newspaper noted Reyes 'almost single-handedly changed the way we view the border' and went so far as to name him 'newsmaker of the year'.[80] Seizing upon the 'success' of the initiative and a wave of popular support, Reyes launched a successful bid for the US Congress, winning 71 per cent of the vote, complete with campaign commercials that emphasised he 'held the line on the border'.

His work, nonetheless, did not meet with universal praise among those opposed to the policy in the border rights community:

> We are talking about racism and the way the picture is fomented by politicians for their own benefit.[81]

> When Reyes justified it, he said we were going to protect the city from transvestites, another incredibly sexual metaphor. All this stuff about AIDS, beggars. He said 'at least now we'll have *our* beggars'. He knows this community really well.[82]

These comments suggest Reyes' role in manipulating public opinion by emphasising the stereotypes and 'disorder' of the border, coinciding with the instrumentalist reading of nationalism discussed earlier.

But Reyes articulated his own vision of the situation before he stepped in:

> The situation was simply out of control. I'd never seen anything like it – you couldn't go anywhere in the city without meeting panhandlers...In short, you had chaos and I didn't like that.[83]

As argued in the pervious section, the operation had a major impact in strengthening socio-spatial separateness as Reyes attempted to create 'order' out of 'disorder' and galvanise 'us' against 'them'.

Inclusion and Exclusion

An analysis of the terminology and symbolisation of these Border Patrol operations reveals the patterns of inclusion and exclusion operating in this border discourse. Operation 'Hold the Line' was designed specifically to exclude 'illegal aliens' from crossing the 'line'. To reinforce national difference, Manzo argues that 'the *idea* of the alien must be ever revived'; hence the painting of undocumented workers as quite literally 'illegal aliens', 'national security threats' that 'invade' in 'tides' and 'waves'.[84] The Border Patrol, in fact, ran an initiative in 1954 called 'Operation Wetback' to prevent similar incursions.[85] But as one borderlander, a specialist in public health along the border, argued:

> We may as well have that intermixing, prepare for it, and understand it as opposed to just having it completely separate.[86]

In response to this kind of sentiment, Operation 'Blockade' and American militarisation efforts complete with Low-Intensity Conflict (LIC) doctrine were introduced to prevent the entry of the morally excluded Other. The rhetoric of the initial launch, though, was coolly received in some quarters, including the Mexican government. As an El Pasoean put it:

> The word 'blockade' was the most unfortunate names ever chosen...it's a word used to define an enemy and it implies stopping all trade and commerce.[87]

The Border Patrol, however, could not be clearer about the policy:

> Operation Hold the Line was very simple – very symbolic of what we were trying to do and the name stuck.[88]

Constructing a Discourse: Walls and Fences on the Border

In conjunction with human barriers, current Border Patrol policy is to construct a variety of ramparts along the US-Mexico boundary itself. This effort is an easily recognisable method or strategy of creating separateness in the political discourse and on the ground.[89] Interestingly enough, the public seemed receptive to the symbol of a 'fence' but not a 'wall'. One respondent pondered this concept:

> They put all this junk underneath so that nobody can dig their way down and they're going to have some barbed wire at the top? Who cares? This is just a terrible a message to send. It is very symbolic. That wall image is real potent.[90]

The Border Patrol has a radically different view of the fence:

> We feel very passionate about the idea of implementing tools that give us more efficiency, more manageability, in troublesome areas.[91]

These are clearly worldviews in opposition; to the Border Patrol the wall is less a symbol than a 'tool' to help 'manage' their monitoring of the line. This kind of strategy represents their efforts to concentrate resources on the 'front line' in the struggle against illegal incursions into the US. The blockade, some felt, was simply a different kind of barrier:

> The interesting thing about the wall – there was a lot of opposition and it was growing in El Paso – everyone thought the Blockade was fine,

but a wall was something different in their minds, aesthetically, metaphorically, whatever. The blockade was just a human wall but they didn't like this idea of this concrete, tangible wall that you can't see through.[92]

Perhaps the physical composition of the barrier does make a difference – since, as noted in the theoretical review, walls and boundaries are 'metaphors of containment' that signify identity and difference, borderlanders may be tacitly acknowledging the interrelationships along the border by embracing a transparent fence and are unwilling to impose further difference with construction of a solid wall that blocks a gaze into Mexico.[93]

Nonetheless, the division of self and Other is paramount in socio-spatial grouping and is forced into play by the construction of these kinds of physical barriers. Here the role of spatiality and division (through the physical manifestation of a fence) can be directly correlated to the construction of otherness.[94] A long-standing local resident, in an editorial for the *El Paso Times*, seemed to strike the heart of the matter:

We have to confront the fact that this isn't one big community anymore. And pretty soon, there will be a wall to remind us about that.[95]

Conclusions

The international scene in the post-Cold War era is marked by the same kind of changes impacting the US-Mexico borderlands: the transformation of the territorial roots of industrialised states through the transnationalisation of capital, communication, and culture. Concomitant with this transformation are new discourses of identity and space and new constructions of boundaries. Identification seems to increasingly have potential for shifting from the traditional, Cartesian nation-state relation; but, as suggested in the theoretical review, in the face of this globalisation, the borders of bounded communities appear to be hardening in an exclusionary fashion, not to capital, but to individuals, particularly in cases where elites manipulate boundaries in an instrumentalist fashion to promote or demote ethnic or national identity. Nevertheless, the territorially demarcated sovereign state is no longer fully able to contain these tendencies, nor can the dominant IR perspectives like neorealism and positivist methodologies alone deal with the associated conceptual changes. New critical perspectives and forms of border analysis, like this one, will be increasingly important for understanding of the nuanced play of identities, borders and order in a turbulent and 'shaken' world.[96]

The global discourses and processes of bordering and of including and excluding appear to be in different fluxes in response to the post-Cold War milieu: on the US-Mexico border, they translate to tightened distinction and difference. To a significant degree, the lines are changing owing to shifts in collective identity, partly brought on by elites who forge national sentiment and conceptions of 'separateness'. Operation Hold the Line is a salient example of this as it fits with a critical understanding of the border as focal point in power relationships that define space.

Ultimately, Hold the Line has helped alter the way El Pasoeans understand their boundedness by changing the dominant territorial discourse of the border. The brief examination of the views of the borderlanders highlighted here suggests the processes and dynamics of this socio-political (re)construction of boundaries. These reconceptions, paradoxically, occur at a time when the region is increasingly tied together economically. Orenstein, in fact, writes that the Operation 'slashed the twin-city economy of El Paso in the north and Juarez to the south, creating a hostile barrier between families and businesses that had long lived in a borderless state'.[97]

Borderlanders often have flexible conceptions of identity and potentially weaker national loyalties than in the 'centre'. Conversi addressees this issue: 'when identities slide into each other, borders "must" be established, although this effort is also presented by nationalist elites as an attempt to maintain a pre-existing or primordial national boundary.'[98] Reyes, from an instrumentalist perspective, helped shift that bond between citizen, ethnicity and state through both policy change and a new discourse strategy that garnered mass support. This was illustrated when the respondents discussed the broadly positive reception of his initiative in the Mexican-American community and public opinion polls which draw the same conclusion.

A composite look at these voices from the border, then, suggests that the discourse and policy of Operation Hold the Line as well as the construction of barriers along the boundary are symbolic and physical representations of difference and a political manifestation of exclusion. The border thus can be seen as a powerful 'othering' device, reinforcing 'the twin concepts of national and alien [which] cannot exist independently of each other; both are simultaneously brought into being by nationalist scriptures that operate as political religions.'[99] Reyes, and others in the policy community, helped draft that scripture. Manzo's perspective is instructive here: 'one of the principle practices of nationalism is the creation of boundaries between national and alien'.[100]

Ultimately Paasi's concept of *spatial socialisation* is perhaps the best tool for understanding the worldview of these borderlanders and is a starting point for explorations elsewhere.[101] Spatial socialisation, he writes, is the 'process through which individual actors and collectives are socialized as members of a specifically territorially bounded spatial entities and through which they...internalize collective territorial identities and shared traditions'.[102] The processes and discourses of Operation Hold the Line, the border, the Other, and collective identity are inherent in the rhetoric, metaphors and symbolisation that constitute this socio-spatial grouping. The 'us' – 'them' or 'I' – 'we' constitution of identity directly follows the 'borderlines between human and "something else"'.[103] Those exclusionary 'borderlines' in the spatial consciousness of residents are being drawn in El Paso and elsewhere in the US-Mexico borderlands.

The future of the US-Mexico border region and other borderlands around the world, as well as the dominant discourse which structures them, remains uncertain and continues to be contested. As economic interdependence is fostered, and as Mexico develops, perhaps a move towards an communitarian-like 'integrated' borderland or a binational political community might be possible. This would pose not only greater theoretical questions for IR with the formation of a new unit of analysis, but also possibly foster the construction of a distinct, binational 'border' identity and ethical community for the residents of the region, ironically through a process of 'debordering'.[104] This evolution would alter the nature of the territorial boundary and Paasi's 'scales'; these 'scales' are produced and contested in social practice and are limits and divisions of community and identity, for example from household to city to state.[105]

This study suggests that the scale for residents along the US side of the border ends along the boundary, but a new integrated community would change the scale of socio-spatial consciousness for border-landers. Anderson's notion of 'imagined communities' – the imagined limits of national communities, their boundedness – might be helpful in such a conception because it suggests the possibility for change, for altering, under the proper conditions, the conscious reconstruction of the limits of the national community.[106] Ultimately, this is the goal of critical theory – to question inclusion and exclusion and ensure the 'fine lines' we draw – our principles of separability – are just and lead to positive social change. At the very least, they may open up the future possibilities for transformation.

Perhaps Gloria Anzaldúa found the best way to understand the border when she wrote

> To survive the Borderlands
> you must live *sin fronteras*[107]
> be a crossroads.[108]

This will increasingly become the challenge of identity for borderlanders in the next century as we continue to produce and contest metaphors, social space and borders in the post-Cold War milieu.

NOTES

1. Anssi Paasi, *Territories, Boundaries, and Consciousness: The Changing Geographies of the Finnish-Russian Border* (New York: John Wiley and Sons 1996).
2. James Rosenau among many others articulates this view, detailing the 'turbulent' world scene. See his *Along the Domestic-Foreign Divide: Governance in a Turbulent World* (Cambridge: Cambridge University Press 1998), *Turbulence in World Politics: A Theory of Change and Continuity* (Princeton NJ: Princeton University Press 1990). See also, for instance, Barry Hughes, 'Rough Road Ahead: Global Transformations in the 21st Century', paper presented at the Annual Conference of the International Studies Association, Toronto, March 1997.
3. William Connolly, *Identity/Difference: Democratic Negotiations of Political Paradox* (Ithaca NY: Cornell University Press 1992) pp.215–16. See also Raimondo Strassoldo, 'The Study of Boundaries: A System-Oriented, Multidisciplinary, Bibliographic Essay', *Jerusalem Journal of International Relations* 2/3 (1977) pp.81–107 and his 'Border Studies: The State of the Art in Europe' in A.I. Asiwaju and P.O. Adeniyi (eds.), *Borderlands in Africa: A Multidisciplinary and Comparative Focus on Nigeria and West Africa* (Lagos: University of Lagos Press 1989) p.384; Michael Kearney, 'Borders and Boundaries of State and Self at the End of Empire', *Journal of Historical Sociology* 4 (1991) pp.52–74; Peter K. Taylor, 'The State as Container: Territoriality in the Modern World-System', *Progress in Human Geography* 18/2 (1994) pp.151–62; Barry Hughes *Continuity and Change in World Politics: The Clash of Perspectives*, 2nd ed. (Englewood Cliffs NJ: Prentice Hall 1994).
4. David Newman and Anssi Paasi survey most of the relevant literature in their 1998 piece 'Fences and Neighbours in the Postmodern World: Boundary Narratives in Political Geography', *Progress in Human Geography* 22/2 (1998) pp.186–207 and space restrictions prevent reproducing this review here, but for a few illustrative examples of new thinking in geography, see, for instance, Gerard O'Tuathail, *Critical Geopolitics: The Politics of Writing Global Space* (Minneapolis MN: University of Minnesota Press 1996); Peter Marden, 'Geographies of Dissent: Globalization, Identity and the Nation', *Political Geography* 16/1 (1997) pp.37–64; John House, *Frontier on the Rio Grande: A Political Geography of Development and Social Deprivation* (Oxford: Clarendon Press 1992); John Agnew, 'Representing Space: Space, Scale, and Culture in Social Science' in J. Duncan and D. Ley (eds.), *Place/Culture/Representation* (London: Routledge 1993); Simon Dalby, *Creating the Second Cold War: The Discourse of Politics* (London: Pinter 1990); W.A. Galusser (ed.), *Political Boundaries and Coexistence* (Bern: Peter Lang 1994); Peter Taylor, *Political Geography* (London: Longman 1993); and Strassoldo, 'The Study of Boundaries' (note 3).
5. For an example of a good recent collection of such efforts, see Paul Ganster (ed.), *Borders and Border Regions in Europe and North America* (San Diego: San Diego State University Press/Institute for Regional Studies of the Californias 1997).
6. See Guntram H. Herb, 'National Identity and Territory' in Guntram H. Herb and David H. Kaplan (eds.), *Nested Identities: Nationalism, Territory, and Scale* (Lanham, MD: Rowman & Littlefield Publishers 1998) and David H. Kaplan's 'Territorial Identities and Geographic Scale', Chap.2 in the same volume.
7. See John Gerard Ruggie, 'Territoriality and Beyond', *International Organization* 47/1 (1993) pp.139–74. For an overview of modernity and international relations, see, among others, Richard Devetak, 'The Project of Modernity and International Relations Theory', *Millennium: Journal of International Studies* 24/1 (1995) pp.27–51.
8. Taylor (note 3) p.152. See also Robert D. Sack, *Human Territoriality: Its Theory and History* (Cambridge: Cambridge University Press 1986).
9. Anthony Giddens, *A Contemporary Critique of Historical Materialism,* Vol. 1 (Berkeley CA: University of California Press 1981) p.45.
10. Ivo D. Duchacek, *The Territorial Dimension of Politics: Within, Among and Across Nations* (Boulder, CO: Westview Press 1986) p.24.
11. Ruggie (note 7) pp.170–74; Samudavanija Chai-Anan, 'Bypassing the State in Asia', *New*

Perspectives Quarterly 12/1 (Winter 1995) p.9. See also Jim George, 'Discourses of Modernity: Toward the Positivist Framing of Contemporary Social Theory and International Relations', in *Discourses of Global Politics: A Critical (Re)Introduction to International Relations* (Boulder, CO: Lynne Rienner 1994) pp.41– 69 and Jim George and David Campbell, 'Patterns of Dissent and the Celebration of Difference: Critical Social Theory and International Relations', *International Studies Quarterly* 34/3 (1992) pp.269-94.

12. On metapatterns, see Tyler Volk, 'Borders', Chap.3 in *Metapatterns: Across Space, Time and Mind* (New York: Columbia University Press 1995). Metapatterns are broad based phenomena occurring repeatedly throughout the social and natural worlds. A basic template for a leaf, for instance, is found in most forms of plants. Similarly, classes are a reoccurring element of societies across time and space. See also Eviatar Zerubavel, *The Fine Line: Making Distinctions in Everyday Life* (New York: The Free Press 1991) p.2, and 'Lumping and Splitting: Notes on Social Classification', *Sociological Forum* 11/3 (1996) p.421. See also Paasi, (note 1) and Anssi Passi, 'Constructing Territories, Boundaries and Regional Identities', in Thomas Forsberg (ed.), *Contested Territory: Border Disputes at the Edge of the Former Soviet Empire* (Brookfield, VT: Edward Elgar 1995), and Newman and Paasi (note 4) p.2.

13. Volk (note 12).

14. Complex processes of social and ethical judgments underlie these differentiations, or in Zerubavels' term, where we draw that 'Fine Line' is of major importance in order to understand our social world. See Eviatar Zerubavel, *The Fine Line: Making Distinctions in Everyday Life* (New York: The Free Press 1991).

15. See also Andrew Linklater, *The Transformation of Political Community* (Cambridge: Polity Press 1998); in anthropology, see the seminal work by Fredrik Barth, *Ethnic Groups and Boundaries: The Social Organization of Culture Difference* (London: George Allen and Unwin 1969) and Deborah Pellow (ed.), *Setting Boundaries: The Anthropology of Spatial and Social Organization* (Westport, CT: Bergin and Garvey 1996), which gives a superb analysis of the way space and boundaries condition social and cultural difference. But it was Gloria Anzaldúa's *Borderlands-La Frontera: The New Mestiza* (San Francisco CA: Spinsters/Aunt Lute Book Co. 1987) which anchored literary explorations of borders and continues to strongly influence the field as the bedrock literary text dealing with large, multidimensional questions of identity and borderlands. Recent work in literary criticism and cultural studies has followed Anzaldúa's lead and is enriching the canon. See, for example, Henry Schwarz and Richard Dienst (eds.), *Reading the Shape of the World: Toward an International Cultural Studies* (Boulder, CO: Westview Press 1996) and the important recent work edited by Scott Michaelsen and David Johnson, *Border Theory: The Limits of Cultural Politics* (Minneapolis, MN: University Of Minnesota Press 1997) which manages the most definitive articulation yet of these concepts, seeking to 'rethink the place of the border in border studies'.

16. Anssi Paasi, 'Constructing Territories, Boundaries and Regional Identities' (note 12) p.42; Newman and Paasi (note 4).

17. Here is one jumping off point for critical theory. While well-beyond the scope of this essay, and in no way a unitary school of thought, the critical approach in IR, influenced by the Frankfurt School (from Horkheimer to Habermas), generally seeks change, emancipatory goals, and ultimately greater freedom by questioning social and political relations in a non-realist, post-positivist way. See David Held, *Introduction to Critical Theory* (Cambridge: Polity 1997); Andrew Linklater, 'The Achievements of Critical Theory', in Steve Smith, Ken Booth, and Marysia Zalewski (eds.), *International Theory: Positivism and Beyond* (Cambridge: Cambridge University Press 1996), Mark Hoffman, 'Critical Theory and the Inter-Paradigm Debate', *Millennium: Journal of International Studies* 16/2 (1987) pp.231–49; and Robert Cox, 'Social Forces, States, and World Orders: Beyond International Relations Theory', *Millennium: Journal of International Studies* 10/2 (1981) pp.126–55.

18. John C. Welchman, *Rethinking Borders* (London: Macmillan Press 1996) p.xii.

19. Kaplan (note 6) p.37.

20. Gloria Anzaldúa, 'To Live in the Borderlands Means You' in *Borderlands-La Frontera: The New Mestiza* (San Francisco: Spinsters/Aunt Lute Book Co. 1987) p.3

21. As Peter Marden argues, 'processes of globalization, such as transnational economic activity, global forms of communication, and social movements operating transnationally, are producing a complex mix of responses centered around identity.' See Marden (note 4) pp.37–64.

22. Anthony Giddens, *The Nation-State and Violence* (Cambridge: Polity Press 1985); Taylor (note 3) p.157.

23. See John Agnew, 'The Territorial Trap: The Geographical Assumptions of International Relations Theory', *Review of International Political Economy* 1 (1994) pp.53–80.

24. Strassoldo (note 3) p.85.

25. See Timothy C. Brown, 'The Fourth Member of NAFTA: The U.S.-Mexico Border', *Annals of the American Academy of Political and Social Science* 550 (March 1997) pp.104–21.

26. Ibid.

27. In the larger bilateral context, Mexico is the third largest trading partner with the United States and the source of 27 per cent of its petroleum imports but also its main conduit for narcotics. See Paul Ganster and Alan Sweedler, 'United States-Mexico Border Region' in *United States-Mexico Border Statistics Since 1900* (Los Angeles: University of California at Los Angeles Latin American Center Publications 1990) p.421. See also Abraham Lowenthal, 'The Intermestic Hemisphere', *New Perspectives Quarterly* 8 (1990) pp.37–46.

28. US Bureau of the Census, 'Population Projections of the United States by Age, Sex, Race, and Hispanic Origin: 1995 to 2050', by Jennifer Cheeseman Day (Washington, DC: US Government Printing Office 1996). See also Jorge del Pinal and Audrey Singer, 'Generations of Diversity: Latinos in the United States', *Population Bulletin* 52/3 (Oct. 1997) pp.2–47.

29. Asiwaju (note 3) p.34.

30. Oscar J. Martínez, *Border People: Life and Society in the US-Mexico Borderlands* (Tucson: University of Arizona Press 1994) p.xvii.

31. Ibid. p.10.

32. An accurate and timely count is nearly impossible. *Twin Plant News*, published monthly in El Paso, publishes periodic counts. Some 275 plants run in Juarez, employing over 170,000 workers including over 10,000 El Pasoeans. This pattern is prevalent along the length of the boundary.

33. Martinez (note 30) p.4.

34. Ibid. p.5.

35. Kearney (note 3).

36. See David Held and Anthony McGrew, 'Globalization and the Liberal Democratic State', in Yoshikazu Sakamoto (ed.), *Global Transformation: Challenges to the State System* (Tokyo: United Nations University Press 1994) pp.57–84.

37. Kearney (note 3) p.55.

38. Marden (note 23).

39. See Mathias Albert, David Jacobs and Yosef Lapid (eds.), *Identities/Borders/Orders New Directions in International Relations Theory* (Minneapolis, MN: University of Minnesota Press forthcoming).

40. See note 17.

41. Andrew Linklater, 'The Achievements of Critical Theory', in Marysia Zalewski, Steve Smith, and Ken Booth (eds.), *After Positivism* (Cambridge: Polity Press 1996) p.280.

42. Ibid. p.282.

43. Ibid. p.282. The normative and emancipatory goals of critical theory cannot be divorced from its analytical components. Discourse ethics and ethical reflexivity, for example, open the space for change and positive social action. For a discussion, see Mark Hoffman, 'Normative International Theory: Approaches and Issues', in A.J.R. Groom and Margot Light (eds.), *Contemporary International Relations: A Guide to Theory* (London: Pinter 1994) and David Held, 'Democracy: From City States to a Cosmopolitan Order', in David Held (ed.), *Prospects for Democracy: North, South, East, West* (Cambridge: Polity Press 1993).

44. See, for example, Anthony McGrew, *Globalization and the Nation State* (Cambridge: Polity Press 1992) and Anthony McGrew (ed.), *The Transformation of Democracy? Globalization and Territorial Democracy* (Cambridge: Polity Press 1997).
45. Zygmunt Bauman, 'Racism, Anti-Racism and Moral Progress', *Arena* 1 (1993) pp.9–22.
46. See David Held, Anthony McGrew, and David Goldblatt (eds.), *Global Transformations: Politics, Economics, and Culture* (Stanford CA: Stanford University Press 1999).
47. Barbara Morehouse, 'A Functional Approach to Boundaries in the Context of Environmental Issues', *Journal of Borderlands Studies* 10/2 (fall 1995) pp.53–73.
48. Andrew Linklater, 'Citizenship and Sovereignty in the Post-Westphalian State', *European Journal of International Relations* 2 (1996) pp.77–103.
49. Eric Hobsbawm, 'Inventing Traditions: Mass-Producing Traditional Europe 1870–1914', in Eric Hobsbawm and Terence Ranger (eds.), *The Invention of Tradition* (Cambridge: Cambridge University Press 1983); Paul Brass, 'Elite Groups, Symbol Manipulation and Ethnic Identity among the Muslims of South Asia', in *Ethnicity and Nationalism: Theory and Comparison* (New Delhi: Sage Press 1991).
50. Alexander J. Motyl, 'The Modernity of Nationalism: Nations, States, and Nation-States in the Contemporary World', *Journal of International Affairs* 45/2 (1992) p.321.
51. Similarly, Brass rejects the primordialist view that every person carries with him or her certain attachments derived from place of birth, kinship, relationships, religion, and language that are 'natural' and not subject to choice. While such attachments may have 'emotive significance', Brass suggests they are 'variable', especially when people command more than one language, change religious affiliation, and move globally through the new milieu of social and economic space – characterised by travel, migration, diasporas, and trade.
52. Rosenau (note 2); Anthony D. Smith, *National Identity* (London: Penguin Books (1991) p.8.
53. Smith (note 52) p.9.
54. Daniele Conversi, 'Reassessing Current Theories of Nationalism: Nationalism as Boundary Maintenance and Creation', *Nationalism and Ethnic Politics* 1 (Spring 1995) pp.75, 78.
55. Paasi (note 1) p.40.
56. Vittorio Lanternari, *Identita e Differenza: Percorsi Storico-antropologici* (Naples: Liguori Press 1986) p.67.
57. Sheldon S. Wolin, 'Fugitive Democracy', in Seyla Benhabib (ed.), *Democracy and Difference: Contesting the Boundaries of the Political* (Princeton NJ: Princeton University Press 1996) p.33.
58. Barth (note 15).
59. Ibid. p.15.
60. Smith (note 52) p.14.
61. Conversi (note 54) p.77.
62. Wolin (note 57); Kathryn A. Manzo, *Creating Boundaries: The Politics of Race and Nation* (Boulder, CO: Lynne Rienner 1996).
63. The 'hardening' of the US-Mexico border is well documented by Williams and Coronado in a 1994 study and by Dunn's work on militarisation and Low-Intensity Conflict Doctrine (LIC). See Edward J. Williams and Irasema Coronado, 'The Hardening of the US-Mexico Borderlands: Causes and Consequences', *International Boundaries Research Unit Boundary and Security Bulletin* 1/4 (1994) pp.6–74 and Timothy J. Dunn, *The Militarization of the US-Mexico Border, 1978–1992* (Austin: The Center for Mexican-American Studies, University of Texas at Austin 1996). Both studies provide extensive empirical evidence for the 'hardening' of the border (such as steel walls, armed border patrol agents, military equipment) and analyze the causes of the hardening including undocumented migration, narcotics trade, and cross border crime. The construction of chain link fences, the use of night-vision goggles and infrared weapons, electronic sensors, helicopters, 'so-called humanitarian aid', and 'psychological operations to influence political and social attitudes among civilian populations', according to Dunn, are all components of LIC doctrine in place to reinforce and 'control' the US-Mexico border (pp.29–30).

64. David Sheppard, 'Silvestre Reyes: His Blockade Changed City, Patrol', *The El Paso Times* (1 Jan. 1994) p.1A. A massive buildup of Border Patrol Agents (in addition to the programmes to construct fortifications of the boundary and increase surveillance through devices borrowed or inspired by the US Military) is underway. Through the 1996 Illegal Immigration Reform and Immigrant Responsibility Act, the US Congress (among other immigration control measures) mandated the US Immigration and Naturalization Service (INS) to hire 1,000 agents per year, for five years, bringing the FY1998 total (nearly 8,000 agents, which represents a doubling of agents since FY 1993) well up. See United States General Accounting Office, 'Illegal Immigration: Southwest Border Strategy Results Inconclusive; More Evaluation Needed' (Report # GAO/GGD-98-21) (Washington, DC: US General Accounting Office 1997) and William J. Krouse, 'US Border Patrol Operations', *Congressional Research Service Report 97-989 EPW* (10 Nov.) (Washington, DC: Congressional Research Service 1997).

65. 'Data' in this study was collected through a series of in-depth, open-ended qualitative interviews conducted by the author in late 1996, designed to access the 'cognitive and interpretive process of people' and allow the respondents full range to describe their thoughts, feelings, and perceptions about Operation Hold the Line, undocumented workers, and the border – in a sense to understand their identity and worldviews. See Michael Quinn Patton, *Qualitative Evaluation Methods* (Newbury Park, CA: Sage Publications 1980) p.207. Interviewees were a cross-section of key participants, both opponents and supporters, in the public discourse in El Paso constructed around (and for) the initiative. Select portions of their comments are reproduced here.

66. Exceptions include Anssi Paasi's work, for example, and approaches coming from other fields. See, for instance, a linguistic perspective from Donna M. Johnson, 'Who is We?: Constructing Communities in U.S.-Mexico Border Discourse', *Discourse and Society* 5/2 (1994) pp.207–31. An excellent compilation from IR on these issues is Michael Shapiro and Haward Alker (eds.), *Challenging Boundaries: Global Flows, Territorial Identities* (Minneapolis, MN: University of Minnesota Press 1996).

67. Mick Presnell, 'Postmodern Ethnography: From Representing the Other to Co-Producing a Text', in Kathryn Carter and Mick Presnell (eds.), *Interpretive Approaches to Interpersonal Communication* (Albany NY: State University of New York Press 1994) p.22. A thorough explication of interpretive and hermeneutic approaches is impossible here, however, the chief objective is to unlock the respondent's construction of social and territorial identity. For an excellent discussion, see Habermas who is paramount among scholars who probe the depths of hermeneutics. In his view, hermeneutics fundamentally seeks to 'understand the meaning of linguistic communication...focus[ing] on the semantic content of speech', but also on the meaning of identity narratives. See Jürgen Habermas, 'On Hermeneutics Claim to Universality' in Kurt Mueller-Vollmer (ed.), *The Hermeneutics Reader: Texts of the German Tradition from the Enlightenment to the Present* (New York: Continuum Press 1994) p.294.

68. Paasi (note 1) p.63.

69. David Campbell, *Writing Security: US Foreign Policy and the Politics of Identity* (Minneapolis, MN: University of Minnesota Press 1998).

70. On 'discourse strategy', see Hugh Mehan, 'The Discourse of the Illegal Immigration Debate: A Case Study in the Politics of Representation', *Discourse and Society* 8/2 (1997) pp.249–70.

71. Paasi (note 1) p.12.

72. David Morley and Kevin Robins, 'Spaces of Identity: Communications Technologies and the Reconfiguration of Europe', *Screen* 30 (1989) pp.10–34; Zdzislaw Mach, *Symbols, Conflict, and Identity: Essays in Political Anthropology* (Albany NY: State University Press of New York 1993).

73. Debbie Nathan, Interview by author, El Paso, Texas (7 Nov. 1996).

74. Doug Mosier, Interview by author, El Paso, Texas (7 Nov. 1996).

75. Suzan Kern, Interview by author, El Paso, Texas (11 Dec. 1996).

76. Paasi (note 1) p.59

77. Daniel Bar-Tal, 'Causes and Consequences of Delegitimisation: Models of Conflict and Ethnocentrism', *Journal of Social Issues* 46 (1990) pp.65–81.

78. Nathan (note 73).
79. Carlos Hamann, 'Public Supports Dramatic Change', *The El Paso Times* (20 March 1994) p.10A.
80. Sheppard (note 64) p.1.
81. Kern (note 75).
82. Nathan (note 73).
83. Quoted in Georgie Anne Geyer, 'Strong Action Finally Puts Teeth Into U.S. Laws', *The El Paso Times* (28 Nov. 1993) p.1G, and Eduardo Montes, 'Border Blockade Put Silvestre Reyes on the Map', *The El Paso Times* (7 Nov. 1993) p.1B.
84. Manzo (note 62) p.220; Dunn (note 63) p.2.
85. Dunn (note 63) p.14.
86. David Steffen, Interview by author, Las Cruces, New Mexico (27 Nov. 1996).
87. Hamann (note 79) p.1A.
88. Mosier (note 74).
89. Most recently, the US Immigration and Naturalization Service is constructing a new 10 foot high fence at the border between Anapra, Mexico (a *colonia* of far northwest Juarez, without water or public utilities) and Sunland Park, New Mexico. Originally envisioned as a steel wall, INS altered its plans amid public protest and built a steel reinforced, chain-link fence with underground barriers prevent digging beneath.
90. Nathan (note 73).
91. Mosier (note 74).
92. Kern (note 75)
93. Barth (note 15); Wolin (note 57).
94. Paasi (note 1).
95. Richard Vela, 'Innocence of Border Christmas is Past', *Norte/Sur: A Monthly Report on The Borderlands of North Central Mexico* 1/6 (Dec. 1993) p.3.
96. See Stephen Chan, 'A Story Beyond *Telos*: Redeeming the Shield of Achilles for a Realism of Rights in IR', *Millennium: Journal of International Studies* 28/1 (1999) pp.101–15.
97. Catherine C. Orenstein, 'Illegal Transnational Labor: Mexicans in California and Haitians in the Dominican Republic', *Journal of International Affairs* 48/2 (winter 1995) p.604.
98. Conversi (note 54) p.79.
99. Manzo (note 62) p.220.
100. Ibid.
101. Paasi (note 1).
102. Ibid. p.8.
103. Ibid. p.9.
104. Mathias Albert and Lothar Brock, 'New Relationships Between Territory and State: The U.S-Mexico Border in Perspective', in David Spener and Kathleen Staudt (eds.), *The U.S.-Mexico Border: Transcending Divisions, Contesting Identities* (Boulder, CO: Lynne Reiner 1998) p.215.
105. Paasi (note 1).
106. Benedict Anderson, *Imagined Communities* (London: Verso Press 1991).
107. 'without borders.'
108. Anzaldúa (note 15) p.194.

African Boundaries and their Interpreters

MAANO RAMUTSINDELA

My map of Africa lies in Europe. Here lies Russia and here ...
lies France, and we are in the middle - that is my
map of Africa. (Otto van Bismarck).[1]

Introduction

The map of Africa imagined by Bismarck in the citation above is an
example of how generations of leaders and ordinary men and women have
thought about places far and near. This visual imagination contributed to the
founding of cartography as 'a body of theoretical and practical knowledge
that map-makers employ to construct maps as a distinct mode of visual
representation'.[2] A growing body of literature has been critical about the
meanings inscribed in the representation of places, and has called for the
deconstruction of the textuality of maps.[3] Such a deconstruction is
increasingly being viewed as a way of understanding maps as social
creations that do not necessarily represent objective 'reality', because maps
are not value free or politically innocent.

In Africa, the political map of the continent has been associated with
both the interests of imperial Europe and the consequent post-colonial
landscape. That landscape continues to inform debate(s) over the
contemporary political geography of the continent.[4] Admittedly, the
reopening of the African boundary discourse on the eve of the twenty-first
century deserves attention for both theoretical and practical reasons. At the
theoretical level, African scholars are seeking approaches to, and
explanations for, what is often derided as the 'African crisis'. Pragmatism,
on the other hand, requires policies and guidelines that can chart the way
forward. The purpose of this essay is to engage in the African boundary
discourse and to debate alternative ways of looking at African boundaries in
the context of the 'African reality' and international experience. I argue that
the intellectual debate over African boundaries as physical lines of
separation imposes severe limitations on our conceptualisation of both the
nature of, and solutions to, boundary problems on the continent. As will be
shown below, the debate over what should happen to Africa's inherited

colonial boundaries hinges on the linear character of boundaries, a perspective that does not pay adequate attention to contemporary conceptualisations of space and boundaries. This is not to argue that such conceptions of space and boundaries should be transplanted into the African context. It is rather to suggest that a narrow view of boundaries does not enhance our understanding of African boundaries.

Evidently, space represented by maps does not exist in the sense of being an object but is, as Lefebvre has noted, produced as a reality in order to serve as a tool of thought and action, a means of control, of domination and power.[5] That is, space is not given and does not exist in absolute terms, but is constructed, represented and lived through its associated images and symbols.[6] Edward Soja aptly captured the spatial turn in the following words:

> contemporary critical studies in the humanities and social sciences have been experiencing an unprecedented spatial turn. In what may in retrospect be seen as one of the most important intellectual development in the late twentieth century, scholars have begun to interpret space and the spatiality of human life with the same critical insight and interpretative power as have traditionally been given to time and history on one hand, and to social relations on the other.[7]

Such conceptualisations of space underscore discourses of boundaries and their meanings. Far from being lines on maps, boundaries are imbued with cultural and social meanings that are constructed and interpreted in many and varied ways.[8]

However, the axis of the academic debate over African boundaries involves two main questions: how the political map of Africa was drawn and what should happen to colonial boundaries in post-independence Africa. Answers to these questions generate at least three interpretations that are very much at the root of this essay. Like the works it engages, the content of this essay is tuned to theoretical evaluation. Where possible, I have attempted to give concrete examples in order to substantiate my point of view.

The Colonial Context

One of the most sustained criticisms of the political map of Africa has been on African boundaries. Although these boundaries have remained intact almost four decades after political liberation swept through the continent, they have been subjected to various interpretations. Of significance to these interpretations is the continuing debate on what should happen to these boundaries. The debate is not new[9] because Pan Africanist stalwarts such as

Kwame Nkrumah of Ghana advocated the change of colonial boundaries since the heyday of the decolonisation process. Nkrumah devoted two of the four pages of the preface to his book, *I Speak of Freedom* (1961), to his argument for the dismantling of colonial boundaries, a process he viewed as a *sina quo non* for the political union of Africa. His remark is worth quoting in some length: 'It is heartening to see so many new flags hoisted in place of the old; it is disturbing to see so many countries of varying sizes and at different levels of development, weak and, in some cases, almost helpless. If this terrible state of fragmentation is allowed to continue it may well be disastrous for us all.'[10]

It was perhaps Julius Nyerere of Tanzania who posed a critical question in the early years of African independence. In his view, the post-independence question was: 'whether Africa shall maintain its internal separation as [it] defeats colonialism or whether the earlier boast "I am an African" shall become a reality'.[11] The essence of the perceptions of Nkrumah and Nyerere is that any meaningful analysis of African boundaries should appreciate the colonial legacy.

Colonialism and its consequent boundaries in Africa provide the context for proponents of boundary change. The origin of African boundaries is commonly ascribed to the Berlin Conference of 1884–85. Many observers viewed the conference as the platform at which Africa was partitioned to serve European interests. As Griffiths wrote: 'Africa was divided up and provided with its sometimes strange colonial boundaries. The Germans insisted on having access to the Zambezi and so the finger of the Caprivi strip was drawn on Europe's map of Africa'.[12]

The view that African boundaries were drawn at the Berlin Conference has come under severe criticism. John Hargreaves has argued that the Berlin Conference did not partition Africa, and pointed out that, 'a widely held myth does associate the Conference with territorial partition, and in a wider sense with the subjection of Black Africa to European colonial control'.[13] In the same vein, Foster, Mommsen and Robinson[14] have argued that the purpose of the conference was not to partition Africa but to regulate the procedure according to which European powers should be entitled to claim formal control over colonial territories. More recently, Katzellenbogen[15] has pointed out that African colonial boundaries existed before the Conference was conveyed as was the case in the present boundary between South Africa and Lesotho, which was fixed by the British and King Moshoeshoe of Lesotho in 1843. The Conference is rather seen as the occasion on which partition received the effective seal of approval by European powers and a stage in the process.[16] The actual partition, it has been argued, is the result of bilateral agreements and arrangements outside the Berlin Conference. In contrast to popular perceptions, Nugent[17] has further argued that boundaries were, in fact, not made for unsuspecting Africans because local people (in the case of the Ghana/ Togo boundary) reinforced such boundaries.

Be that as it may, the present map of Africa is largely a result of European interests in Africa. It is these interests in colonial and post-colonial times, and the state of instability on the continent, that have conditioned the re-emergence of the call to change African boundaries. The logical association of African boundaries with the colonial project is that decolonisation has failed to pay adequate attention to colonial boundaries, hence the need to complete the decolonisation agenda by redrawing the African map.

There is a school of thought that argues that social, political and economic problems on the continent are partly ascribed to the continuing existence of colonial boundaries. Stock,[18] in fact, thinks that colonial structures (including boundaries) have contributed significantly to African underdevelopment. Mazrui[19] estimated that two million lives have been lost defending the colonial boundaries of countries such as Nigeria, Zaire, Sudan and Ethiopia. More recently, a bloody border war that broke out in mid-1998 between Eritrea and Ethiopia over the disputed north-west Tigray region is an indication of the effects of colonial boundaries. McKinley

TABLE 1
SOURCES OF BOUNDARY DISPUTES IN AFRICA

Countries with disputes	Disputed areas
Algeria	Part of south-eastern region claimed by Libya
Botswana	Uninhabited Kasikili (Sidudu) Islands
Cameroon	Lake Chad
Chad	100,000 sq km Aozou Strip between Chad and Libya
Congo	Boundary along the Congo River
Egypt	Boundary with Sudan
Equatorial Guinea	Boundary with Sudan over Corisco Bay
Eritrea	Dispute with Yemen over Hanish Islands
Ethiopia	Dispute with Somali over Ogaden
Gabon	Dispute with Equatorial Guinea in Corisco Bay
Libya	Aozou Strip between Chad and Libya
Malawi	Dispute with Tanzania over Lake Nyasa
Mauritania	Boundary with Senegal
Morocco	Over Western Sahara and islands off the coast of Morocco
Namibia	Dispute with Botswana over Kisikili Islands
Niger	The 19,000sq km area north of Niger claimed by Libya
Nigeria	Dispute with Cameroon over the Bakassi Peninsula
Somalia	Dispute with Ethiopia over the Ogaden
Tanzania	Dispute with Malawi over Lake Nyasa
Tunisia	Maritime dispute with Libya
Western Sahara	Claimed by Morocco
Zaire	The indefinite section of the boundary along the Congo River
Zambia	Quadripoint with Botswana, Namibia and Zambia
Zimbabwe	Quadripoint with Botswana, Namibia and Zambia

Source: Adapted from Central Intelligence Agency, *The World Fact Book* (New York: CIA 1996).

described the colonial legacy of the dispute as follows: 'Ethiopia asserts that it has jurisdiction over a number of areas that used to be part of the Ethiopian administrative provinces of Tigray, but Eritrea claims those regions are within its territory and has cited turn-of-the-century treaties between the Italian colonisers and Ethiopian emperor as proof.'[20]

Generally, more than half the states on the continent have been involved in border disputes since independence (Table 1). In this context, a group of scholars has come out in support of boundary changes. As Asiwaju recently remarked: 'the caliber of the opinion leaders who favo[u]r boundary revision as a solution to Africa's deepening political and development crises makes it difficult to ignore their arguments.'[21] Hence, suggestions have been made to redraw African boundaries. These suggestions reveal a particular interpretation of boundaries.

The Unfinished Business: Interpretation I

Mazrui[22] and Gakwandi[23] have argued that unless boundaries are changed, decolonization in Africa remains an unfinished business. Against the backdrop of this position, Gakwandi proposed a political map of Africa with seven states (see Figure 1). The proposal is underscored by the following main assumptions:

First, it is assumed that the new map would ease existing tension within states, eliminate threats of domination of one ethnic group by another, and thereby reduce conditions leading to the problem of refugees. The logic of the assumption is rooted in the colonial legacy of 'partitioned Africans' whereby different population groups were placed in the same territory while groups from the same territory were split asunder. Asiwaju[24] provides a checklist of one hundred and three (103) African boundaries that divide ethnic groups. It is assumed that such a division led to the emergence of dominant groups that suppress minorities – a condition that led to incidents of bloody conflict in some parts of the continent. Gakwandi[25] argues that such a situation can be rectified by demarcating larger states in which there would be no dominant group (something along the balance of forces thesis).

The creation of larger states to counteract ethnic domination appears to be a simplistic solution. In fact, the viability of the multi-ethnic post-colonial state is being called into question elsewhere in Africa and the world. Clapham[26] observed that the Tigray People's Liberation Front (TPLF) of Ethiopia demanded an Ethiopia organised as an ethnic confederation. The attempt to enlarge states will, undoubtedly, increase the plurality of states. If the problem of ethnic tension caused by multi-ethnic pluralism has not been solved within the present small states and islands, it is doubtful whether it could be solved in larger states. The proposal to

FIGURE 1

THE RE-IMAGINED MAP OF AFRICA

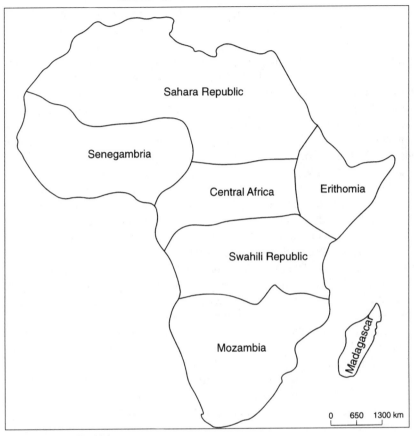

Sahara Republic

Senegambria

Central Africa   Erithomia

Swahili Republic

Mozambia   Madagascar

0   650   1300 km

Source: Gakwandi, 1996.

enlarge states is being made at the time when global trends are pointing towards the shrinking of states under the emerging force of self-determination.

The second assumption is that including the disputed areas and the disputant states in one country can solve existing border disputes. As the number of border disputes (Table 1) shows, disputes over boundaries on the continent are a serious concern. In stark contrast to the proposed way of solving border disputes by amalgamating states, international experience shows that border disputes are solved through legal channels such as the International Court of Justice and methods such as boundary commissions, arbitration, buffer zones, safe havens, transit corridors, condominia, joint development areas, and so on. The experience in many African countries is that the conceivable way of resolving colonial boundary disputes has been by reference to the colonial order.[27] The current boundary dispute between Namibia and Botswana over two minute islands in the Chobe River is, for instance, mainly ascribed to lack of respect for colonial boundaries negotiated by the Germans and the British during the heyday of colonialism.

Thirdly, it is assumed that the proposed map would banish the phenomena of landlocked states thereby easing the flow of commercial goods and services and promote the sharing of resources. Research shows that the developing landlocked states of Africa face more difficult obstacles in attaining access to marine resources.[28] The seriousness of the condition of landlocked states on the continent is shown by the findings that the seven landlocked states were among the eleven poorest states in Africa in 1981.[29] Access to water transport is important because the initial scramble for Africa was about access to coastal areas and navigable rivers. In southern Africa, the apartheid state turned the landlockedness of neighbouring states into a geopolitical tool in order to launch its destabilisation programme on the region. It sabotaged alternative facilities such as the Beira Corridor that was planned as a freight and trading route between Zambia, Zimbabwe, Malawi and Mozambique in order to deny these countries access to port facilities in Beira (Mozambique), and to force them to use South African ports for their trade – a strategy that was adopted in order to maintain the hegemony of apartheid South Africa in the region.[30] The problems of landlockedness fall into two broad categories: access to and from the sea, and the uses of the sea. These problems can be solved without necessarily redrawing maps. European landlocked countries such as Switzerland, the former Czechoslovakia, and Hungary 'have long operated high-seas merchant fleets that fluctuate in size and profitability'.[31] African landlocked states need mechanisms by which transit trade will not be frustrated by international boundaries. The 1982 Law of the Sea Convention provides the legal framework to safeguard the right of access of landlocked states to and from the sea, and freedom of transit.[32] This legal framework and other measures can be used by landlocked states in Africa to enter into transit arrangements and agreements in order to overcome restrictions and obstruction to transit trade.

It can reasonably be assumed that mechanisms which facilitate the flow of people and goods will also enable Africans to share the resources of the continent. Attempts to bundle states together, as the proposed map suggests, would certainly open the available limited resources to larger populations than those existing today. There is already a 'scramble' for resources within the existing small states. At local levels, the manipulation of space aimed at the redistribution of resources has had a fair share of problems. Case studies on strategies intended to promote access to resources in the United States show that redistricting and other forms of spatial manipulation have a limited record of success.[33] More recent examples are found in a number of new local governments in post-apartheid South Africa, where the mixing of racial and ethnic groups within common resource boundaries did not automatically make resources accessible to all.[34] Access to historically white schools, for example, has not been easy for some African families who relocated to former white cities and towns after the abolition of apartheid laws.

The fourth assumption is that 'the newly consolidated states would be able to command greater power and respect in the world than existing states are able to do'.[35] The assumption reduces the occluded density of political power to the mere size of states. It has a bearing on the traditional geopolitical thinking of Halford Mackinder, Friedrich Ratzel, and others who thought that states could be powerful if they were big in terms of territorial size and population numbers. At the dawn of the twenty-first century, few people, if any, would endorse the idea that the political power of a state lies in its territorial size. There is, in fact, a shift in the conceptualisation of power in global politics. The location of power has shifted to actor-networks, among other things.[36] Nye and Owens[37] even went to the extent of speculating that the country that can best lead the information revolution will be more powerful than all others.

The proposed map raises a fundamental question: which criteria have been used to draw the boundaries of the proposed states? The map does not show any meaningful set of criteria. The north and south boundaries of the proposed Central Africa, for instance, are simple horizontal lines which cut across existing states, and tend to create the same 'Berlin effect' they aim to remedy. It is, however, important to note that the map itself is a modification of the regional (in a loose sense) division of the continent into north-, west, south-east-, north-east-, central- and southern Africa, and the islands.[38]

Reconfiguring the Local: Interpretation II

Besides plans to enlarge African states, some scholars have mooted the idea of changing colonial boundaries in order to create even smaller states which accord national divisions more nearly with ethnic ones. The argument is that if parts cannot go together they would be better off divorced. Sudan, where the northern Muslim Arabs are at war with Christians and animists in the south, might be better off divided.[39] Proponents of this argument such as Adebayo Bello[40] argue that multi-national and multi-lingual states carved through colonial boundaries have failed, as they were bound to. The main logic of this proposition is not necessarily a return to the pre-colonial era of

African states which would lead to the creation of thousands of states, but to reconfigure some of the states which suffered as a result of the forced coexistence of communities. Bello argues that, 'linguistic and cultural differences have always been the most compelling factors on which regional and national loyalties are based in all parts of the world and no one should expect it to be different in Africa'.[41] De Blij appears to be supportive of the disintegrative course of African states. He remarked that, 'the map of Africa may show the political boundaries of a dozen states, but does not show the homelands of several hundred tribal peoples, many of whom would put their territory first and the state second in their scheme of priorities.'[42]

Here De Blij overestimated the potential for 'homeland' development on the continent. Even, in the case of South Africa, where the creation of 'homelands' was so pronounced, those 'homelands' (better known as bantustans in the radical lexicon) did not develop from the will of the people they were meant for, but were largely a creation of the white minority government – designed to facilitate the policy of divide and rule.

The use of linguistic and cultural homogeneity in state- and nation-building by Bello (and others) cannot be applied as universal principles. Language and culture are very fluid and tend to yield different results in nation-building projects. In this context, Werbner's observation that 'the story of ethnic difference in Africa threatens to overwhelm the larger debate about post-colonial identity politics across the continent'[43], is worth noting.

What comes to mind about creating smaller states in Africa is the breaking up of the former Soviet Union as a larger state in which different 'nationalities' were forced into co-existence. The disintegration of the Soviet Union should be understood in its context, if advocates of smaller states in Africa are to draw lessons from that experience. There the restructuring of the republics (*perestroika*) required the replacement of conservative bureaucracy with a progressive one for a successful opening up or liberalisation of society (*glasnost*). Smith[44] is of the opinion that these progressives and the demand for a democratic society used the local platform to advance local self-expression and self-determination. The breaking up of states in the former Soviet Union and elsewhere has mainly occurred as a result of the demand for self-determination and secession. In Africa, few attempts were actually made to implement such sentiments by ethnoregional groups, for example Biafra from Nigeria, Katanga from Zaire and Eritrea from Ethiopia. Eritrea succeeded in breaking away from Ethiopia in 1991, after a prolonged war. More recently, the demand for local autonomy has been articulated by the Nuba Mountain faction of Sudan (with the consequent tension between Sudan and Uganda),[45] the right-wing Afrikaners of South Africa, and secessionist movements in Moheli and Anjouan Islands in the Comoros. Given the multi-ethnic character of

African states, one would have expected an increase in the number and intensity of demands for local autonomy. That has not been the case because, in most cases, ethnic groups compete for control of the very state whose limits are defined by colonial boundaries.[46]

The idea that instability in Africa can be contained by eliminating the coexistence of communities is based on the simplified assumption that instability on the continent is a function of forced coexistence. It can be contended that other factors such as the legacy of colonialism, the political culture, external manipulation and influence, the military, and so forth, affect stability within states on the continent. The idea also assumes that Africans from different ethnic background cannot live together - an assumption which is highly contentious.

The Sanctity of the Legacy: Interpretation III

> *We must take Africa as it is, and we must renounce any territorial claims ... African unity demands of each of us complete respect for the legacy we have received from the colonial system, that is to say: maintenance of the present frontiers of respective states* (Modibo Keito, President of Mali).[47]

The reasons for not changing colonial boundaries can be divided into two groups for convenience. The first is that colonial boundaries are irrelevant to Africa's problems.[48] This reason has been dismissed by many observers as historically incorrect. The second reason is that the only way to maintain stability and peace on the continent is by observing inherited boundaries however colonial they might be. This reason was endorsed by the OAU. In its second summit conference in Cairo in 1964, the OAU resolved that all member states should respect the borders existing on the achievement of independence. The OAU resolution was based on the recognition of the perceived danger of widespread disagreement and conflict over common borders.[49] Redrawing boundaries either to create bigger or smaller states was considered a recipe for chaos and unimaginable blood-letting. It is sensible to seek consensus within the inherited boundaries, the argument goes. In line with this thinking, Uzoigwe has argued that 'the map of Africa after partition made more practical sense than it did, for example, in 1879'.[50] The implication of Uzoigwe's argument is that partition has brought territorial order to Africa, in spite of it being the source of serious boundary disputes and battles which continue to threaten Africa's peace and stability. In a similar vein, Austin[51] has mooted the point that though Africa's boundaries are artificial, they have some advantages over uncertain ones.

The view that boundaries should not be changed has overwhelming support because of the durability of colonial boundaries, the protection they enjoy under international law and (more significantly) the interest of past and present governments in maintaining the territorial status quo. Touval[52] has pointed out that only four African states (Somalia, Togo, Ghana and Morocco) rejected their colonial boundaries after independence. Current trends show that African leaders have strong intentions to maintain the territorial status quo, no matter how 'fragile' or 'failed' African states appear to be.[53] A convincing case in point is the state of Lesotho which Anthony Lemon described as 'the only sovereign state in the world (apart from the micro-states of San Marino and the Vatican) to be wholly surrounded by the territory of a single neighbour'.[54] Despite its dependence on South Africa, Lesotho has remained an independent state.

Reconceptualising African Boundaries

The concerns over problems caused by colonial boundaries are genuine and cannot be dismissed as irrelevant to issues affecting the continent. However divergent these concerns are, they all share a common ideal for a peaceful and stable continent. Added to this ideal is the wish to forge unity among the people of the continent. As Julius Nyerere has suggested most recently, 'we should build the broader Pan-Africanism. There is still the room – and need.'[55] The quest for unity in Africa is more urgent in the continent, given the fact that even highly industrialised countries of the North are still pursuing political and economic unity among themselves - as the example of the European Union (EU) shows.

A critical question on African boundaries is whether changing international boundaries physically would solve boundary problems and also enhance political and economic unity. It is my contention that it is not necessary to change boundaries physically in order to achieve these noble goals. Boundary problems in Africa do not necessarily need a blanket solution in the form of a second 'Berlin conference' (the redrawing of the map). The causes of African boundary problems themselves are not the same (see Fugre 1), nor should the solutions be. Some boundary problems require boundaries to be adjusted, as was the case with the boundary problem between Burkina Faso and Mali, which was solved by a new demarcation following the ruling of the International Court of Justice in December 1986. A border dispute caused by 'serious armed incidents' such as that which took place between Cameroonian and Nigerian forces in the Bakassi Peninsula on 3 February 1996[56] does not necessarily require boundary changes as a solution. This problem could be left in the hands of the newly formed Preventive Diplomacy Forum of Eminent Persons whose principal objective is to mediate political disputes in Africa. This could be a viable alternative since Nigeria wants the affected countries (Nigeria and Cameroon) to settle the boundary dispute themselves. It would also be useful to consider that Africa's boundary problems are sometimes caused by the position of boundaries, the use of resources, the way they are perceived (by border peoples and officials), the way they function, and so on.

A viable change that is urgently needed is that of the functions performed by African boundaries - without reducing boundaries to a narrow functionalism. Many critical observers agree that African colonial boundaries were not meant to promote the unity of Africans both within and between states.[57] It could be argued that changing the appearance of colonial boundaries does not, in itself, guarantee the realisation of African unity. Even if people of the same language and culture are 'bounded' together in space, national unity could still remain difficult to achieve as examples of the Basques (Spain), the Irish (Ireland), the Muslims (Pakistan and Bangladesh), and so on show. These examples point to another element that advocates of boundary changes in Africa aim to achieve: national identity. African states are considered to have problems of national identities because the former colonial powers imposed states over heterogeneous groups. Reducing or enlarging these groups could still remain a weak basis on which a new nationalism should emerge because the roots of nationalism and national identities are many and varied. Identities, too, are very fluid and can no longer be confined to state boundaries alone.

If Europe were indeed Africa's mentor of a nation state, it would be useful to learn that the (apparent) unity of Europe through the European Union (EU) has very little, if anything, to do with changing the physical boundaries of states. Rather, the EU has, among other things, focused on the functions of international boundaries of member states. These boundaries have become more porous and integrative for EU member states. Of course, the political, historical and material conditions obtainable in Europe are not the same as those in Africa. These differences notwithstanding, a case can still be made for a regionalisation that seeks to transcend Africa's colonial boundaries.

Notwithstanding the 'danger' of transplanting European models to Africa, which does not need any rehearsal here, research shows that African boundaries hardly represent a genuine partition, as they tend to encourage interaction.[58] This interaction should be built into the new roles of African boundaries. The intended divisive nature of colonial boundaries should be counteracted by efforts to make the same boundaries integrative through commercial activities, development projects, and so forth. As Asiwaju has suggested,

FIGURE 2

TRANS-BORDER CORRIDORS IN SOUTHERN AFRICA

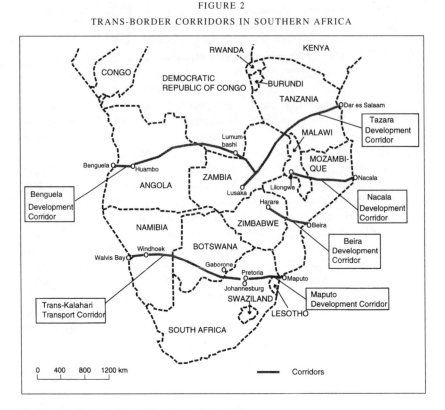

Source: Development Bank of Southern Africa, 1997.

what the African crisis call for is a whole range of policy revisions, including aspects that have hindered the equitable management of transboundary resources within and across national territories and boundaries, so that these may be transformed from being factors of conflict into becoming veritable windows of opportunities for cooperation between and within the states.[59]

Transborder cooperative projects in southern Africa and elsewhere on the continent are the viable and pragmatic ways of infusing new meanings into colonial boundaries. The new Spatial Development Initiatives (SDI) in post-apartheid South (ern) Africa, for instance, encompass a range of economic sectors designed to facilitate economic growth and development in the region through the establishment of development corridors.[60] The most well known of these corridors is the Maputo Development Corridor which is, as

Rogerson[61] puts it, 'anchored on major cross-border infrastructural improvements ...' This corridor has been dubbed the largest infrastructure project on the African continent.[62] Although these corridors (see Figure 2) are still at their initial phase, they have the potential to redefine the divisive nature of colonial boundaries. The Maputo Corridor between South Africa and Mozambique, in particular, is set to transform cross-border movements as the South African Home Affairs Department has agreed to prioritise the streamlining of travel visas and operation of border posts similar to those of the European Union.[63]

In addition to the corridors, other transborder schemes and activities promise to transform the legacy of colonial boundaries from zones of separation to that of integration. The proposed Transfrontier Conservation Areas (TFCAs), for example, straddle national boundaries, thereby not only facilitating the integration of ecological zones (see Figure 3), but having the potential to promote regional integration and prospects for employment.[64] As President Mandela summed up, '[the TFCA] would be a victory not only of the more cohesive management of [the] regions' ecology, but [are] a concrete symbol of regional unity and a spur to development'.[65] The TFCAs are part of the conceptual shift (supported by the World Conservation Union) away from the idea of strictly protected national parks towards greater emphasis on multiple resource use by border communities. Despite their prime focus on conservation, the TFCAs have the potential to open up resources that have hitherto been restricted to national boundaries for use by communities across those borders. In this sense, it could be possible for Africans to share the resources that national boundaries restricted them from so doing.

The launching of a joint regional passport by Kenya, Uganda and Tanzania[66] – and the mooted plan to introduce a regional visa for South Africa, Swaziland and Mozambique – appear to be sound and practical steps to effect changes on the functions of inherited colonial boundaries. Similar steps include the formation of the Exercise Blue Hungwe (SADC peacekeeping force) in 1996/97[67] and the launching of the South Africa-Lesotho Highlands Water Project which was officially opened on 22 January 1998. More recently (June 1998), the launching of the Trans-Lebombo railway linking South Africa, Swaziland and Mozambique has raised hopes for an African Renaissance in the region. These examples have not been used in this essay to assess the failure or success of regional integration,[68] but rather to present trans-border and regional schemes and activities as viable and pragmatic options needed to redefine African boundaries - as opposed to a call for redrawing physical boundaries.

FIGURE 3

TRANS-FRONTIER CONSERVATION AREAS IN SOUTHERN AFRICA

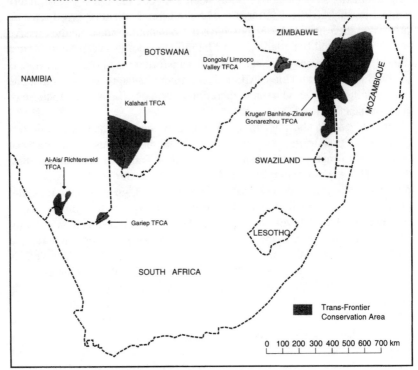

Source: Peaceparks Foundation, 1997.

Conclusion

The purpose of this essay has been to reflect and engage in the ongoing debate on African boundaries. What underlies the debate is the textuality of the map of Africa and practical problems facing the continent. Advocates of boundary changes view the map (of the continent) as perpetuating visible and invisible evils.[69] What African boundary scholars need is to rethink African boundaries within the growing body of boundary literature, which reflects the density of the concept of a boundary.[70]

It can be concluded that the quest for creating new larger or smaller states in Africa appears to be a mixture of ambitions to eradicate the colonially imposed territorial limits, a desire to reclaim the continent's past political institutions, and the search for a 'new start' in state building. Such a quest is genuine and understandable, but need not be reduced to aspirations rather than achievable objectives. Given the fact that Africa is the most divided and troubled continent, concerns over colonial boundaries cannot be dismissed. These concerns need to be accommodated within the changing African reality, lest they become another rhetoric. The analysis presented in this essay suggests that priority in the decolonisation of the map of Africa should be given to changing the character of colonial boundaries rather than their physical appearance. There is no need to draw a new map and impose it on the continent. Whose boundaries will that map be representing? Will that map be compatible with the existing territorial conceptions of African communities? Viewed from a different angle, are they not facing the danger of reproducing 'imposed' boundaries by a new script? As I have suggested elsewhere,[71] drawing politically relevant boundaries for a new order could release other boundary meanings that do not necessarily resonate with the intended broader ambition. Perhaps the question for Africa is not whether or not to draw new boundaries, but how to transcend the limitations imposed by colonial boundaries. I would suggest that the new map should be left to 'evolve' from the (possible) success of regional integration. After all, the new political map suggested by Gakwandi is, in essence, a quest for a regional map!

NOTES

1. R.J. Gavin and J.A. Betley, (eds.) *The Scramble for Africa: Documents on the Berlin West African Conference and Related Subjects, 1884/5* (Ibadan: Ibadan University Press 1973) p.646.
2. R.J. Johnston, D. Gregory and D.M. Smith (eds.), *Dictionary of Human Geography* (Oxford: Blackwell 1994) p.44.
3. H. Lefebvre, *The Production of Space* (Oxford: Blackwell 1991); J.B. Harley, 'Silences and Secrecy: the Hidden Agenda of Cartography in Early Modern Europe', *Imago Mundi* 40, (1988) pp.57–67; J.B. Harley, 'Deconstructing the map', *Cartographica* 26 (1989) pp.1–20; P.J. Taylor, 'Politics in maps, maps in politics: A tribute to Brian Harley (Editorial comment)', *Political Geography* 11/2 (Feb. 1992) pp.127–9; D. Dorling and D. Fairbain, *Mapping: Ways of Representing the World* (Harlow: Longman 1997).
4. *African Studies Association of Political Science Newsletter*, 11 June 1993; M.F. Ramutsindela, 'Southern Africa: A Regional Geography of the Other', in M. Naish (ed.), *Values in Geography* (London: Institute of Education 1998) pp.21–8.
5. H. Lefebvre, *The Production of Space* (Oxford: Blackwell 1991) pp.30–32.
6. J. Agnew and S. Corbridge, *Mastering Space: Hegemony, Territory and International Political Economy* (London: Routledge 1995), Ch.4; S. Duncan and M. Savage, 'Space, Scale and Locality', *Antipode* 21/3 (July 1989) pp.179–206.
7. E.W. Soja, 'Thirdspace: expanding the scope of geographical imagination', in D. Massey, J. Allen and P. Sarre (eds.) *Human Geography Today* (Cambridge: Polity Press 1999) p.261.
8. A. Paasi, *Territories, Boundaries and Consciousness: the Changing Geographies of the Finish-Russian Border* (New York: Wiley 1996); D. Newman and A. Paasi, 'Fences and neighbours in postmodern world: boundary narratives in Political Geography', *Progress in Human Geography* 22/2 (June 1998) pp.186–207.

9. A.I. Asiwaju, 'Fragmentation or integration: what future for African boundaries?', paper delivered at the Fifth Conference of the International Boundaries Research Unit on Borderlands under Stress, Durham, July 1998.
10. K. Nkrumah, *I Speak of Freedom* (London: Panaf Books 1961) p.xi.
11. M.J. Nyerere, *Nyerere: Freedom and Socialism* (Nairobi: Oxford University Press 1986) p.207.
12. I.L. Griffiths, *An Atlas of African Affairs* (London: Routledge 1985) p.45.
13. J.D. Hargreaves, 'The Berlin Conference, West African boundaries, and the eventual partition', in S. Forster, W.J. Mommsen and R. Robinson (eds.), *Bismarck, Europe and Africa: The Berlin Africa Conference 1884-1885 and the Onset of Partition* (Oxford: Oxford University Press 1988) p.313.
14. Ibid. Forster; Mommsen and Robinson introduced their edited volume which was timely produced to mark the 100th year of the Berlin Conference by arguing against the view that Africa was simply partitioned at the Conference.
15. S. Katzellenbogen, 'It didn't happen at Berlin: politics, economics and the ignorance in the setting of Africa's colonial boundaries', in P. Nugent and A.I. Asiwaju (eds.), *African Boundaries: Barriers, Conduits and Opportunities* (London: Pinter 1996) pp.21–34.
16. R. Robinson, 'The conference in Berlin and the future in Africa, 1884–1885', in S. Forster, W.J. Mommsen and R. Robinson (eds.), *Bismarck, Europe and Africa* (Oxford: Oxford University Press 1988) pp.1–32; J.D. Hargreaves, *Decolonization in Africa* (New York: Longman 1996); S. Katzellenbogen, 1996 (see note 15), pp.21–34.
17. P. Nugent, *National Integration and the Vicissitudes of State Power in Ghana: The Political Incorporation of Likpe, a Border Community, 1945–1986* (London: University of London 1992) PhD thesis.
18. R. Stock, (1995) *Africa South of the Sahara* (New York: Guilford Press 1995). There are many other theories of African underdevelopment that cannot be dealt with in this essay.
19. A.A. Mazrui, 'The Bondage of Boundaries', *Economist* 24 Sept. 1993.
20. J. McKinley, 'Eritrea battles Ethiopia', *Mail & Guardian* 5–11 June 1998.
21. Asiwaju was referring to the 1986 Nobel Prize winner (in literature) Wole Soyinka and the famous US-based African political scientist, Ali Mazrui. See A.I. Asiwaju, 1998 (see note 9), pp.1-2.
22. A.A. Mazrui, 'The bondage of boundaries', *Economist* 24 Sept. 1993.
23. A.S. Gakwandi, 'Towards a new political map of Africa', in T. Abdul-Raheem (ed.), *Pan Africanism: Politics, Economy and Social Change in the Twenty-first Century* (London: Pluto 1996) pp.181–90.
24. A.I. Asiwaju, 'Partitioned Culture Areas: A Checklist', in A.I. Asiwaju (ed.), *Partitioned Africans: Ethnic Relations Across Africa's International Boundaries 1884–1984* (London: Hirst and Co. 1985) pp.252–9.
25. A.S. Gakwandi 1996, (see note 23), pp.181–90.
26. C. Clapham, 'Boundary and territory in the horn of Africa', in P. Nugent and A.I. Asiwaju (eds.), *African Boundaries: Barriers, Conduits and Opportunities* (London: Pinter 1996) pp.237–50.
27. D.K. Zormelo, *Integration Theories and Economic Development: A Case Study of the Political and Social Dynamics of ECOWAS* (London: University of London 1994) PhD Thesis.
28. M.I. Glassner, 'Resolving the problems of land-lockedness', *Geopolitics and International Boundaries* 2/1 (1997) pp.197–208.
29. I.L. Griffiths 1985, (see note 12) p.104.
30. J.P. Hayes, *Economic Sanctions on Southern Africa: Thames Essay No.53* (Aldershot: Gower 1987).
31. M.I. Glassner, 1997, (see note 28) p.199.
32. Ibid. pp.201–2.
33. R. Morrill, 'Redistricting, region and representation', *Political Geography Quarterly* 6 (1987) pp.142-160; R. Morrill, 'Spatial engineering and geopolitical integrity', *Political Geography* 15/1 (Jan. 1996) pp.95–7.
34. A. Lemon, 'The new political geography of the local State in South Africa', *Malaysian*

Journal of Tropical Geography 27/2 (1996) pp.35-45; M.F. Ramutsindela, 'The survival of apartheid's last town council in Groblersdal, South Africa', *Development Southern Africa* 15/1 (1998) pp.1–12.

35. A.S. Gakwandi, 1996 (see note 23)
36. G. O'Tuathail, 'Post-modern Geopolitics? The modern geopolitical imagination and beyond', in G. O'Tuathail and S. Dalby (eds.) *Rethinking Geopolitics* (London: Routledge 1998) pp.16–38.
37. J.S. Nye, and W.A. Owens, 'America's information edge', *Foreign Affairs* 75 (1996) pp.20–36.
38. E.A. Boateng, *A Political Geography of Africa* (Cambridge: Cambridge University Press 1978).
39. Editorial, 'Darkest Africa', *Economist*, 13 Feb. 1993, p.17.
40. A. Bello, 'The boundaries must change', *West Africa*, (10–16 April 1995), p.546.
41. Ibid. p.546.
42. H.J. De Blij, *Systematic Political Geography* (New York: Wiley and Sons 1973) p.1.
43. R. Werbner, 'Introduction: multiple identities, plural arenas', in R. Werbner and T. Ranger (eds.) *Post Colonial Identities in Africa*, (London: Zed Books 1996) p.1.
44. G. Smith, 'The Soviet federation: from corporatist to crisis politics', in M. Chicholm and D.M. Smith (eds.) *Shared Space: Divided Space* (London: Unwin Hyman 1990) pp.84–105.
45. *Electronic Mail & Guardian*, 'Pitched battles between Uganda and Sudan', 22 April 1997.
46. C. Ake, *Democracy and Development in Africa* (Washington DC: Brookings Institution, 1996).
47. A.F. Burghardt, 'The bases of territorial claims', *Geographical Review* 63 (1973) p.227.
48. Editorial, 'Africa's bizarre borders', *Economist*, 25 January 1997, p.15. The article opened up with the following words: 'imposed arbitrarily, defended illogically, and blamed incessantly, Africa's frontiers are largely irrelevant to its problems.' These words provoked an immediate dismissal (through published letters) from Josefien Berse and Antje van Driel (The Hague) and the Kenyan High Commissioner in London, M. Ngali (see *Economist*, 15 February 1997, p.8).
49. J.V.R. Prescott, 'Africa's boundary problems', *Optima* 28/1 (1980) pp.3–21; M.I. Glassner, *Political Geography* (New York: Wiley 1996).
50. G.N. Uzoigwe, (1988) 'The Results of the Berlin West Africa Conference: an assessment', in S. Forster, W.J. Mommsen and R. Robinson (eds.) 1988 (see note 13) p.546.
51. D. Austin, 'Africa repartitioned', *Conflict Studies* 193 (1986).
52. S. Touval, (1985) 'Partitioned groups and inter-state relations', in A.I. Asiwaju (ed.), *Partitioned Africans: Ethnic Relations Across Africa's International Boundaries 1884–1984* (London: Hurst and Co. 1985) pp.223–32. Since 1985, the number of independent states that opted to change colonial boundaries has increased. Namibia's international boundaries changed in 1994 as a result of the re-incorporation of the Walvis Bay enclave from South Africa (see D. Simon, 'Strategic territory and territorial strategy: the geopolitics of Walvis' Bay's reintegration into Namibia', *Political Geography* 15/2 (Feb.1996) pp.193–219).
53. P. Chabal, and J. Daloz, 'The Political Instrumentalization of Disorder', paper read at the African Studies Association of the UK Biennial Conference on Comparisons and Transitions, London, September 1998 (See P. Chabal and J. Daloz, *Africa Works: Disorder as Political Instrument* (London: James Currey 1999).
54. A. Lemon, 'Lesotho and the New South Africa: the question of incorporation', *Geographical Journal* 162/3 (Nov. 1996) pp.264.
55. I. Bunting, 'The heart of Africa, Julius Nyerere interviewed on anti-colonial resistance', *New International*, Jan-Feb 1999, pp.12–15.
56. International Court of Justice, 'World Court to hold hearing on provisional measures in Cameroon, Nigeria Boundary Case', *International Court of Justice Press Release*, 28 February 1996.
57. J.S. Coleman, (1994) *Nationalism and Development in Africa* (Berkeley: University of California 1994); J. Lonsdale, 'The conquest state of Kenya, 1895–1905', in B. Berman and J. Lonsdale, *Unhappy Valley (Book 2)* (London: James Currey 1992); K. Nkrumah, *I Speak of Freedom* (London: Panaf Books 1961).

58. P. Nugent and A.I. Asiwaju, 'Introduction: The Paradox of African Boundaries', in P. Nugent and A.I. Asiwaju (eds.), 1996 (see note 15) pp.1–17.
59. A.I. Asiwaju, 1998, (see note 9) p.12.
60. Development Bank of Southern Africa, (1997) *Annual Report* (Midrand: Development Bank of Southern Africa 1997); C.M. Rogerson, 'Restructuring the Post-Apartheid Economy', *Regional Studies* 32 (April 1998) pp.187–97.
61. C.M. Rogerson, Ibid, pp. 190.
62. *Electronic Mail & Guradian*, 'Maputo Corridor gets under way', 8 June 1998.
63. African National Congress, 'Economic renaissance takes off in Maputo', *ANC Briefing* (26 Aug. 1998).
64. *Electronic Mail & Guardian*, 'Mugabe approves game park plan', 3 Aug. 1998.
65. N.R. Mandela, 'Peace Parks Foundation Review', *Africa-Environment and Wildlife* 6 (1998)
66. *Electronic Mail & Guardian*, 'East African States resurrect commonwealth', 28 April 1997.
67. *Electronic Mail & Guardian*, 'Regional Peacekeeping force shapes up', 7 April 1997.
68. A detailed discussion on post-apartheid regional dynamics in southern Africa is presented in D. Simon (ed.) *South Africa in Southern Africa: reconfiguring the region* (Oxford: James Currey 1998).
69. P. Nugent and A.I. Asiwaju (eds.), 1996 (see note 15); A.S. Gakwandi, 1996 (see note 23); E. Wamba-dia-Wamba, 'Democracy, Social Movements and Mass Struggles', in T. Abdul-Raheem (ed.), *Pan Africanism: Politics, Economy and Social Change in the Twenty-first Century* (London: Pluto 1996) pp.541–50.
70. P. Nugent and A.I. Asiwaju (eds.), 1996, (see note 15): A. Paasi, 1996 (see note 8) D. Newman and A. Paasi, 'Fences and neighbours in postmodern world: boundary narratives in Political Geography', *Progress in Human Geography* 22/2 (June 1998) pp.186–207.
71. M.F. Ramutsindela, 'The changing meanings of South Africa's internal boundaries', *Area* 30/4 (Dec. 1998) pp.291–9.

Common Cause for Borderland Minorities? Shared Status among Italy's Ethnic Communities

JULIAN V. MINGHI

Introduction

Italy's three major non-Italian speaking ethnic minority regions are located along its northern boundary with France (the French-speaking Val d'Aosta); with Austria (the German-speaking South Tyrol); and with Slovenia and Austria (the Slovene-speaking area of eastern Friuli). In each region, the ethnic minority is distinct in its location and size, its relative importance within the region, its transborder relations with the neighbour state, and its role in the Italian body politic. Taken together, these three regions account for a sizeable proportion of Italy's official minority language speakers, and over 80 per cent if one excludes Friulian and Sardian. Each has evolved political parties to protect its linguistic and territorial integrity and to articulate its cultural interests – the Union Valdôtaine (UV) in the Val d'Aosta, the Südtiroler Volkspartei (SVP) and the Partito Autonomista Trentino Tirolese (PATT) in the South Tyrol, and the Solvenska Skupnost (SSK) in eastern Friuli. Throughout their history these parties operated totally independent of one another and exclusively within their own regions in partisan support for the ethnic group they represent and for their vested interest in cultural autonomy from the Italian state. There is no record of meetings held among them and certainly no example of collective action prior to 1994. Indeed, the Italian government had always treated these borderland minorities separately and hence had discouraged any common policy. Yet on 18 November 1994, in Bolzano, capital and largest city of the South Tyrol, and again on 28 February 1996 in the mountain resort and gambling casino town of Saint-Vincent in the Val d'Aosta, the leaders of these political parties met together to discuss common problems and to agree upon a collective political agenda for the following year – a 'common cause' that would best support their own aims by joint action in gaining recognition and concessions from the national government in Rome, and also from the regional government of the particular region.[1] Clearly, by late 1994, the political situation in Italy had deteriorated to a point at which these minority groups felt so threatened that they agreed upon this unprecedented step – to join in a common cause.

The paper examines the joint declarations that emerged from these meetings in the context of the changing priorities expressed, the reactions to them in the Italian political hierarchy, and the viability of such novel 'common cause' strategies among minorities sharing the same state. As such, the study fits into the context of the changing nature of Europe's borderland communities, a context that has been extensively studied, especially during the past decade – on the one hand, the unchanging constant of minority/majority ethnic relations, and on the other, the dynamic of rapid change in European spatial relations as a result of the spreading influence of the European Union.[2] Several contributions for understanding better the impact changes in boundary functions are having on borderland communities are to be found in the Europe segment of the 1994, Eurasia, volume in the *World Boundaries* Series.[3] The proceedings of the May 1994 Basel conference on 'Political Boundaries and Coexistence' contain a score of European case studies directly relevant to this context.[4] But this study calls particular attention to the unique aspects of traditional borderland ethnic communities suddenly acting together within this particular dynamic Italian polity. This particular twist, while being part of the European changing borderland scene, is without precedent and deserving of political geographical analysis.

The Italian Political Setting

These meetings were indirectly a result of the deterioration in the Italian government's ability to hold together, in the wake of scandals showing widespread corruption among the parties making up the multi-party coalition governments that had ruled Italy in the late 1980s and early 1990s. Following an 18-month period under an emergency government of technocrats, the meetings were actually precipitated by the formation of the centre-right Berlusconi government as a result of the Italian national elections of March 1994, elections under a reformed system which was meant to avoid complex coalitions and so eliminate the causes of past corruption. Silvio Berlusconi's new Forza Italia party won most seats but not a majority, and hence formed a centre-right coalition government with two strange bedfellows – the Lega Nord of Umberto Bossi and the neo-fascist Alleanza Nazionale led by Gainfranco Fini.[5] Bossi was calling for the introduction of *macroregioni* in a loose federal system and for doing away with smaller 'autonomous' ethnic regions such as the Val d'Aosta, the South Tyrol and Friuli-Venezia Giulia, a proposal hardly designed to inspire confidence among the minority regions' political leaders. Meanwhile, the Alleanza gained several key cabinet positions – including the Culture and Heritage, Ports and Telecommunications, and Transport and the Merchant

Fleet portfolios, all of which had some particular significance for one or more of these borderland minority regions, particularly as the Alleanza had a clear nationalistic agenda against granting any special rights to linguistic minorities in Italy's borderlands and for doing away with the few that had been given.[6] In the 1994 election, the Alleanza had gained solid support among the Italian-speaking urban minority in the South Tyrol and hence its nationalist agenda had become an active local issue.[7]

Not since the fall of the Fascist regime at the end of World War II had a government in Rome included ideological elements so inimical to the cultural and political aspirations of these ethnic minorities. Not surprisingly, the three minority ethnic groups felt under immediate and common threat and hence banded together to discuss their situation. Even after the fall of the Berlusconi government over the Christmas/New Year break of 1995/96, followed by the installation of yet another 'technical' government, this perceived threat was not sufficiently removed and hence the group met again in early 1996 to reassess the situation for the immediate future, as a new national election seemed likely. Only after the election of the centre-left Prodi government under the Partito Democratico della Sinistra (PDS) and its allies in April 1996 was the immediacy of the threat seen to fade and, as of this writing, there have been no subsequent meetings. The Prodi government gave high priority to reassuring minority groups in Italy that it will revamp policy towards them by establishing a commission to suggest legislation that would for the first time adopt a common and more liberal policy towards such groups.

The Three Minority Regions

All three groups are located in regions that fall into the 'autonomous' category Italy was forced by pressure from neighbours to create after WWII.[8]

The Val d'Aosta, with about 115,000 mostly French-speaking population, has remained stable in political status, but has expanded in its importance in recent decades with the opening of the Mount Blanc and Great Saint Bernard tunnels in the late 1960s and their connections with the French and Italian superhighway systems, vastly improving the region's linkages with western Switzerland and the Savoie region of France, and the expansion of foreign and domestic tourism and casino gambling.[9] The South Tyrol, gained by Italy from Austria in 1919, was subjected to extreme Italianisation policies under Fascism – attempts at linguistic conversion, inundation by Italian immigrants from the Mezzogiorno, and ethnic cleansing of German-speakers from 1939 to 1943. After the Second World War, this ex-Austrian region was included in the Trentino-Alto Adige autonomous region made up of the provinces of Bolzano and Trento. Although the PATT still represents the small German-speaking minority in the province of Trento, a more liberal government policy adopted in 1972 created a separate autonomous province of Bolzano (Bozen) which better fitted the size and shape of the original southern portion of Austria's traditional Tyrol province and also the contemporary distribution of the German-speaking majority of 300,000, about 68 per cent of the total provincial population. The region sits astride the major European historic north/south route over the Brenner Pass, a critical European Union 'bridge' over the Alps linking Germany and Italy through Austria, and this prosperous region now has Italy's highest per capita income and lowest unemployment rate.[10]

The Friuli-Venezia Giulia region of northeastern Italy was specifically created to accommodate the large Friulian-speaking population concentrated in the region around the capital, but it also contains on its eastern margin about 96,000 Slovene-speakers in a narrow north-south band along the Austrian and Slovenian (ex-Yugoslav) borders. Unlike in the other two cases, a very substantial shift in the location of the international boundary took place in 1947, with a major gain of territory by Yugoslavia and the consequent disruption of the regional economy of the Italian borderland – the severance of Trieste and Gorizia from their hinterlands, the build-up of NATO military concentrations at a perceived weak point in Western defences, the confrontation of the Cold War, and the absorption of over 150,000 Italian refugees, most of whom were purposely located in the borderland, so reducing the Slovene population proportion of the region to about 60 per cent. This region, disadvantaged for several decades after the war, has also undergone rapid economic development over the past few years, especially with adjacent Austria joining the European Union in 1995. Hence, the region has taken full advantage of its hitherto peripheral border location, given the end of the Cold War and the breakup of Yugoslavia which have served to increase dramatically exchanges with the newly-created neighbour state of Slovenia in 1991 as well as with the rest of central and eastern Europe.[11] Hence, by the mid-1990s, all three regions were in a most advantageous situation, both enjoying the highest standards of living of any Italian regions and with the potential for further economic growth by exploiting their borderland location.

The dissimilarities among these regions are obvious – unique locations, distinctive histories, contrasting sizes of areal extent and population, populations varying from 53 per cent to 68 per cent of the total being of the linguistic minority as opposed to the Italian-speaking segment of the region, and variations over time in their relative value status to the Italian state.[12] Nevertheless, the elements the three regions hold in common are quite striking. They all fall within Italy's alpine zone, they are all borderland locations near minorities from relevant sponsor-neighbours, with whom links have been forged and maintained through metaphor and narrative based on common culture, all have undergone a period of separatist policy in recent history, all faced ethnic-linguistic repression during the Fascist period, all share the status of regional autonomy since World War II, all have made considerable gains in cultural autonomy since the early 1970s, and all have felt the impact of fundamental economic changes in improved international access and relative location over the past two decades.

The Two Joint Declarations – A Common Cause

The preamble to the 1994 Joint Declaration makes reference to the political swing to the right in Italy towards 'authoritarianism and nationalism' including proposals for reforms that 'are against the interests of minorities and contrary to general trends in Europe' and hence identifies the need for joint action. The group resolved, among other things, to keep one another informed of the contemporary situation in their regions, to offer mutual help in a show of solidarity, to coordinate electoral activity so as to ensure maximum representation of their respective minorities, and, very significantly, to collaborate for the first time with minority parties from all over Europe in establishing an international convention and empowering minority groups through European legislation. At the second meeting 15 months later and a few weeks after the fall of the Berlusconi government, the political situation is seen, if anything, as even cloudier and more difficult for linguistic minorities, especially given the tendency towards 'ungovernability', placing Italian democracy in jeopardy. The preamble mentions multiple attacks and arguments being made against minority rights 'by arrogant and aggressive centralist forces'. A proposed amendment to Article 6 of the Italian constitution, which would have favoured especially the Slovene language group, had just been defeated in the Italian Chamber of Deputies and the Lega Nord had launched a propaganda campaign to discredit the regions' special autonomy status as an 'unjustly privileged institution'. Hence the Second Joint Declaration included several of the original resolutions but in a revised and more specific form. For example, the electoral cooperation clause called for the development of several specific campaign themes 'to win support for positions consistent with the historic and cultural patrimony of our communities'. The most important common element between the two declarations is the emphasis given to the growing role of the European Union in guaranteeing the rights of linguistic minorities within the states of the Community.

Implications for the Future

The minorities of these three regions are seen by White as all grouped under 'Type 7' in his classification of linguistic minorities – groups that are close-knit and are contiguous to the external majority state.[13] Such groups are obviously prone to irredentist movements, especially if the minority was created by a change in frontier dividing a particular group from its linguistic homeland, as in the case of the South Tyrol. White concludes that 'Type 7' minorities have a distinct advantage over others in a state. Size, economic importance and political articulation from a close-knit group are not enough to guarantee the protection of human rights, but location in a borderland adjoining an external sponsor – if the state's regime values a good working relationship with its neighbour – gives such a group a definite edge.[14] Hence, in making common cause among all three regions sharing such an edge, these joint declarations can be seen as most effective instruments in blunting the challenge from Rome. With Austria's accession to the European Union in 1995 and Slovenia's inclusion in a 1998 exclusive list of the next wave of acceptable future members, all neighbouring states to Italy in reference to these three regions are most definitely in the category of states with which Italy wishes to retain a good working relationship.

Soon, despite the complex and often bitter history of ethnic conflict and territorial rearrangements, questions of free political expression and ethnic rights in all three regions will be seen more as internal matters for the European Union and less as exclusive problems for the Italian state.

One can also take the approach that a 'common cause environment' had developed over the years leading up to the 1994–96 period, allowing for the successful joint action undertaken by these parties. These regions share the basic need to preserve their pristine alpine environment while exploiting their tourism advantages; to protect their superior standard of living, with high levels of public spending and per-capita income in relation to neighbouring regions; to exploit the advantages of their multi-lingualism in tourism and trade, and generally in giving them an edge in the new Europe; and, in general, to get the full beneficial impact of being part of borderland euroregions moving from periphery to centre status, especially in the case of the Slovene minority and its privileged location regarding the end of the Cold War, market economy development in Central Europe and EU expansion.[15] While perhaps, with closer relations among neighbouring states, the traditional 'guarantor card' cannot now be individually played successfully (as the SVP played it for decades, working with the Tyrol provincial and the Austrian national governments to pressure Italy diplomatically), the regions can now play in unison the 'European card' in reaction to perceived threats to their collective interests from the parent state (see Figures 1 and 2).

FIGURE 1

THE OLD-TRADITIONAL MINORITY BORDERLAND RELATIONS IN ITALY

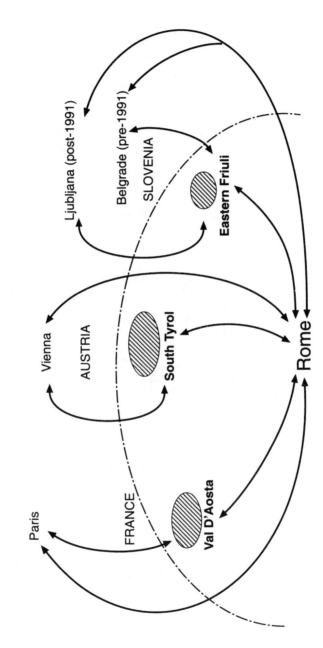

FIGURE 2

THE COMMON CAUSE APPROACH TO MINORITY BORDERLAND RELATIONS IN ITALY

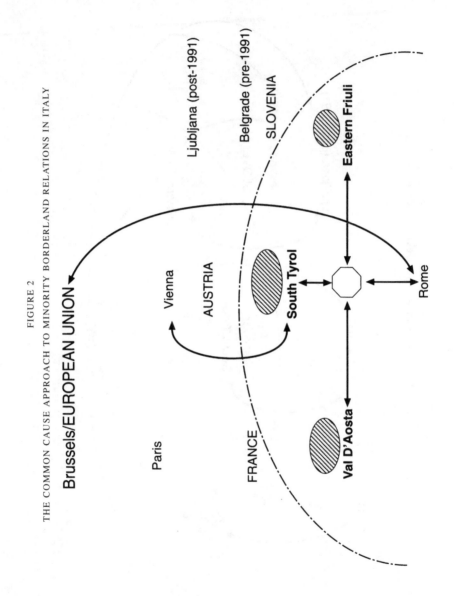

There is no doubt whatsoever that the resolution in the group's 1994 declaration to plead their case for guaranteed linguistic and cultural minority rights beyond Italy and beyond the neighbour-sponsor states to a European Union level played a role in denying the Berlusconi government a sufficient level of acceptability among Italy's major partners in the Union. In particular, French and German leaders and media made constant reference to the inclusion of neo-fascist elements in the Berlusconi government, which helped to assure its fall after less than nine months in office. Hence, both at the foreign policy level of neighbour European states and by the overtly supportive policies for linguistic minorities of organs of the European Union in Brussels such as the Commission on the Regions, the Italian government of Berlusconi was being forced to abandon any moves that would lead to a decline in the rights of these borderland linguistic minorities.

Conclusion

In 1997 the Prodi government established a constitutional reform commission under PDS leader Massimo D'Alema whose task included proposing legislation that would guarantee rights and representation equally for all ethnic-linguistic minority groups. The D'Alema Commission, which included several leaders of the political parties who were signatories to the 1994 and 1996 joint declarations, was due to publish its findings in 1998, but the Commission suspended its work when the Berlusconi group in parliament refused to participate further. As a consequence, in the autumn of 1998, separate legislation was introduced concerning the rights of regional ethnic-linguistic minorities, but excluding national border minorities, although efforts continue to develop a standard approach to such minorities within the framework of general constitutional reform. Clearly the trend in Europe towards the creation of transborder regions of cooperation and exchange, together with the traditional instability of Italian politics, provide a timely context for an examination of the effectiveness of this common cause strategy.

The two joint declarations that form the basis of this paper, while clearly changing permanently the status of these three ethnic communities within the Italian state, may well turn out to be a flash-in-the-pan in the greater context of European borderlands. Time will tell, but all this suggests that we may be in transition from one era in the political geography of borderlands to another as illustrated in the models for Italy illustrated in Figures 1 and 2, whereby, in moving into a new era, a strategy of common cause has far greater assurance of success than the former policy by which minorities sought help uniquely through neighbour guarantors. The results of this study suggest that this cooperative action by the representatives of these three ethnic-linguistic minority regions in challenging Italian tendencies seen as a threat to their interests was most effective and successful at consolidating and expanding local political control over the cultural life of each linguistic group, while at the same time enabling the regions to continue to enjoy political peace and economic prosperity. This development during the last decade of this century may well be a harbinger of change in the process by which European borderland minorities go about doing business with their central national governments in the twenty-first century.

NOTES

1. *Dichiarazioni congiunte dei rappresentanti dei movimenti politici delle comunità etnico-linguistiche e dei movimenti autonomisti*, Bolzano, 18 Nov. 1994 and Saint-Vincent, 25 Feb. 1996.
2. For examples of this changing context see S.Cassese and L. Torchia, 'The Meso Level in Italy', in L.J. Sharp (ed.), *The Rise of Meso Government in Europe* (London: Sage 1993); Commission of the European Communities, *Linguistic Minorities in Countries belonging to the European Community* (Luxembourg: Office for Official Publications of the European Community 1986); C. Desideri, 'Italian Regions in the European Community', in J. Jones and M. Keating (eds.), *The European Union and the Regions* (Oxford: Clarendon Press 1995).
3. C. Grundy-Warr (ed.), *Eurasia: World Boundaries*, Vol.3 (London: Routledge 1994).
4. W.A. Gallusser (ed.), *Political Boundaries and Coexistence* (Berne: Peter Lang 1994).
5. John Agnew, 'The Dramaturgy of Horizons: Geographical Scale in the 'Reconstruction of Italy' by the New Italian Political Parties', *Political Geography* 16/2 (Feb. 1997) pp.99–121.
6. J.V. Minghi, 'Voting and Borderland Minorities: Recent Italian Elections and the Slovene Minority in eastern Friuli-Venezia Giulia', *GeoJournal* 43/3 (Nov. 1997) pp.263–71.
7. S. Tiella, 'Quelques Remarques concernant la Proposition d'une Eurorégion Alpine Italo-Autrichienne', in H. Goetschy and A-L. Sanguin (eds.), *Langues Régionales et Relations Transfrontaliéres en Europe* (Paris: Harmattan 1995) p.265.
8. Sicily and Sardinia are the remaining two of a total of five official autonomous regions in Italy.
9. P. White, 'Geographical Aspects of Minority Language Situations in Italy', in Colin H. Williams (ed.), *Linguistic Minorities, Society and Territory* (Clevendon: Multilingual Matters 1991) pp.44–65.
10. S. Tiella (note 5) pp.263–71.
11. V. Klemencic and M. Klemencic, 'Structures Nationales des Groupes Ethniques et des Minorités Nationales dans l'Eurorégion Alpe-Adria', in Goetschy and Sanguin (note 7) pp.173–203.
12. P. Nedle, M. Strubell, and G. Williams, *Euromosaic* (Luxembourg: Office for the Official Publications of the European Community 1996).
13. P. White (note 9) p.50.
14. Ibid. pp.62–3.
15. This attitude is perhaps best captured from a statement in an election poster for the late Darko Bratina as a candidate for the 'Slovene' seat in the Italian Senate in 1994: 'From a mutilated territory to a region where we can live and plan our future together with new personal and cultural contacts, new ways of exchange and development, new opportunities for work and business. In finding ourselves once again in a nodal location between east and west, the challenge now is to quit being on the periphery and to consciously push ourselves into the center of Europe'.

Bounding Whose Territory?
Potential Conflict between a State and a Province Desiring Statehood

DAVID B. KNIGHT

Introduction

There is a belief that as the world becomes increasingly economically integrated, the power and influence of the state will be threatened more and more by the rising importance of regions, whether the latter are totally within states or cut across shared boundaries between two and more states. The outcome of such threats will, among other things, involve the interplay between group politico-territorial identities, territory (and its bounding and organisation), self-determination, and political decision-making. These elements, when linked, can have dynamic consequences for the world's political map.

A consequence of globalization, many authors maintain, is the weakening of the state.[1] As Waterman observes:

> as sovereignty is weakened, whether by people identifying with some 'world-culture' rather than a national one, or through the increased activities of multinationals operating as economic units within the open lattice-work of nation-states, the power of the nation-state to determine the futures of its citizens is slackened too. However, the weakening of the power of the nation-state within its own borders tends to unleash countervailing forces to the global ones in the form of intensely nationalist sentiments.[2]

Consequences of the latter include, first, a bravado reaction, such as the expression of competing nationalisms and resulting aggression between Argentina and Britain over the Falklands/Malvinas. Second, a reaction to changing external circumstances can take a bullying form, as with the extraterritorial (especially trade) decisions of the US Congress, the members of which, responding to nationalist ideology, are seeking to maintain the 'place' of the USA in the world by trying to force its will on businesses operating in other states. In contrast, third, other states may express their nationalism by linking it to a form of internationalism, illustrated by the UN peacekeeping activities in East Timor by Australia,

New Zealand and other smaller states. However, fourth, a quite different consequence can result. Waterman continues:

> [Nationalist sentiments] play upon related pressures *within* the societies of the nation-states [causing], in turn, increasing instability within the state. If the instability is spatially distinct, then a solution involving separation of the contestants, segregation by state, if you will, becomes a possibility.[3]

This paper is concerned with selected possible outcomes of competing nationalist sentiments within states. Specifically, it is concerned with the consequences of the interplay of elements identified above, in the context of a state within which a regionally dominant minority, as a nation, wants independence within its own sovereign state. The central question addressed is, to what territory would the minority be entitled if secession were to occur?

Theorising Some Consequences of Spatial Distinctiveness

'Instability' that is 'spatially distinct', to use Waterman's phrase, is an interesting turn of phrase, one that takes on special meaning when we consider 'peoples' located within regions of states who advance their desire for political independence.[4] With particular reference to Europe, some recent postmodernist writers hold that we have entered a new phase of understanding pertaining to the political organisation of territory, one that will permit multi-identities to exist peacefully in shared space, but Newman provides an important caution:

> While processes of globalization have been important in creating and promoting the dialogue of peace, the implementation on the ground takes place at the local level and, as such, remains constrained by many of the ethno-exclusive attitudes which caused the conflict in the first place.[5]

Despite advances towards the increased integration of Europe, wherein people of existing states are willing to give up degrees of national authority to new international institutions and, for many, to identify with a European identity, there are some sub-state peoples in Europe who want to gain statehood for themselves. Ironically, in so doing, they too may identify as European – but not through the intermediary of the state within which they find themselves. Such is the case with Scottish nationalists, for example; they want to have their own state of Scotland – standing apart from the UK – recognised internationally, but it would be but one of many regions within Europe. The same presumably holds true for the most ardent separatists – or nationalists – in Catalonia and Euskade, for instance, who may also accept themselves as Europeans, but not as Spaniards. The issue of identity, and levels of attachments to different levels of identity, is a fascinating matter, for at root there is the key question – to what level of identity is primacy given? At issue is the scale of primary allegiance.[6]

If an overwhelming majority within a state give primacy to the 'nation' that is allied to the state, there is likely not to be internal conflict because of nationalism (though conflict within the state may well occur because of other 'normal' ongoing societal issues). People who have an attachment to the 'nation' will also have attachments to other, lower-level expressions of 'self', be it to a region of the state, to a village or a city and, perhaps, to neighbourhoods within them, to family, and to various voluntary organisations. The interplay between these various measures of 'self' can reinforce each other. Further, while there are many states with multi-cultural and multiethnic populations, wherein there may be competing senses of group self, conflict does not necessarily exist as a given. However, if a well-defined people within a state gives primacy to a level of identity that is 'less' than the state-wide national one, tension and possibly outright conflict may result as the national group politico-territorial identity seeks to maintain control of the local group politico-territorial identity. Each group may use its own formulation of national 'self' and its nationalism, with the regionally-dominant group politico-territorial identity seeking to create an appreciation for why 'ethno-exclusivity' is necessary for the survival of 'the nation' which, from both international and the state's national perspectives, may be classed as a sub-state nation.[7]

Any national government having to contend with a sub-state nation will seek effectively to accommodate, manipulate, subdue, or crush any notion of separateness if coincident with the desire for territorial separation and the attainment of sovereignty. Many systems of government permit the expression of the minorities' needs and aspirations, whether within a unitary or a federal state system. The key to success in accommodating contrasting needs and aspirations is not the system of government, however, as much as it is the will of the people to accept differences. Indeed, distinctiveness may be accepted for each cultural community within a multi-cultural, multiethnic state even as, at the same time, there is the acceptance of a shared 'national' identity that transcends regions and lower-level group identity attachments. James and Jackson identify, however, that a general characteristic of multinational and multiethnic statehood is that 'one linguistic or cultural or religious group' dominates, with minorities 'at best only tolerated and protected but [not accepted as] equal partners'.[8] If a minority that is regionally-focused within the state comes to believe that their aspirations cannot be met within the existing state, no matter how much goodwill there is on the part of the majority to make accommodations for the distinctiveness of the minority, secession may be sought by that minority.[9] In these instances, regionally-dominant but national-minority senses of separateness can be so profound – for the minority – that separate statehood is deemed to be an inevitable 'right'. Examples abound of group politico-territorial identities being willing to fight and even die for the achievement of statehood. In this, the sub-state nationalisms have expressed one of the key ideals of all nationalisms.[10]

A call for self-determination – that is, full independence and self-control within one's own sovereign territory – may, in part, reflect a desire by the minority to counter globalising processes that undercut cultural pluralism, or it may simply be that they do not want to continue to be dominated by the 'other' people and 'their' state, from whom they feel they must separate. Whether separation and independence is the best recourse is, of course, open to debate, for larger, not smaller, forms of political integration are seen by many to make the most sense. But who is to decide the best interpretation of 'reason'?! The acceptance by states of self-determination is often easy – as long as it is in someone else's territory!

Two contrasting 'rights' can be identified here:

• the right under international law for an existing state to protect and maintain its existing territory;

• the (not clearly delineated) right of a regionally-dominant, sub-state people, self-defined as a nation, to have control over itself in its own state through the application of self-determination and territorial secession, whereby the fundamental character of a state and of statehood is achieved.

The fundamental difference between these two perspectives on rights is that the first stresses territory over identity, while the second stresses identity over territory.[11] The issues of identity, territory and control, when tied to recognition within the international system of states, clearly are intertwined. This is not the place to discuss the legalities of any right to secession, for contrasting stances are held, but it is clear from changes to the world's political map in recent decades that secessions can occur.

If it is accepted that a people can secede from the state within which they currently find themselves, then what territory can they take with them? Is there a historical basis for dividing the national territory? Is it simply a matter of the regional minority declaring that it knows what territory is at issue and that is that? Or must there be negotiations over the extent of the territory, that is, assuming the existing state is willing to negotiate such a negation of part of itself? Or will 'might' decide? The use of negotiations and the general lack of violence applied in the division of Czechoslovakia into two states – the Czech Republic and Slovakia – on 1 January 1993, with good relations prevailing, as also happened when Sweden and Norway divided in 1905 and though with a lesser presence of good will when Slovenia seceded from Yugoslavia in 1991. However, as in Biafra's attempt to separate from Nigeria, Bangladesh's separation from Pakistan, Eritrea's secession from Ethiopia, the breakup of former Yugoslavia and, even as these words are being written, in parts of Indonesia and several regions of the former USSR, carving territory from an existing state and the acceptance of a new statehood can be a vicious process, with disastrous consequences for the general population.[12]

The 'nation without a country' syndrome expresses itself in many forms, and not all lead to national conflict with loss of life. For instance, it is instructive to consider Scotland as a region within the UK. There is at least a minority desirous of secession from the UK, and it may be that Scots will in time find that they have more meaningful links with Europe than with England (another region in the UK). This realisation could, in time, threaten the structure of the existing state. But apart from on-screen rewrites of a heroic history, toughly fought rugby games, and ongoing soccer hooliganism, violence between Scotland and England is not expected if each country were to find its way – each as a region (within the UK and within Europe) and as an integral part of the UK (within changing Europe) – into separate status in the international system of states. However, if Scots reached the point of separation from the UK, would it be enough to base the international boundary with England on the well-established Scottish nation-territory link, with the Scots' defined territory becoming sovereign? The boundary between the two 'regions' has been subject to past periodic relocations. Would the remainder of the UK be content to accept the current boundary as the basis of territorial separation?

Mention of the potential for a change in territorial definition for Scots and the issue of boundary definition raises the general point that all secessionists must logically and immediately face, that is, what territory can a seceding people 'take with them' as they create a new state. And who is to decide? Should one or another group dominate, that is, the leaders of the seceding people, or the government of the existing state to be divided? Inevitably agreement, however reached and under whatever form of duress, would eventually have to be accepted by both parties. One can theorise that the seceding population could be granted – or be able to take – only that territory within which they maintain numerical and cultural dominance. But what if they claim a territory far larger than just that within which they are dominant? And what if the broader territory is not widely settled? Perhaps the answer to these questions is that the territory should be that over which the seceding people have the ability to maintain effective control. But what if that same territory can legitimately be said to be under the effective control of the existing state? If conflicting claims exist then some form of conflict resolution – victory in war or via negotiation or mediation – will be required to effect the territorial secession.

Of all the questions raised here, we maintain that the most important pertains to territory – specifically, with what territory can a people secede? It is not possible to answer this question in a general way, for in each case it is necessary to consider the particular circumstances pertaining to the attributes of, and historical claims to, the territory in question.[13] As a result, it is only by considering the specifics of secession processes, influenced as they are by the manner in which secession is accepted and agreed to, that it will be evident what territory is to be carved from the existing state.[14] Notwithstanding this caution, it is likely to be possible in advance to identify what each party's stance is, though this in itself will guarantee nothing in terms of what will actually occur, that is, if the secession process proceeds.

Another point needs to be identified here. The process of territorial separation, whereby two states are created out of one involves a mix of input and feedback within the political system and need not involve violence if there is the will on both sides to keep the process peaceful, if not also tension free. However, as suggested above, history has demonstrated that existing states will often use all means possible, including military force, to try to prevent secession.

The above thoughts help frame a case study of identity-territory conflict, wherein one party – the Quebec separatists – want to have 'their' territory divided from Canada as a new state. The outcome of the ongoing conflict over priority of allegiance remains uncertain.[15] The secessionist process and federal counteractions are not the prime concern here.[16] Rather, we focus on the territorial bounding dimension of the conflict. Any change in Canada's international boundaries as a consequence of the creation of an independent State of Quebec necessarily would entail a complex series of issues – and not just for Quebec but of these only the matter of territory is highlighted in this paper.

We begin by highlighting contrasting perspectives on the claim to independence from within Quebec and, more generally, within Canada, commenting on the importance of a land base and territorial size, and identifying evolutionary highlights of Quebec's politico-territorial partitioning, before considering the problems of 'which territory?'

Contrasting Perspectives on Quebec and Canada

The current government of the Province of Quebec seeks to take Quebec out of the Canadian confederation to become a sovereign State. The federal government, in turn, seeks to undermine the sovereignist agenda. There are essentially four points of view:

- separatists within Quebec maintain that the Quebecois nation has the right to separate from Canada and so have its own separate, independent country;

- federalists, both within Quebec and across the remainder of Canada, maintain that Quebec will remain part of Canada;

- a small minority of Canadians outside Quebec, fed up with constitutional wrangling and threats from Quebec, have declared, 'just let *them* go!'; and

- Aboriginal people in Quebec declare that not only must they decide their own future (within Quebec and within, or apart from, Canada), and not have it be decided for them by others, but have recorded in referenda their nonacceptance of secession by Quebec.

Not put off by federalist opposition, which has maintained the majority in two provincial referenda, the Parti Quebecois [PQ] government and its supporters state that it is not a matter of 'if' Quebec will become independent but 'when'. Indeed, as Jacques Parizeau, former Premier of Quebec, recently told me: 'There will be referenda until we get a majority vote for separation!'

During the 1970s and 1980s, the federal government, notably through its former prime minister Pierre Trudeau, advanced classic arguments in favour of a multicultural, multiethnic nationalism within a federal state. Under a different prime minister, Jean Crétien, the government, stung by the near defeat in the second referendum, asked the Canadian Supreme Court to rule on the right of Quebec to secede, given that there is no provision for such in the constitution. The court's decision was dual in character: there is no such right, however, if a 'clear majority' of Quebeckers vote for independence then the federal government must enter into negotiations with the secessionist leaders.[17] No definition of 'clear majority' was given, so this point is being much debated.[18] That aside, if we suppose that Quebec, sooner or later, eventually does succeed in gaining independent status then, among many other things, new international boundaries would have to be created.[19] What might these be?

The PQ has declared that the existing provincial-territorial bounds are inviolable, hence they must also be the boundaries for an independent Quebec. But could Canada agree to existing inter-provincial boundaries being transformed into international ones? If separation is agreed upon, might not Canada insist on a territorial 'price' for Quebec to 'pay' as a condition for secession? If the latter question is deemed to have merit and

Canada's territorial demands could be upheld, what parts of what is now Quebec would be contentious? This question is not merely of academic interest for, to the anger and dismay of Quebecois separatists but the satisfaction of minorities within Quebec, the prime minister of Canada has declared that if Quebec can secede from Canada then parts of Quebec can secede from Quebec.

A Land Base and the Issue of Size

Why should there be conflict over what territory an independent state of Quebec would be entitled to? Since the most fundamental necessity for any state is a territorial base and its contents – for without territory a state cannot exist[20] – Quebecois want no less than what is now said to 'belong' to the Province of Quebec. But this territory is not *separately* Quebec's, for it forms part of Canada. The state of Canada has a bounded territory and, under international law, all within it is held to be part of the state. The basis for conflict is clear.

The territory of Canada is today divided into ten provinces and three territories. Canada benefits, and suffers, from having a mammoth national territory – the second largest in the world, after Russia. There is great areal variation in the territorial units within Canada: Quebec, one of the ten provinces, with 1,540,680 sq. km. is larger than the combined area of the provinces of Alberta, Saskatchewan, New Brunswick, Nova Scotia, and Prince Edward Island. Ontario, the second largest province, while smaller than Quebec is nevertheless huge by any measure (1,068,582 sq. km.). The Northwest Territories (divided in 1999 into NWT and Nunavut) is 3,379,684 sq. km. Thus, in a sense, Quebec is 'small', yet Quebec is roughly equal in size to northern Europe and is nearly three times the size of France (547,026 sq. km.). Quebec currently represents 15.4 per cent of the total area of Canada.

The issue of the moment is what territory would Quebec be entitled to take out of confederation, that is, if Canada permitted secession to occur? Would it be entitled to take the current land base that is bounded by existing inter-provincial boundaries, or perhaps a territory greater or lesser than that? To appreciate the conflicting contemporary perspectives, it is necessary to outline the manner in which Canada's boundaries, notably as they pertain to Quebec, came into being.

Historical Considerations: The Changing Bounds of Quebec[21]

Formal international and internal delineation of territories by Europeans occurred as a result of competing claims in North America by the French and English. French territorial claims began to have meaning with the founding of Quebec 'city' and other fledgling settlements in New France. Meanwhile, the English had settled Virginia and had formally delineated a claim in Acadia for the colony of Nova Scotia, an area located within French-claimed territory between Cape Cod and Cape Breton. The bounds of the French and English territorial claims thus overlapped, and were to remain in contention for more than a century. In 1627 the King of France granted a charter for the development of government of New France, in an area encompassing the lands and waters from Florida to the Arctic Circle, and from Newfoundland to the 'great fresh water sea' in the west, including the 'lands in the watershed of the St. Lawrence and its tributaries, and of the other rivers of Canada which flows into the sea, as well as any other lands which the company may extend the French authority.' Fighting with the English occurred in 1627–32, intermittently from 1656 to 1667, and later. The two countries' monarchs agreed in 1686 that a boundary between their respective territories was needed, but war occurred again in 1689–97 and yet again in 1702–13. By the 1713 Treaty of Utrecht, the French surrendered their claims to Nova Scotia (Acadia) and Newfoundland.

Another area of contention pertained to the area north of the St. Lawrence lowlands. The huge watershed of the Hudson's Bay territory which came to be known as Rupert's Land was given by the British Charter of 1670 to the Hudson's Bay Company (HBC). France disputed the Charter but eventually relinquished its claim to Rupert's Land in the Treaty of Utrecht. Thereafter, the French sought to lay claim to lands in the interior of North America, west of the Great Lakes, but in 1741 war again broke out between France and England. Three attempts were made to settle the boundaries between the contending powers, first by an international joint commission, thereafter by direct diplomacy, but when these failed, by warfare from 1756 until the decisive conclusion in 1763 with the British conquest of Quebec. The War of the Boundary Lines led to all of eastern North America, with the exception of the islands of St. Pierre and Miquelon, becoming British. The formation of boundaries around the various colonies thus resulted from the changed power and territorial circumstances. But further changes followed: six years of Revolutionary War ended with territories to the south of Newfoundland, Nova Scotia, and Quebec, as well as the extensive Indian territories claimed by the French between the Ohio and Mississippi rivers, becoming part of the new US. In sum, both Canada (that is, British North America, divided into several colonies) and the US emerged from the Treaties of Paris of 1763 (Figure 1) and, more especially, 1783, as did the basis for their shared boundaries.

French settlement was initially confined to two long narrow bands of land on the north and south shores of the St. Lawrence river, anchored by

FIGURE 1

THE CHANGING BOUNDS OF QUEBEC 1763–1927

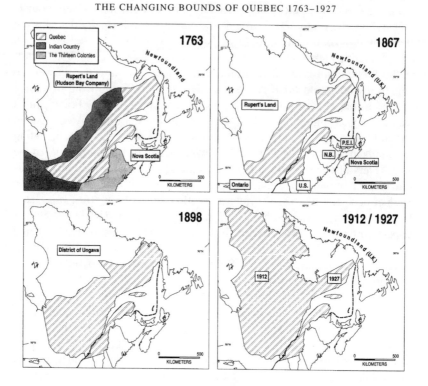

the cities of Quebec and Montreal.[22] This territory lay in the core of what is now the province of Quebec or, as Louder and colleagues nicely affirm, 'the heart of French Canada.'[23] The boundaries of a territory extending far beyond the limits of settlement were described in the 1763 Royal Proclamation. Nicholson notes that 'all parts of the mainland north of the St. Lawrence not included in Quebec, Newfoundland, or the territory granted to the Hudson's Bay Company were assigned to the Crown'.[24]

Quebec's territory thus went north as far as the boundary between the drainage basins of the St. Lawrence and Hudson's Bay. This remained the northern limit when Quebec was divided in 1791 into two colonies, Lower Canada and, in what was to become Ontario, Upper Canada. In 1841 these two territories – called Canada East (formerly Lower Canada) and Canada West (Upper Canada) – were linked within the quasi-federal United Province of Canada. The latter still stood as a separate colony from Newfoundland, Nova Scotia, New Brunswick, and Prince Edward Island, though all remained under the control of the Crown's designate, the

FIGURE 2

POPULATION DISTRIBUTION IN QUEBEC

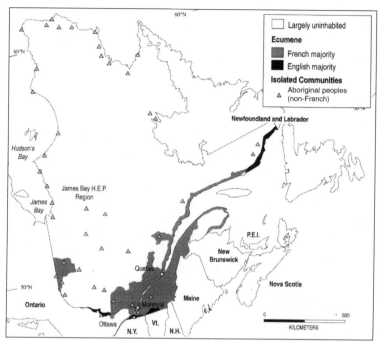

Governor-General of British North America. The boundaries dividing Quebec, New Brunswick and Maine (and, thus, between Canada and the US in this region) were in contention from 1798 to 1842.

Continuous and fractious discord within the Province of Canada led to its demise, but out of this emerged confederated Canada, created on 1 July 1867.[25] The new Dominion of Canada initially included Quebec (formerly Lower Canada/Canada East), Ontario (formerly Upper Canada/Canada West), New Brunswick, and Nova Scotia (Figure 1). In 1867, the old (pre-1841) boundary between Quebec and Ontario was reinstituted. Other boundaries were not altered, thus the northern boundaries of both Quebec and Ontario remained the geomorphological division between the Hudson's Bay and St. Lawrence drainage basins. Canada continued to expand, with the incorporation of new territories: Manitoba and the North-West Territories (1870), British Columbia (1871), Prince Edward Island (1873), Saskatchewan and Alberta (1905), and Newfoundland (1949). In 1898 the Yukon Territory was divided from the Northwest Territories and part of the latter was split off as Nunavut in 1999. All of these changes involved lands that were already Canadian. The present limits of Canada thus date from

1949. Crown (formerly HBC) lands north of the St. Lawrence watershed were in time transferred to Ontario and Quebec; in the case of Quebec, the boundaries were extended northwards in 1898 and 1912 (Figure 1). The Quebec-Ontario boundary, identified in 1791, was clarified in 1889. Elsewhere, the boundary with Newfoundland and Labrador was altered on a number of occasions. Although the present boundary was confirmed by the Privy Council in 1927 (Figure 1), included in the Terms of Union between Canada and Newfoundland in 1949, and enshrined in the Canadian constitution in 1982, many Quebecois maintain that the boundary remains unacceptable.[26]

The presence of Aboriginal peoples in Quebec must be acknowledged. Many different groups live in disparate parts of the province, including in many small widespread settlements in the north where they form the dominant people (Figure 2). Of note here, 'reserves' adjacent to the Ottawa and St. Lawrence rivers, through and by which travellers en route to Montreal traverse, give cause for concern due to conflicting perspectives on which government has – or would have – ultimate control. Other Aboriginal peoples, elsewhere in the province, have land claims and claims for self-government that also remain to be settled to their satisfaction.

Whose View is Right?

With the above as background, we now turn to the possibility of Quebec seceding from Canada. The following discussion first summarises the 'PQ View', the 'Federal View', and selected minority perspectives before points raised by selected authors' writings are discussed as they pertain to the issue of territory. Two broad categories of minority groups exist in Quebec, Aboriginal peoples and others. Non-French in Quebec comprises 20 per cent of the population: ten per cent 'English' (but of very varied background), eight per cent Allophones (non-French speaking/non-English speaking), two per cent Aboriginal peoples, or First Nations and Inuit.

PQ View

Quebec is Quebec! All territory now held to be within the Province of Quebec would form the new State of Quebec, according to sovereignists. This territory, this land, as the homeland of Quebecois, is held to be inviolable. René Levesque, the fascinating leader of the PQ when it first became the government in Quebec, stated in 1976 that 'The territory of Quebec is there on the map and we will not be disrupted by any kind of loose hypothesis'.[27] The PQ holds that the Quebecois, as *the* 'people' of Quebec, have the right to declare independence for all territory within the current province's territorial bounds. PQ ministers declare that under

Canadian law, provincial boundaries may be altered only if the province consents and, they say, Quebec will never agree to change its boundaries. Further, these PQ representatives hold that once Quebec becomes independent its boundaries will remain inviolable under international law. In addition, they maintain that the secession of any regions now within Quebec would be unacceptable since self-determination applies to 'peoples' and 'nations' such as, they claim, the Quebecois, and not to minorities. This argument sidesteps the issues of Quebeckers being a minority within Canada and of the many Aboriginal peoples within Quebec also having rights as 'people' in the international legal sense.[28] The PQ's perspective on who can and cannot be recognised is fascinating:

- The PQ maintains that Anglophones cannot be considered as a 'people' within Quebec since they are part of the *'English* Canadian nation' (whatever that may be). As such, they are given rights in that capacity and so do not qualify for similar rights (as a minority) within Quebec. The PQ does not accept that there is an all-encompassing *Canadian* nation for to do so would raise the spectre of having to admit that many Quebeckers are part of that nation.

- PQ members maintain that minorities – including Jews, Italians, Scots, Haitians, Portuguese, etc. – within Quebec do not have any rights in this regard for they do not qualify as separate 'peoples'. However, the Quebecois notion of an *'English* Canadian nation' is not pertinent to Allophones, though the notion of *Canadian* nation is.

- The PQ believes that Quebecois, Acadians (in New Brunswick), and Aboriginal peoples are 'nations' and, therefore, as per international law, 'peoples' within Canada. As such, they have the right to self-determination. However, in 'granting' such recognition to Aboriginal peoples, the PQ also maintains that, nevertheless, Aboriginal peoples do not have the right to secede from Quebec.

These twists of logic raise many questions. To select but one: if self-determination but not secession applies to Aboriginal peoples, why does such a limitation not also pertain for the Quebecois?!

Separatists are firmly set on the 'fact' of the bounding of the areal extension of current-day Quebec as inviolable, no matter how well (notably the settled extreme south) or how little (notably the north) is actually known. Some separatists call for the expansion of territory. For example, Brossard suggests that eastern Ontario Franco-Ontarians and northern Franco-New Brunswickers would want to join an independent Quebec; however, this is in no way a dominant view.[29]

Federal View

Canada is Canada! Canada includes Quebec and all other territories and peoples therein that are bounded by Canada's international boundaries, operating within the federal system. The basic stance is that Canada is indivisible. Building on that belief, federalists for long maintained naively, as was shown in 1996, that the majority of Quebeckers would always want to remain in Canada in response to the force of reasoned discourse. The 1980 referendum result within Quebec, when the vote was 40.5 per cent for separation and 59.5 per cent against, led to complacency on the federalist side. Thus it was that the 49.4 per cent in favour of separation versus 50.6 per cent in favour of remaining in Canada shocked federalists. The following question thereafter became increasingly possible: what if a PQ government succeeds in getting a majority of the population in the province to support the call for separation and sovereignty?

A plan to divide the country has not been enunciated by Ottawa, for understandable reasons. However, in contrast to the earlier assumption that the majority of Quebeckers would ultimately opt for Canada, the federal minister assigned to deal with the separatist challenge has advanced a 'Plan B' scenario. The latter bluntly and boldly maintains that there would be a high price for Quebec to pay before separation would ever to be agreed on, with one of the 'costs' being territorial division, although the federal government will not elaborate on its thinking, unless and until the matter of secession and territorial (and other) issues have definitely to be dealt with. Some federal options are identified below.

Minority Views in Quebec: Aboriginal Peoples

Canada's Aboriginal peoples, with some notable exceptions, have a treaty relationship with the Crown, now vested in the federal government.[30] In this sense, these peoples are 'federalists'. While interaction exists with the provincial government in Quebec City, Cree, Mohawk and other First Nations and Inuit assert their inherent right to *their* land and to self-government.[31] They observe that their lands are in Canada, not just within Quebec. They live in cities in the south, on reserves mainly in the south, and in widespread small settlements in various parts of the province, notably in disparate areas of the north where there is an association with traditional hunting and trapping territories that are huge in areal extent. The largest clusters of people are located on or around lands designated as theirs just south of Montreal, at Kahnawake, and westward near the confluence of the St. Lawrence/Ottawa Rivers.

The Aboriginal peoples have made it clear that they will insist on the right to decide for themselves whether they would continue to live in Quebec if the PQ succeeded in getting a majority vote for independence.

Referenda results indicate that the Aboriginal communities are overwhelmingly against Quebec's secession from Canada, with Aboriginal lands and self-government *within Canada* being 'part of the deal' for their acceptance of Quebec's independence. This stance presents significant problems for the PQ.

Minority Views in Quebec: 'Others'

A high percentage of the English and Allophones in Quebec are federalists; only a small minority are supporters of the call for independence. The majority of 'others', and a sizeable percentage (but still an overall minority) of Francophones, wish to remain in Canada without having to relocate to do so. Their attachment to Canada reflects a long-term commitment to that country, plus experiences related, in part, to schooling and language laws in Quebec, being regarded as 'incomplete' citizens by ardent separatists, and being targets of disturbing racial or ethnically-biased statements by some PQ leaders and supporters. About 80 per cent of these 'others' are metropolitan in location, especially in and around Montreal. Most are on Montreal Island, in the centre and westwards from Montreal's downtown core, but also in some surrounding communities, ranging from Rawdon in the north to Huntingdon in the south, Cowansville in the east, and Rigaud in the west. There are also sizeable clusters elsewhere in the province: in the Ouataouais (in counties near to and across the Ottawa River from the City of Ottawa); north in the Timiskaming region; in the Eastern Townships south of Montreal; in the Chateauguay Valley; and in the Lower North Shore of the St. Lawrence.

Partitionists

Some Quebec federalists, organised in their opposition to secession, are referred to as 'partitionists'. They will demand the partitioning of Quebec and the retention of selected regions within Canada if Quebec is to secede from Canada. Partitionist organisations have got more than one hundred village/town/township councils to declare support for remaining in Canada if secession occurs. The PQ maintains that partitioning is unacceptable, for that would undercut their stance that the current territory of Quebec is inviolable. However, opposition to partitionists has been weakened by some PQ members who have suggested that Franco-Canadians in neighbouring provinces – in the Ottawa Valley and in New Brunswick – should have the right to declare whether or not they wish to join an independent Quebec. By this they are unwittingly giving support to Federalists who would insist on the partitioning of Quebec. A related aspect of the desire for control over an expanded territory is evidenced in Quebecois desires to have control over Labrador. This is sometimes revealed by showing an unbounded Quebec incorporating Labrador on Quebec maps. In response, some partitionists have suggested that an 'Eleventh Province' could be created out of a section of western Quebec, to encompass most of those in Quebec desirous of remaining in Canada; however, it is wrong to believe that federalists in Quebec are clustered in this one region.

Related to the issue of partition is the current perceived 'intrusion' of the federal government within Quebec. Territorially-based tensions regularly arise from Quebec separatists' concern about the large presence of the federal government in the Hull region in western Quebec – across the Ottawa River from Ottawa, within the federal National Capital Region [NCR], which includes federal lands and buildings within both Ontario and Quebec. Separatists do not accept that the federal government has any rights whatsoever on the Quebec side of the Ottawa River. Indeed, the Quebec government views the federal government's National Capital Commission's land ownership and planning and landscape development involvements within the NCR as a violation of Quebec's territorial integrity. Interestingly, however, this stance smacks of hypocrisy when parallelled with the PQ stance against the Cree in 'occupied' James Bay, as identified below.

Opinions Regarding Territorial Restructuring

If federalist partitionists were to have their way, and partitioning were done on a cluster by cluster basis, Quebec would look like Swiss cheese! It seems unreasonable to assume that this would be the result. Many possible opinions have been expressed about the territory issue that will have to be faced if Quebec ever succeeds in getting a majority vote for separation.[32]

Warnings

Political geographer Burghardt, drawing from Hungarian experiences within the Hapsburg Empire, identified what could happen to Quebec if secession from Canada were to occur.[33] Among other things, he commented on the serious detrimental effect secession would have on Montreal if, in the manner of Vienna, it was cut off from its economic hinterland (in Ontario and to the west). The end of the Empire resulted in Vienna experiencing severe economic depression and then major violence. Calls for cutting off trade with Quebec (and, therefore, Montreal), if secession were to occur, have been voiced in many parts of Canada, though such threats raise concerns in Ontario owing to the closeness of the Ontario and Quebec economies.

Another political geographer, Knight, fascinated by people's acceptance of the political boundary between Quebec and Ontario as immovable, considered a territorial redivisioning of Canada so as to stimulate others' thoughts. Assuming that Quebec would some day secede from Canada,

Knight developed several scenarios of possible territorial consequences that would flow from Quebec's separation.[34] The identified pedagogical device of 'future maps' was subsequently used in many Quebec and Ontario schools and universities to get students to think about the ramifications of secession.[35] The task of creating future maps of altered politico-territorial organisation and the lively discussions that these stimulated proved to be highly successful within Ontario, but Quebec students and their teachers were deeply troubled by the exercise because the issue was so near to their hearts and everyday living. While Knight's original tongue-in-cheek scenarios were developed for teaching purposes, they caused a considerable stir because of a rise in support for the PQ, which was elected to power in the following year.[36]

PQ 'History'

It is important to remember that history can be quite subjective, as illustrated by a PQ book produced for the 1980 referendum. It claimed that since Quebecois had long settled the land and were 'owners', the territory in the 'physical frame of present State [*sic.*] of Quebec, is properly theirs'.[37] That maps can be used for propaganda purposes is wonderfully illustrated in the book. Examples include: ignoring of the reality of Rupert's Land having been British from the early 1600s; conveniently showing France's claims a year before the diminishing effects of the Treaty of Utrecht and not afterwards; on maps after 1713, referring to British territories (including the thirteen colonies) as British 'acquisitions' to contrast, cleverly, with French 'possessions'; falsely showing Prince Edward Island, Cape Breton, Anticosti Island and Newfoundland as part of the province of Quebec in 1763; ignoring the existence of the 1841–67 Province of Canada because, presumably, to do otherwise would admit that Quebec was not a separate province when Confederation came into being but simply part of a larger political unit; not showing Canada at the time of Confederation, undoubtedly since to do so (for readers contemplating secession from Canada) would show that Quebec did not include the northern territories in 1867; showing southern Upper Canada/Canada West/Ontario smaller than reality, surely to emphasise the larger extent of Quebec; and so on, but with reasonably accurate maps for 1898, 1912, and 1927. At least for the poorly educated or undiscerning reader, the book fed a mythic understanding of the past and thus supported the PQ line that Quebec was entitled to the full areal extent of the province's currently existing bounds.

Playing with Percentages

Jacques Brossard, a professor of law and a PQ constitutional adviser, maintained that an independent Quebec should not only keep most of what it has now but must *gain* lands currently in Labrador and New Brunswick, and also the territorial waters in Hudson's Bay.[38] In return, Brossard was willing to cede some small sections of Quebec to 'Canada', but only in those areas where the local Anglophone population was 80 per cent or more, that is, had the same majority that Francophones have in the province as a whole. This condition would 'give' to 'Canada' small parts of Pontiac County west of Ottawa, two small islands in the Magdalen Islands archipelago, and one township south of Labrador, along the St. Lawrence.

The Right to Choose

In an examination of the ethics of sovereignty and secession, philosopher O'Grady believes that the principle of individual choice must apply.[39] For him, the resulting map of an independent Quebec would roughly equate with Quebec at the time of Confederation, but with some areas in the north shore, Eastern Townships, Montreal area, the Ottawa Valley, and northern Quebec all remaining in Canada. He is unsure about the vast James Bay area. Sociologist Gerber also feels that individual choice, demonstrated by electoral results, would lead to Quebec potentially being split into several sections.[40]

Quebec Anglophone Federalists

Albert (a Montreal businessman) and Shaw (a former independent member of Quebec's provincial legislature) reflect on the loss of territory Quebec would have to face before it could become independent.[41] The authors persuasively argue that Quebec should be deprived of more than three-quarters of its current territory (Figure 3a). This, they state, is because the territory of Rupert's Land was given by Britain to Canada under the Crown. Quebec was granted these lands 'in trust' *as part of Canada*, hence if Quebec is to leave then it cannot retain those lands. Crown sovereignty was retained, hence the lands do not 'belong' to Quebec.

With respect to the territory on the south shore of the St. Lawrence, they argue that an independent Quebec should lose the whole area because it was not part of New France and because it was by the Treaty of Paris of 1763 that the bounds of the territory were established by the British, not France. They also argue that the Gaspé and the bounds between Quebec and New Brunswick were, in the 1790 words of Lord Dorchester, Governor General, 'annexed' by the British 'for the present'.[42] The argument with respect to the south shore, at base, has a strategic dimension:

> ...if separation were to occur then Canada could not agree to relinquish to a foreign country territory that was not originally French, that was added to the province of Quebec strictly to suit British

FIGURE 3
PROPOSALS FOR A REPUBLIC OF QUEBEC

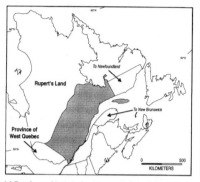

(a) Province of Laurentia: Albert and Shaw (1980)

(b) Republic of Quebec: McDonald (1991)

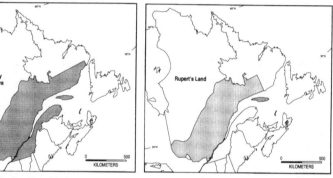

(c) Republic of Quebec: Varty (1991)

(d) Republic of Quebec: Bercuson and Cooper (1991)

administrative convenience and objectives, that was in large part first settled by the English-speaking and which is of vital strategic importance to Canada's sea traffic with the Great Lakes and to her overland communication with her Maritime provinces.[43]

Shaw and Albert do not adequately take into account the shift of English-dominated settlement in the south shore – notably in the Eastern Townships, but also Gaspé – to French, as a reflection of the overall change in societal status of the English 'from majority to minority status'.[44] Nor do they deal with a fundamental within international law and the claims to territory, effective occupation of territory.[45] This apart, the issue of the south shore is critical, for rather than providing merely a corridor through (independent) southern Quebec to link 'eastern Canada' – New Brunswick, Nova Scotia, Prince Edward Island, and Newfoundland and Labrador – with 'western

Canada' (Ontario and west), as some other authors have suggested, Shaw and Albert propose that the 'whole ball of wax' should remain in Canada.

In addition to northern Quebec and the south shore remaining in Canada, these authors maintain that Canada should retain the west half of Montreal Island – the divide being along St. Denis Street in downtown Montreal City – plus the Outaouais region and part of the easternmost north shore of the lower St. Lawrence, in order to reflect cultural realities. While Shaw and Albert provide convincing research-based findings and recommendations which cannot be fairly revealed in this all-too-brief summary, their work has an interesting twist: they maintain that their proposals will never be needed for 'the fever [for independence] will break'.[46]

Tough Talk

Taking a very tough line, McDonald argues that Canada must be ruthless in insisting on only a small territory for Quebec as the price to pay for secession (Figure 3b).[47] By so doing, he argues, separatists would then be forced to back down and to accept a reconstituted federalism. Strangely, McDonald does not retain federalist Montreal Island within Canada, but he splits off much of western Quebec to keep in Canada. In the latter region, he thereby would force 40 per cent of Francophones living in the region to live on Canadian soil while only 20 per cent of Anglophones would.[48] It is hard to take McDonald's proposal seriously though it stands as a warning to separatists that Canada need not simply accept Quebec's territorial demands. Separatists, however, dismiss such proposals as dreamy nonsense!

Raising the Temperature

While Shaw and Albert hold that separation is not likely to happen, Alberta's historian Bercuson and political scientist Cooper not only think otherwise but would seem to welcome it – but with a loss of territory. Indeed, Bercuson and Cooper declare that 'we believe … that the rest of us would be better off if Quebec were a small country and not a large province'.[49] Rupert's Land is to be retained by Canada (Figure 3d). They follow Shaw and Albert in identifying the south shore as Canadian, despite the fact that this would deny thousands of Francophones a 'right' to be in an independent Quebec, or to express, via a referendum, that they might want to stay there – with 'there' still being part of Quebec. On the other hand, Bercuson and Cooper maintain that non-Francophones must be given the right to self-determination. A double standard? A challenge to thought is provided in their suggestion that Canada will necessarily have 'to resort to extra-constitutional procedures' to resolve territorial and other issues. Why? In part because the Canadian constitution does not allow for secession, and because everything around secession will amount to 'something like a revolutionary founding or refounding of the regime'.[50] This provocative statement raises the fundamental question of how 'Canada' and 'Quebec' would ever agree on the territorial issues and by what process. Starting a territorial discussion between Canada and Quebec from the perspectives offered by Shaw and Albert or Bercuson and Cooper would surely lead to a highly charged first discussion. With respect just to the south shore, the legal basis for a claim to it by Canada is distinctly questionable. Reid thus notes, 'it is illogical to use legalistic historical claims to justify openly *illegal* seizure of territory'.[51]

Legal Sense about the North

An analysis of legal principles and instruments led lawyer Varty to conclude that Quebec has no right to the lands transferred to it in 1898 and 1912 (Figure 3c).[52] Focusing on the north – called Ungava, or what was once Rupert's Land – he concluded that the territories were given to a province *within* Canada. 'This was an explicit condition'; thus, if Quebec changes 'its status in the Canadian federation by declaring independence', it will have broken 'the condition upon which jurisdiction to the lands was granted'.[53] He holds that the lands were given to Quebec 'in trust', with Canada having 'retained part of the jurisdiction to the lands which it can exercise at any time', thus

> Quebec, in the position of trustee, would be required to turn over the trust property to Canada at the termination of the trust. [Equally, since] civil law principles of trust operate in a way similar to those of common law, ... the underlying title [is] vested in the Crown ... [hence there is] the temporary right of Quebec to manage the trust property, and the return to Canada of Quebec's part of the jurisdiction should Quebec breach the terms of the trust.[54]

Varty observes that Canada may wish to permit Quebec – if the majority Francophone residents in the area decide by referendum to remain in Quebec – to purchase a portion of southern Ungava. Varty does not consider the south shore. He does, however, note that if Quebec were to secede, Ontario would retain a physical link through still-Canadian Ungava Territory with Newfoundland and Labrador, though the Maritimes would remain cut off from any direct link with Ontario. A Francophone Quebec, he maintains, would return to its core territory in the lower St. Lawrence watershed, essentially as it has been for three and more centuries.

Varty notes too that an independent Quebec within the bounds he records would be reduced to approximately 500,100 square kilometres, about one third its present size yet essentially the size it was at the time of its creation as a province in 1867. It would be reduced from being a third larger than

Ontario to about half of Ontario's size. This would leave Ontario huge, which would suggest that Ontario should be carved into perhaps six units, which would set the stage for western provinces also to be divided. Varty and others hold that such an action could strengthen Canada's federation by helping to undercut provincially-based regionalisms that often operate against the federal 'centre'.

Reid warns that if Quebec chose to remain under the Crown, within the Commonwealth of Nations, then Varty's legal arguments could not prevail; why should a country that continues an allegiance to the Crown have to 'return' territory to Canada so the land can remain under the Crown?[55] Varty feels anti-monarchy sentiment is too strong in Quebec for such to happen, however, as Reid observes, separatists might do anything to be able to retain the two-thirds of their current territory that would be in question.

Counterviews about the North and Aboriginal Self-determination

Clearly, the north would be a major and highly contentious issue. As suggested above, Quebec is not entitled to the north, *if* one accepts that it did not hold rights to it before Confederation. However, a Quebecois claim can be made for at least the James Bay region, on an effective occupation basis, given that a mammoth hydroelectric power generation scheme has been constructed with the transmission lines clearly linking the region to southern Quebec. A 1975 James Bay and Northern Quebec Agreement was reached with the Aboriginal people of that region, the Cree. Now, however, the Cree say they were under duress and oppression when the James Bay agreement was entered into, so they are challenging the agreement's validity. This stance is highly problematic for the Quebecois. While the PQ maintains that it is the destiny of the 'people' of Quebec to be independent – and for the PQ this implicitly and necessarily includes both the self-defined Quebecois, other Europeans, as well as the Cree, Naskapi, Inuit, Mohawk, and other Aboriginal peoples – yet the Aboriginal people refuse to relinquish their own right to self-determination, as 'people', under international law.[56]

Partitioning: Which Territorial Units?

While Aboriginal people located within Quebec have already declared against Quebec's separation from Canada, there is also the issue of others within the populace who would want to remain in Canada. If the assumption is that the majority (living within the total area of the current province) rules then minorities within Quebec could not affect the outcome. What might be the outcome if people were able to have their ballot-box desires identified by territorial units smaller than the whole province instead of being amassed with the majority's desires?

Assuming a democratic approach to territorial divisioning could prevail at the local scale, with people in sub-provincial territories located along the boundaries between Quebec and Newfoundland-Labrador, New Brunswick and Ontario being permitted to vote in referenda, there would still be the problem of which unit of organisation would be appropriate. Reid indicates that there could be significant differences in territorial consequences if the territorial units used are counties (only one of which has a majority English population), municipalities, electoral districts (either provincial or federal, there being more of the former than the latter, with provincial ridings averaging 52,000 inhabitants), or polls within ridings (each containing about 250 voters and a single polling station). Use of any of these increasingly smaller units would result in contrasting territorial consequences. To illustrate this, Reid prepared maps that identify which sections of Montreal Island might remain in Canada by assuming a majority (based on English versus French) as the basis for territorial divisioning. His results identify that the territory thus to remain in Canada would be dependent upon the level for recording votes – ridings, polls, or municipalities (Figure 4, based on Reid's several maps).[57] Using the smallest areal unit, the poll, would result in the best measure of acceptance of who and what should remain in 'Canada' versus in 'Quebec'.

An issue arising from Reid's and others' work pertains to whether or not to permit exclaves/enclaves within the consequent two States. If affirmative, the resulting Swiss cheese pattern would cause problems for movement and communication. If negative, there would likely be relocations of people fearful about the future, which could give rise to violence.

Another issue pertains to the degree to which people within Quebec will be able to truly express their desire *not* to be in an independent Quebec. This is no idle matter for clusters of English-speaking Canadians, Allophones, and also French-speaking federalists in the Montreal region (notably on Montreal Island), in the Ottawa Valley, the Eastern Townships south of Montreal, the Gaspé, and on the north shore near Newfoundland and Labrador, would want to remain Canadian. A problem with Reid's analysis, and that by some others, is the assumption that French-speaking Quebeckers would vote to remain in Quebec and that Anglophones and Allophones would not. Some among the latter two groups may vote to remain in an independent Quebec. With respect to French-speaking people, whether or not they may call themselves Quebecois, many would prefer to remain in Canada, though there is no clear understanding of the numbers apart from when referenda results are recorded, since the numbers fluctuate from opinion poll to opinion poll. Thus while the linguistic-heritage measure may represent a rough guide to affiliation-leanings, it is important to remember that the actual outcome of a referendum on independence, with territorial divisioning, may produce some surprises.

FIGURE 4

DIVIDING THE MONTREAL AREA

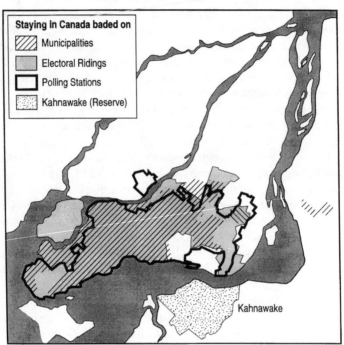

On the Need for Communication Corridors

The retention of communications across Canadian territory would be a key concern for Canada if Quebec were to secede; thus federalists have discussed the need to insist on the creation of Canada-controlled 'corridors' across the territory of an independent Quebec. Such corridors are believed to be essential so that the Atlantic provinces would be able to have physical contact with Ontario and the rest of the country; there is no desire to repeat the failed East/West Pakistan fragmentation lesson.

But would Quebecois separatists agree to having corridors running across their territory? (Figure 5). A road-rail corridor from Ontario through Quebec to the Maritimes would be contentious since the most logical option would be via a route through the south shore of Quebec. There is no certain route for a corridor within that region. One possibility would be a corridor through the south shore, along or adjacent to existing major transport routes, with east-west access to and north/south crossing of the corridor controlled by Canada. Robertson, a corridor advocate, acknowledges that the south

shore of Quebec contains many Francophones, many of whom would opt
for independence.[58] Even a small corridor anywhere east-west across the
region would create a northern and a southern population, divided by the
corridor. But rather than the width of, say, a four-lane highway and an
adjacent railway, Robertson, for security reasons, proposes a corridor 30–50
kilometres wide. People within this corridor would have to decide to be
'Canadians' – and so remain where they live – or to relocate to a part of
independent Quebec. Robinson suggests, as an alternate route, that the
corridor be along the boundary with the US, but this would mean the
Canadian territorial 'strip' would cut Quebec off from direct contact with
the US. The latter suggestion also would be problematic for it ignores the
geographical nature of the land involved, notably in the east where
communications are very poor owing to rugged terrain.

FIGURE 5

LINKING A DIVIDED CANADA

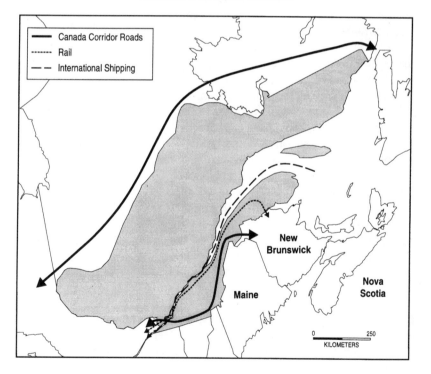

Varty proposes the construction of a northern corridor development for redirected roads and powerlines (from Churchill Falls to Ontario) to maintained surface links between Ontario and Newfoundland and Labrador (Figure 5). While extremely difficult to maintain owing to rugged terrain and climatic constraints, especially in the depth of winter and during the muddy transition months in spring and autumn, this corridor route would be either in Canada, assuming the north *did* remain Canadian, or in the 'foreign' territory of the State of Quebec, assuming the north *did not* remain part of Canada.[59]

If Quebec were to secede within a smaller territory than at present, another concern would be how to keep Canadian those partitioned areas within Quebec, the population of which would opt for Canada. For instance, parts of Montreal Island and the Ottawa Valley may stay Canadian. A corridor could be maintained from Ontario along the current Ottawa-Montreal limited access highway 417 to Montreal Island. An alternative could be a road-rail corridor along the north shore of the St. Lawrence from near Cornwall in Ontario to Montreal. Any Canadian exclaves within Quebec would present additional problems for movement of people and goods. Would several mini-corridors be necessary?

Another 'corridor' would necessarily pertain to the St. Lawrence Seaway, for the latter would serve three states: Canada, the US, and Quebec. Since the Seaway is already regarded as an international waterway, under the shared control of the US and Canada, this may not be particularly controversial, but Quebecois nationalists would be loath to be forced into having to accept that they could not have full control of movement through their territory. At issue also would be air transportation routes across an independent Quebec. This identification of potential transportion issues serves to indicate that an independent Quebec would also have to deal with the US, not just Canada. There is no expectation that an independent Quebec could expect to automatically be dealt with fairly by the US, with, for instance, a simple rewrite of states' names in the Free Trade Agreement and numerous other legal instruments and treaties between Canada and the US, but that is the subject of another paper.

Likelihood of Negotiations

If a *clear* majority (but what constitute such remains an unknown) of people in Quebec express their support for independence and thus separation, the Canadian federal government, as already directed by the Supreme Court, would likely accept the situation and start negotiations about dividing assets, debts and territory. A civil war would not be an expected outcome of any final push to independence by Quebec, given Canada's concern for democracy and the long-standing relationships between the 'two founding societies'. Simeon uses interestingly guarded language on this point: 'a peaceful transition to an independent Quebec is by no means implausible'.[60] Nevertheless, it is likely that at least some instances of localised violence would erupt if passions were to overflow.

There is a lot of talk! Nothing is on the table formally, though PQ leaders remain adamantly against any talk about any parcelling up of Quebec's current territory even as some federalists openly espouse the 'divisioning' of present-day Quebec if secession is pursued. No formal plans by the federal government have been presented and likely none will be until necessity pertains. Quebeckers are to be given a 'next' referendum; the PQ remains committed to holding such.[61] As this paper is being written, polls indicate a decreased interest in secession, but this may well change in the future. If negotiations are ever held it is reasonable to assume that bitter debate will occur about many issues, not least territorial ones. It is instructive that discussants of possible territorial consequences for a seceding Quebec generally write in English. Quebecois separatists unquestioningly accept the principle that 'when Quebec becomes sovereign, its borders will be the borders of the current province of Quebec'.[62] For them, there is thus no point in discussing the issue. Meanwhile, academics and federalists continue to present their ideas on an issue that one day may become volatile.

NOTES

1. See selectively in G.J. Demko and W.B. Wood (eds.), *Reordering the World: Geopolitical Perspectives on the 21st Century* (Boulder CO: Westview 1994), and the 'globalization and geography' special issue of *GeoJournal* 45/1–2 (1998). On some consequences within states, see D.B. Knight and A. E. Joseph (eds.), *Restructuring Societies: Insights from the Social Sciences* (Ottawa: Carleton University Press 1999).
2. S. Waterman, 'Partition, secession and peace in our time', *GeoJournal* 39 (1996) p.351.
3. Ibid.
4. D.B. Knight, 'The dilemma of nations in a state structured world', in N. Kliot and S. Waterman (eds.), *Pluralism and Political Geography: People, Territory and State* (London: Croom Helm 1983) pp.114–37; and two pertinent case studies, M. Keating, 'Spain: peripheral nationalism and state response', in J. McGarry and B. O'Leary (eds.), *The Politics of Ethnic Conflict Regulation*, (London: Routledge 1993) pp.204–25, and D.H. Kaplan, 'Two nations in search of a state: Canada's ambivalent spatial identities', *Annals of the Association of American Geographers* 84 (1994) pp.585–606.
5. D. Newman, 'Introduction: postmodernity and the territorial discourse of peace', *GeoJournal* 39 (1996) p.328.
6. On the importance of scale when considering identities and political partitioning, see G. Herb and D.H. Kaplan (eds.), *Nested Identities* (Lanham, MD: Rowman and Littlefield 1999).
7. Other names cited in the literature for sub-state nationalisms include mini-nationalisms, ethnic nationalisms, autonomist nationalisms, and subnations.
8. R.H. Jackson and A. James, 'The character of independent statehood', in R.H. Jackson and A. James (eds.), *States in a Changing World* (Oxford: Clarendon Press 1993) p.22.

9. M.W. Mikesell and A.B. Murphy, 'A framework for comparative study of minority-group aspirations', *Annals of the Association of American Geographers* 81 (1991) pp.581–604.

10. Whereas people once fought for the overlord (be it a king, prince, duke or whomever), with the development of nationalism people became willing to fight in the name of their nation and its territory. Political and religious leaders, poets and writers helped forge a patriotism that was called upon by the citizens as they acted to protect the nation and its territory. In the case of a sub-state politico-territorial identity, the call to achieving statehood similarly involves a mobilization of followers who, as citizens with passions aroused, may resort to violence, as an expression of the nationalism and patriotism.

11. D.B. Knight, 'Territory and people or people and territory: thoughts on postcolonial self-determination', *International Political Science Review* 6/2 (1985) pp.248–72.

12. For useful systematic and world regional examinations of changes see Jackson and James (note 8).

13. See A.B. Murphy, 'Historical justifications for territorial claims' *Annals of the Association of American Geographers* 80 (1990) pp.531–48; and A.B. Murphy, 'Territorial ideology and international conflict: the legacy of prior political formations', in N. Kliot and S. Waterman (eds.), *The Political Geography of Conflict and Peace* (London: Belhaven 1991) pp.126–41.

14. C.F.J. Whebell, 'A model of territorial separation', *Proceedings of the Association of American Geographers* 5 (1973) pp.295–8.

15. See C. Williams, 'A requiem for Canada?' in G. Smith (ed.), *Federalism: The Multiethnic Challenge* (London: Longman 1995) pp.31–72; and D.B. Knight, 'Canada and its political fault lines: reconstitution or disintegration?' in D.G. Bennett (ed.), *Tension Areas of the World* 2nd ed. (Dubuque, Iowa: Kendall/Hunt 1998) pp.207–27.

16. D.B. Knight, 'Regionalisms, nationalisms, and the Canadian state', *Journal of Geography* 83/5 (1984) pp.212–20.

17. Judgement of the Supreme Court of Canada, 20 Aug. 1998. And see G. Fraser, 'The Quebec ruling: Canada must negotiate after yes vote – Supreme Court rejects unilateral secession, but says Quebeckers' wishes can't be ignored', (Toronto) *Globe and Mail* (21 Aug 1998) p.1.

18. See, for example, R. Mackie, '50% plus 1 too little, Quebec majority says: 60 per cent vote needed to leave Canada, latest poll of Quebeckers finds', *Globe and Mail* (Toronto), 31 Aug. 1998, p.1.

19. Canada and pre-independent Quebec would be forced to deal with a variety of issues, including citizenship, money and banking, taxing, trade links, language protection for minorities, public service workers, military matters, international treaties and associations. For a discussion of some of these issues, see A. Freeman and P. Grady, *Dividing the House: Planning for a Canada Without Quebec* (Toronto: HarperCollins 1995).

20. See volumes on international law or D.B. Knight, 'Statehood: a politico-geographic and legal perspective', *GeoJournal* 28/3 (1992) pp.311–18.

21. The following historical material is based on N.L. Nicholson, *The Boundaries of the Canadian Confederation* (Toronto: Macmillan of Canada 1979), C.E. Heidenreich, 'European territorial claims, 1713–1763', in R.C. Harris (ed.), *Historical Atlas of Canada*, Vol.I, *From the Beginning to 1800* (Toronto: University of Toronto Press 1990) Plate 40, and N.L. Nicholson and C.F.J. Whebell, 'From sea to sea: territorial growth to 1900', in R.L. Gentilcore (ed.), *Historical Atlas of Canada*, Vol.II, *The Land Transformed* (Toronto: University of Toronto Press 1993) Plate 21. In this paper Aboriginal peoples and their pre-European territories are not considered.

22. R.C. Harris and J. Warkentin, *Canada Before Confederation: A Study in Historical Geography* (Ottawa: Carleton University Press 1991), notably figures 2–4 and 2–5, p.35.

23. D. Louder (ed.), *The Heart of French Canada: From Ottawa to Quebec City* (New Brunswick, NJ: Rutgers University Press 1992).

24. Nicholson (note 21) p.21.

25. W.L. Morton, *The Critical Years: The Union of British North America 1857–1873* (Toronto: McClelland and Stewart 1964) and D.B. Knight, *Choosing Canada's Capital: Conflict Resolution in a Parliamentary System* (Ottawa: Carleton University Press 1991).

26. Due to concerns about the province's 'territorial integrity' the Quebec Government created

a commission to study the boundaries. Its reports included H. Dorion, *La Frontière Québec-Terre-Neuve* (Quebec: Presses de l'université Laval 1963).

27. Cited in W. F. Shaw and L. Albert, *Partition: The Price of Quebec's Independence* (Montreal: Thornhill 1980) p.56, and see R. Lévesque, *La passion du Quebec* (Montréal: éditions Quebec/Amérique 1978).

28. D. B. Knight, 'Self-Determination for Indigenous Peoples: The Context for Change', in R.J. Johnston, D.B. Knight and E. Kofman (eds.), *National Self-Determination and Political Geography* (London: Croom Helm 1988) pp.117–34; S.H. Venne, *Our Elders Understand Our Rights: Evolving International Law Regarding Indigenous Rights* (Penticton B.C.: Theytus 1998).

29. Jacques Brossard, *L'accession a la souveraineté et le cas du Quebec* (Montreal: Les presses de l'université de Montréal, 1976).

30. See especially O.P. Dickason, 'Iron men, true men, and the art of treaty-making', in Knight and Joseph (note 1) pp.105–22; and, for the broader historical context, O.P. Dickason, *Canada's First Nations: A History of the Founding Peoples from Earliest Times* (Toronto: McClelland and Stewart 1992).

31. On these general issues see J. Wolfe-Keddie, 'Listening and Heeding: Challenges of Restructuring the Relationship Between Aboriginal Peoples and Canada', in Knight and Joseph (note 1) pp.123–63.

32. The following discussion is partly reflective of a thoughtful discourse in S. Reid, *Canada Remapped* (Vancouver: Pulp Press 1992).

33. A.F. Burghardt, 'Quebec Separation and the Future of Canada', in R.L. Gentilcore (ed.), *Geographical Approaches to Canadian Problems* (Toronto: Prentice-Hall 1971) pp.229–35.

34. D.B. Knight, 'Maps as constraints or springboards to imaginative thought: future maps of Canada', *Bulletin, Association of Canadian Map Libraries*, 18 (1975) pp.1-9.

35. D.B. Knight, 'Future maps of Canada as a pedagogical device', *The Monograph* 30/2 (1979) pp.3–5.

36. Shortly after the publication of the 1975 article the author was visited by a member of the RCMP terrorist squad who believed the article was seditious in intent. It took some time for the officer to develop an appreciation for the pedagogical importance of such writing.

37. Parti Québécois, *L'Option* (Quebec: 1979), which is accessible in Shaw and Albert (note 27) pp.57–64.

38. Brossard (note 29).

39. W.D. O'Grady, *The Quebec Problem: An Inquiry into the Ethics of Sovereignty and Secession* (Ottawa: Borealis Press 1981).

40. L. Gerber, 'Referendum results: defining new boundaries for an independent Quebec', *Canadian Ethnic Studies* 24/2 (1992) pp.22–34.

41. Shaw and Albert (note 27).

42. Ibid. p.91.

43. Ibid. p.96.

44. G. Caldwell and E. Waddell (eds.), *The English of Quebec: From Majority to Minority Status* (Quebec: Institute québécois des reserche sur la culture 1982).

45. A.F. Burghardt, 'The Bases of Territorial Claims', *Geographical Review* 63 (1973) pp.225–45.

46. Shaw and Albert (note 27) pp.194–99.

47. K. McDonald, *Keeping Canada Together* (Toronto: Ramsey Business Systems 1990).

48. Reid (note 32) p.42.

49. D.J. Bercuson and B. Cooper, *Deconfederation: Canada Without Quebec* (Toronto: Key Porter Books 1991) p.157.

50. Ibid. p.144.

51. Reid (note 32) p.45.

52. L. Varty, *Who Gets Ungava?* (Vancouver: Varty and Co. 1991) pp.21–41.

53. Ibid. p.41.

54. Ibid.

55. Reid (note 32).

56. Grand Council of the Crees, Eeyou Astchee, *Never Without Consent: James Bay Crees' Stand Against Forcible Inclusion into an Independent Quebec* (Toronto: ECW Press 1998).
57. Reid (note 32) pp.97–9.
58. I.R. Robertson, 'The Atlantic provinces and the territorial question', in J.L. Granatstein and K. McNaught (eds.), *English Canada Speaks Out* (Toronto: Doubleday 1991).
59. Varty (note 52).
60. R. Simeon, 'Scenarios for separation', in R. Simeon (ed.) *Must Canada Fail?* (Montreal: McGill-Queen's University Press 1977) p.197.
61. R. Séguin, 'Bouchard vows to use mandate to hold sovereignty referendum: timing is the only unknown, Quebec premier says', (Toronto) *Globe and Mail* (8 Dec 1998) p.A4.
62. National Executive Council of the Parti Québécois, *Quebec in a New World: The PQ's Plan for Sovereignty*, R. Chodos, translator (Toronto: Lorimer 1979) p.49.

Seeking the Common Ground

FREDERICK W. BOAL

In Anthony Smith's 1981 book *The Ethnic Revival* we find the following:

> The dissolution of ethnicity. The transcendence of nationalism. The internationalisation of culture. These have been the dreams, and expectations, of liberals and rationalists in practically every country, and in practically every country they have been confounded and disappointed. Although in the latter half of the twentieth century the world has become more unified, and its states more interdependent, than at any previous period of history, the hopes of cosmopolitans everywhere seem farther than ever from being realised, and ethnic ties and national loyalties have become stronger and more deep-rooted than ever.[1]

The homogenising tendencies of advanced industrialisation, and the processes encapsulated in the term 'globalisation', could be expected to reduce ethnicity to the folkloristic margins of society in a situation where neither multinationals nor mass electronic communications have any regard for ethnic or national boundaries.[2] Moreover, the needs of industrial capitalism have been seen as requiring homogeneity, while the mass media may convince humanity of its global interdependence. Additionally, over the past two hundred years a series of imperial powers – from the British, French, German, Austro-Hungarian and Russian empires of the nineteenth and early twentieth centuries to what Michael Ignatieff refers to as the Soviet and American joint imperium after the Second World War[3] – have in the past imposed a more-or-less effective policing authority on many preexisting ethnicities.

In his 1981 book Anthony Smith clearly acknowledges expectations of homogenisation, yet he finds reality to be markedly different. We have, indeed, been recent witnesses to a vast up-welling of ethnic sentiment and action. On the other hand it may be incorrect, as Anthony Smith and Alberto Melucci separately assert,[4] to see the ethnic revival as a recent phenomenon. Both Smith and Melucci see the ethnic revival as being rooted as far back as the French Revolution, a stance also adopted by Milton Esman when he writes:

The revised manuscript of this paper was submitted in August 1999.

The French Revolution ushered in the era of political democracy and the associated ideology of political nationalism. The dominant version of this ideology endowed all peoples, all self-declared nations, with the right of 'self-determination'. Foreign rule was inherently unjust, therefore illegitimate ... . Thus ethnic nationalism and the doctrine of national self-determination stimulated and legitimated unprecedented activism among previously passive and compliant ethnic communities. National self-determination, first the rallying cry for numerous hitherto subordinated peoples of Europe ... then spread globally to areas of European colonisation in Asia, Africa, the Middle East and the Caribbean.[5]

Nonetheless, whilst accepting that the ethnic revival has deep temporal roots, it is also evident that developments since the Second World War have contributed significantly to the recent ethnic up-welling. Many of these developments are basically the obverse of those processes outlined above that were seen as key factors in the decline or suppression of ethno-national movements. For instance the collapse or retreat of most of the imperial empires has meant that, since 1989, we have entered the first era in which there is no framework of imperial order.[6] This has meant, as Ignatieff puts it, that

> huge sections of the world's population have won the right to self-determination on the cruellest possible terms: they have been left simply to fend for themselves ... . Small wonder then, that, unconstrained by stronger hands, they have set upon each other.[7]

In addition, it can be asserted that electronic communications have provided ethnic and ethno-national groups in post-industrial societies with dense cultural networks that they might otherwise lack. Mass literacy and the impact of television and radio, while contributing to the construction of the global village, have also contributed to an awareness of ethnic differences, thereby fuelling ethnic antagonisms.

It has also been argued that the revival of ethnicity and ethno-nationalism is a form of resistance to the 'disruptive, impersonal impact of globalisation'.[8] The sheer pace of technological change creates an atmosphere in which security and identity are felt by many to be under threat. In these circumstances, according to this view, ethnic identification and indeed nationalism offer a sense of identity and an association with history and place.[9] It could also be argued that the economic disruptions attributed to globalisation have a malign effect on ethnic relations within a given society, as de-industrialization etc. lead to an intensification of inter-ethnic competition for what is perceived as a shrinking supply of the more 'traditional' jobs.

Once a process of ethnic self-determination gets underway, it then provides a stimulus to action amongst others, particularly when, as so often seems to be the case, the achievement of self-determination by one group seldom inspires tolerance on its part for the claims of ethnic minorities within the boundaries of a newly independent or autonomous polity. In Esman's words 'yesterday's victims become tomorrow's oppressors'.[10] This, in turn, triggers further ethnic self-assertion.

Finally it has been noted that the ideology of state nationalism has experienced a notable decline since the Second World War, especially in much of Europe and North America (though not, it must be stressed, amongst what Rogers Brubacker would refer to as 'nationalising states'[11]). This development, according to Esman, has opened political space, especially for indigenous ethnic minorities but also for immigrant diasporas, to mobilise for political action and claim making on the state. Perhaps here the ethnic revival does not lead to ethno-national separatist claims – rather it sustains the burgeoning of multiculturalism. Might we claim, indeed, that multiculturalism is a form of ethnic self-expression that does not threaten to lead to the break-up of existing states – unlike ethno-nationalism, which does? Critically, in the multicultural case ethnic groups rarely exist as homogeneous regional concentrations; in the ethno-national case they do.[12]

One final factor likely to encourage the emergence of ethno-nationalisms is the growing advantages that accrue to small states. Recent work by Alberto Alisina and his colleagues suggests six conditions that now favour smallness – a lessened need for security now that the two superpowers no longer glower at each other, the decline in trade barriers, the opportunity this offers for specialisation, improved communications, the use of 'small' languages encouraging multilingual skills in the population, and finally the fact that small countries tend to be ethnically homogeneous. In sum, as Alisina sees it, trade liberalisation and political separatism go hand in hand. In a world of free trade and global markets, even relatively small cultural, linguistic or ethnic groups can benefit from forming small and homogeneous political jurisdictions that trade peacefully and are economically integrated with others. 'Today the costs of going it alone are probably smaller that they have been for at least the last couple of centuries.'[13]

I hope I have made the point. Globalisation does not mean the suppression or dissolution of ethnic difference – rather, the reverse seems to be the case.

Ethnic Conflict 'Solutions'

We have attempted to indicate the reasons for a globally invigorated ethnicity. However it even more important to examine ways in which ethnic conflict may be moderated or terminated. A useful contribution to this end has been made by Brendan O'Leary and John McGarry who, after an undoubtedly extensive review of conflict regulation measures, have presented a taxonomy comprised of eight distinct macroscale methods of national and ethnic conflict regulation.[14] They present their scheme under two general heads – methods for the elimination of differences and methods for managing differences:

Methods for Eliminating Differences
> Genocide
> Forced mass population transfers
> Partition and/or secession
> Integration and/or assimilation

Methods for Managing Differences
> Hegemonic control
> Arbitration (third party intervention)
> Cantonisation/federalism
> Consociation or power sharing

I would like to offer a broader, more generic schema, in which ethnic conflict resolution or ethnic conflict management strategies are seen as falling into one of three categories – territoriality, dominance and mutuality. The first two distinctions are drawn from the work of Robert Sommer. He has argued that territoriality and dominance-subordination behaviours are used by communities to build security and limit aggression.[15] On the small spatial scale an individual either refrains from going where he is likely to be involved in disputes or, based on his knowledge of who is above or below him socially, engages in ritualised dominance-subordination behaviour rather than in actual conflict. The spatial scale of this dichotomous choice can be expanded to the level of ethnic communities. In this case ethnic relations are sorted out on the basis of territorial separation or on the basis of hegemonic control (dominance) by one of the ethnic groups involved. Interestingly, in the Irish case, the territoriality/dominance alternatives were outlined as early as 1901 by the Irish Catholic journalist D.P. Moran when he wrote '...the only thinkable solution to the Irish national problem is that one side gets on top and absorbs the other until we have one nation, or that each develops independently'.[16]

The third category of solutions I am proposing here is that of mutuality. Here there is what we might refer to as a mutual or reciprocal acknowledgment of rights. Each group recognises the legitimacy of the other's culture and political aspirations and then contributes to the search for some form of mutually acceptable inter-group accommodation.

Briefly returning to the O'Leary and McGarry taxonomy, we can rearrange their methods of regulation as below:

Territoriality
> Genocide
> Forced mass population transfer
> Partition and/or secession
> Cantonisation/federalism
> [integration and/or assimilation]

Dominance
> Hegemony

Mutuality
> Consociation/power sharing

I have excluded the O'Leary/McGarry category of 'third party arbitration' from my list as I feel that such external intervention is not a long-term regulator of conflict. Rather it will likely involve an attempt to move the situation towards one of the remaining categories – in particular partition or cantonisation/federalism or consociation/power sharing. Integration and/or assimilation lie uncertainly between territoriality and dominance. Such a process would in the long run create a homogeneous territory, while the process itself would probably be characterised by dominance-subordination behaviour.

Northern Ireland

It is evident that the ethnic conflict in Northern Ireland has not yet been fully resolved, despite the signing of the Belfast Agreement on 10 April 1998. Indeed one could argue that this conflict has been flaring up, on-and-off, for the past 400 years, no matter what stimulus may have been gained from the global circumstances outlined earlier. The twentieth century has witnessed attempts at conflict resolution/termination based on territoriality – the partition of Ireland at the macrospatial scale combined with localised population concentration and population relocations. Dominance had also been evident – in the reality of Protestant unionist majority control of the Northern Ireland sub-state between 1921 and 1972 and in the aspirations of Catholic Irish nationalism for a unitary state in the whole island where, undoubtedly, they would have been the dominants.

Both territoriality and dominance can regulate, if not necessarily resolve, ethnic conflict. However dominance/hegemony is likely to be particularly unpalatable to the dominated. On the other hand territoriality can be quite successful if, thereby, ethnically homogeneous spaces are demarcated. In many instances this is not the case, as amply demonstrated by Northern Ireland, where a recalcitrant ethnic minority, comprising over one third of the population, found itself involuntarily encapsulated.

This leaves the mutuality approach. This is fundamentally the same as that recently advocated by a number of members of the Global Security Fellows Initiative in their discussion of the concept of 'accommodating differences'.[17] In this they understood such an accommodation:

> 1. as a philosophy, an attitude and a set of values which involve a coexistence of broadly understood differences (the 'live-and-let-live principle'), a tolerance (a respect of 'otherness') and civility of intergroup relations. This implies affirmation of differences as natural social phenomena that should be equally valued and dealt with on the basis of partnership rather than domination;

> 2. as a certain sociocultural and political strategy and practical method of policy making which is oriented towards search for compromise, consensus and peaceful settlement of tension and conflicts which might arise from differences. As its ultimate goal, such a policy might lead to the new understanding of democratic citizenship aimed at the preservation and even promotion (rather than discouragement) of cultural, ethnic and other diversity.

To explore and indeed to unashamedly promote this approach, two colleagues of mine at the Queen's University of Belfast (Colin Irwin and Tom Hadden) and I decided to survey Northern Irish opinion on a range of matters judged to be ethnically contested. Critically, however, respondents were not asked merely what outcomes they favoured most, but on each item what their second preference would be, and so on.[18] Underlying this strategy was a belief on our part that, on many issues, members of the two ethnic groups could not expect realistically to get quite what they wanted. Rather compromise would have to be the central philosophy within which inter-ethnic negotiation would be grounded.

The survey was carried out across Northern Ireland in the spring of 1996. Seven hundred and fifteen completed questionnaires were subsequently analysed. Most importantly the findings were publicised in a series of articles in Northern Ireland's principal (and only cross-community) daily newspaper – the *Belfast Telegraph*.[19] The results were also made available to the public through a special supplement to the news and comment magazine *Fortnight*.[20]

Let me now examine some of the survey results, pinpointing in particular where common ground is to be found – where in other words we can hope to find the bases for a mutuality solution. However, before commencing this analysis one key criterion must be established. This we will refer to as *sufficient consensus*. For the condition of *sufficient consensus* to be met there must be majority support separately from each of the ethnic communities – any proposal must have the support of at least 50 per cent of Catholics *and* 50 per cent of Protestants.[21] For the purposes of this paper I intend to examine seven fields of activity, ranging from the macro-political framework to issues of policing, employment equality, parades, school and housing integration and the language of street signs.

Each respondent in the survey was presented with a number of possible situations and was then asked to rank these in order from their top preference to their least preferred scenario. The charts that follow present the Catholic and Protestant responses for each item, indicating the percentage choosing each item as their first preference and then displaying the cumulative percentages of first and second preferences, first, second and third preferences and so on. The cumulative percentages that achieve a level of fifty or higher are highlighted. Let us now turn to the analysis itself.

Macro-Political Level

In many ways the constitutional preferences are the most crucial, both because they involve the overall framework within which other, more micro-scale concerns exist and have to be worked out, and because constitutional matters emerge as the most complex and most severely contested. The chart (Figure 1) tells us a great deal. First it can be seen that there are a number of possible constitutional arrangements that achieve over fifty per cent support from one of the ethnic groups, but that fail to achieve *sufficient consensus*. Thus, for Protestants there is strong support for the full incorporation of Northern Ireland into the British state, for the continuance of the current set-up of so-called 'direct rule' from Westminster and – to a lesser extent – for a separate (independent) Northern Ireland state. With Catholics, on the other hand there is strong majority support for Northern Ireland to be governed in a structure of joint authority between the Republic of Ireland and the United Kingdom, and, less emphatically, for Northern Ireland to be fully incorporated into the Irish state (the 'united' Ireland solution). However, as with the Protestant preferences, the Catholic top preferences fail the *sufficient consensus* test. There are only two possible scenarios (amongst the eight presented) that pass the *sufficient consensus* test – (1) power sharing within Northern Ireland, with overall sovereignty responsibility lying with the UK, but with the Irish Republic having a consultative role and (2) power sharing with the addition of institutional

FIGURE 1

CONSTITUTIONAL PREFERENCES

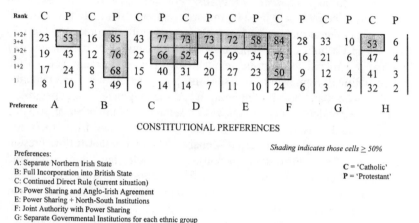

ETHNIC GROUP

Rank	C	P	C	P	C	P	C	P	C	P	C	P	C	P	C	P
1+2+3+4	23	53	16	85	43	77	73	73	72	58	84	28	33	10	53	6
1+2+3	19	43	12	76	25	66	52	45	49	34	73	16	21	6	47	4
1+2	17	24	8	68	15	40	31	20	27	23	50	9	12	4	41	3
1	8	10	3	49	6	14	14	7	11	10	24	6	3	2	32	2
Preference	A		B		C		D		E		F		G		H	

CONSTITUTIONAL PREFERENCES

Shading indicates those cells ≥ 50%

Preferences:
A: Separate Northern Irish State
B: Full Incorporation into British State
C: Continued Direct Rule (current situation)
D: Power Sharing and Anglo-Irish Agreement
E: Power Sharing + North-South Institutions
F: Joint Authority with Power Sharing
G: Separate Governmental Institutions for each ethnic group
H: Full Incorporation into Irish State

C = 'Catholic'
P = 'Protestant'

structures that would involve action on matters of common concern to the two political entities on the island of Ireland. As with the first scheme Northern Ireland would remain within the overall ambit of the United Kingdom.

Thus at the macro-political level of constitutional frameworks, one or more mutuality solutions appeared to be available. However for such solutions to be reached it was evident that considerable compromise would be required, with both ethnic communities having to move a significant distance from their preferred options.

Micro-Political Level

Moving below the macro-political level we can explore a number of other matters, many of which, of course, are not detached from the macro-political. Just as macro-political solutions are necessary to provide the foundations for conflict management and/or resolution at the local level, so local conflict resolution or amelioration, desirable in its own right, will also help to provide a day-to-day underpinning for whatever higher level constitutional accommodation has been achieved. There is thus a profound complementary relationship between the local and the national (and indeed the international).

FIGURE 2

POLICING PREFERENCES

ETHNIC GROUP

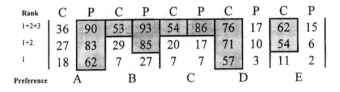

Rank	C	P	C	P	C	P	C	P	C	P
1+2+3	36	90	53	93	54	86	76	17	62	15
1+2	27	83	29	85	20	17	71	10	54	6
1	18	62	7	27	7	7	57	3	11	2
Preference	A		B		C		D		E	

POLICING PREFERENCE

Shading indicates those cells ≥ 50%

Preferences:
A: No Change in Structures, but Recruit More Catholics   **C** = *'Catholic'*
B: New Community Policing Units within RUC   **P** = *'Protestant'*
C: New Community Policing Units outside the RUC (RUC to Deal with "Ethnic" Crime)
D: A New Single Police Force (RUC Disbanded)
E: A Number of Regional and City Police Forces (RUC Disbanded)

Here we examine the survey responses on a number of topics – policing, employment, housing, parades, the language of street signs and, finally, schools. All these matters are of general societal concern, but it must also be underlined that, in particular, they all have major spatial/territorial dimensions. Thus the nature of policing of ethnically segregated communities will be a highly sensitive matter. The extent to which ethnically mixed residential areas should be encouraged, the extent to which parades are seen as being territorially assertive, the extent to which the language of street signs are seen as indicators of local territorial 'ownership'/ control, the extent to which schools are viewed as local spaces for the reproduction of the ethno-national cultures of particular groups – all these will impact profoundly on ethnic community relations.

Firstly, the thorny issue of policing. Here it is evident (Figure 2) that there is marked ethnic polarisation with regard to most preferred outcomes – Protestants want the policing structures to remain basically the same as at present; Catholics, on the other hand, have a strong preference for the disbanding of the RUC (the present police force, the Royal Ulster Constabulary). However options B and C do present *sufficient consensus* outcomes, where community policing units within the current RUC would be introduced, or, alternatively, where such community policing units would be separate from the RUC, the latter continuing to deal with 'terrorist' related crime. So, once again, a mutuality solution is available, but one which is far from the most preferred outcomes of each of the ethnic communities.

FIGURE 3

FAIR EMPLOYMENT PREFERENCES

ETHNIC GROUP

Rank	C	P	C	P	C	P	C	P	C	P
1+2	5	41	59	72	55	36	52	26	29	25
1	3	28	42	47	20	10	23	8	12	7

| Preferences | A | B | C | D | E |

FAIR EMPLOYMENT LAW

Shading indicates those cells ≥ 50%

Preferences:
A: Stop Fair Employment Activities
B: No Change
C: Preference to Under-represented Community
D: Require Selection from Under-represented Community
E: Areas of High Unemployment – Allow Recruitment from One Community Only

C = *'Catholic'*
P = *'Protestant'*

For many of the other topics examined in our survey, mutuality solutions are quite readily to hand. In terms of fair employment law, which exists to counter discrimination and to ensure employment equity, there is strong cross-community support for the continuation of the present system, which has been described as perhaps the most vigorous employment equity legislation in the European Union.[22] Lying behind this consensus, however, can be seen a greater reluctance amongst Protestants to support the current laws and a greater enthusiasm among Catholics for the application of a more full-blown affirmative action strategy (Figure 3).

Public sector (social) housing in Northern Ireland is characterised by high levels of ethnic segregation.[23] Here the survey data indicate clearly that most people do not want a situation where either separation or integration would be enforced. Rather they opt for a situation where residents would have a choice between segregated and integrated housing – indeed a situation where integration would not only be available but would even be encouraged is clearly a strong *sufficient consensus* outcome (Figure 4).

Two other matters that involve the occupation and claiming of space display some contrast in their preference patterns. As is well known through the media attention received, Northern Ireland has a high frequency of parades. While both communities partake in this ritualistic activity, it tends to be predominantly Protestant. Thus, as Figure 5 shows, Protestants favour situations where all parades would be allowed, or at least where the police force would rule on those that were disputed. (these are usually parades of one community that are interpreted by the other as going through their

FIGURE 4
PUBLIC HOUSING PREFERENCES

ETHNIC GROUP

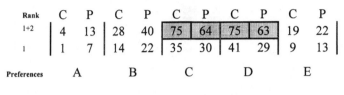

Rank	C	P	C	P	C	P	C	P	C	P
1+2	4	13	28	40	75	64	75	63	19	22
1	1	7	14	22	35	30	41	29	9	13
Preferences	A		B		C		D		E	

PUBLIC HOUSING POLICY

Shading indicates those cells ≥ 50%

Preferences:
A: Separation-Separate Estates/Projects and Ethnically Separate Housing Authorities
B: No Change-People Have to Choose Between Predominantly Catholic or Predominantly Protestant Estates
C: Guaranteed Choice   **C** = '*Catholic*'
D: Choice with Incentives for Mixed Housing   **P** = '*Protestant*'
E: Integration – Require Occupancy of Mixed Estates

FIGURE 5
PREFERENCES REGARDING DECISIONS ON CONTENTIOUS PARADES

ETHNIC GROUP

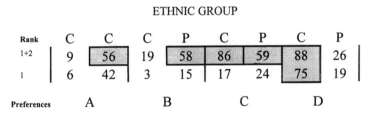

Rank	C	C	C	P	C	P	C	P
1+2	9	56	19	58	86	59	88	26
1	6	42	3	15	17	24	75	19
Preferences	A		B		C		D	

DECISIONS ON CONTENTIOUS PARADES

Shading indicates those cells ≥ 50%

Preferences:
A: Allow All Parades   **C** = '*Catholic*'
B: RUC (police) to Rule on Disputed Parades   **P** = '*Protestant*'
C: Independent Body to Rule on Disputed Parades
D: No Parades Where They are not Wanted (Majority of Residents Decide)

FIGURE 6

PREFERENCES WITH REGARD TO STREET NAMES

ETHNIC GROUP

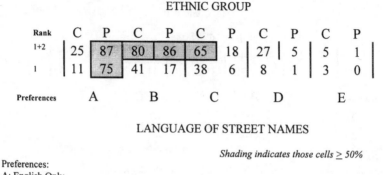

Rank	C	P	C	P	C	P	C	P	C	P
1+2	25	87	80	86	65	18	27	5	5	1
1	11	75	41	17	38	6	8	1	3	0
Preferences	A		B		C		D		E	

LANGUAGE OF STREET NAMES

Shading indicates those cells ≥ 50%

Preferences:
A: English Only
B: English with Addition of Irish where Majority of Residents in Street Wishes
C: Bilingual (English and Irish)   C = '*Catholic*'
D: Sometimes Irish Only – but Only Where Majority in Street Wishes   P = '*Protestant*'
E: Irish Only

territory – and are thus seen as invasive, triumphalist and thereby displaying dominance). On the other hand Catholics want the residents of any area to have the final say as to whether or not a given parade should be permitted to pass through. None of these strongly held preferences attain the *sufficient consensus* criterion of majority support from both groups. However option C (an independent body to rule on disputed parades) does achieve the *sufficient consensus* level, albeit more vigorously for Catholics.

Another contentious issue, with strong territorial connotations, is the question as to what language or languages should be used on street signs – should they be in English only, in Irish only or in some combination? While English is the shared language for both ethnic groups, Irish is symbolically very significant as a marker of Irish culture and Irish national identity. Inevitably, therefore, Irish provides a bone of contention as seen in the chart (Figure 6). Protestants favour English-only signs, while Catholics favour bilingual signs on all streets, or at least on those streets where such an arrangement has the support of a majority of those resident therein. A compromise is available, however, with *sufficient consensus* to be found for the latter solution which, incidentally, is the current law anyway.

Finally we can look at the very important topic of education. Schools in Northern Ireland tend to be very polarised in the ethnic composition of their student bodies – Catholic schools for Catholics and state schools for Protestants. There is, however, a small but growing integrated sector where

FIGURE 7
PREFERENCES WITH REGARD TO SCHOOLS

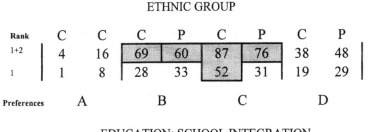

ETHNIC GROUP

Rank	C	C	C	P	C	P	C	P
1+2	4	16	69	60	87	76	38	48
1	1	8	28	33	52	31	19	29
Preferences	A		B		C		D	

EDUCATION: SCHOOL INTEGRATION

Shading indicates those cells ≥ 50%
C = *'Catholic'*
P = *'Protestant'*

Preferences:
A: Separation-Separate Authorities and Separate Schools – No Integrated Schools
B: No Change-People Have to Choose Between Catholic and Protestant Schools
C: Guaranteed Choice between Separate and Integrated Schools
D: Integration-Single Authority with No State Funded Catholic or Protestant Schools

both Catholics and Protestants attend and where the ethos of the schools is carefully designed in terms of the ethno-religious balance of staff, students, symbolism and curriculum. As Figure 7 demonstrates there is a moderately strong cross-ethnic preference to leave things as they are. Significantly, however, there is an even stronger *sufficient consensus* for the provision of a school system where parents and students would have a choice between separate (Catholic and Protestant) and integrated schools.

Where did all this survey material leave us? Potentially in a nervously hopeful situation. On a wide range of issues compromise positions were to be found; indeed in some situations the two ethnic groups were in agreement even in terms of their first preferences. On a more cautious note, however, it needed to be stressed that with some matters a considerable degree of compromise would be required in the search for a common ground – for instance on constitutional matters, on policing and on parades.

'Stings in Tails' etc.

Beyond these issues of whether or not a willingness to compromise exists and, more importantly, can be attained, lie two other concerns – what I will refer to as 'stings in tails' and the 'slippery slope/dynamite process' dichotomy.

Our survey data demonstrated that compromise positions carrying *sufficient consensus* were available. By definition, these positions (as compromises) can obtain majority support from both ethnic communities. Unquestionably, however, noncompromising minorities remain. In one sense, since *sufficient consensus* exists, these minorities can be ignored in the process of operationalising agreement. However – and here is found the 'stings in the tails' – within these non-compromising minorities are to be found further minorities who in the past have resorted to violence to attain their ends. This ability to take violent action still exists, providing thereby an environment of considerable unease. The question is, could *sufficient consensus* compromise be destabilised by terrorism, or are the British and Irish governments willing to undertake the fraught task of containing or, better, suppressing this violence, thus enabling the delicate creations of compromise to take root?

The existence of elements within the two ethnic communities who are less attracted to the compromise positions – and who are, indeed, obsessed with a zero-sum view – can be illustrated by briefly examining the preference patterns of two of the five main political parties, Sinn Féin and the Democratic Unionists. In no sense are all the adherents of these parties active or even passive supporters of out-and-out violence, but within this support undoubtedly is encapsulated a significant number of 'hard liners', for whom compromise is anathema.

The biggest 'sting in the tail' of compromise resided at the macro-political constitutional level. The highly polarised constitutional preferences of Sinn Féin and Democratic Unionist supporters are starkly evident in Figure.8. Even when we aggregate preferences to include fourth ranked scenarios, no constitutional arrangement amongst the eight presented succeeds in attaining *sufficient consensus*. Similarly with parades. On the other hand, even with these two parties who see themselves as upholders of the core objectives and values of their respective communities, many other matters still indicate the presence of mutuality solutions – fair employment, social housing policy, the language of street names, school integration and even (with difficulty) policing.

The second concern about the feasibility of mutuality solutions derives from what I label the 'slippery slope/dynamic process' dichotomy. The compromises we have delineated here require movement from dearly held, preferred positions. However, at the time of the survey there was a significant asymmetry in the interpretative stances of many in the two ethnic communities. With Protestants there was a deep-seated concern that movement to a compromise position would be rather like stepping onto a slippery slope. In other words the compromise would not be the final position – instead it would merely be a way-station en route to the other

FIGURE 8

CONSTITUTIONAL PREFERENCES OF SUPPORTERS OF THE SINN FÉIN AND
THE DEMOCRATIC UNIONIST PARTIES

POLITICAL PARTY

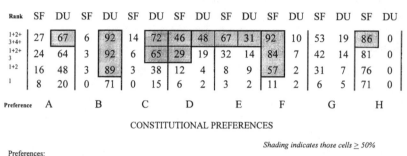

Rank	SF	DU	SF	DU	SF	DU	SF	DU	SF	DU	SF	DU	SF	DU	SF	DU
1+2+3+4+	27	67	6	92	14	72	46	48	67	31	92	10	53	19	86	0
1+2+3	24	64	3	92	6	65	29	19	32	14	84	7	42	14	81	0
1+2	16	48	3	89	3	38	12	4	8	9	57	2	31	7	76	0
1	8	20	0	71	0	15	6	2	3	2	11	2	6	5	71	0
Preference	A		B		C		D		E		F		G		H	

CONSTITUTIONAL PREFERENCES

Shading indicates those cells ≥ 50%

Preferences:
A: Separate Northern Irish State
B: Full Incorporation into British State
C: Continued Direct Rule (current situation)
D: Power Sharing and Anglo-Irish Agreement
E: Power Sharing + North-South Institutions
F: Joint Authority with Power Sharing
G: Separate Governmental Institutions for each ethnic group
H: Full Incorporation into Irish State

SF = *Sinn Féin*
DU = *Democratic Unionist*

community's preferred destination. On the other hand leaders of the Catholic community are wont to declare that negotiation is part of a broader 'dynamic process'. Again, the compromise position is not seen as the end of the story but as a possible bridge to a more desirable final outcome. Thus, one ethnic community fears that the process of compromise will be on-going; the other community hopes that it will be just that – on-going. In consequence one community may be hesitant in the search for the common ground; the other community, in aspiring to an open-ended process, may overplay its hand thereby providing the very evidence that reinforces that hesitancy.

The Belfast Agreement

Much has happened since the survey discussed above was carried out in the spring of 1996. In May of that year elections were held in Northern Ireland as a means of putting in place teams of negotiators representative of those political parties that could achieve a prescribed minimum of electoral support. The subsequent discussions became stalled for over a year on the issue of 'decommissioning' of paramilitary arms. However, by September

1997 the newly elected Labour Government at Westminster stated its intention that substantive negotiations should begin with a view to reaching a conclusion by May 1998. Any agreement thereby reached should then be put to the people of both parts of Ireland (separately and concurrently).

All parties entering the talks were required to commit themselves to what were known as the 'Mitchell Principles' of democracy and non-violence. These had been set out in January 1996 by an international body chaired by former US Senator George Mitchell. Commitment was required:

- to democratic and exclusively peaceful means of resolving political issues;
- to the total disarmament of all paramilitary organisations;
- to agree that such disarmament must be verifiable to the satisfaction of an independent commission;
- to renounce for themselves and to oppose any efforts by others, to use force, or threaten to use force, to influence the course or the outcome of all-party negotiations;
- to agree to abide by the terms of any agreement reached in all-party negotiations and to resort to democratic and exclusively peaceful methods in trying to alter any aspect of that outcome with which they may disagree;
- to urge that 'punishment' killings and beatings stop and to take effective steps to prevent such actions.[24]

After many weeks of intensive negotiations, which included interventions by American President Clinton, British Prime Minister Blair and Irish Taoiseach Ahern, the parties that remained at the talks[25] and the British and Irish governments signed what became known as the 'Good Friday' or the 'Belfast' Agreement on 10 April 1998.

The Agreement is founded on a 'three stranded approach'. The essence of this is found in Clause Three of the 'Declaration of Support' issued by the signatories:

> We are committed to partnership, equality and mutual respect as the basis of relationships within Northern Ireland, between North and South, and between these islands.[26]

It has been agreed that Northern Ireland should remain part of the UK, since this is the wish of a majority of the population, but that in the future, should a majority favour a united Ireland, then that wish would be expedited by both the UK and the Irish governments. A democratic institution (The Assembly) was agreed, this to exercise executive and legislative authority over a wide range of matters, with safeguards to ensure that all sections of the community can participate. This is to be achieved by the operation of proportionality in the sharing of ministerial posts and membership of committees. In addition the principle of *sufficient consensus* is to be brought to bear, whereby decisions on key issues are to be taken on a cross-community basis – either there is parallel consent where there must be a majority of those present and voting, including a majority of both unionists and nationalists, or there must be a weighted majority (60 per cent) of members present and voting, including at least 40 per cent of each of the nationalist and unionist blocs present and voting.[27]

The second and third strands of the Agreement are given substance through the setting up of a 'North-South Ministerial Council' to bring together those with executive responsibilities in Northern Ireland and the Irish Government to 'develop consultation, co-operation and action within the island of Ireland' (Strand Two), and a British-Irish Council 'to promote the harmonious and mutually beneficial development of the totality of relationships among the people of these islands' (Strand Three).

The basis constitutional framework agreed on 10 April 1998 is very close to the *concurrent consensus* indicated in the 1996 survey. Many other matters remain to be resolved, however. There is a plethora of general statements in the Agreement, but specifies are thin on the ground. A Human Rights Commission is to be established to maintain an overview in the rights field. An Equality Commission is to undertake the work that currently falls within the ambits of the Fair Employment Commission (ethnic employment equality), the Equal Opportunities Commission (gender equality), the Commission for Racial Equality and the Disability Council. Linguistic diversity is to be promoted – 'all participants recognise the importance of respect, understanding and tolerance in relation to linguistic diversity, including in Northern Ireland, the Irish language, Ulster-Scots and the languages of the various ethnic[28] communities... .' In particular the Irish language is to be promoted 'where appropriate and where people so desire it', including a statutory duty placed on the Department of Education to encourage and facilitate Irish medium education in line with already existing provision for integrated education. More generally, as 'an essential aspect of the reconciliation process is the promotion of a culture of tolerance at every level of society, including initiatives to facilitate and encourage integrated education and mixed housing.'

Policing, one of the most difficult areas to achieve *sufficient consensus* proposals, is highlighted in the Agreement – 'the participants recognise that policing is a central issue in any society'... 'They consider that this opportunity [the Agreement] should inform and underpin the development of a police service representative in terms of the make-up of the community as a whole and which, in a peaceful environment, should be routinely unarmed.' To this end the Agreement mandates the establishment of an independent commission to make recommendations for future policing arrangements. 'Its proposals on policing should be designed to ensure that policing arrangements, including composition, recruitment, training, culture, ethos and symbols[29] are such that in a new approach Northern Ireland has a police service that can enjoy widespread support from, and is seen as an integral part of, the community as a whole'.

The Belfast Agreement attempts to confront the existence of paramilitarism in its proposals with regard to two extremely sensitive issues – prisoners and the decommissioning of paramilitary weapons. On the former it was agreed that both the British and Irish governments would put in place mechanisms to provide for an accelerated programme for the release of those prisoners who had been convicted of 'scheduled' offences (offences of a terrorist nature, where conviction was obtained in non-jury courts) and who were affiliated with organisations maintaining 'a complete and unequivocal cease fire'.[30] Our *sufficient consensus* survey had earlier indicated a great unwillingness, on the part of the Northern Ireland public, to accept any form of amnesty, though it must also be stressed that Protestants were much more strongly opposed than Catholics. However, despite this great unease, it was found necessary to install a prisoner release programme, in order to obtain signatures to the Agreement from those parties with paramilitary linkages (Sinn Féin, Ulster Democratic Party, Progressive Unionist Party).

Decommissioning (that is the disarming of paramilitary organisations) became part of the 'peace process' before the Agreement was signed. As noted earlier in this paper an international body on decommissioning, chaired by former US Senator George Mitchell, set out what became known as the 'Mitchell Principles'. These included a commitment on the part of all involved in the 'peace process' 'to the total disarmament of all paramilitary organisations'. By September 1997 an Independent International Commission on Decommissioning had been set up and the decommissioning theme was subsequently built into the Belfast Agreement itself:

> all participants … reaffirm their commitment to the total disarmament of all paramilitary organisations. They also confirm their intention to continue to work constructively and in good faith with the Independent Commission and to use any influence they may have, to achieve the decommissioning of all paramilitary arms within two years following endorsement in referendums North and South of the agreement and in the context of the implementation of the overall settlement.[31]

Post Agreement Actions

Following the signing of the Agreement in April 1998, concurrent referenda were held on 22 May in Northern Ireland and the Republic of Ireland. In the Irish Republic constitutional changes[32] required by the Agreement were approved by 94 per cent of those voting. The objective of the referendum in Northern Ireland was the Agreement itself. This was approved by 71 per cent of the voters. However this two-thirds-plus majority hides a significant ethnic differential – approximately 95 per cent of Catholics who voted approved the Agreement, but the Protestant vote was quite deeply split, with some 55 per cent in favour, 45 per cent against. Following the referenda, elections to the new Northern Ireland Assembly took place on 25 June.

Commentary

The constitutional compromise that forms the linchpin of the Belfast Agreement is very close to the *'concurrent consensus/mutuality'* solution indicated in the 1997 survey. Beyond this the Agreement contains much good intention, mostly couched in highly general terms, including a good helping of vague or compromise terminology – 'these islands', 'North and South', 'parity of esteem', 'the community/the two communities', ' ethos', 'traditions'. Of course it can be argued that vagueness and ambiguity were necessary to achieve a document that all the disparate parties at the negotiating table could sign up to. Such an approach has been referred to as 'constructive ambiguity'!

Many of the other issues explored in the 1997 survey have been shunted off in the Agreement to commissions – the Human Rights Commission, The Equality Commission, the Commission on Policing – while a variety of other commissions had earlier been established to deal with a range of other difficult and sensitive matters. These cover decommissioning of paramilitary arms, parades, prisoners (Sentence Review Commissioners) and victims (the Victims Commission).[33]

At the end of the day, if the 'peace process' is to reach a successful conclusion, the various commissioners are going to have to produce recommendations very close to those indicated by the earlier 'mutuality' survey. At the same time, there is an underlying concern (as noted earlier with reference to the survey) that while all the parties to the Belfast Agreement signed up to the same set of words, a number of them may have 'read' those self-same words in diametrically opposed ways, or, at least, may have seen the structures proposed in the Agreement as serving diametrically opposed ends – transitional arrangements to a united Ireland, on the one hand (the nationalists, and particularly Sinn Féin); structures securing Northern Ireland's place in the UK, on the other (those unionists who remained at the negotiating table).[34]

Undoubtedly crunch times lie ahead, as the warm glow of the Agreement has to be translated into specific proposals and actions. The devil, undoubtedly, will be in the detail. Throwing the biggest shadow of all is the issue of decommissioning paramilitary armaments. This has the potential to derail the whole process. Initially it was suggested that paramilitary arms should be turned in *before* the paramilitary related parties could participate in talks. Then decommissioning was to take place *during* talks ('parallel decommissioning'), then *at the end* or the talks, and now, according to the Agreement, *within two years* of the 22 May referenda. Is this really a process of compromise, or is it one where society in general repetitively yields to the intransigence of the paramilitaries?

Conclusion

Globally we have been witnessing an ethnic revival. The deep-rooted and long present ethnic conflict in the northern part of Ireland has undoubtedly been reinvigorated, partly because of the general societal and political processes that have underpinned this revival. As we have noted earlier, ethnic conflict can be resolved (terminated) in one of three ways – by territorial, separationist strategies, by the dominance of one group over one or more others, or by a process we have designated 'mutuality'. Such approaches, I would claim, are not ones to be restricted to the Northern Ireland situation – they are universal. At the same time John Darby has warned us that 'it is dangerous to overgeneralise about ethnic conflict and to impose lessons from one setting to another'.[35] He goes on to stress that any approach to conflict resolution must pay respect to its local characteristics, while searching for its general features. Thus, just as I would argue that the territoriality-dominance-mutuality alternatives are of general applicability, I would certainly also agree that their working out must be place specific. It is evident to me, therefore, that my approach and that of Darby are closely aligned. Consequently I would certainly support Darby's claim that:

> The NI [Northern Ireland] experience illuminates three of the most fundamental choices in considering ethnic conflict: whether it can be resolved or if regulation is a more realistic objective, whether ethnic minorities should be assimilated into the general culture, or their differences recognised through pluralistic institutions; and whether minority aspirations can be better satisfied by secession or by internal constitutional reform.[36]

In the Northern Ireland case Darby concludes that 'the only serious option is a compromise arrangement which seeks to satisfy through negotiation the aspirations of all interests'.[37] He also underlines the need for a subtle approach to ethnic conflict environments. Such an approach is evidenced in his conclusion that 'it often makes sense to maintain elements of both assimilative and accommodation policies in divided societies, even if occasionally they sit uneasily beside each other. *In dealing with pluralism, pragmatism is always preferable to dogma*' (my emphasis).[38]

Our survey data have indicated the possibilities for compromise in Northern Ireland. Such compromise is not easy to attain, however (particularly when we apply the *sufficient consensus* rule). Nonetheless the subsequent Belfast Agreement has provided a framework[39] that offers the opportunity to develop the many *sufficient consensus* compromises that must follow if the Agreement's generalities are to be translated into actions en route to an accommodationist solution to the Irish ethnonational conflict. No matter how difficult it is to attain compromise, I would still argue that it is fundamentally worth trying, on the one hand if we can thereby avoid the travails of territorial separation and involuntary population movement and on the other if we can avoid situations where one group feels it has lost and has subsequently been forced to live in circumstances not of its choosing under the hegemony of its foe. The lessons in this for elsewhere in the world are obvious.

NOTES

1. A.D. Smith, *The Ethnic Revival* (Cambridge: Cambridge University Press 1981), p.1.
2. J. Hutchinson and A.D. Smith, 'Introduction', in J. Hutchinson and A.D. Smith (eds.), *Ethnicity* (Oxford: Oxford University Press 1996), pp.3–14.
3. M. Ignatieff, *Blood and Belonging* (London: BBC 1993), p.8.
4. A. Melucci, 'The post-modern revival of ethnicity', in J. Hutchinson and A.D. Smith, *Ethnicity*, pp.367–70.
5. M.J. Esman, *Ethnic Politics* (Ithaca NY: Cornell University Press 1994), p.4.
6. Michael Ignatieff likewise notes that 'the cosmopolitan order of the great cities –London, Los Angeles, New York, Paris – depend critically on the rule-enforcing capacities of the nation state. When this order breaks down, as it did during the Los Angeles riots of 1992, it becomes apparent that civilised, cosmopolitan multi-ethnic cities have as great a propensity for ethnic warfare as any Eastern European country' (Ignatieff (note 3), p.9).
7. Ignatieff (note 3), p.8.
8. Robert J. Holton, *Globalisation and the Nation State* (London: Macmillan 1998), p.155.
9. Ibid, pp.156–7.
10. Esman (note 5), p.5.
11. R. Brubacker, *Nationalism Reframed: Nationhood and Nationalism in the New Europe* (Cambridge: Cambridge University Press, 1996).
12. There is an intriguing angle to this in the case of the United States. Samuel P. Huntington has recently noted that American foreign policy has been increasingly driven by the concerns of a plethora of ethnic diasporas, rather than by a focused 'national interest'. As Huntington expresses it 'the ideologies of multiculturalism and diversity ... deny the existence of a

common culture in the United States, denounce assimilation and promote the primacy of racial, ethnic and other sub-national cultural identities and groupings' (see S.P. Huntington, 'The erosion of American national interests', *Foreign Affairs* 76, [1997], p.33). Ethnicity here, in the form of multiculturalism, does not lead to the break-up of the existing state, but it does have a fragmenting effect, albeit at a lower level.

13. The Economist, 'Small but perfectly formed', *The Economist*, 3 January 1998, pp.63–6.

14. B. O'Leary and J. McGarry, 'Regulating nations and ethnic communities', in A. Breton, G. Galleotti, P. Salmon and R. Wintrobe (eds.), *Nationalism and Nationality* (Cambridge, Cambridge University Press, 1995), pp.245–89.

15. R. Sommer, *Personal Space: The Behavioural Basis of Design* (Englewood Cliffs, NJ: Prentice Hall 1969).

16. Quoted in A.C. Hepburn, *The Conflict of Nationality in Modern Ireland* (London: Edward Arnold 1980), p.64.

17. Global Security Fellows Initiative, 'Accommodating Differences: from Philosophical Concept to Political Strategy', paper presented at GSFI Conference, Kielce, Poland, 16–18 Sept. 1998.

18. Ranking establishes the order of preference in which the various alternatives are seen by each respondent. However the method does not establish whether something is 'acceptable' or not. Thus a scenario ranked 3 might be 'acceptable' to someone (though clearly not their top preference). On the other hand the same scenario (ranked 3) might, nonetheless be quite 'unacceptable'. Subsequent survey work carried out by Colin Irwin on related (but by no means the same) issues has employed a scale 'preferred', 'acceptable', 'tolerable', and 'unacceptable'. This methodology overcomes the problem as to whether scenarios are being rejected or not, though great care is needed to ensure that respondents fully understand the shades of meaning attached to each of the four response categories. See C. Irwin, *The Search for a Settlement: The People's Choice*, (Belfast: Fortnight Educational Trust, 1998).

19. C. Irwin, Series of articles in *Belfast Telegraph*, 4 July, 2 Aug., 12 Sept., 30 Sept., 22 Oct., 20 Nov., 3 Dec. 1996.

20. T. Hadden, C. Irwin and F. Boal, *Separation or Sharing?* (Belfast: Fortnight Educational Trust 1996).

21. A. Guelke, 'Consenting to agreement', *Fortnight,* 366 (1997), pp.12–13; F.W. Boal, 'Integration and division: sharing and segregating in Belfast', *Planning Practice and Research*, 11 (1996), pp.151–8.

22. R. Cormack, 'The Queen's University of Belfast: a case study of a university operating in a divided society', paper presented at CC-HER Forum, Conference on Higher Education for Tolerance in Europe, Ljubljana, 18–20 Oct 1995.

23. M.A. Poole and P. Doherty, *Ethnic Residential Segregation in Northern Ireland,* (Coleraine: University of Ulster Centre for the Study of Conflict 1996); M.C. Keane, 'Segregation processes in public sector housing', in P. Doherty (ed), *Geographical Perspectives on the Belfast Region,* (Newtownabbey: Geographical Society of Ireland 1990), pp.88–108.

24. The 'Mitchell Principles' are available at http://www.nio.gov.uk/mitchrtp.htm#MP.

25. Eight of the ten originally elected. The Democratic Unionist Party (DUP) and the United Kingdom Unionist Party (UKUP) withdrew from the talks due to the failure to achieve any paramilitary decommissioning.

26. 'North' and 'South' refer respectively to Northern Ireland and the Republic of Ireland. 'These Islands' refers to what otherwise have been labelled 'The British Isles'.

27. Belfast Agreement page 5 clause 5d. The Belfast Agreement is available in printed form: *The Agreement,* (Belfast, Northern Ireland Office, 1998). It is also accessible on the Web at http://www.nio.gov.uk/agreement.htm.

28. Here the term 'ethnic' is used in the peculiarly restrictive sense employed by the population census in Great Britain – that is it refers basically to 'non-white' persons.

29. Some years ago Raymond Breton noted that people 'expect some consistency between their private identities and the symbolic contents upheld by public authorities, embedded in the societal institutions, and celebrated in public events'. (see R. Breton, 'The production and allocation of symbolic resources: an analysis of the linguistic and ethnocultural fields in Canada', *Canadian Review of Sociology and Anthropology*, 22, 1984). A similar signal is

sent out by the Belfast Agreement: 'All participants acknowledge the sensitivity of the use of symbols and emblems for public purposes, and the need in particular in creating the new institutions to ensure that such symbols and emblems are used in a manner which promotes mutual respect rather than division' (Belfast Agreement, page 20, clause 5).

30. Officially it is stressed that this is a system for early release, not amnesty, as the prisoners are released under licence – that is they can be recalled to serve out the remainder of their sentences should they re-offend.
31. Belfast Agreement, page 20 – Decommissioning: clause 3.
32. Belfast Agreement, pages 3–4, Annex B.
33. If one can be permitted a certain degree of cynicism, one could suggest that the biggest task of all will be for the Decommissioning Commission to decommission all the other commissions before, as a final act, decommissioning itself!
34. Those unionists that withdrew from the negotiations (DUP and UKUP) would see the Agreement in the same light as Sinn Féin.
35. John Darby, *Northern Ireland: Managing Differences,* (London: Minority Rights Group, 1995), p.29.
36. Ibid..
37. Ibid.
38. Ibid., p.30.
39. Interestingly, the constitutional proposals in the Belfast Agreement represent a shift from a conflict of ethnic nationalisms to a competition of civic ones. Unionists in the Agreement have committed themselves to the creation of an inclusive Northern Ireland within the United Kingdom (a brand of civic British nationalism), while Irish nationalists have really committed themselves to an aspiration for an inclusive civic Irish nationalism. The essence of this shift from ethnic to civic nationalisms is found in one of the clauses of the Agreement between the British and the Irish governments, which in turn forms an integral part of the overall Belfast Agreement. Clause 5 states that the two governments:

affirm that whatever [constitutional] choice is freely exercised by a majority of the people of Northern Ireland, the power of the sovereign government [the British or the Irish, as the case may be] with jurisdiction there shall be exercised with rigorous impartiality on behalf of all the people in the diversity of their identities and traditions, and shall be founded on the principles of full respect for, and equality of, civil, political, social and cultural rights, of freedom from discrimination for all citizens, and of parity of esteem and of just and equal treatment for the identity, ethos and aspirations of both communities. [Belfast Agreement, page 28 Article 1, clause (v)].

Borders in a 'Borderless' World

VICTOR PRESCOTT

Carlos Fernandez de Casadevante Romani, *La frontière Franco-Espagnole et les relations de voisinage* [The Franco-Spanish boundary and relations within the borderland], Bayonne: Harriet 1989.

D. Rumley and V.J. Minghi, *The Geography of Border Landscapes,* London: Routledge 1991.

J.C. Wilkinson, *Arabia's Frontiers: the Story of Britain's Boundary Drawing in the Desert,* London: Tauris 1991.

Bernard Gay, *La nouvelle frontière lao-vietnamienne: Les Accords de 1977–1990,* Histoire des frontières de la Peninsule Indochinoise, No.2. General editor P.B. Lafont. Paris: L'Harmattan 1993.

Richard Schofield, *Kuwait and Iraq: Historical Claims and Territorial Disputes,* London: Royal Institute of International Affairs 1994.

World boundaries, Volume 1: *Global Boundaries,* C.H. Schofield (ed.) London: Routledge 1994.

World boundaries, Volume 2: *The Middle East and North Africa,* C.H. Schofield & R.N. Schofield (eds.). London: Routledge 1994.

World boundaries, Volume 3: *Eurasia,* C. Grundy-Warr (ed.) London: Routledge 1994.

World boundaries. Volume 4: *The Americas,* P.O. Giro (ed.) London: Routledge 1994

A. Paasi, *Territories, Boundaries and Consciousness: The Changing Geographies of the Finish-Russian Border,* Chichester: John Wiley 1996.

The books reviewed in this essay have two common characteristics. They deal almost exclusively with international boundaries on land and they were published between 1989 and 1996. These books fall into three categories. First there are those by Wilkinson, Schofield and Gay which deal in detail with the evolution of one or more international boundaries in a specific area. Second there is the *World Boundary* series of four volumes that present conference papers on a variety of boundary topics arranged by continents. Third there are the studies of boundary landscapes.

Wilkinson tells the story of Britain's efforts to draw boundaries in Arabia from 1913 to 1971. The Prologue which introduces the reader to the book is a fine essay which establishes that none of the states in Arabia possess boundaries with their Arabian neighbours which could be defended with confidence according to the tenets of international law. This situation has arisen because international law is ill-suited to determine sovereignty issues in sparsely populated deserts, because local concepts of territorial organisation were largely ignored in attempting to draw boundaries, and because Britain resolutely tried to preserve a sphere of influence by arguments and means that were at best devious and at worst dishonest. Wilkinson faces squarely the problem of bias on the part of many writers on this subject including himself and describes how his position shifted from the view that Britain was the defender of poor, small Gulf states against greedy Saudi and Omani dominance to a realisation that Britain's prime interest was preserving its sphere of influence rather than the quasi-independence of the Gulf states (p.xxxi). The material is arranged in a logical structure and Part I reviews the geopolitical setting of the regional powers, Saudi Arabia, Yemen and Britain and the Gulf territories of Greater Bahrain, Qatar and Greater Oman. The Blue and Violet Lines of the 1913 and 1914 Anglo-Ottoman Conventions are then reviewed in separate chapters which comprise Part II. Part III recounts the development of Britain's relations with Ibn Saud from before 1914, through World War I and the post-war period to the early 1930s and the particular problem of the Yemen-Aden boundary. The discovery of oil in Bahrain in 1932 ended the conventional wisdom that there was no oil on the Arabian side of the Gulf and led to a period of negotiations that were terminated as World War II loomed over Europe. These negotiations are the subject of Part IV. The end of World War II coincided with America's claim to the continental shelf and the rush to follow that lead in areas with high petroleum potential including the Persian Gulf. A formal Saudi claim to territory prompted further negotiations which ended in the crisis that followed Saudi's occupation in 1952 of the Buraimi Oasis which Britain believed belonged either to Abu Dhabi or Oman. These events are dealt with in Part V. Part VI covers the crisis that followed this occupation and events up to the withdrawal of British troops in 1971.

Wilkinson concludes that the main cause of the boundary problems was Britain's desire to retain a sphere of influence and this persistence allowed the peripheral states to occupy territory up to the limits claimed by Britain. It was not a dispute mainly over oil but concerned Saudi self-respect. The future will tell whether Saudi Arabia is prepared to allow the peripheral states to retain the territory which British actions helped them to secure.

The primary and secondary sources used by Wilkinson are comprehensively listed and there are eleven useful maps bound at the end of the book and a useful index. My only slight criticism of this work is that readers might have benefited from more maps, but this is a splendid study not only for the detailed analysis and explanation of events but also for the quality of the writing which is uncomplicated and flows smoothly throughout. I finished reading this book with the same feeling that I had after reading Alistair Lamb's 1966 study of the McMahon Line – I wish I could write a book like that.

Schofield's study of the Kuwait-Iraq boundary was first published in 1991. The second edition includes two new chapters and six new maps. This study is an example of the best contributions of political geographers in unravelling the evolution of international boundaries whether or not they have been the subject of serious dispute. The text follows a strictly chronological order from the early eighteenth century to delimitation of a boundary between Kuwait and Iraq by the United Nations Iraq-Kuwait Boundary Demarcation Commission in 1993. Schofield makes the strong case that the Commission might have acted outside its terms of reference in delimiting a territorial sea boundary through the Khor [inlet] Abdullah. The effect of that delimitation is to leave most of the principal navigation channels, dredged and maintained by Iraq since 1961, on the Kuwaiti side of the boundary. Kuwait and its allies are presumably aware that a legitimate Iraqi grievance has been stored for the future.

Gay's latest volume completes his earlier study of the Laos-Vietnam boundary from 1893 to 1987, which was published in 1989 by the same publisher. This volume deals with six previously secret agreements between the two countries during the period from July 1977 to March 1990. These treaties, accords and reports deal with the delimitation, demarcation and administration of the boundary extending for 2,130 km.

The first chapter reports on the processes of delimitation and demarcation. Delimitation involves definition of a line or the principle by which the line will be determined. In this case the two countries adopted the principle of *uti possidetis juris* which provides that former colonial teritories will inherit the existing colonial boundaries at the time independence is achieved. It is a principle which was invoked in the cases before the International Court of Justice between Burkina Faso and Mali in West Africa and El Salvador and Honduras in central America (Prescott 1998). This agreement was signed on 10 February 1976 when it was agreed that the critical date for selecting the boundary was 1945 and it would be the boundary marked on the 100,000 series produced by the Geographical Service of Indochina. Arrangements for the demarcation of the boundary were settled by a treaty dated 18 July 1977 and the Mixed Commission placed 202 pillars along the boundary in the period 25 July 1978 to 24 August 1984.

Gay provides an excellent, detailed description of the demarcated boundary arranged in 14 sections stretching from the tri-junction with China to the tri-junction with Cambodia. This description is admirably integrated with two general maps and 13 large scale maps which also display the areas exchanged by each side where the final line deviates from the 1945 line for reasons of mutual administrative convenience.

The six agreements are presented in Lao, Vietnamese and French and the whole is supported by lists of large scale maps and indexes of provincial names and exchanged territories. Gay's record of a long period of constructive and successful negotiations could serve as a handbook for any countries that have emerged from a colonial situation, have good relations with their neighbours and find that there are uncertainties about the location of the former colonial boundary.

The International Boundaries Research Unit at Durham University has just celebrated its first decade and during that time it has reached a position of pre-eminence as an organisation focusing precisely on international boundaries. The first three volumes considered here include papers presented at the Unit's second annual conference in 1991 which examined fresh boundary perspectives. Volume 4 contains papers from a conference organised on boundaries in Ibero-America in Costa Rica during 1990. There is a fifth volume, not considered here, which deals with maritime boundaries. All the volumes have the same format with a common series preface and a particular preface for the contents. They are all illustrated with maps, figures and occasional plates and have a satisfactory index.

The title of 'Global Boundaries' for Volume 1 is misleading because the contents include four chapters dealing with aspects of boundary studies, a brief review of a collection of Mahan's papers published in 1900, a longer useful examination of the role of borderlands for regional integration in Africa and three chapters on Antarctica. The emphasis on Antarctica was appropriate during the thirtieth anniversary of the signing of the Antarctic Treaty although there is inadequate treatment of the continent's continental shelf which might prove a contentious field in the future. The chapters I found most interesting and most likely to re-read were by Matinez on the dynamics of border interaction, by Harbottle on peace-keeping operations and by Asiwaju on African borderlands. This is a slim volume and since all volumes are the same price it seems expensive.

Volume 2 covers North Africa and the Middle East, but North Africa is only considered in two chapters. The first is by Joffe who provides a very short, illuminating discussion about the relationships of nation, state and territory in the Islamic world. Blake tells the story of Captain Kelly's contribution to the demarcation of the Uganda-Sudan boundary, which was such a pleasure to read that I wished for a whole book devoted to biographical sketches of surveyors of colonial boundaries, who often provided geographical descriptions that were invaluable at the time. The ten chapters concerned with the Middle East consist of four on Israel and Palestine, two on Iraq and Kuwait and one on each of Beirut, Syria, Oman and the United Arab Emirates and the Iraq-Jordan boundary.

The analysis by Drysdale of traffic across Syria's boundaries is elegant and could be used by others as a model for similar studies in other areas. Walker and Amadouny both describe the evolution of boundaries in the Middle East with sharply contrasting styles. Amadouny follows a conventional plan in discussing the Transjordan-Iraq boundary during the period 1915–40. He places much reliance on treaties and archival material supported by the writings of others. Walker seems to rely on his memory for there are no references to the works of others and, perhaps worse still, no maps. Further he seems to prefer the word 'frontier' to 'boundary' despite the fact that most political geographers would have thought the battle had been won to use those terms in their distinctive meanings. Newman's long and comprehensive examination of the continued significance of the Green Line after it was erased in 1967 seems to be a classical example and extension of what Hartshorne (1936) called a relict boundary. Hartshorne was identifying boundaries that are no longer exist but where landscape differences built up during their existence survive. The Green Line is a line which still affects the lives of people living near it.

The volume on Eurasia has a good balance of five chapters on European boundaries and six on Asian boundaries. Black delivers a seminal account of the evolutions of concepts of frontiers and boundaries in Europe and the role of maps in their delineation, especially in the eighteenth century. Bucholz is concerned with the present and future as he reviews the significance of the establishment and abolition of the boundary separating East and West Germany. Grundy-Warr considers the effect of peace-keeping operations in Cyprus and reaches the encouraging, but surprising, conclusion that such activities do not tend to preserve partition.

The five chapters on Asia are all located on the continent's periphery. No doubt recent events in central Asia will make studies of international boundaries there more common. Certainly the conference on boundaries and energy in 1996 at Durham contained three excellent papers on disputes over oil and pipelines in central Asia including one by Vinogradov that raised the question of whether boundaries in the Caspian Sea were governed by the Convention on the Law of the Sea or by the various techniques for dealing with international lakes (Blake *et al.*, 1998, pp.140–42). The peripheral case-studies under review included excellent analyses by Nazam on water distribution between India and Bangladesh, by Goodstadt on Hong Kong's boundary as re-union with China loomed and by Hara on the Japan's Northern Islands and the dispute with Russia. Hara's contribution to this long-standing divisive question is refreshingly balanced and shows that Russia's case is not as bankrupt as some other authors have suggested.

The fourth volume dealing with the Americas is also well balanced with three chapters on North America and four chapters each on central and south America. The studies of the United States boundaries with Canada and Mexico are uniformly good but the most novel is the study of pollution along the Mexican boundary by Robles. This sets a standard against which similar studies will be measured. Three of the studies set in central America deal with borderlands and the study by Lavell on the classification of borderlands could inspire a decade of postgraduate theses in the region. The fourth study by the Girot, who edited the volume, considers the relationships between the alignment of canal projects and the international boundary between Nicaragua and Costa Rica. The south American studies provide two admirable, conventional presentations of boundary disputes between Chile and Bolivia and Ecuador and Peru by St. John and Geisse and Arenas respectively. A third elegant study by Bandieri explores the impact of administrative decisions by Argentina and Chile on the Chilean area of Neuquén using simple language and a clear structure.

Generally I have reservations about the publication of collections of conference papers. For a scholar there is often disappointment with the quality of some conference papers which seem to have been cobbled or thrown together with the sole aim of securing travel and accommodation expenses from universities and institutes. For a member of the board of a university press there is a worry that the market for such volumes is often compromised by the facts that the papers were distributed to persons who attended the conference and that the best ones have been copied and circulated to interested parties who were not in attendance. Some publishers also are appalled by the length of time it takes hard-working academic editors to cajole authors of conference papers to polish and complete them in the light of comments made at the conference. Fortunately these four volumes do form a useful addition to the libraries of scholars and organisations interested in international boundaries. Several of the chapters will be read and reread by boundary scholars not only for their factual and theoretical content but also for their stylish structure and language.

The book on border landscapes edited by Rumley and Minghi is another collection of conference papers which fortunately does not match my general suspicions. The conference on border landscapes was held in Perth, Australia in August 1988 and was organised by the Study Group on the World Map as part of the 26th International Geographical Union Congress. The book contains 14 chapters which provide a wide range of topics and approaches on the general subject of border landscapes. Four chapters deal with border landscapes in southern Europe involving the borders of France and Italy, France and Switzerland, Switzerland and Italy and Italy and Yugoslavia, and the fifth European example looks at the northern border of Bavaria. Another five chapters consider Asian examples extending from Afghanistan and Pakistan in the west via Malaysia and Thailand, Papua New Guinea and Indonesia and the Torres Strait to southern Sakhalin when it was a Japanese borderland with Russia from 1905 to 1945. Other chapters deal with borderlands in the Gulf of Aqaba, Botswana and South Africa and the American-Mexican border in the vicinity of the Colorado River. Finally there is a chapter on peace-keeping forces in the area of international boundaries.

The general aim of the book, which is successfully achieved, is to clarify the nature and extent of border landscapes and the methods by which they might be studied. Border landscapes are the geographical context of international boundaries and the main pioneers of the the study of international boundaries, whether we think of Ratzel, a geographer, or Lapradelle, a lawyer were certain that those boundaries had to be considered in their geographical context. Of course they must also be considered in their historical context but it is the area within which the boundary is located that is under examination here. There is a multitude of relationships between a boundary, its flanking areas, their residents and the governments which administer them. Rumley and Minghi make the important point that borderlands might also differ in important characteristics from other areas in the same state and that could apply either to core areas or borderlands in a different sector of the boundary. They suggest four themes for investigation (p.296).

The *social differentiation* between and within states would require excursions into aspects of cultural geography, such as the social consciousness of border dwellers and their perception of the boundary and of the people living across the boundary or in the core of their own state. The *economic differentiation* between and within states would be concerned with the nature of economic activities, patterns of land-use, the existence of subsidies or the imposition of quotas and levels of cross-boundary trade and cross-boundary employment. The *political differentiation* between and within states would include security issues, systems of government, electoral inclinations and administrative subdivisions. The nature of *interaction between states* would pose the challenge to rank the political outcomes in terms of inter-state relations from war through grudging accommodation to *entente cordiale*.

Rumley and Minghi believe these four themes provide the basis for the description, classification and explanation of the nature of borderlands and changes that occur within them. They also point to the principal path that might lead to a comprehensive understanding of border landscapes (p.297). It is the path of comparative studies. This would encourage the study of categories of borderlands where at least one important element was kept as constant as possible. Such categories could include borderlands in major deserts, borderlands where the people on opposite sides of the boundary speak the same language and were once part of the same country, borderlands where the separated countries belong to the same security bloc, borderlands separated by a boundary coinciding with the thalweg of a major river which provides an arterial route for trade and water for irrigation, and borderlands where the location of the boundary has changed on a number of occasions over distances up to 20 km.

Advances in the field of landscape studies will be greatly assisted by the production of more case studies including straightforward descriptions of borderlands. General concepts, for example, about the stages of evolution of international boundaries was only possible because for a long time the nuts and bolts of almost all the world's international boundaries have been described in terms of treaties and the existing political aims of competing countries. Such information was found in collections and descriptions by writers such as Hertslet (1875–91), Ireland (1938) and Brownlie (1971). Alas there are not yer any equivalent continental or even sub-continental texts regarding border landscapes. The collection edited by Rumley and Minghi shows that there is no lack of scholarly talent to produce wide-ranging descriptions; we can only hope that some have the enthusiasm for such a major endeavour.

The original study by de Casadevante Romani was produced in Spanish as a doctoral thesis in the Faculty of Law in 1985 at the Universidad del País Vasco in Bilbao. The volume being reviewed is a revised version of that thesis and its publication was suggested and encouraged by Daniel Bardonnet, Professor of Law at the Université de Paris II. In his Preface Bardonnet points out that the general view, supported by Bruhnes and Vallaux (1921, p.353), that the boundary along the Pyrenees is 'dead or fossilised' is incorrect. That view is based on the delimitation and demarcation of the boundary according to the treaties of Corbeil in 1258, the Pyrenees in 1659, Elizondo in 1785 and Bayonne in 1856–68. In contrast De Casadevante Romani reveals a boundary that has a lively and changing reality.

The originality of this study is closely related to the sources used by the author. Information from the archives of the Foreign Affairs Departments in Madrid and Paris has been matched with information contained in the archives of the municipalities on both sides of this boundary and available about the current arrangements between municipalities separated by the boundary. This great volume of material has enabled de Casadevante Romani to understand and explain the present mechanisms to reduce boundary friction affecting commerce, travel and development. The volume also provides a fine foundation on which future changes can be built confidently as the European Economic Community continues to develop.

This study is organised in three parts. The first (pp.15–90) examines cross boundary relations from the viewpoint of international public law. The three chapters deal in turn with general aspects of international public law and boundaries, including consideration of the contradiction created between sovereignty and cross-boundary cooperation; state organisations with borderland responsibilities; and the new structures created by the European Economic Community. The second part (pp.91–148) focuses on the Basque sector of the Franco-Spanish boundary by reviewing the origins of the boundary and the regimes in respect of adjacent sea in Fontarabie (Figuier) Bay at the western terminus of the boundary on the coast of the Bay of Biscay and in respect of the fluvial Ile des Faisans which belongs jointly to France and Spain. The third section (pp.149–336) explores the mechanisms developed jointly by France and Spain to simplify and control trans-boundary activities including those involving pasture, mail, trains, tourism, fishing, pollution, overflights and the distribution and allocation of water. The Conclusion (pp.337–48) includes 18 numbered paragraphs. The first few paragraphs make general points about boundaries and international public law and the boundary through the Pyrenees, but the conclusions then become quite specific and relate to particular arrangements and particular areas of discordance between law and practice.

The text is supported by a long, superb, classified bibliography and copies of certain texts. My only criticism of this book is that it has too few maps but that is a general criticism of many extremely valuable articles and texts about boundaries written by lawyers. That aside this book should be read in whole or part by anyone interested in the ways by which friendly neighbouring states can organise activities within their borderlands to their mutual advantage. It is rather like the legal equivalent of the commendable geographical investigation by Suzanne Daveau (1959) of the Jura Mountains between France and Switzerland.

P.J. Taylor, editor of the third volume in the Belhaven Studies in Political Geography describes this book in the following terms. Anssi Paasi has produced a theoretically sophisticated treatment of nationalism by focusing on boundaries in the construction of territories and on discourses in the representation of others. Drawing on a range of relevant social science and humanitarian literature, he has woven together an original argument that links traditional geographical understanding of regions with national territorial constructions through the symbolic role of boundaries in national socialisation. All this is revealed in an unusual empirical context with, first, national level study of the meaning of Finnishness and, second, a detailed study of a community dominated by the Finnish boundary with the USSR/Russia (pp.xv–xvi).

Paasi sums up his work as follows.

> This book provides a theoretically informed analysis of the social and historical construction of territories, boundaries and socio-spatial consciousness, particularly in the case of the Finnish state and the Finnish/Soviet/Russian boundary. The rise of the Finnish state, the nation-building process and the changing positions of this state in the European and world geopolitical and ideological landscape will be traced. The aim is to combine two geographical perspectives which have typically been pursued separately in geographical research – a structurally based analysis of the construction of boundaries as part of the nation-building process, and an interpretative analysis of local, personal experience of this process (p.xvii).

The book consists of three sections. The first, entitled 'Territories and Boundaries in Regional Transformation', contains four chapters (pp.1–76) that provide the theoretical foundation for the other sections. The role of boundaries in the traditional of geographical concepts is discussed to reveal boundaries as an essential element in the formation of territoriality, and a framework is suggested that will promote understanding of the generation of territorial units in the transformation of regions. Boundaries are then examined as a factor in creating nationalism and the contributions which education plays in national socialisation.

The second section, entitled 'The Institutionalization of the Finnish Territory', consists of three chapters (pp.77–200). It provides an application of theoretical constructs by exploring the rise of the Finnish state and the roles of boundaries in various locations and representations of those boundaries in that development. Aspects of Finnish society's impressions of itself and of the Soviet and Russian state are examined because since 1945 the two states have exhibited sharp political, economic and strategic contrasts.

The third section, entitled 'Towards Local Experience' (pp.201–99), comprises three chapters relating the meaning of local, social and international boundaries to the population of the Commune of Vartsilä which was divided by the boundary settled after World War II.

The Epilogue (pp.300–309) is entitled 'Towards a Global Sense of Place'. It deals mainly with the views that boundaries '… are phenomena that are 'located' in the socio-spatial consciouness and collective memories of people living in territorially constructed units on various spatial scales whether communes, provinces or states' (p.301) and that those territorial units are in a constant state of flux (p.302). The Epilogue is densely written and lacks the practical examples that would have made it easier to understand for those not steeped in theoretical and conceptual forms of discourse. It concludes, in the words of Massey (1993), with a plea for a global sense of the local. The text is supported by several photographs and maps at generally small scale, an excellent bibliography and a name and general index.

The main impression which the book made on this reviewer is that it focuses more on the neighbourliness of Russia, the Soviet Union and again Russia than on any of the actual boundaries that have marked the eastern limit of Finland since 1323. While inferences are drawn repeatedly about the role of the boundary in creating Finnish nationalism and in affecting the lives of individuals in some small defined areas of eastern Finland, it is often unclear whether the role was played by the boundary or by the existence of the Russian or Soviet state. For example Chapter 5, 'Nationalism, Geopolitics and Changing Territories: The Case of Finland', is an unremarkable historical political geography of Finland without close attention to the role of the boundary as opposed to Finland's situation between Sweden and Russia.

Only general information is provided about the boundary. The treaties that defined it are not discussed in any detail, nor, with the possible exception of the Finnish frontier-zone, is there close examination of any decrees of Finland or the Soviet Union that governed economic, industrial, settlement or land-use arrangements close to the boundary. The reasons why one particular boundary alignment was selected rather than another are presumably to be found in the archives. The account of the consciousness and memories of individuals living close to the boundary is considered in great detail and generally produces results that might have been expected. There are important differences between respondents who are old and young. The closeness of the boundary caused some mainly older people to be fearful and sad because they could see areas in Russia where they once lived happily. Some young people found that the presence of many border guards made them feel more secure. Tourism from Finland to western Russia has boomed since 1990 as some Finns search for evidence of their family history in Karelia. But it is disappointing that there is no clear exposition of the extent to which people living in the borderland are similar to or different from people living in central or western Finland in terms of attitudes, for example, to Russia, domestic political affiliations, thriftiness, holiday destinations or education opportunities.

In Chapter 7 that deals with the use of representations of Finland's eastern boundary exploited to signify territoriality there is a very interesting account of the role of Finnish political geographers who in some cases allowed patriotism to overwhelm their scholarly responsibilities. It will be surprising if there are not similar skeletons in cupboards other than those of Germany. Curiously, although there is a quotation from one of the geographers who 'prostituted' his science that 'The maritime boundaries are Finland's natural boundaries' (p.191), there appears to be no discussion of the significance of Finland's loss of a coastline on the Barents Sea. Nor is there any comment on the very successful maritime boundary delimitation with Russia through the Gulf of Finland.

This is a book which will stimulate and guide those who wish to produce similar studies of national, regional or local spatial consciousness, but in my view it will be of marginal interest to those who are interested in boundaries as such.

This review supports the conclusion that the interest especially of political geographers in international boundaries has been well maintained throughout the 1990s. The scope of that interest has been expanded to give proper weight to the importance of border landscapes. Although not discussed in this review it is undeniable that the volume and quality of published studies concerned with maritime international boundaries matches the output concerned with international land boundaries. This leads to the conclusion that there is a better all-round balance in the consideration of international boundaries today than at any time in the past. In my view the discipline can look forward with confidence to the next century in 2001.

REFERENCES

G. Blake, M. Pratt, C.H. Schofield and J.A. Brown, 1998. *Boundaries and Energy: Problems and Prospects* (London: Kluwer Law International 1998) pp.137–214.
I. Brownlie, *African Boundaries: a Legal and Diplomatic Encyclopaedia* (London: Hurst 1971).
Jean Bruhnes and Camille Vallaux, 1921. *La géographie de l'histoire* [The geography of history] (Paris: Alcan 1921) 2nd edition.
Suzanne Daveau, *Les régions frontalières de la montagne Jurassienne* [Frontier regions of the Jura Mountains], Paris: Trevoux 1959.
R. Hartshorne, 'Suggestions on the Terminology of Political Boundaries', *Annals*, Association of American Geographers, 26 (1936) pp.56–7.
E. Hertslet, *The Map of Europe by Treaty*, (4 volumes with continuous pagination) (London: Butterworth 1875–91).
G. Ireland, 1938. *The Possessions and Conflicts of South America* (Cambridge, MA: Harvard University Press 1938).
D. Massey, 'Power Geometry and a Progressive Sense of Place', in J. Bird, B. Curtis, T. Putnam *et al.* (eds), *Mapping the Futures: Local Cultures, Global Change* (Routledge: London 1993).
V. Prescott, 1998. 'Contribution of the United Nations to Solving Boundary and territorial disputes', in *The United Nations at work*, (M.I. Glassner ed.) (London: Praeger 1998) pp.239–84.

Notes on Contributors

Jason M. Ackleson is a PhD candidate in the Department of International Relations at the London School of Economics and Political Science, having studied on a British Marshall Scholarship. He is former editor of 'Millennium: Journal of International Studies' and works on questions of borders, identity, and International Relations theory.
E-mail: j.m.ackleson@lse.ac.uk

Frederick W. Boal is Professor Emeritus of Human Geography at the Queen's University of Belfast. His interests focus on ethnic relations in urban contexts, with a particular emphasis on territorial behaviour. In 1982 the Gill Memorial Award was conferred on him by the Royal Geographical Society for 'contributions to social geography'. In 1999 he was granted an OBE 'for contributions to regional planning and urban development'.
E-mail: f.boal@qub.ac.uk

Stanley D. Brunn is Professor of Geography in the Department of Geography at the University of Kentucky, Lexington, KY 40506. He is former editor of the *Annals of the Association of American Geographers*. He is also an active member of the Commission on the World Political Map (WPM) of the International Geographical Union (IGU). Among his current interests are human geographies and the geographies of the Internet.

Fabrizio Eva is contract professor at the Institute of Human Geography, State University of Milan. He is corresponding member of IGU World Political Map Commission. His academic interests include current geopolitical dynamics, international relations, borders and nation-state issues, ethnonationalisms, political and economic dynamics in Eastern Asia (particularly China and Japan), the geopolitical legacy of Elisée Reclus, Piotr Kropotkin and anarchic thought.
E-mail: fabrizio_eva@planet.it

Richard Grant is Associate Professor in the Department of Geography and Regional Studies, University of Miami, Coral Gables, Florida, USA. He is currently undertaking research sponsored by the National Science Foundation in Washington D.C. on economic globalisation and urbanisation in developing countries. In particular, he is studying the effects of economic globalisation in Accra, Ghana and Mumbai, India. His research interests are international trade, foreign aid, and the geographical effects of liberalisation policies. He is a co-editor of the Global Crisis in Foreign Aid, published by

Syracuse University Press (1998). His work has been published in journals such as the Annals of the Association of American Geographers, Political Geography, Environment and Planning A.

E-mail: rgrant@miami.edu

Nurit Kliot is Professor of Geography at Haifa University and chair of the Department of Natural Resources Management. Her fields of interest focus on Political Geography, the impact of ideology on the landscape, Refugees, Cultural Geography, places and landscape, social Geography, time-space Geography, Philosophy of Geography, Humanistic Geography, sense of place, the Geography of peace and war. Her published works include studies of the geopolitics of water in the Middle East, political geography of refugees and the geographical implications of the Egypt-Israeli peace process.

E-mail: nuritk@geo.haifa.ac.il

David B. Knight is Professor of Geography at the University of Guelph in Ontario, Canada, and a past Dean of its College of Social Science. He is a political and cultural geographer who has taken a particular interest in the links between group identities, territory and self-determination. He served as the first Chair/President of the International Geographical Union Commission on the World Political Map. His work appears in geography, political science, and international law publications. His most recent (co-edited) book is 'Restructuring Societies'.

E-mail: dbknight@uoguelph.ca

Virginie Mamadouh is Associate Professor of human geography (especially political and cultural geography) at the University of Amsterdam and is currently affiliated with the Amsterdam Study Centre for the Metropolitan Environment (AME). She received her doctoral degree in 1992 from the University of Amsterdam.

E-mail: V.D.Mamadouh@bgumail.bgu.ac.il

Julian V. Minghi is Professor of Geography, University of South Carolina since 1973. Minghi is a political geographer with particular interests in the changing dynamics of borderlands and in the transformation of relations between western and ex-socialist Europe. PhD, University of Washington, 1962. Formerly on the faculties of the University of Connecticut (1961–4) and the University of British Columbia (1964–73).

E-mail: minghi@garnet.cla.sc.edu

David Newman is Professor of Political Geography and Chairperson of the Department of Politics and Government at Ben Gurion University of the

Negev, Israel. He is the editor of GEOPOLITICS, a member of the Commission on the World Political Map (WPM) of the International Geographical Union (IGU), and contributes a weekly political commentary column to the Jerusalem Post. He has published extensively on territorial issues relating to the Israel-Palestine conflict and peace process.
E-mail: newman@bgumail.bgu.ac.il

John O'Loughlin is Director of the 'Globalisation and Democracy' graduate training program, funded by the National Science Foundation, in the Institute of Behavioral Science at the University of Colorado, Boulder. His research interests are in the diffusion of democracy, the relationship between economic and political transitions in Russia and Ukraine, and the changing identities of the peoples of the post-Soviet states. He is editor of *Political Geography*.
E-mail: Johno@colorado.edu

Victor Prescott is Professor Emeritus in Geography at the University of Melbourne. For the past 40 years, his principal focus of research has been international boundaries on land and sea. He has written books and papers on these topics and political geography in general and some have been translated into Arabic, Chinese, German and Italian. He has also served as an expert witness in cases decided at the International Court of Justice, the United States' Supreme Court and Land Rights Tribunals in the Northern Territory of Australia.
E-mail: johnrvp@myriad.its.unimelb.edu.au

Maano Ramutsindela teaches geography at the University of the North in South Africa and was formerly a Canon Collins scholar at Royal Holloway, University of London. He has published on land reform, local government restructuring, boundaries and identities in post-apartheid South Africa. He has recently completed a project on the reconstruction of the post-apartheid state.
E-mail: maanor@unin.unorth.ac.za

Dennis Rumley is an Associate Professor of Geography at the University of Western Australia and is a Visiting Fellow at the East-West Center. He is a Full Member of the Commission on the World Political Map of the International Geographical Union. He has published more than 80 papers, books and reviews in international academic journals. On behalf of the IGU Commission he has organised two international Conferences – one at the University of WA and one at the United Nations University in Tokyo – and co-edited two books based around these Conferences – *'The Geography of Border Landscapes'* (London: Routledge, 1991) with Julian Minghi and

'Global Geopolitical Change and the Asia-Pacific: A Regional Perspective' (London: Avebury, 1996) with Tatsuya Chiba, Akihiko Takagi and Yoriko Fukushima. The latter has recently been translated into Japanese by the co-editors. He has recently published *'The Geopolitics of Australia's Regional Relations'* (Dordrecht: Kluwer, 1999).

Gearóid Ó Tuathail (Gerard Toal) is Associate Professor of Geography at Virginia Tech. He is the author of *Critical Geopolitics* and an editor of *The Geopolitics Reader, Rethinking Geopolitics* and *An Unruly World? Globalization, Governance And Geography* (all published by Routledge). He is based at the Virginia Tech Washington-Alexandria Centre, 205 South Patrick Street, Alexandria, VA 22314, USA.
E-mail: toalg@vt.edu

Abstracts

The Worldviews of Small States: A Content Analysis of 1995 UN Speeches
Stanley D. Brunn

171 UN members gave speeches at the organisation's 50th anniversary in New York in October 1995. In the fifteen minutes allowed each state, the leaders expressed their views about themselves and others in the world community. I investigate the addresses of 78 small states (less than 5 million) to answer three questions: how they see themselves in the world, how they envision the world, and what role they see the UN playing? Some focused on global problems, others on their own place on the world map. Small African states emphasized human welfare issues (hunger, AIDS, refugees), those in Europe human rights, and those in the South Pacific nuclear testing. Many members expressed gratitude for peacekeeping forces and UN support in times of severe hardship.

Ordering the 'Crush Zone': Geopolitical Games in Post-Cold War Eastern Europe
John O'Loughlin

In the aftermath of the Cold War, no consensus has emerged in American political circles on a replacement for the containment geopolitical code of the 1945–1990 era. Various geopolitical paradigms are on offer, each emanating from a world-view that is heavily colored by domestic political ideologies.

Seven of these paradigms are described and considered in light of the momentous geopolitical decision in 1998 to expand NATO into Eastern Europe. Eastern Europe has been considered a 'crush zone' by political geographers for over a century and the region has been intimately involved in the geopolitical re-orderings of this century. Strenuous avoidance of geopolitical issues, including long-term relations with Russia, was notable during the NATO expansion debates. The stark contrast of 'chaos' (Russia and its neighbors in the former Soviet Union) to 'cosmos' (the European Union and three new members of NATO) dominated the NATO enlargement debate. The end-consequence of recent NATO and US foreign policy decisions will be a re-drawing of the geopolitical divide across Europe from the eastern Baltic to the Black Sea. Fear of being placed on the eastern side of this new 'iron curtain' has caused many East European states to re-discover their 'European' credentials and claim entry to the West.

Economic Globalisation: Politics and Trade Policy in Ghana and Kenya
Richard Grant

This paper studies economic globalisation in Ghana and Kenya by examining both the domestic national policy environment that mediates globalisation and by measuring the nature and level of global engagement. Global engagement is measured in two ways: first, by indexing international business perceptions of the reform process and second, by creating one of the first indexes of economic globalisation by compiling data on economic flows such as foreign direct investment, multinational activity, etc. These analyses lead to the main conclusions that globalisation is geographically differentiated and that the impact of economic globalisation is a function of trade policy, institutional and ethnic variables.

Geopolitical Change and the Asia-Pacific: The Future of New Regionalism
Dennis Rumley

The main purpose of this paper is to outline a preliminary framework for the analysis of the nature of geopolitical change in relation to interactions among globalisation, the state and regionalism for the Asia-Pacific region. Overall, it is clear that the combination of globalisation with the 'collapse' of bipolarity has ensured that regionalism and regionalisation will become increasingly important in world politics. There is a need for post-realist spatial structures and policies to cope with all of these outcomes, and regionalism can potentially play an important 'intermediary' role in which the reestablishment of security and stability can be facilitated. The emergence of 'new regionalism' in the Asia-Pacific is potentially well suited to these requirements, although its structure and function are highly contested as the paper demonstrates.

Global Stability Through Inequality Versus Peace Processes Through Equality
Fabrizio Eva

This paper intends to demonstrate the existence of a world order founded upon the inequality of states. It will also show that this order is the result of historical events and is tacitly accepted. A group of countries, almost all of which belong to the West, guide and control world stability in the name of what are deemed to be universal principles, despite the fact that the behaviour of these major powers often seems to run counter to these same principles. The paper proposes the principle of equality as an ideal pragmatic point of reference for developing real peace processes that remain stable through time. The discussion of equality versus inequality draws on current geopolitical dynamics. In the conclusion is stressed the potential for geographic thought to not only play an active role in understanding international relations, but also in orienting these relations.

Borderless Worlds? Problematising Discourses of Deterritorialisation
Gearóid Ó Tuathail (Gerard Toal)

The supposed waning significance of territory in a world of instantaneous communication and speeding flows has given rise to multiple discourses of deterritorialization which seek to chart the world after the 'death of distance' and the 'end of geography.' This paper reviews various discourses of deterritorialization and seeks to problematize their general claims by examining one of the more precise articulations of deterritorialization, the so-called 'end of geography' in financial markets. It argues that discourses of deterritorialization are ideological, involve a re-arranging not transcendence of territory, and deepen inequalities across the globe. Borderless worlds rhetoric, ironically, helps produce even more bordered worlds. The paper concludes by identifying a techno-political sphere that political geographers need to engage in order to understand the changing 'world political map.'

Discourses of Identity and Territoriality on the US–Mexico Border
Jason M. Ackleson

This article analyses recent 'border control' policies implemented in the US-Mexico borderlands—specifically 'Operation Hold the Line', an initiative designed to seal the boundary from unofficial incursions of undocumented workers into the US. Through an interpretative, qualitative, and critical 'border analysis' that reads the relationships between borders, territoriality, and collective identity in an increasingly transnational and 'turbulent' moment of late modernity, the piece examines both the policy manifestations of the 'hardening' of the borderlands and the discourses which support it. The analysis is informed by new thinking about borders, widely defined, in International Relations as well as other disciplines.

African Boundaries and their Interpreters
Maano Ramutsindela

African states and their boundaries have been a long running research theme on the continent. The re-opening of the debate over African boundaries is important for theoretical and practical reasons. The purpose of this essay is to engage in recent trajectories of the African boundary discourse, and to debate alternative ways of looking at the future of hitherto colonially inscribed boundaries. I argue that priority in the decolonization of the African map should be given to changing the character of colonial boundaries rather than their physical appearance.

Common Cause for Borderland Minorities? Shared Status among Italy's Ethnic Communities
Julian V. Minghi

Following the 1994 Italian national elections, a new center-right government was perceived by Italy's ethnic borderland communities as a threat to their hard-won cultural autonomy. Representatives of the political parties of the Slovene-, French-, and German-speaking communities met together for the first time to formulate declarations for a collective political agenda – a common cause to protect and guarantee their autonomous status within the Italian state.

Relations among all elements in the political hierarchy – including the European Union – were consequently all transformed. The paper examines the impact of this coordinated effort in the context of the evolving Italian body politic, and speculates about the broader implications this process may hold for the future of European borderland minority communities in general.

Bounding Whose Territory? Potential Conflict between a State and a Province Desiring Statehood
David B. Knight

A basic requirement of statehood is a territorial base. The secession of a regionally-focussed minority within an existing state will necessarily require territorial separation. But to what territory is a seceding people entitled for a new state? This is not an easy question to answer, for until territorial secession occurs, the territory in question is part of the existing state. A case study of Canada and Quebec is presented, with reference to the historical growth of the Canadian and the Quebec provincial territorial limits, to claims by Quebecois separatists and the federal counter perspective, and to proposals for territorial restructuring if Quebecois ever want to negotiate secession from Canada.

Seeking the Common Ground
Frederick W. Boal

Claims can be made that globalizing processes reduce or even eliminate the significance of ethnicity. Equally, claims can be made that an 'ethnic revival' is evident, that, at least in part, is a response to globalising forces. This ethnic revival has created or renewed ethnic conflict in many parts of the world, no more so than in Northern Ireland. This paper focuses on strategies that may eliminate or at least reduce conflict. Three such conflict resolving or regulating processes are posited – territoriality, dominance and mutuality. The paper draws on a survey whose objective was to provide pointers towards a mutuality solution to the Northern Ireland conflict. It is suggested that the Northern Ireland mutuality experience, for all its difficulties, provides helpful pointers for those elsewhere who are concerned to find solutions to ethnic or ethno-national conflicts in this 'globalising world'.

Index